HANDS-ON

AI
TRADING

with Python™, QuantConnect™,
and AWS™

HANDS-ON
AI
TRADING

with Python™, QuantConnect™, and AWS™

Jiri Pik
Ernest P. Chan
Jared Broad
Philip Sun
Vivek Singh

WILEY

Copyright © 2025 by Jiri Pik, Ernest P. Chan, Jared Broad, Philip Sun, and Vivek Singh. All rights reserved.

Published by John Wiley & Sons, Inc., Hoboken, New Jersey.
Published simultaneously in Canada.

No part of this publication may be reproduced, stored in a retrieval system, or transmitted in any form or by any means, electronic, mechanical, photocopying, recording, scanning, or otherwise, except as permitted under Section 107 or 108 of the 1976 United States Copyright Act, without either the prior written permission of the Publisher, or authorization through payment of the appropriate per-copy fee to the Copyright Clearance Center, Inc., 222 Rosewood Drive, Danvers, MA 01923, (978) 750F400, fax (978) 750-4470, or on the web at www.copyright.com. Requests to the Publisher for permission should be addressed to the Permissions Department, John Wiley & Sons, Inc., 111 River Street, Hoboken, NJ 07030, (201) 748-6011, fax (201) 748-6008, or online at http://www.wiley.com/go/permission.

Trademarks: Wiley and the Wiley logo are trademarks or registered trademarks of John Wiley & Sons, Inc. and/or its affiliates in the United States and other countries and may not be used without written permission. All other trademarks are the property of their respective owners. John Wiley & Sons, Inc. is not associated with any product or vendor mentioned in this book.

Limit of Liability/Disclaimer of Warranty: While the publisher and author have used their best efforts in preparing this book, they make no representations or warranties with respect to the accuracy or completeness of the contents of this book and specifically disclaim any implied warranties of merchantability or fitness for a particular purpose. No warranty may be created or extended by sales representatives or written sales materials. The advice and strategies contained herein may not be suitable for your situation. You should consult with a professional where appropriate. Further, readers should be aware that websites listed in this work may have changed or disappeared between when this work was written and when it is read. Neither the publisher nor authors shall be liable for any loss of profit or any other commercial damages, including but not limited to special, incidental, consequential, or other damages.

For general information on our other products and services or for technical support, please contact our Customer Care Department within the United States at (800) 762-2974, outside the United States at (317) 572-3993 or fax (317) 572-4002.

Wiley also publishes its books in a variety of electronic formats. Some content that appears in print may not be available in electronic formats. For more information about Wiley products, visit our web site at www.wiley.com.

Library of Congress Cataloging-in-Publication Data:
Names: Pik, Jiri, author. | Chan, Ernest P., author. | Broad, Jared, author. | Sun, Philip, author. | Singh, Vivek, author.
Title: Hands-on AI trading with Python, QuantConnect and AWS / Jiri Pik, Ernest P. Chan, Jared Broad, Philip Sun, Vivek Singh.
Description: This book is a comprehensive guide designed for finance students, traders, and quantitative analysts who aim to elevate trading strategies with artificial intelligence. It is tailored for readers with a foundational understanding of Python and basic financial concepts. It provides a practical approach to integrating AI into trading, emphasizing intuition, real-world applications, and ease of experimentation. Key concepts include AI algorithms, data preprocessing, and model selection, focusing on practical implementations. The book features a hands-on approach using QuantConnect, eliminating the need for complex data management or infrastructure setup. It covers essential AI techniques like regression models, hidden Markov models, reinforcement learning, and generative AI, highlighting how these methods optimize risk management, trend prediction, and trading efficiency. Pre-trained models from AWS Bedrock, and PredictNow.ai are utilized, making AI applications accessible and actionable. The book demystifies algorithmic trading by providing over 20 fully implemented AI algorithms with detailed source code examples. It balances theoretical knowledge and practical insights, enabling readers to understand AI's impact on modern finance, experiment effectively, and adapt trading strategies to evolving market conditions. The book is a valuable resource for those seeking to leverage AI for financial success.
Identifiers: LCCN 2024039575 (print) | LCCN 2024039576 (ebook) | ISBN 9781394268436 (hardback) | ISBN 9781394267675 (ebook) | ISBN 9781394267668 (epub)
Subjects: LCSH: Artificial Intelligence – Applications in Finance. | Algorithmic Trading – Computer Programs. | Financial Engineering – Data Processing. | Machine Learning – Financial Applications. | Investment Analysis – Technological Innovations. | Quantitative Finance – Software.
Classification: LCC HG4515.95 .P428 2025 (print) | LCC HG4515.95 (ebook) | DDC 332.64/20285—dc23/eng/20240911
LC record available at https://lccn.loc.gov/2024039575
LC ebook record available at https://lccn.loc.gov/2024039576

Cover Image(s): © sore.studios/Shutterstock, © Troundless/Shutterstock
Cover Design: Jon Boylan
SKY10093739_121624

This book is dedicated to Singapore, a place that has become my home and fostered my professional growth. I am deeply grateful for the supportive and inspiring environment Singapore has provided, which has significantly contributed to the development of this book. Thank you, Singapore, for being a constant source of inspiration and support.
—*Jiri Pik*

To my family: Ben, Sarah, and Ethan.
—*Ernest Chan*

This book is dedicated to my parents, who are my guiding light, and my family, Ranu and Adri, who are my source of joy.
—*Vivek Singh*

Dedicated to my loving and supportive wife, Maria.
—*Jared Broad*

This book is dedicated to James Harris Simons (April 25, 1938–May 10, 2024), a genius mathematician, an accomplished entrepreneur and innovator, and above all a teacher and inspiration for math students and quants.
—*Philip Sun*

Contents

Biographies		xiii
Preface: QuantConnect		xv
Introduction		xxiii
Part I	**Foundations of Capital Markets and Quantitative Trading**	1
Chapter 1	**Foundations of Capital Markets**	3
	Market Mechanics	3
	Market Participants	4
	Trading Is the "Play"	4
	The Stage and Basic Rules of Trading—The Limit Order Book	4
	Actors—Liquidity Trader, Market Maker, and Informed Trader	5
	Liquidity Trader	5
	Market Maker	5
	Informed Trader	6
	AI Actors Wanted!	7
	Data and Data Feeds	7
	Custom and Alternative Data	9
	Brokerages and Transaction Costs	10
	Transaction Costs	11
	Security Identifiers	13

	Assets and Derivatives	15
	US Equities	15
	US Equity Options	19
	Index Options	21
	US Futures	21
	Cryptocurrency	23
Chapter 2	**Foundations of Quantitative Trading**	**25**
	Research Process	25
	Research	25
	Backtesting	26
	Parameter Optimization	26
	Paper and Live Trading	26
	Testing and Debugging Tools	26
	Debuggers	27
	Logging	27
	Charting	27
	Object Store	28
	Coding Process	28
	Time and Look-ahead Bias	29
	Look-ahead Bias	29
	Market Hours and Scheduling	30
	Strategy Styles	30
	Trading Signals	31
	Allocating Capital	31
	Regimes and Portfolios of Strategies	32
	Parameter Sensitivity Testing and Optimization	33
	1. Remove	33
	2. Replace	34
	3. Reduce	34
	Parameter Sensitivity Testing	34
	Margin Modeling	35
	Equities	35
	Equity Options	36
	Futures	37
	Diversification and Asset Selection	37
	Fundamental Asset Selection	38
	ETF Constituents Asset Selection	39
	Dollar-Volume Asset Selection	40
	Universe Settings	40
	Indicators and Other Data Transformations	41
	Automatic Indicators	41
	Manual Indicators	41

	Indicator Warm Up	42
	Storing Objects	42
	Indicator Events	42
	Sourcing Ideas	42
	Hypothesis-driven Testing	43
	Data Driven Investing	44
	Quantpedia	44
	QuantConnect Research and Strategy Explorer	45
Part II	**Foundations of AI and ML in Algorithmic Trading**	**47**
	Step-by-step Guide for AI-based Algorithmic Trading	48
Chapter 3	**Step 1: Problem Definition**	**49**
Chapter 4	**Step 2: Dataset Preparation**	**53**
	Data Collection	53
	Exploratory Data Analysis	53
	Data Preprocessing	54
	Handling Missing Data	55
	Handling Outliers	58
	Feature Engineering	61
	Normalization and Standardization of Features	62
	Transforming Time Series Features to Stationary	64
	Identification of Cointegrated Time Series with Engle-Granger Test	70
	Feature Selection	76
	Correlation Analysis	76
	Feature Importance Analysis	77
	Auto-identification of Features	78
	Dimensionality Reduction/Principal Component Analysis	80
	Splitting of Dataset into Training, Testing, and Possibly Validation Sets	83
	How to Split Your Data	83
Chapter 5	**Step 3: Model Choice, Training, and Application**	**87**
	Regression	88
	Linear Regression	89
	Polynomial Regression	91
	LASSO Regression	93
	Ridge Regression	96
	Markov Switching Dynamic Regression	99
	Decision Tree Regression	103

	Support Vector Machines Regression with Wavelet Forecasting	105
	Classification	110
	Multiclass Random Forest Model	110
	Logistic Regression	114
	Hidden Markov Models	117
	Gaussian Naive Bayes	119
	Convolutional Neural Networks	122
	Ranking	127
	LGBRanker Ranking	127
	Clustering	130
	OPTICS Clustering	130
	Language Models	132
	OpenAI Language Model	132
	Amazon Chronos Model	135
	FinBERT Model	137
Part III	**Advanced Applications of AI in Trading and Risk Management**	**141**
	Getting Started with Source Code	141
Chapter 6	**Applied Machine Learning**	**143**
	Example 1—ML Trend Scanning with MLFinlab	143
	Example 2—Factor Preprocessing Techniques for Regime Detection	148
	Example 3—Reversion vs. Trending: Strategy Selection by Classification	154
	Example 4—Alpha by Hidden Markov Models	158
	Example 5—FX SVM Wavelet Forecasting	170
	Example 6—Dividend Harvesting Selection of High-Yield Assets	176
	Example 7—Effect of Positive-Negative Splits	181
	Example 8—Stop Loss Based on Historical Volatility and Drawdown Recovery	185
	Example 9—ML Trading Pairs Selection	197
	Example 10—Stock Selection through Clustering Fundamental Data	207
	Example 11—Inverse Volatility Rank and Allocate to Future Contracts	214
	Example 12—Trading Costs Optimization	221
	Example 13—PCA Statistical Arbitrage Mean Reversion	228
	Example 14—Temporal CNN Prediction	233

	Example 15—Gaussian Classifier for Direction Prediction	242
	Example 16—LLM Summarization of Tiingo News Articles	250
	Example 17—Head Shoulders Pattern Matching with CNN	256
	Example 18—Amazon Chronos Model	265
	Example 19—FinBERT Model	272
Chapter 7	**Better Hedging with Reinforcement Learning**	**281**
	Introduction	281
	A New AI Trading Assistant	281
	Continuous Hedging Is Not Required	282
	Machine Learning Comes to the Rescue	283
	A Simplified but Effective Reinforcement Learning Approach	284
	Overview of the Reinforcement Learning	285
	Identification	285
	Simulation	286
	Refinement Training on Actual Market Data	287
	Testing and Implementation	287
	Implementation on QuantConnect	288
	Primary Research Notebook	289
	The Policy Network	290
	Model Functions	292
	Fine-tuning with Market Data	296
	Results	300
	Conclusion	303
Chapter 8	**AI for Risk Management and Optimization**	**305**
	What Is Corrective AI and Conditional Parameter Optimization?	305
	Feature Engineering	308
	Applying Corrective AI to Daily Seasonal Forex Trading	312
	What Is Conditional Parameter Optimization?	318
	Applying Conditional Parameter Optimization to an ETF Strategy	319
	Unconditional vs. Conditional Parameter Optimizations	320
	Performance Comparisons	322
	Conditional Portfolio Optimization	322
	Regime Changes Obliterate Traditional Portfolio Optimization Methods	322
	Learning to Optimize	324
	Ranking Is Easier Than Predicting	325
	The Fama-French Lineage	327

	Comparison with Conventional Optimization Methods	327
	Model Tactical Asset Allocation Portfolio	331
	CPO Software-as-a-Service	333
	Conclusion	340
	Definitions of Spread_EMA & Spread_VAR	340
Chapter 9	**Application of Large Language Models and Generative AI in Trading**	**341**
	Role of Generative AI in Creating Alpha	341
	Selecting an LLM for Building a Generative AI Application	342
	Prompt Engineering	344
	Prompt Engineering in Practice	345
	Addressing Model "Hallucination"	346
	Question Answering Using a Retrieval Augmented Application in SageMaker Canvas	347
	RAG Application Costs and Optimization Techniques	350
	Testing Our Infrastructure	351
	Summarization	356
	Useful AI Platforms and Services	359
	ChatGPT	359
	Gemini	359
	Bedrock	359
	SageMaker	359
	Q Business	360
References		361
Subject Index		363
Code Index		379

Biographies

Jiri Pik

Jiri Pik is the founder and CEO of RocketEdge.com, a creative consultancy specializing in cloud computing, artificial intelligence (AI), and ultra-low-frequency financial trading. He has more than 20 years of experience in financial technology, working with leading banks and hedge funds, such as Citi, Goldman Sachs, JPMorgan, and UBS, to build and optimize trading, risk management, and market data systems. As a cloud architect, he holds all 12 Amazon Web Services (AWS) Certifications and several Microsoft Azure Certifications. He lives in Singapore.

Jared Broad

Jared Broad is the founder and CEO of QuantConnect, an open-source algorithmic trading platform that has served thousands of quantitative trading funds since 2012. He obtained his biomedical engineering degree from the University of Auckland. QuantConnect provided the full support of their team, including Derek Melchin, a senior quant at QuantConnect, to create the suite of examples.

Ernest Chan

Ernest Chan (Ernie) is the founder and chief scientific officer of Predictnow.ai, a machine learning Software as a Service (SaaS) and consultancy for risk management and adaptive optimization. He started his career as a machine-learning researcher at IBM's T. J. Watson Research Center's Human Language Technologies group, which produced some of the best-known quant fund managers. He was also one of the first few employees of Morgan Stanley's AI group. He is the founder and non-executive chairman of QTS Capital Management, a quantitative CPO/CTA, and the acclaimed author of three books on quantitative trading (*Quantitative Trading, Algorithmic Trading, Machine Trading*), all published by Wiley. He obtained his Ph.D. in physics from Cornell University and his B.Sc. in physics from the University of Toronto.

Philip Sun

Philip Sun, CEO of Adaptive Investment Solutions, automates the construction and trading of options overlay strategies utilizing innovative approaches, including ML/AI. Philip teaches algorithmic and high-frequency trading as an adjunct faculty in the Mathematical Finance Program at Boston University. Before Adaptive, Philip led quantitative research at Sentinel Investments and was a senior quant at Fidelity Investments and Wellington Management.

Vivek Singh

Vivek Singh, senior product manager at AWS, is part of the core leadership team developing generative AI suite of services and leads GenAI data annotation, fine-tuning and evaluation services to improve the performance, trust, safety, and responsible use of LLMs and GenAI applications. Before AWS, Vivek worked at a large hedge fund performing fundamental stock analysis.

Preface: QuantConnect

QuantConnect provides a comprehensive environment for researching, backtesting, optimizing, and deploying live algorithmic trading strategies. Founded in 2012 it has a community of more than 300,000 registered quants, engineers, and data scientists.

QuantConnect supports 11 asset classes, including equities, futures, forex, options, and cryptocurrencies, in a cloud or on-premise environments. It provides a comprehensive data library, including price, fundamental, and alternative data.

It hosts a professional caliber, co-located, low-latency live-trading environment with direct connectivity to 20 brokerages and routing to more than 1,200 destinations (qnt.co/book-cloud-live-trading).

Transparency, freedom, and security are key focuses of the community ethos. Users own all their intellectual property (IP) and code, and can use the open-source version of QuantConnect, LEAN (https://www.lean.io), to run independently hosted strategies.

Maintaining equal access to the technology is an important part of QuantConnect's mission.

A robust framework helps create, evaluate, and launch trading algorithms much more efficiently. For video walk-throughs of QuantConnect, see qnt.co/book-videos.

Benefits of Using Frameworks

We wanted this book to focus on fully implemented algorithmic trading strategies, allowing our readers to wrestle with code and explore the markets for alpha, rather than learning about scaffolding or parsing data. By using a robust framework, all of the data loading and basic portfolio management are handled, saving you weeks to years of effort.

Efficiency

Frameworks offer hundreds of ready-made components and libraries, which save development time. These include basic alpha signals, portfolio construction systems, and open-source execution algorithms. Through building on top of a framework, you can leverage thousands of lines of code within a few statements.

Standardization

Frameworks provide demonstration template algorithms and a community of members familiar with the Application Program Interface (API).

Error Reduction

Leveraging frameworks will dramatically reduce the likelihood of coding errors and potential losses in production trading. No quant or engineer is perfect; for a critical system managing capital, you need something with a track record and reviewed by thousands of people. Frameworks generally have less errors as they are covered with unit and regression tests.

Focus on Strategy

The traditional process of building an algorithmic trading strategy devotes 95% of efforts to the same three activities: data parsing and loading, brokerage connectivity, and dashboards or user interfaces, none of which improve your investment performance. By harnessing a framework, traders can focus on their trading strategies instead of infrastructure.

QuantConnect Framework

QuantConnect serves an open-source algorithmic trading engine, LEAN, with an extensive library of financial data and cloud-computing resources. With minimal effort, you can start a quantitative trading technology stack and deploy strategies for production trading (see Figure 0.1).

Its technology centers around three elements:
- Cloud Platform (qnt.co/book-cloud)—A cloud-hosted managed environment that lets your team focus entirely on alpha creation and trading. Data updates, cloud infrastructure, and team onboarding are all handled automatically.
- Local Platform (qnt.co/book-local)—An on-premises environment serving the same cloud user interface but giving you the freedom to add custom libraries, load proprietary datasets, and operate entirely on your organization's servers.
- LEAN CLI (qnt.co/book-cli)—A simple PIP package, CLI offers LEAN's entire power via an easy-to-use command line interface. Results are rendered as JSON objects for processing with your favorite charting program.

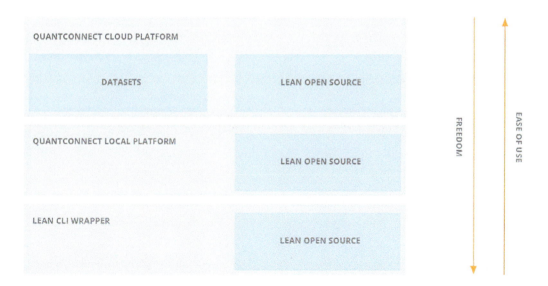

Figure 0.1 QuantConnect enables you to run LEAN via three platforms.

For all these platforms, the loading and parsing of data is handled automatically. There are integrations to historical and live-streaming data vendors and 60 alternative data vendors letting you focus on alpha research.

Creating an Account

To run most of the examples in this book, you will need an account on QuantConnect. Creating an account is free and takes less than 2 minutes. Register at quantconnect.com/signup.

Research

QuantConnect cloud-based research terminals attach to terabytes of financial, fundamental, and alternative data, preformatted and ready to use (Figure 0.2). Hosted alternative data are linked to the underlying securities, tagged with the FIGI, CUSIP, and ISIN to facilitate building strategies. Users can access popular machine learning and feature selection libraries to quantify factor importance, and install custom packages on request.

Backtesting

With minimal-to-no code changes, clients can move from research to point-in-time, fee, slippage, and spread-adjusted backtesting on lightning-fast cloud cores (Figure 0.3). It is easy to perform multi-asset backtesting on portfolios comprised of thousands of securities with realistic margin-modeling.

xviii   PREFACE: QUANTCONNECT

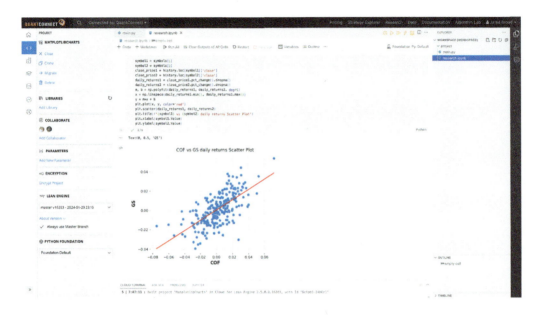

Figure 0.2 QuantConnect cloud-hosted Jupyter research environment.

You can import custom and alternative-data, linked to underlying securities, for realistically modeling live-trading portfolios and avoiding common pitfalls like look-ahead bias. More than 20,000 backtests are performed by the QuantConnect user-base daily.

Optimization

The parameter sensitivity testing allows you to run thousands of full backtests on scalable cloud compute, completing weeks of work in minutes. Visualize all the iterations of parameters on heatmaps to quickly understand your strategy's sensitivity to parameters for robust out-of-sample trading. Explore further by opening each result and seeing its individual trades and backtest logs to completely understand the source of your alpha, and how sensitive it is to parameter changes (Figure 0.4).

Live Trading

QuantConnect has deployed more than 300,000 live strategies to a managed, co-located live-trading environment (Figure 0.5). The platform processes more than $45B in notional volume per month, serving hundreds of fund clients. Quants can execute trades directly through our 20 integrations, or route to 1,200 liquidity providers.

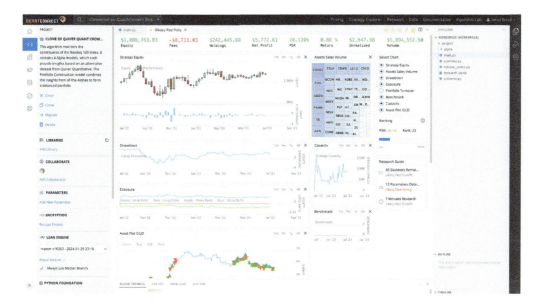

Figure 0.3 Accurate point-in-time backtesting, across 11 asset classes, down to tick resolution data.

Figure 0.4 Scalable cloud parameter optimizer for rapid sensitivity testing.

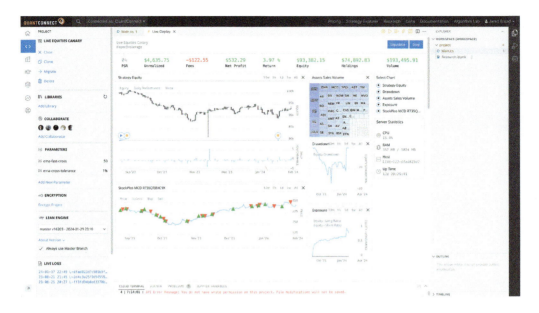

Figure 0.5 Instantly deploy strategies to live-trading with all data, user-interface, and order management handled automatically.

Powered by an Open-source Core

QuantConnect is powered by LEAN (qnt.com/book-lean), an open-source algorithmic trading engine designed to handle the entire life cycle of a trading strategy through research, backtesting, optimization, and live deployment.

LEAN has a permissive, commercially friendly license so you are free to download it and run it on your own servers. The LEAN engine is built in C# for the data parsing and loading, and bridges to python for the algorithm analysis.

Emphasizing its commitment to open-source, QuantConnect has built the LEAN CLI—a command line interface to run the research, backtesting, optimization, and live trading technology anywhere in the world.

Its high-level architecture diagram is illustrated in Figure 0.6.

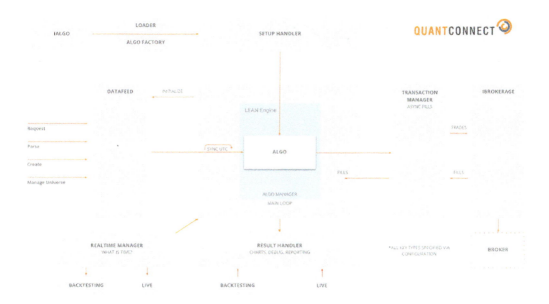

Figure 0.6 LEAN architecture.

The detailed description of the engine is outside the scope of this book, and we recommend that readers review the LEAN documentation (qnt.co/book-lean-docs).

Introduction

Target Book Audience

This book has been written for students interested in finance; traders and quants in hedge funds and pension funds; and investment firms looking to build intuition into when (or when not) and why (or why not) modern trading strategies work well and how to enrich a strategy with artificial intelligence (AI) algorithms to make it more robust.

The book builds upon the following:

- A working knowledge of Python 3.x, including pandas, numpy, and sci-kit libraries.
- Some familiarity with modern finance and trading.
- A reader's constant curiosity to keep asking himself/herself what a change of any part of the algorithm would result in.

Book Goals

We had three principal goals in writing this book:

1. To provide an overview of the key artificial intelligence (AI) algorithms, techniques, and best practices used in modern financial trading,
2. To teach intuition behind the algorithms via a significant number of worked-out real-world examples with detailed explanations, and
3. To provide an easy-to-setup and use environment where readers could instantly experiment with the algorithms to build their confidence without spending any time setting up the required infrastructure.

Unlike other books on financial trading, this book does not focus on setting up market data, backtesting, and trading infrastructure. Such setups are notoriously difficult, expensive, and require major investments. Consider the issue of market data quality, which requires a permanent team of data scientists and software engineers to ensure the data is correct and always delivered without delay.

Instead, the book fully utilizes **QuantConnect**, an open-source, financial-trading-as-infrastructure platform that allows you to start building your trading algorithms and test trading hypotheses using QuantConnect's market data feeds, backtesting, and trading infrastructure.

Similarly, the book does not focus on explaining the intricate details of training large language models or sophisticated financial models. Instead, it depends on **AWS Bedrock**, which has already trained foundation models, or **MLFinLab** or **PredictNow.ai** trained financial models.

Book Organization

The book is organized as follows:

- In the Preface, we introduce the QuantConnect platform.
- In Part I, we introduce foundational concepts of modern markets (Chapter 1) and quantitative trading (Chapter 2).
- Part II introduces foundational concepts of designing a robust AI algorithm, starting with defining your inputs and output, shaping your data, and choosing the right models to use.
- Part III is the core of the book, describing more than 20 fully implemented algorithms that harness different data sources, models, and technology platforms. Included are algorithms built on QuantConnect with source code and results, allowing readers to see each algorithm from different perspectives, which is critical for mastering its applications in readers' strategies.

Accompanying Book Materials

Book Examples

The fully worked-out real-world examples have been designed to illustrate key components of modern algorithmic trading strategies.

Their parameters, such as the assets to be traded or the backtesting start and end dates, have been chosen to illustrate the algorithm's performance. Readers are encouraged to modify the input parameters to see the effect of their changes.

The source code of all book examples is available in QuantConnect's library for readers to clone and experiment with. To access them, navigate to hands-on-ai-trading.com/examples, and you'll be directed to complete, maintained examples with which to experiment. To see how to modify an algorithm's parameters, see Parameter Optimization in Chapter 2.

Feedback

For readers with issues regarding bugs in the book code examples, please create an issue in the GitHub repository for the book (qnt.co/book-repo), and the QuantConnect team will address them directly.

For general support regarding issues related to QuantConnect, please log in to the QuantConnect Discord server at quantconnect.com/discord, where the QuantConnect team, AI-quant support agents, and thousands of community members can assist.

Acknowledgments

We're incredibly grateful to the *dozens of contributors* who helped to make this book possible. There were combined efforts from *teams* of people at RocketEdge, QuantConnect, PredictNow, and Agile Finance.

Specifically, we're grateful for Derek Melchin's outstanding work over almost a year of researching, designing, building, and debugging more than 20 QuantConnect demonstration strategies. In addition, we're grateful for the QuantConnect team who built entirely new application program interfaces (APIs) to make the book example code more elegant.

PredictNow thanks Sergei Belov, Haoyu Fan, Akshay Nautiyal, Sudarshan Sawal, and Quentin Viville for their research that contributed to the successes of the CAI and CPO methods. We thank Pavan Dutt, Nancy Khullar, and Jai Sukumar for their assistance in features engineering, software implementation of the CPO method, and Guillaume Goujard for his mathematical insights. Client feedback has been indispensable for improving these methods, and we thank all of our cannot-be-named clients for them. Finally, we appreciate the insightful questions raised by the audiences at UBS & Cornell Financial Engineering Manhattan AI Speaker Series, NYU Mathematical Finance and Financial Data Science seminar, CIBC's Finance-AI seminar, Fidelity AI Asset Management group, Google Innovation Day, and many other public and private forums where we presented CPO.

Philip Sun would specifically like to thank Yilin Liu, a research assistant responsible for some of the initial AI hedging model development; Hao Xing, associate professor of finance at Boston University; and Chris Kelliher, senior quant researcher at Fidelity and adjunct faculty of Boston University's Mathematical Finance Program, who provided valuable guidance for AI hedging research.

Finally, thank you to Chris Bartlett of Algoseek.com for bringing the author team together and providing the sample data for the book; and all of the team at Wiley, Bill Falloon, Katherine Cording, Delainey Henson, Purvi Patel, Rajesh Venkatraman, Sudhagaran Thandapani, Sheryl Nelson, and Susan Cerra for their patience as we stretched the deadlines.

Part I

Foundations of Capital Markets and Quantitative Trading

Chapter 1

Foundations of Capital Markets

This chapter introduces the core concepts of modern financial markets and how they're represented in QuantConnect. We'll cover the modern US markets, data feeds, and the asset classes used in later chapters. Readers who are familiar with QuantConnect may skip this chapter.

Market Mechanics

The United States has 11 major stock exchanges. The two largest are the New York Stock Exchange (NYSE) and the National Association of Securities Dealers Automated Quotations System (NASDAQ). Trades on these exchanges are compiled by the Securities Information Processor (SIP) into a single data feed. This feed helps the Securities and Exchange Commission (SEC) determine the national best bid or offer (NBBO), which shows the best prices posted on public markets in the United States. When a new quote for more than 100 shares offers a better price, it is flagged as the NBBO. Quotes or trades involving fewer than 100 shares, known as odd lots, are excluded from this pricing. Figure 1.1 illustrates this flow.

Brokerages often send orders to market makers to be executed "off the market." Market makers executing these orders are required to provide fills within the NBBO price range. Furthermore, these off-market trades are reported to the Trade Reporting Facility (TRF) and eventually are included in the SIP data feed. Some brokers offer

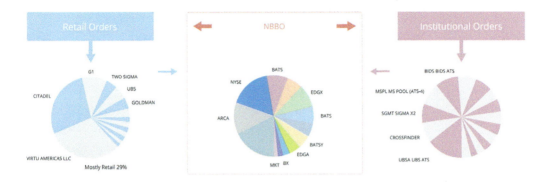

Figure 1.1 Flow of retail and institutional traffic across public and private markets, and the origin of national best pricing.

Direct Market Access (DMA), which allows your orders to be routed directly to a specific exchange. However, using DMA might not always get you the best national price for the asset, so it's important to be careful when using this option.

Market Participants

Trading Is the "Play"

If markets are theaters, then trading is the "play." Like a Shakespearean play, trading, especially algorithmic trading, is a highly coordinated and scripted activity. Comparing trading to the Bard's plays will probably make Shakespeare turn in his grave. But he will forgive this literary enthusiast for the forced metaphor.

The Stage and Basic Rules of Trading—The Limit Order Book

To stretch this analogy further, the stage of trading is the "limit order book," which is a ledger of some sort that lists limit order prices of a security in columns. On the left side is the column of bid prices, that is, prices traders are willing to buy a security at, and the amounts or "sizes" of the orders (for stocks, the sizes are typically in multiples of round lots of 100 shares; and for futures and options, in numbers of contracts). On the opposite side of this ledger is the column of ask prices, that is, prices traders are willing to sell a security at, and sizes. The prices are usually sorted from high to low from top to bottom, with the best bid and ask meeting in the middle. Bid prices cannot be higher than ask prices, that is, bid and ask prices do not cross, otherwise the buyers and sellers will be able to fulfill each other's order in a way that benefits one or both sides. Any buy orders that enter the market higher than current best ask price is effectively a market order and will be matched up to the size of the best ask price, and then the next best ask price and so on, until entire buy orders are filled in a process called "walk-the-book," or when remaining ask prices are above the best bid price. Because of this, a trader who posts limit orders will usually post bid prices below the best ask price and ask prices above the best bid price.

Because there is a spread between the best bid and ask prices, limit orders do not get filled right away, and indeed sometimes, not filled at all. To ensure immediacy of trades, in a sufficiently liquid market, a trader can post a "market order," which gets matched with the best bid for a market sell order and matched with best ask for a market buy order. If there is not enough size at the current bid and asks, the market sell and buy orders will walk the book as described previously: the market buy order will pay progressively higher prices; and conversely, the market sell order will accept progressively lower prices. If the size of the market order is large compared to sizes of available limit orders, the order will walk deeper (i.e., higher for buyer or lower for seller) in the order book, causing an immediate rise or decline in the trade price of the securities. This is a form of adverse price impact of trading.

Actors—Liquidity Trader, Market Maker, and Informed Trader

Now that the stage is set, let's introduce the actors, or more appropriately, the characters or roles in the play. Just like actors, traders can play multiple roles, sometimes in the same play or even at the same time.

Liquidity Trader

A "liquidity trader," also called "fundamental trader" or derogatively "noise trader," is a trader whose primary goal is to get in or out of a position for purposes other than profiting from advantaged information (not always insider information). For example, a mutual fund manager decides to rebalance her stock portfolio to match a benchmark index. The trader acting on the instruction of the fund manager is a liquidity trader. The same fund manager may be a macro forecaster, sector specialist, or stock picker basing her trades on publicly available information and deciding to buy or sell some stocks to profit from her mosaic view. Still, such a fund manager does not possess any advantaged information. The trader who executes her trades may be respectfully called a "fundamental trader," even though fundamentally she is no different from a liquidity trader. Finally, you also have undisciplined traders who are trading for the sake of trading—and we can safely call them "noise traders". Whether the traders are fundamental or noise, their objective is to complete buy or sell orders with no advantaged information.

Market Maker

If a liquidity trader wants liquidity, who is there to pour him a drink? Well, it could be the liquidity trader on the other side of the trade. It is likely that most liquid stock transactions occur by matching simultaneous market orders on opposite sides of the trade. And much of those orders are matched by your broker dealer before they reach the stock exchange. This is done by internally "crossing" or "netting" the orders, usually done at the mid-price, that is, halfway between best bid and ask in the limit order book.

If there is not enough market order from the opposite side, a market order will "hit the bid" or "lift the offer." It will walk the book if there is not enough size at the best bid or ask, as we discussed previously. Here, it is the other limit orders that will fulfill the liquidity-seeking market order. Exchanges will pay a rebate on a filled limit order to reward the trader for liquidity.

Strategies that facilitate trading and improve transaction prices, or immediacy, are strategies typically deployed by a "market maker." Traditionally, when trading was conducted on the floor of a stock exchange (e.g., NYSE), dedicated market makers were physically located in booths and their jobs were to match trades for their assigned list of stocks. They stood ready when the listed buy and sell (limit) orders were not sufficient to clear the market of open orders (e.g., when the market was at a standstill because the best bid and ask prices were too far apart). In situations like that, it was the market maker's job and her opportunity to post orders that get in between the best bid and ask prices to encourage liquidity traders to transact at her better prices. In return, the market maker would profit from the bid and ask spread, that is, she bought at her bid price and sold higher at the current or improved ask price. The previous narrative is in the past tense because the majority of market-making activities have shifted to electronic trading platforms. Some floor trading still exists for less liquid stocks and other asset classes. For example, the Chicago Board of Options still operates a pit to trade equity and equity index options, while the Chicago Mercantile Exchange ceased pit trading in March 2020 due to COVID-19 and decided the closure would be permanent.

In the modern era of electronic trading, market makers are now almost exclusively algorithmic and high-frequency trading programs. There are still traders whose primary or exclusive job is to make markets in certain stocks, but anyone can make markets intentionally or unintentionally by deploying strategies that improve outcomes—better prices and immediacy—for liquidity traders.

Informed Trader

Wait, a market maker helps only liquidity traders? What about other types of traders? Doesn't the market maker help everyone? Yes, market-making activity helps everyone, except other market makers who are competing against each other. That being said, market makers are more wary of "informed traders" than other market makers. To skirt the controversy about insider trading, we shall broadly define informed traders as ones who possess advantaged or privileged information that is only known to a small number of agents and is not released to the public. As we discussed previously, a trader or fund manager might have her unique opinion about the future outcome of financial markets and of individual securities. And she might have superior forecasting or analytical skills. But if she does not have advantaged information that others don't have, she is not considered an informed trader. On the other hand, advantaged information does not always have to be about the fundamental values of financial securities. For example, say a broker has the knowledge that a particular fund manager is about to make a large block trade that will have a significant impact on the market price. A trader who has this information can profit, illegally, by trading ahead of the fund manager, in a scheme called front-running.

It is not this author's job to argue the benefit or harm of insider trading or trading on privileged information. The point is that an informed trader has a huge advantage over other traders, as she knows about future outcomes with much greater certainty than other traders do. Those uninformed traders include both liquidity traders and market makers. Even a market maker with high-frequency trading rigs cannot win against low-tech informed traders. It is very difficult to know whether the counterparty is an informed trader. This means that market makers need to adjust their strategies to incorporate the risk of trading against informed traders.

AI Actors Wanted!

One of the exciting promises of machine learning and artificial intelligence (AI) is that we can train an algorithm to detect patterns of activities by informed traders. It is no longer humanly possible to sift through the terabytes of trading data generated each day by markets, not to mention analyzing and recognizing tradable patterns. Even if a human can recognize patterns, he will not be fast enough to react to them. Gone were the days when traders could sharpen their stock picking skills and find trading opportunities by studying the stock tables in the *Wall Street Journal* or the tiny thumbnail sized price charts on *Investor's Business Daily*. Therefore, it has become critical to rely on fast computers running powerful machine-learning algorithms to process and analyze market data sufficiently fast in order to detect and act on tradable signals.

Data and Data Feeds

As market participants enter bids, asks, or execute trades, an event is created that is broadcast through the market. Over millions of traders and investors, this creates a constant stream of events during the trading day and an enormous volume of data. Interestingly, the stream tends to drop off around lunchtime and picks back up around 3 pm when traders tune in for market close. The market open and close volumes can be two to three times mid-day volume.

Until the 1960s, this stream of trades and quotes was written to reels of paper tapes for posterity, creating a ticker tape. The saying "replaying the tape" comes from repeating those streams as they appeared in order.

```
self.time            # Time in backtesting and live trading
```

If the data streams are recorded as they appear, despite any potential errors or imperfections, they become a point-in-time dataset. Point-in-time data is a raw representation of the data at the precise moment it was captured but may include errors in the feed connectivity or exchanges themselves.

A classic regular example of this is the late reporting of trades performed. Although exchanges require participants to report trades within 90 seconds, some may report much later than that, at prices from trades that occurred earlier in the day. This appears like a price discontinuity and can be quite disconcerting for new quants who don't take care to filter them out.

Recently, some rapid market declines were exacerbated by algorithmic trading programs. The most famous is the 2010 Flash Crash, which started at approximately 2:30 pm and lasted about 35 minutes on May 6, 2010 (see Figure 1.2). In the aftermath of the 2010 Flash Crash, stock exchanges announced new trading curbs or circuit breakers. Several exchanges led by the NYSE and NASDAQ began retroactively canceling trades that occurred at very low prices during crashes. These cancelations occur minutes to hours after the trades and are impossible to know beforehand.

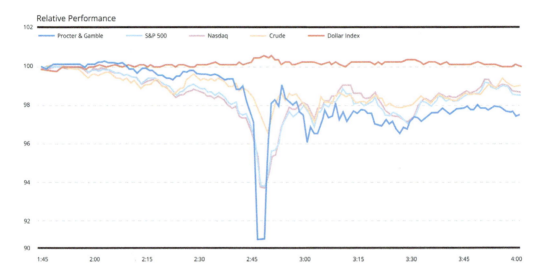

Figure 1.2 Relative performance of various assets during the market crash on May 6, 2010.

Market data feeds generate three primary data types of tick data:

Trade ticks—A sales report of an order filled, along with flags to convey information about the order, such as the exchange venue and delay.

Quote ticks—An offer to buy or sell a specific quantity of shares for a price. The difference between the best or highest bid prices (offers to buy) and the best or lowest asking price (offer to sell) forms the bid-ask spread. For US markets, the best quotes in the country form the National Best Bid or Offer (NBBO). These ticks are broadcast with a special flag to inform the market of the current best prices.

In QuantConnect, this data is delivered on each data event as a list of ticks. Note, "tick_type" is an attribute that identifies whether the data point is a trade tick or a quote tick.

```
def on_data(self, slice):
    ticks = slice.ticks.get(self._symbol, [])    # Empty if not found
    for tick in ticks:
        price = tick.price                        # Price limit or trade
        trade_or_quote = tick.tick_type           # TickType.TRADE or QUOTE
```

Consolidated Data—Tick data creates billions of events per day. It consumes a lot of disk space and is slow to process. To make the dataset smaller and easier to perform research on, ticks can be aggregated into bars. Most commonly, aggregations represent prices (open, high, low, close), volume traded, last bid, last ask, and so on, over a fixed interval of time. QuantConnect consolidates the market's stream of ticks into trade and quote bars (see qnt.co/book-consolidate). A trade bar represents the sale prices over a period, while quote bars represent the bids and asks aggregated over a bar period (Figure 1.3).

```
def on_data(self, slice):
    trade_bar = slice.bars.get(self._symbol)        # Fetch trade bar
    quote_bar = slice.quote_bars.get(self._symbol)  # Fetch quote bar
```

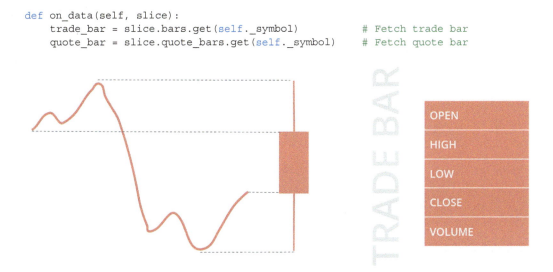

Figure 1.3 Trade bar formation and properties.

Each quote bar carries child bid and ask bars as properties, representing the aggregation of bid and ask data over a fixed interval. They are also in the form of an Open-High-Low-Close (OHLC) bar. In QuantConnect, when quote data is available for an asset, it is used for the modeling of order fills as it is a more accurate representation than using the previous trade price (Figure 1.4).

```
quote_bar.bid.close       # Close of aggregated bid price bar
quote_bar.ask.close       # Close of aggregated ask price bar
```

Custom and Alternative Data

In addition to price, a multitude of other data sources are available to provide insight into the movements of asset prices. Broadly, this category of data is called alternative data and includes imaging, real estate, weather, shipping, regulation, and a suite of customer tracking, including geolocation, reviews, sentiment, and transactions.

QuantConnect hosts more than 60 datasets (qnt.co/book-datasets) and frequently onboards new ones. Data can be added to the strategies with a couple of lines of code. The following example delivers news articles about Apple from a streaming news service, TiingoNews:

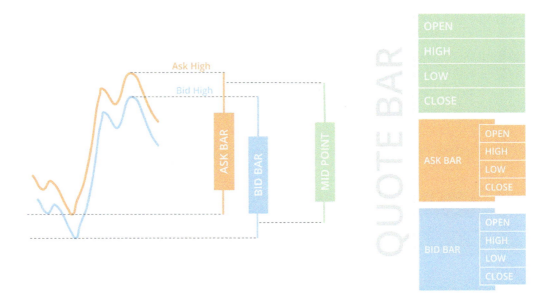

Figure 1.4 Quote bar formation and properties.

```
self._aapl = self.add_equity("AAPL", Resolution.MINUTE).symbol
self._dataset_symbol = self.add_data(TiingoNews, self._aapl).symbol
```

Generating tradable signals from alternative data is a science, and we'll go into more detail on how to analyze these datasets in later chapters. If QuantConnect does not have the data you need, you can upload custom datasets by defining the data format as a class and using the add_data method to add it to your strategy. In the following snippet, we're passing a custom class MyFactorDataset, which will define the properties of the data and parse a source CSV file:

```
self._custom_symbol = self.add_data(MyFactorDataset, "Factors").symbol
```

Brokerages and Transaction Costs

Brokers act as intermediaries between the capital markets and clients. They hold client assets, clear trades from the exchanges, and ensure clients remain within margin limits, enforcing SEC and FINRA margin rules. Brokerages typically clear and settle their trades with clearing firms. The majority of institutional and retail trades are executed through brokerage firms. We will not discuss the functions of the clearing firms in this book as they do not concern the readers here.

Brokers have varying fee structures, supported assets, and order types (qnt.co/book-order-types). Some brokerages route to market makers to fill trades, earning rebates from directing order flow to a specific market maker. Some may fill orders internally in a process called "netting" with other client orders. All internally filled orders must be executed within the national best bid-ask prices from public markets.

Brokerages can support many different types of orders, including some proprietary order types that seek optimal fills. Other brokerages have nuanced limitations, such as the inability to update an order once it has been placed.

QuantConnect implements 12 order types. Following are examples of two commonly used order types that are used in the later examples:

```
# On exchange open attempt to fill in the opening auction
self.market_on_open_order(symbol, quantity, tag, order_properties)

# On hitting a stop_price, place market order.
self.stop_market_order(symbol, quantity, stop_price, tag, order_properties)
```

Note, some order types may not be supported by the brokerage. In QuantConnect, all orders return an *order ticket* (qnt.co/book-order-ticket), which can be used to update or cancel an order before it is filled. Think of this as a coat ticket that lets you retrieve your coat from the cloakroom.

Figure 1.5 Order messaging between the algorithm and brokerage.

Transaction Costs

In trading, there are many types of transaction costs. Some are explicit, such as fees from the brokerage (qnt.co/book-fee-model) and taxes, and others are more implicit—incurred simply from the act of trading. For quantitative research, it's important to understand where these costs come from, so you can model them—and optimize your trading to reduce these costs.

Trading Fees

Brokers charge fees per order or share, which are charged directly to your brokerage account. In QuantConnect, this can be modeled with fee models to simulate specific trade fees or, more generally, a brokerage model that enforces a specific broker's limitations and costs.

```
# Setting a custom fee model of $1 for this security
security.set_fee_model(ConstantFeeModel(1))
```

```
# Setting all the fees and limitations of a broker
self.set_brokerage_model(BrokerageName.INTERACTIVE_BROKERS_BROKERAGE)
```

Bid-Ask Spread

For market orders, the most substantial of these implicit costs is the bid-ask spread: the difference between the best bid and ask prices (usually estimated from the NBBO, covered earlier) of an asset in the market. When a market order is filled, it crosses the spread and fills at the best available price (Figure 1.6). Some practitioners optimistically assume fills will occur at the last trade sale price, which is generally somewhere in the middle of the spread. In live trading, the spread can significantly impact profitability and should be accounted for in research.

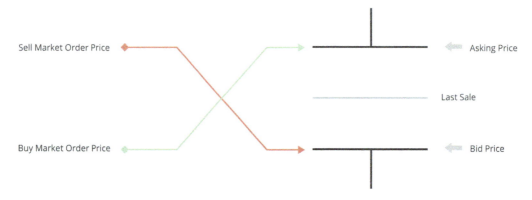

Figure 1.6 Spread crossing: sell market orders fill at the bid price, and buy market orders fill at the ask price. The last sale can be at the bid, at the ask, or somewhere in between them.

In QuantConnect, orders are filled using quote data, accounting for this spread. If the default fill behavior doesn't fit your use case, you can customize the behavior with plugins.

```
security.set_fill_model(ImmediateFillModel())
```

Slippage

Trade slippage (qnt.co/book-slippage-model) is the difference between the expected execution price and the final fill price for your trade. The most common cause for small orders, on liquid assets, is time as the asset prices change while the order is filled (Figure 1.7).

For illiquid assets or large orders, slippage can come from the temporary or permanent price impact of the trade order itself. A direct mechanism of price impact is through a process called "walk-the-book," which we discussed previously. The order book combines bid-ask prices at multiple levels with indicated sizes. A large market order to buy (i.e., an order to be executed immediately at the best ask price in the order book) will be filled with the best ask price first, then sequentially filled with higher and higher ask prices until the entire order is filled. This causes the traded price to move up by

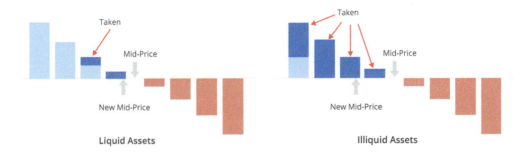

Figure 1.7 Slippage costs are different between liquid and illiquid assets.

"walking the book". The sell market order will walk the book downward in price following the same logic. The price impact can be temporary for liquid markets, as market makers replenish the order book at prices close to the original price before the market order arrived. However, if market makers suspect informed trader activity, they will replenish the order book with higher or lower prices near the last traded price (or worse). In this case, the price impact becomes permanent. A temporary price impact can be ameliorated by trading in smaller increments, while an anticipated permanent price impact will require more sophisticated trading algorithms to disguise the actual size of the trade.

QuantConnect assumes assets are liquid by default but offers several alternative models to customize more nuanced fill behavior:

```
# Assume instant fill at top of order book
security.set_slippage_model(NullSlippageModel())

# Model-estimated market impact in fills
security.set_slippage_model(MarketImpactSlippageModel(self))
```

Security Identifiers

Uniquely identifying assets is important to track them over time reliably. In equities, corporate events, such as renames, mergers, and exchange delistings, can render backtests misleading and inaccurate. Spotting these issues can be challenging if you're trading a portfolio of hundreds of stocks. There have been many unique asset identifiers developed in the last few decades to assist with asset tracking:

- CUSIP—A proprietary system limited to the United States and Canada that covers several asset classes. CUSIP is an eight-digit alphanumerical string, or nine digits, if it includes a "check-digit" encoded from the first eight digits.
- FIGI—Bloomberg's free, proprietary database look-up service.
- ISIN—For most US and Canadian assets with CUSIPs, the ISIN is a concatenation of the country code, for example, US, CA, and the eight-digit CUSIP.

A quant trader can access these identifiers by subscribing to a third-party asset price dataset that contains these identifiers such as Algoseek—or subscribe to identifier datasets directly from the providers. However, there are some key limitations to using these identifiers:

- They are proprietary datasets that often require expensive and restrictive licenses.
- Identifier datasets may not be self-contained and require a parallel database to look up information about the company.
- Coverage of different asset classes or country markets is limited.

QuantConnect solves these limitations by implementing an open-source encoding technique. The identifier (see qnt.co/book-security-id) is a hash of data required to "fingerprint" the asset, making it entirely self-contained, so no database lookup is required. This identifier is called the "Symbol," which supports up to 99 asset classes in 255 countries and handles derivative asset types. It has no licensing fee.

In 2014, Google performed a ticker swap and initial public offering (IPO) of Class C shares (qnt.co/book-goog-ipo) without voting rights. They listed GOOCV and GOOAV as temporary assets to facilitate the swap, and then flipped the tickers so the former Class A share ticker was used for class C (Figure 1.8).

```
self._goog = self.add_equity("GOOG").symbol      # Store the symbol for trading
self._googl = self.add_equity("GOOGL").symbol
self.debug(str(self._goog.id))                   # Prints "GOOCV VP83T1ZUHROL"
self.debug(str(self._googl.id))                  # Prints "GOOG T1AZ164W5VTX"
```

Figure 1.8 Security identification for a complex ticker change history.

The symbol object does not change despite the ticker rename, remaining a consistent connection to the company represented. The `id` property of the Symbol object stores the encoded hash, which can be useful for transport (encoding to JavaScript Object Notation [JSON]) or storing on disk (Figure 1.9).

Using the symbol object for trading ensures the referenced entity remains the same through ticker renames and corporate mergers. When serialized to a string, it looks something like `SPY R735QTJ8XC9X` and is stored in the symbol.id property. This two-part string is a base64 encoded set of data that contains the IPO ticker, security type, a date, the option strike, right, and the market the asset is listed in. The `market` property

Chapter 1. Foundations of Capital Markets

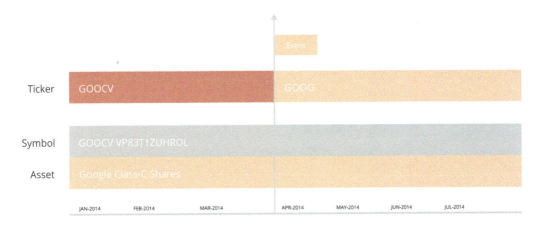

Figure 1.9 Security identification for a simple ticker change history.

distinguishes between tickers that have the same string value but represent different underlying assets—for example, BTCUSD is listed on Coinbase and on Kraken, but they have different prices and are treated as different venues because they're not easily sold on the other exchange.

Assets and Derivatives

For the purposes of the book, the following chapter is focused on five asset classes that are used in the later examples. We'll explore adding the assets to your algorithm and how to access the data used in later examples.

Quant modeling is easiest in liquid markets where well-formatted and maintained data exist. The majority of QuantConnect price data is supplied by Algoseek (algoseek.com). Established in 2015, Algoseek provides excellent, point-in-time data recorded directly from the exchanges and low latency real-time feeds. It offers scalable pricing plans that include leasing data, so quants can access large datasets for lower prices.

Most assets are listed and eventually delisted. In QuantConnect assets are called *securities* (qnt.co/book-securities) and are stored in a central securities collection. Most asset classes share common properties, such as market hours, margin requirements, profit-loss accounting, and security properties like contract multipliers.

```
self.securities["SPY"]                    # SPY security from collection
self.securities["SPY"].price              # Current price of SPY
self.securities["SPY"].symbol             # SPY symbol object
self.securities["SPY"].holdings.quantity  # Shares of SPY held
```

US Equities

Founded in 1817, the US Equity market is the largest and most liquid market in the world. It represents half of the world's market capitalization and has roughly 9,000 companies listed.

Events in a company's life cycle, such as the IPO, regular and special dividends, stock splits and reverse splits, mergers and acquisitions, and so on, are called corporate actions. These events impact the value of a company and are important factors to understand. In the following chapters, we will explore examples of how AI trained on corporate actions may be deployed in trading strategies.

Corporate financial performance data, such as revenue, costs, and profitability reported on financial statements–balance sheets, income statements, cash flow statements, and earnings forecast data—are a company's fundamental data. Fundamental data providers dutifully record company quarterly filings to the SEC. Some standardize (or harmonize) reported items into adjusted numbers that can be compared across industries and markets with different accounting conventions or practices. From financial statement data, financial analysts formulate financial ratios such as the price-earnings (PE) ratio and free-cash flow to asset ratio as common metrics to compare different companies' valuations. In the following chapters, we will explore examples of applying machine-learning techniques to predict asset prices or formulate trading strategies based on these fundamental ratios.

In QuantConnect you can easily fetch fundamental data for individual companies and develop a stock screen based on fundamental data.

```
self.add_universe(self._filter)    # Add a filtered equity data universe

def _filter(self, fundamental):    # Select symbols based on pe_ratio
    return [c.symbol for c in fundamental if c.valuation_ratios.pe_ratio < 10]
```

Some ratios used later in the book are described here:

- PE Ratio—Close price of the asset divided by earnings per share.
- Revenue Growth—Growth of the company revenue in percent from income statements.
- Free Cash Flow Percent—Free Cash Flow as a percentage of operating cash flow.
- Dividend Payout Ratio—Ratio of the dividend payments to net earnings.

US Equity Corporate Events

Over a company life cycle, many of the same corporate events occur, starting with the IPO, secondary offerings, cash or stock dividends, stock splits and reverse splits, ticker and company name changes, mergers and acquisitions, and finally delistings. In QuantConnect, these are modeled as follows:

Splits—Companies can divide or consolidate shares to make them more accessible to market participants when the price changes dramatically (Figure 1.10). As company valuation grows, the price per share can exceed the purchasing power of retail investors. A classic example is Berkshire Hathaway Class-A stock, which has never split and is worth more than $200,000 per share today. This leads to lower transaction volume and a potentially less efficient market. Similarly, as an asset price falls, it encounters pressure from the exchanges to keep the price above $1 to remain listed—by consolidating shares (e.g., swapping two for one) in a **reverse split,** a company can double its list price to remain compliant with exchange rules.

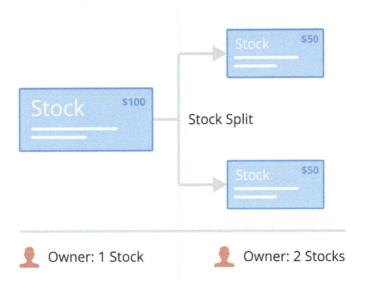

Figure 1.10 Stock value and number of shares owned before and after a split event.

In QuantConnect, splits are events passed to the split event handler that can trigger an algorithmic response for trading or incorporate in the data series for research:

```
def on_splits(self, splits):              # Dedicated splits event handler
    split = splits.get(self._symbol)

def on_data(self, slice:                  # Splits in on_data events
    split = slice.splits.get(self._symbol)
```

Splits change the price of an asset instantly, so care is needed to reset algorithm states, such as indicators that might depend on continuous prices.

Dividends—As companies pass profitability, some elect to issue dividends to shareholders. These dividends are usually paid quarterly, but ultimately, the distribution amount and frequency are up to the company's chief financial officer and the board. Dividends are quoted in dollars per share and distributed as cash to your brokerage. In QuantConnect, these dividends are passed into the dividend event handler and can be used to elicit an algorithmic response:

```
def on_data(self, slice):
    dividend = slice.dividends.get(self._symbol)

def on_dividends(self, dividends):
    dividend = dividends.get(self._symbol)
```

You can request historical data for both splits and dividends. This is helpful to manually calculate an asset's dividend yield or forecast dividend trends.

```
# Fetch all dividends for symbols paid in the last year
history = self.history[Dividend](symbols, timedelta(365))
```

The value received from paid dividends can then be modeled as a payment in cash, or applied to the price of the asset through a process called data normalization.

Data Normalization—To accurately compare two securities, we need to adjust the historical prices to account for price splits and dividend payments in a process called data normalization. These adjustments use a formula to change historical prices to reflect their value growth as accurately and smoothly as possible. There are issues with data normalization, which we won't go into in this book. Still, as a first pass, the adjusted price data does a good job of simplifying the research process by incorporating splits and dividends. For more realistic accounting of the impact of dividends and splits on your investment strategies, QuantConnect supports a *raw* mode, which applies the dividends as cash to your portfolio and lets you decide how and when to reinvest them.

In QuantConnect, you select the data normalization mode while adding the assets to your strategy:

```
# No adjustment of historical prices, and dividends paid as cash
self.add_equity("AAPL", data_normalization_mode=DataNormalizationMode.RAW)

# Full split and dividend adjustment of historical prices
self.add_equity("AAPL",
data_normalization_mode=DataNormalizationMode.ADJUSTED)

# Only adjusting for splits, and paying dividends as cash
self.add_equity("AAPL",
data_normalization_mode=DataNormalizationMode.SPLIT_ADJUSTED)
```

Security Changes—IPO, Renames, Spin-offs, Mergers, and Delistings—A company's regular activity generates many modeling challenges for a quant. Although these corporate events do not impact price, they track the listing status on the exchange. Handling them is important to ensure your portfolio's value is continuous through the change. We'll briefly review some of these next and show how they're handed in QuantConnect.

IPO—When a company is ready, it can apply to be publicly listed on an exchange. Once approved it will be formally listed in an IPO. When any asset is added to your algorithm, it generates a securities-changed event with the details of the new listing.

```
def on_securities_changed(self, changes):
    for security in changes.added_securities:
        Pass
```

Renames—Companies often rebrand to reflect their new business lines or to swap for a better market tickers. These ticker changes are handled in symbol-changed events, which provides the new and old ticker to your strategy. Swapping to the new ticker is not required, as QuantConnect uses the Symbol object to track assets.

```python
def on_symbol_changed_events(self, changes):
    for symbol, change in changes.items():
        self.log(f"Change: { change.old_symbol} -> {change.new_symbol}")
```

Spin-offs and Mergers—Companies occasionally acquire smaller companies, engulfing the smaller company in the transaction. This is modeled as a simple delisting of the smaller company. Mergers are similar but can result in a new ticker; this is modeled as a delisting and a rename.

Delistings—Most asset classes have some form of delisting. For equities, this is the removal of the company from the public markets. The event is captured in the delistings event handler. In addition, it will show up in the securities changed event as a removed security.

```python
def on_delistings(self, delistings):          # Asset delisting events
    delisting = delistings.get(self._symbol)

def on_securities_changed(self, changes):     # Removal from selected screen
    for security in changes.removed_securities:
        self.log(f'Security {security.Symbol} removed from universe')
```

US Equity Options

An option is a contract stipulating the *right* but not obligation to purchase an asset at a specific predetermined price (called the "strike price") on a specific date in the future (called "expiration date" or "expiry"). They are classified as a derivative—where the option's theoretical price strongly depends on the underlying asset. At the option expiration, in-the-money options are exchanged for shares of the underlying security.

Following are key properties of US equity options:

- Underlying Asset—This is the underlying equity for the contract, accessed with the `underlying` property.
- Option Right—Calls give the holder the right to buy stock at a specific price, while puts give the holder the right to sell the stock.
- Strike Price—Strike is the contractual price for the option and is important for determining the option's value and how it will be exercised at expiration.
- Expiration Date—The last date the options can be traded or exercised. American options may be exercised at any time and are settled by physical delivery of the underlying stock.

- Contract Multiplier—In equity options, each option contract represents 100 shares of the underlying assets. This contract multiplier should be multiplied to the listed prices to compute actual "invoice" prices and payout of the option contract.

Options data are disseminated by the Options Price Reporting Authority (OPRA), which aggregates the prices from the US options exchanges. Due to the regularly expiring contracts and strike prices, options generate orders of a magnitude more price data than equities. On a given day, roughly 1.5 million option contracts are available on approximately 4,000 of the most liquid companies. This generates hundreds of terabytes of financial data and can be challenging to process and analyze.

In QuantConnect, options data can be added individually or filtered from a universe of assets. Each underlying asset has hundreds of option contracts available, forming a universe based on each asset.

```
option = self.add_option("SPY")    # Requesting a universe of options on SPY
option.set_filter( … )             # Filter the option contracts returned

self.add_option_contract(contract_symbol)   # Specific option contract

def on_data(self, slice):                   # Using option chain in on_data
    chain = slice.option_chains.get(option.symbol)
```

When the underlying stock price is higher (lower) than the strike price of a call (put) option, the option is said to be in the money (ITM). That is, if exercised, the option will lead to positive cash flow to the buyer of the option; conversely when the underlying stock price is lower (higher) than the strike price of a call (put) option, the option is said to be out-of-the-money (OTM). OTM options can be used as an insurance policy to hedge against unlikely events.

The majority of US equity options are settled physically—through the transfer of shares according to the terms stipulated in the option contract. Although US equity options are mostly "American" options, meaning these options can be exercised before the expiration date, it is unlikely that a call option will be exercised early, as Option Pricing Theory predicts that the value of the call option before expiry should always be higher than the intrinsic value, which is the value if you exercise the option. To lock-in a gain for an ITM call option, the correct action is to "sell to close" the call option position. If you hold the ITM call option to expiry, your broker will automatically exercise on your behalf, and you will receive the underlying shares and pay for them with cash at the strike price. Of course, in this case, since the strike price is below the market price of the underlying, you may turn around and sell the shares for an immediate gain (mind the tax consequences if you sell).

On the other hand, American put options can be and often do get exercised early. If you sell a put option, the buyer may exercise their right to sell their shares to you before expiry. In this case, you will be "assigned" to buy and receive the shares above market price, incurring a loss. As an insurer, you are responsible for paying the claim. If the ITM put is held till expiration, then the put will be exercised automatically by the broker of the buyer of the put. The "assignment" process for early exercise and exercise expiry is managed by the options exchange and facilitated by your broker on a first in, first out (FIFO) basis.

Index Options

Options on equity indices work similarly as individual equity options except for two important differences: they are "European," that is, they can only be exercised on the expiration date, and they are cash settled, with the payout computed based on the difference between the index level and the strike level multiplied by the contract multiplier.

QuantConnect supports three index option monthly option chains, along with their weekly counterparts: VIX (VIXW), NDX (NQX), and SPX (SPXW).

NDX—NASDAQ lists regular (NDX) European options on Nasdaq-100 indices. The NDX's reference index is the level of Nasdaq-100, with a contract multiplier of 100.

SPX—Chicago Board of Option Exchange (CBOE) lists regular SPX European options on S&P500 indices. The SPX's reference index is the level of S&P500, with a contract multiplier of 100.

VIX—The CBOE lists regular VIX European options calculated using SPX option bid/ask quotes that estimates the 30-day measure of the expected volatility of the S&P500 Index. It has a contract multiplier of 100.

These indexes can be added to an algorithm as follows:

```
self._index_symbol = self.add_index('SPX').symbol    # Add index to algorithm
option = self.add_index_option(self._index_symbol)   # Add options on index
option.set_filter(-2, 2, 0, 90)                      # Filter contracts
```

Due to the cash settlement, the US Internal Revenue Service also has different tax treatments for index options and equity options. Please consult your tax advisor for details. Many brokerages require special permission to trade index options. Some do not allow trading index options due to the different tax treatments. Inquire with your broker to determine your accounts' eligibility for index option trading.

US Futures

The US futures markets were originally created for agricultural products, such as wheat, corn, and soybeans in the 1850s, and later expanded into other commodities like meat, lumber, industrial and precious metals, energy resources, and financial instruments, such as bonds, indices, and currencies. They allowed commodity producers to reduce their market risk and fix a price for their produce ahead of time, so that the producers could plan their production with relative certainty of future revenue. The Chicago Mercantile Exchange (CME) Group is the largest collection of futures exchanges in the United States, closely followed by the Intercontinental Exchange (ICE) Group.

Futures contracts have an expiry date for when the settlement is performed. Contracts are generally categorized into monthly or quarterly contracts. QuantConnect supports the 160 most liquid future products. Each product has a collection of future contracts representing their discrete expiry dates, and forms a universe:

```
future = self.add_future(Futures.Indices.SP_500_E_MINI)  # Add ES future
future.set_filter(0, 90)                                 # Filter 90 days
```

For each future product ("chain"), there are many, overlapping future contracts active with different expiry dates and different prices. The future contract that tracks the underlying commodity or securities (called spot) most closely is called the front month. "Rolling" is the process of selecting the next front-month contract. When this roll occurs, the price of the front-month contract jumps, as they are two different contracts with different expiry dates.

To create a normalized price series for the front contract for analysis, a virtual continuous front contract was created that stitches many contracts together to form a price series. Note, the continuous front contract price is not the true price of the underlying contract, but a normalized price series to capture the continuous movement of the fundamental value for data analysis. There are many methods of creating this normalized series, but as it is only a representation of the price moment there is no one "correct" way. There are nine possible combinations of normalization methods available in QuantConnect, which can be specified by the `add_future` method.

In QuantConnect, this continuous front contract is referenced as the *canonical* contract. The current underlying, tradable, contract is called the *mapped* asset. This can be accessed as follows:

```
future = self.add_future(Futures.Indices.SP_500_E_MINI)    # Canonical asset
adjusted_price = self.securities[future.symbol].price      # Adjusted price
raw_price = self.securities[future.mapped].price           # Raw price
```

When routing trades, you need to use the underlying mapped assets as the continuous contract is not tradable.

```
self.market_order(future.mapped, 1)      # Buy 1 contract of mapped asset
```

In live trading when the front contract rolls, there will be a discontinuity in the continuous price of mapped assets. Therefore, any indicators built on the continuous "canonical" prices should be reviewed and reset to adjust for the jump in the price of the mapped asset after a roll. After settlement, the exchange will delist the contract, triggering a delisting event in QuantConnect.

Most modern futures markets settle profit and loss daily in cash, so there is not a big cash payment at expiry. But the majority of commodities and financial futures are still settled in kind, requiring delivery of physical assets. Therefore, speculative traders, who normally do not intend to take or make delivery, should close or roll their futures position ahead of expiry. Many brokerages have an automatic liquidation policy in place when physical-delivery futures are near expiry. This eliminates the risk of delivery that financial brokers do not support. Such liquidations can have unintended and likely negative consequences on your investment portfolio, so traders are advised to consult their brokers for an early liquidation date in order to close or roll their futures positions ahead of forced liquidation.

Cryptocurrency

In the last decade, cryptocurrency has exploded as a new global asset class. As a decentralized store of value and business ecosystem, it had wide appeal. Early adopters were well rewarded with enormous gains in value.

Trading is split between centralized exchanges and decentralized exchanges (DEX). Most exchanges were built by technologists with modern application program interfaces (APIs) but limited knowledge of the financial infrastructure underpinning traditional financial markets. As such, they operate in a similar way to mid-century US exchanges—disconnected and independent before the SIP connected them with a nationwide feed. Most rely on private market makers to provide liquidity, and other funds who perform inter-exchange arbitrage to balance asset prices between exchanges.

However, the crypto-trading infrastructure is rapidly catching up to those of traditional financial markets. The first crypto exchanges were launched with spot-price trading on cash accounts only. Now there are hundreds of exchanges offering margin trading, and trading on crypto derivatives similar to continuous futures or options.

As they have different prices and no centralized feed, crypto exchanges are considered different markets. They can be added with the add crypto API:

```
# requesting price feed for both exchanges by market
coinbase_btcusd = self.add_crypto("BTCUSD", market=Market.COINBASE).symbol
kraken_btcusd = self.add_crypto("BTCUSD", market=Market.KRAKEN).symbol
```

As each exchange has different supported margins, assets, and order types, it's important to set the brokerage model for the relevant exchange. Here you can also set the account type (cash or margin).

```
self.set_brokerage_model(BrokerageName.KRAKEN, AccountType.MARGIN)
```

Chapter 2

Foundations of Quantitative Trading

Quantitative trading is a mix of art and science. In this chapter, we seek to introduce some of the core concepts to comfortably understand the examples in later chapters. These are in no way comprehensive, and due to quantitative trading's artistic nature, many parts are reasonably opinionated, but we'll endeavor to paint a balanced picture. If you're a professional quant or familiar with QuantConnect, feel free to skip this chapter.

Research Process

The classic quant research process flows from research, backtesting, parameter optimization, paper trading (out of sample), and live trading. Researchers following this path tend to reduce their time spent on ideas that may not result in profitable signals, eliminating ideas quickly in research before testing them in a highly accurate backtesting environment for merit once the realities of trading costs are accounted.

Research

A Jupyter notebook (qnt.co/book-cloud-research) provides a space for rapid exploration of ideas in an iterative way. Large datasets can be loaded into memory and plotted easily to visualize signals and test their effectiveness. This allows researchers to quickly explore ideas with a few lines of pandas code. Generally, this research applies vector operations on in-memory datasets, so care should be taken to avoid look-ahead bias.

Backtesting

Backtesting (qnt.co/book-cloud-backtesting) provides you with an accurate representation of your strategy performance, with many details of the market modeled, including trade fees, spreads, slippage, and interest penalties. Like live trading, data from a moment of time is injected into your strategy code bar by bar, allowing you to define how you will set up algorithm state and handle corporate events like splits and dividends. By carefully abstracting code, your research and backtesting code can translate directly to live trading with almost no changes.

Parameter Optimization

A parameter (qnt.co/book-cloud-optimization) is a variable in your strategy that controls the outcome of your backtesting. Try to minimize the number of parameters whenever possible to reduce the likelihood of overfitting. With 5–10 parameters, it is easy to make any strategy perform well in-sample. All strategies have parameters, from implicit ones in your date range and starting capital, to explicit ones in your indicators or signal definition. Your goal at this phase is to test a strategy's sensitivity to its parameters. This robustness testing can give you confidence that the strategy will perform in many environments and that you have not cherry-picked a good set of variables.

Paper and Live Trading

Deploying a strategy to live trading (qnt.co/book-cloud-live-trading) lets you ensure the algorithm signal works out of sample and can highlight potential issues in mechanical aspects of the algorithm, such as processing times, order fill delays, or data delays. Many of these issues don't come to light until after the first trade has been placed, so some practitioners believe it is best to jump straight from idea to live trading with a small amount of capital.

Testing and Debugging Tools

Building a robust algorithmic trading strategy is a challenging endeavor, and even seasoned practitioners rarely get it right on the first try. Using the right tools, you can quickly debug issues and deploy your strategy. In addition, by adopting an iterative build-test, you can dramatically reduce the complexity of the errors encountered. In this section, we'll review the tools and coding processes to build strategies quickly.

There are four key tools for designing and debugging.

Debuggers

Debugging (qnt.co/book-cloud-debugging) should be the first step to understanding errors in backtesting code execution. Debuggers pause program execution to inspect the state of variables or execute code snippets to test executions. To trigger debugging in QuantConnect, click the border next to the line of code where you'd like the program to pause, then press the backtest button with the small bug icon (see Figure 2.1).

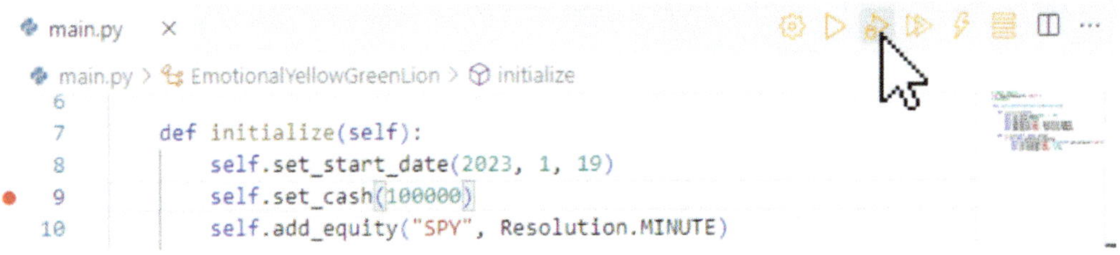

Figure 2.1 Running backtests in QuantConnect Cloud with debugging mode.

Separate from the IDE debugger tool, QuantConnect can stream messages to the cloud console environment during a backtest or live trading. This is a crude way to confirm that signals are being triggered and get a sense of your strategy execution.

```
self.debug(f"Signal triggered, placing limit order: {limit}")
```

Logging

Log (qnt.com/book-logging) statements are strings recorded during backtests. It is best to record key decision moments because backtests can replay millions of data events. A log statement placed in the wrong place can generate millions of lines of text that are difficult to analyze. Take care when placing the log to keep them readable. Unlike streamed debug messages, log statements are permanent and can be referred to later if needed.

```
self.log(f"Signal triggered, placing limit order: {limit}")
```

Charting

Plots help to visualize models and help you understand edge cases for debugging. They can quickly reveal outliers in data and the signal's distribution of values.

When generating custom plots, you should first develop an intuitive guess about what you should see before you draw it. This can help you reject the results and debug the underlying issues. For example, a plot of an asset's price standard deviations should be between −4 and +4, with any outliers occurring during extreme market conditions, such as during the COVID-19 pandemic in March 2020.

In QuantConnect, there is a powerful custom charting application program interface (API, qnt.com/book-charting). Default plots can be created with a single line of code or customized ones with two or three lines if the chart is defined first.

```python
# Create a line plot with default options
self.plot("deviations", "AAPL", asset_deviation)

# Instantiate with custom colors and series type
chart = Chart("deviations")
chart.add_series( Series("AAPL", SeriesType.SCATTER, "$",
                  Color.GREEN, ScatterMarkerSymbol.TRIANGLE)
)
self.plot("deviations", "AAPL", asset_deviation)
```

Object Store

The QuantConnect Object Store (qnt.co/book-object-store) is a key-value data store for low-latency storage and retrieval of information. Objects can be stored and retrieved there programmatically across all the layers of QuantConnect technology (research, backtest, optimization, and live trading).

During a backtest, you can build large objects you'd like to analyze and store them for later analysis. This can be helpful when the objects are too large to plot, or when you'd like to perform analysis across many backtests.

```python
self.object_store.save("key", "value")          # Save a string to object store
string_data = self.object_store.read("key")     # Retrieve the object

self.object_store.save_bytes("key", bytes)      # Store a serialized object
byte_data = self.object_store.read_bytes("key") # Retrieve byte data array
```

It can be useful to pair this with the end of the algorithm event handler to write the object for analysis at the end of your strategy's backtest.

```python
# At the end of algo, write data to object store under project id folder
def on_end_of_algorithm(self):
    self.object_store.save(f"{self.project_id}/backtest", self._data)
```

Coding Process

The most common mistake beginners make is writing hundreds of lines of code without running a single backtest. As long as you're using backtests to verify the *mechanics* of your implementation plan and not tune the value of a parameter, they are an excellent tool for building and debugging your strategy. Using backtesting to tune the strategy parameters risks overfitting, which we'll cover later in this chapter.

Using an iterative build process of a "build-test," you can add one layer at a time to your strategy and then backtest it over a short window of time, verifying it behaves as you expect with debug statements, or verifying the order times and quantities match your expectations. At each layer, take the time to write clean, commented code with any necessary abstractions. This can feel clunky and slow initially, but the time saved in debugging a complex strategy can be enormous.

Time and Look-ahead Bias

Financial data comes in two different "shapes" according to the period it covers: point values or period values. As a backtest progresses, data is emitted in a precise sequence to prevent seeing future data points before they should be available to strategy code. This is done to prevent look-ahead bias—a form of quant research error caused by having knowledge of the future in an algorithm.

Point data only has a single timestamp. Examples include a trade tick, a measurement of weather, or a customer transaction. Period values have two timestamps: a start time and an end time of the period they cover. Examples include a daily bar for stocks, opening at 9:30 am and closing at 4 pm (Figure 2.2).

Figure 2.2 A data event occurs at the end of the data consolidation period. Tick data does not have a consolidation period, so data events occur when a new tick arrives.

In QuantConnect, period values are represented by the time and end_time data properties.

```
tick.time           # Instant of time trade or quote occurred
tradebar.time       # Start of the price bar
tradebar.end_time   # End of the price bar
```

Look-ahead Bias

Look-ahead bias occurs when knowledge of future events is used in an algorithm, causing the performance to look better in backtesting than it would in out-of-sample performance. It is very easy to fall into this bias. Some examples include the following:

- Designing strategies based on knowledge of recent major market movements.
- Timestamping data at the start time of a period rather than when it was available, which may be several days later. For example, government data representing "May-2024" likely won't be available until June 10, the following month.
- Filling trades based on the close price of daily bars, which occurs when the market is closed.

- Using a large language model (LLM) trained and released in 2024 on a backtest that starts in 2018.

Market Hours and Scheduling

Every asset class has a set of market hours (qnt.co/book-market-hours) to describe when they are open for trading. This can be as simple as crypto, which is 24 hours a day, or as complex as futures markets that open and shut multiple times within a day. Most markets include market holidays when the market is closed entirely or shortened market hours around Christmas or other holidays. The collection of days and hours when a market is open for transactions is called a market calendar.

With robust time handling, you can model a market calendar in your algorithm. QuantConnect accurately accounts for these market hours for all supported asset classes. You can schedule code (qnt.co/book-scheduled-events) to run based on the market status using the scheduling API in QuantConnect:

```
# At the end of trading week, trigger rebalance function 30 minutes after
# market open - accounting for market holidays and trading hours.
symbol = Symbol.create('SPY', SecurityType.EQUITY, Market.USA)
self.schedule.on(
    self.date_rules.week_end(symbol),
    self.time_rules.after_market_open(symbol, 30),
    self._rebalance
)
```

For AI models, it's imperative to retrain them on recent data. This training is ideally done frequently to adjust to the latest market conditions. Using the built-in train method, you can schedule a function callback premarket and launch a long-running training method to refresh your model.

```
self.train(self.date_rules.every(DayOfWeek.SUNDAY),
           self.time_rules.at(8,0), self._training_method)
```

Strategy Styles

Most strategies are variants of four core ideas: momentum, reversion, scalping, or arbitrage. Momentum strategies use signals, such as technical indicators, sentiment, or news, to invest with the larger up-and-down swings of the market—attempting to exit before the trends lose momentum. Reversion strategies seek turning points in an asset's rapid rise and bet it will return to historical mean prices or industry benchmarks. Scalping strategies look for tiny fluctuations in asset prices and enter and exit quickly for small gains. Arbitrage strategies typically buy and sell the same or similar assets in different locations to benefit from small variations in the asset price.

Trading Signals

Strategies typically fall into two types of signal categories: a binary flag or a continuous signal. These signals are part of a strategy's alpha or factor creation.

Continuous signals are numeric and indicate the strength or rank of the idea being tested. Examples of this could include calculating a factor score based on the price-earnings (PE) ratio of a universe of assets. Assets could be assigned a score, and then allocated capital based on the score's strength.

Binary signals are discrete, generally signaling long, flat, or short investment directions. They could use the same data but only generate a trade signal when reaching some target criteria—for example, only emitting a signal when the PE ratio of an asset is less than five. More natural applications of discrete signals arise from event trading, such as the approval of a new drug release for a pharmaceutical company.

There are no fixed rules around these categories, and you can build hybrids together. For example, you could convert a binary news event announcing the FDA approval of a drug into a continuous signal, by calculating the probability that the drug has been approved based on the premarket trials and other emerging public information. Once the final announcement is made, the probability would go to 100%. This allows your strategy to take positions before the final announcement.

Allocating Capital

Using these signals, traders then decide how to allocate their buying power for the best performance. There are three basic styles of capital allocation: discrete trade/bet placements, continuous portfolio allocations, or tactical allocations (a hybrid of these approaches). The allocation is typically the responsibility of a portfolio construction system.

Classic quantitative finance focuses on portfolio allocators' desire to keep capital invested at all times, following the old adage "time in market is more important than timing the market." They focus on continuous signals that generate a ranking of assets and create a diversified portfolio with the best assets possible. A whole field of portfolio allocation science, and most notably, Modern Portfolio Theory, emerged seeking to carefully weight portfolio assets to improve portfolio performance. An example of this could be ranking companies in the S&P500 by fundamental performance and allocating to the top 20 companies, with the allocation sizes inversely proportional to their trailing volatility. These strategies are best measured by alpha, beta, and Sharpe ratio, and benchmarked to the major indices.

```
# Rebalance portfolio to allocation by weights
targets = [PortfolioTarget("AAPL", 0.5), PortfolioTarget("MSFT", 0.5)]
self.set_holdings(targets)
```

Discrete trading strategies scan markets for specific criteria, and then enter trades with sizing and risk allocations independent of other holdings in the portfolio.

The entry and exit signals are typically discrete (short −1, flat, or long 1). Because this is closer to how humans trade, it is a common bridge for professional traders automating their trading strategies. The performance of such strategies is often uncorrelated with wider markets and benchmarked by absolute returns—a target percent return per year. For risk control, more advanced versions of discrete trading use a modified Kelly criterion, treating asset trades as bets with individual payoffs and risk criteria. These strategies are commonly measured by win-rate, expectancy, and Sharpe ratio. Quantitatively minded discrete traders tend to put on many bets across a wide universe of assets to smooth their overall performance.

```python
# Manually create and route orders for individual stocks or strategies
long_straddle = OptionStrategies.straddle(symbol, strike, expiry)
self.buy(long_straddle, 50)

# Volatility adjusted order position size with stops
trading_range = self.atr("SPY", 30)
quantity = risk_capital / trading_range.current.value
self.market_order("SPY", quantity)
self.stop_market_order("SPY", -quantity, data["SPY"].close - trading_range)
```

Tactical asset allocation is like classic portfolio allocation, in that it aims to be invested at all times but adjusts its allocation according to strategy signals. This could be small reweights of existing portfolio items or a complete replacement of the portfolio contents. An example of this is a strategy allocating to primary indices during bullish markets but reducing position sizes in equities and allocating to bonds during market volatility. These strategies are typically benchmarked to major indices and measured by alpha, beta to indices, and Sharpe ratio.

Regimes and Portfolios of Strategies

Striving for perfection across all market regimes is often a risky path that leads to overfitting. Unless your strategy is market agnostic—like a high-frequency trading strategy profiting from exchange rebates and routing trades, or a market-neutral strategy profiting from arbitrage opportunities—you must embrace that there will likely be drawdowns in your strategy. Many of the world's top-performing funds, such as Renaissance Technologies or World Quant, use a "many alpha" approach with complex portfolio management systems that decide how to weigh the signals of their millions of alphas.

Bullish, strongly trending markets might best fit long-only, levered, trend-following strategies seeking to capitalize on the strong markets. During market turbulence, such as uncertainty about elections or interest rate hikes, the markets may tend to "range"—trading up and down within a narrow band of values until more clarity arrives. In these periods, mean-reversion strategies may perform better, buying the local price minima and selling the local price maxima. Finally, during bear markets, a portfolio manager may select defensive strategies like bonds or short-biased equities, and algorithms that react faster to market news due to the higher volatility in bear markets. Planning and building a suite of these strategies helps ensure you have the right portfolio bias during market regime changes.

Although price is quite challenging to predict, volatility tends to have momentum. Investors often panic together and cause rapid price movements. Some quant's design strategies focused on high- or low-volatility environments using options or shorting volatility.

Parameter Sensitivity Testing and Optimization

Parameters (qnt.co/book-cloud-optimization) are variables in every algorithm that impact its performance. These variables can be very subtle, and you often need to carefully review your strategy code to identify them all—even very subtle properties like starting date and initial capital can have substantial impacts. One of the most common errors of quantitative research is overfitting a strategy to past data.

Overfitting occurs when a function is too closely fit to a limited training data set. Overfitting can occur in your trading algorithms if you have many parameters or select parameter values that worked very well in the past but are sensitive to small changes in their values. In these cases, your algorithm will likely be fine-tuned to fit the detail and noise of the historical data to the extent that it negatively impacts the *live* performance of your algorithm. Figure 2.3 shows examples of underfit, optimally fit, and overfit functions.

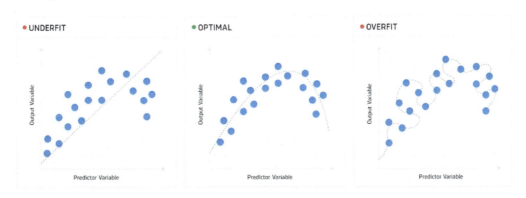

Figure 2.3 Overfitting and underfitting a model leads to poor predictions on samples outside of the training dataset.

A strategy that may be optimally fitted would not necessarily have the smoothest equity curve. It would have parameter choices that showed the strongest performance over a wide range of potential values. To lower the chances of overfitting, we recommend following the following steps:

1. Remove

Remove as many parameters as possible from your strategy. Ideally, the parameter can simply be removed entirely, such as eliminating a signal that isn't contributing significantly to the strategy returns. For machine learning, this can be done with PCA (discussed in later chapters) to transform the original dataset into its key components.

2. Replace

When it's not possible to remove a parameter, seek to replace it with a probability, natural (real-world) reason, or a data source.

Imagine your strategy was looking for news releases every hour at minute zero (10:00 am), seeking to aggregate the last hour of sentiment and rebalancing the portfolio every hour. Rather than optimizing to see which minute *off* the hour (e.g., 10:03, 10:06, 10:07 am) gives the best performance, it would be more natural to **remove** this parameter and build a rolling window of sentiment and perform the analysis continuously. Alternatively, you could **replace** this parameter by finding a data source for the news feeds and perform the sentiment analysis when there is a news release for your assets—a real-world replacement for a parameter.

Once you've built the new sentiment analysis technique, it would be tempting to introduce another parameter, such as rebalancing when you see a sentiment jump of ±10%. Instead of introducing this arbitrary parameter, you could replace it by calculating a rolling sentiment standard deviation score. This could emit a constant sentiment signal strength 'stdev/4' that a portfolio construction system uses in its allocations decisions—dynamically scaling the allocation according to sentiment. Although this unfortunately introduces another subtle parameter—the lookback window period for the standard deviation—it is at least a dynamically changing probability, rather than an arbitrary fixed target score.

3. Reduce

Finally, and potentially the hardest step to take, is to avoid the lure of backtesting while adjusting parameters to improve performance. Whenever possible, build your strategy on a small window of time, testing its mechanics and preserving as much recent data as possible for the out-of-sample test. Before you put the algorithm into forward trading, you can test it on out-of-sample data, but aim to only use this data two or three times before discarding an idea.

Parameter Sensitivity Testing

QuantConnect offers a powerful grid search parameter testing tool to quickly explore all possible combinations of a backtest's parameters. This is somewhat dangerous in the wrong hands, and with great power comes great responsibility. In QuantConnect, parameters for this tool are set in the side panel of each project and loaded into your code as shown here:

```
# retrieve stored parameter
parameter_value = self.get_parameter("parameterName")
```

We recommend that our tool be used for *parameter sensitivity testing*—exploring the decay in performance across a range of parameter values. Your algorithm is likely robust if total performance is similar across a wide range of parameter values. If you see a concentration of returns on a narrow range of parameter values, it is likely an artifact in the data, or a few isolated trades are dramatically improving your performance. In recent history, the biggest cause of these outsized returns is a perfectly timed short of the March 2020 COVID crash, a 6-sigma global event unlikely to happen again soon. If your combination of parameters is shorting COVID-2020, you're likely overfitting.

The Sharpe ratio does not detect these hidden outliers underlying the equity curve, as it only considers the total mean and variance of the returns and relies on a normal distribution of returns in the data. Given enormous empirical evidence showing that returns *do not* follow a normal distribution, Bailey and De Prado (2012) proposed the Probabilistic Sharpe Ratio (PSR) as a probability measure calculated from a sample of the returns. Using the discrete daily or trade returns, the PSR informs us of the probability that the estimated Sharpe ratio is greater than a chosen benchmark (i.e., whether the estimate is statistically significant).

In QuantConnect, this is calculated and included in the backtest results using a benchmark Sharpe ratio of 1.0. You can interpret the PSR scores generated as a percent probability that the true Sharpe ratio exceeds 1.0—i.e., a PSR score of 77% indicates a 77% chance your strategy has a Sharpe ratio above 1.0.

Margin Modeling

Every strategy starts with a capital allocation and seeks to deploy it as efficiently as possible. To do this, algorithms must manage their buying power well to open their desired positions (qnt.com/book-buying-power).

Margin is a calculation of a trading account's maximum allowed purchasing power. It is based on its assets on hand (including cash), the account type, and your brokerage. There are a few different ways to model margin defined by the SEC and FINRA, but ultimately, it's a line of credit. This makes it your broker's decision on how much leverage it will provide based on the market risk and collateral in account.

The margin available and the total margin used at any time are available as properties of the portfolio object in your QuantConnect strategy. These properties calculate the portfolio-wide margin across all asset types.

```
self.portfolio.margin_remaining    # Buying power available for allocation
self.portfolio.total_margin_used   # Buying power allocated on holdings
```

Equities

Equities have three main forms of margin available for investors:

Cash Accounts—Buying power is restricted to cash on hand. After a trade, it can take up to three days to settle the cash and transfer ownership of the shares. In QuantConnect, this can be specified with the brokerage model.

```
# Set cash account and all broker models
self.set_brokerage_model(BrokerageName.INTERACTIVE_BROKERS_BROKERAGE,
                         AccountType.CASH)
```

Margin Accounts—Brokers can offer up to 2x overnight or 4x intraday of additional buying power with margin accounts. Order settlement is also instant, allowing fast redeployment of capital. Most of the examples in this book rely on leverage margin accounts.

```
# Set cash account and all broker models
self.set_brokerage_model(BrokerageName.INTERACTIVE_BROKERS_BROKERAGE,
                         AccountType.MARGIN)
```

Portfolio Margin—A dynamic risk-based estimate of the margin available based on holding volatility and liquidity. If you have safe, cash-like assets, they will be useful collateral for the broker and your available margin will remain high. Portfolio margin accounts settle instantly and offer up to 6.7x your initial cash as buying power. QuantConnect does not have portfolio margin modeling yet, but you can achieve a crude approximation of it by setting leverage to 7.

```
self.add_equity("SPY", leverage=7)
```

Equity Options

Equity option contracts provide leveraged exposure to the equity assets. They can be used in combinations as betting instruments for many investment theses, including insurance, high volatility, low volatility, ranging, or trending strategies. The notional value of the contract is 100x the list price of the option contract as it represents 100 underlying equity shares.

Option strategies are combinations of option contracts that reduce the total exposure of an investment. Dozens of investment strategies are available, and QuantConnect models 16 of them. They can be accessed with the shortcut helpers, as shown in the following example. This example adjusts its asset trading strategy according to the forecast volatility, selecting the closest expiry date when it's a low volatility short strategy:

```
if low_volatility:
    contracts = OptionStrategies.short_straddle(option_symbol, strike,
min(expiries))
else:
    contracts = OptionStrategies.straddle(option_symbol, strike,
max(expiries))

# Using the OptionStrategies helper, get the contracts to buy
order_tickets = self.buy(contracts, 1)
```

Generally, when buying an option, risk is constrained to the purchase of the option contracts. Margin requirements increase when selling options, which require potentially settling the agreement with 100 shares of the underlying per contract in the event of a loss. This is where hedged strategies shine, by providing a reduction in the total risk exposure of the strategy.

In QuantConnect, the hedging margin requirements are calculated automatically for you, allowing you to focus on the alpha of the strategy and make better use of available capital.

Futures

Future contracts charge a fixed amount per contract, called the initial margin, and then require a minimum amount to be kept in the brokerage account to keep the contract open, called the maintenance margin. As with equities, if the account falls below the minimum requirements, the exchange or broker can liquidate the position.

Each contract has a varying initial and maintenance margin requirement that the exchange periodically updates according to contract price and volatility movements. The notional value for a future contract (total value controlled) is the unit asset price multiplied by the contract multiplier. The contract multiplier was originally the typical unit of sale for the commodity (e.g., 100 barrels of oil), but now with the rise of financial futures, it is typically a scaling factor to provide contracts with similar exposure to other listed futures.

In QuantConnect, all the prices, contract multipliers, and initial and maintenance margin requirements are modeled to provide accurate point-in-time buying power. This happens automatically, but if you'd like to explicitly get the number of contracts or shares you can buy or sell with a fixed capital allocation, you can use the following method:

```
# Fee-adjusted quantity of contracts for 20% buying power
contract = canonical_future.mapped
quantity = self.calculate_order_quantity(contract, 0.2)
```

Diversification and Asset Selection

Diversification is when you invest in a variety of assets to earn better overall returns. If you combine assets correctly, you can reduce your overall portfolio risk, as the drawdowns of one investment will be offset by gains in another.

"Diversification is the only free lunch in investing."

— *Harry Markowitz*

With QuantConnect, you can add multiple stocks and asset types to your portfolio and explore the benefits of harnessing diversification. The most straightforward form of diversification is selecting assets with different industries, customer bases, and risk-return profiles. By choosing fundamentally diverse investments, you can improve your portfolio's chances of surviving market crashes. On QuantConnect, you can select stocks based on their industry to diversify within US equities or even invest across one of the 11 asset classes we support. Additionally, through our exchange traded fund (ETF) support, you can trade bonds and international market ETFs.

```
# Purchase a portfolio of targets, processing orders intelligently
self.set_holdings([
    PortfolioTarget("SPY", 0.6), PortfolioTarget("BND", 0.4)
]))
```

To improve your portfolio diversification, you can measure asset correlations and add them to your portfolio when they are relatively uncorrelated with your existing holdings. Correlation is a measure of how similar a new asset is to your existing portfolio returns. A value of 1.0 indicates the new asset moves identically to the current portfolio, and −1.0 shows it moves precisely opposite the current portfolio. A value of 0 means the asset moves independently.

```
def beta(self, asset_returns, benchmark_returns):
    covariance = np.cov(asset_returns, benchmark_returns)[0, 1]
    variance = np.var(benchmark_returns)
    return covariance / variance
```

A common mistake is adding stocks to a portfolio that seem independent but move together when the market experiences volatility. Seemingly uncorrelated assets often become correlated in market corrections, so a critical review of historical correlations is essential to surviving future downturns.

Fundamental Asset Selection

In QuantConnect, the selection of assets is called universe selection (qnt.co/book-universe-selection). Universe selection is the picking of the assets for your strategy based on codified criteria. Codifying the selection removes human bias from the decision of assets. Precisely, what filter you apply depends on your strategy investment goals, but the common root of universe selection is avoidance of *selection* or *survivorship* bias through the use of a system or algorithm to include the assets in your algorithm.

Selection bias is an incomplete or unscientific selection of constituents for use in your strategy. The most common form of this is selecting an asset simply due to personal attachment to the brand or company.

Survivorship bias is a type of selection bias where the universe of assets for an investment is limited to those that are still available today. The most common form of this bias would be using today's top performing assets as your universe for a multi-year backtest. Over the last 10–20 years, many companies have failed and been delisted. By selecting assets listed today, you are implicitly applying knowledge of the future.

For example, in hindsight, it is easy to tell Apple or NVIDIA were breakout successes for investors, but at the time, picking them out from thousands of other technology stocks was a much harder task.

Even in the definition of the universe selection function, it is easy to overfit your strategy. If you've hardcoded revenue or profitability filters for your asset universe, keep in mind they could be favorably screening assets. Once the core selection criteria have been defined, you should return to test the sensitivity of the new parameters.

In the following QuantConnect example, we perform selection on corporate fundamental data. In the fundamental object, approximately 900 properties of each company are available for selection.

```python
def select(self, fundamental):
    filtered = [f for f in fundamental if not np.isnan(f.valuation_ratios.pe_ratio)]
    sorted_by_pe_ratio = sorted(filtered, key=lambda f: f.valuation_ratios.pe_ratio)
    return [f.symbol for f in sorted_by_pe_ratio[:10]]
```

Scheduled universe selection reapplies the universe filters at a fixed cadence based on the market calendar. This can increase the algorithm's backtesting speed and reduce portfolio churn by selecting assets for longer. By default, universe selection runs daily, which is too frequent for many strategies.

```python
# Re-run selection at the start of every trading calendar month of SPY.
self.universe_settings.schedule.on(self.date_rules.month_start("SPY"))

# When selection happens, fetch daily bar data from selected assets
self.universe_settings.resolution = Resolution.DAILY

# Add universe selection function
self.add_universe( lambda fundamental: [ ... ] )
```

When a selection should result in no universe changes, you can return the special flag `Universe.UNCHANGED` to return the previously selected universe. This action prevents asset churn in your portfolio and speeds up backtesting.

ETF Constituents Asset Selection

ETFs are baskets of securities seeking to outperform the markets. Many ETFs passively follow popular indexes like the S&P500, providing a cost-efficient way to invest in index constituents with a cost per share 1/100th of the index cost. Indices and overlayed ETFs are also a good list of constituents for stock selection as they follow a well-defined formula for the addition and removal of assets from the universe, which has not changed in many years.

In QuantConnect, you can select an ETF as a data source to power universe selection, closely tracking the index or underlying active strategy. From this universe, you can use the filtering function to request fundamental data of each asset to further narrow your range of instruments.

```python
# Add and filter ETF constituents
self.add_universe(self.universe.etf("QQQ", universe_filter_func=self.filter))

# Narrow universe with other data
def filter(self, constituents):
    return [ c.symbol for c in constituents
            if self.fundamentals(c.symbol).valuation_ratios.pe_ratio > 10
    ]
```

Dollar-Volume Asset Selection

The simplest and fastest method for universe selection is a price and dollar-volume (price times shares traded) filter. This dataset contains the daily price values and volume traded. Using price information, you can construct any technical indicator required and filter and rank by the most liquid assets available.

QuantConnect has short-cut methods to add this automatically with one line of code. The following automatically selects five assets with the highest dollar-volume from the previous trading date:

```python
self.add_universe(self.universe.dollar_volume.top(5))
```

To build more advanced universe types on top of universe data, we recommend using a class to store data and initialize per security properties that keeps your algorithm organized. Using the SymbolData class pattern avoids the common mistake of creating parallel dictionaries to store asset information. As a universe presents its data for selection, the SymbolData constructor can build complex states and track if the asset should be included in the universe.

The following example is pseudocode to share the concept, but the possibilities of each asset's selection and modeling are limitless:

```python
class SymbolData:
    # Construct initial state. Use algorithm to setup state
    def __init__(self, algorithm, symbol, period):
        self._symbol = symbol
        self._sma = SimpleMovingAverage(period)
    # Update internal state with required data, train models
    def update(self, time, price, volume):
        self._sma.update(time, volume)
```

Universe Settings

Universes have many configurable settings (qnt.co/book-universe-selection-settings) to set their desired behavior and control the properties of the assets they add to your strategy. These settings need to be configured during the algorithm initialization. Notable properties that we use in the subsequent chapters are as follows:

Scheduling—Defining a cadence to trigger the universe selection. This improves algorithm performance and reduces asset churn. By default, universes are selected daily.

```python
self.universe_settings.schedule.on(date_rule)
```

Extended Market Hours—By default, data feeds contain normal market hours only. By setting this to true, data from pre- and post-market hours will also be passed to your algorithm.

```python
self.universe_settings.extended_market_hours = True
```

Data Resolution—Defines the resolution of the asset data added from universe selection.

```
self.universe_settings.resolution = Resolution.HOUR
```

Data Normalization Mode—Defines the data adjustment technique to use for asset data added from selection. By default, full split and dividend data normalization are applied.

```
self.universe_settings.data_normalization_mode = DataNormalizationMode.RAW
```

Indicators and Other Data Transformations

Quant practitioners have created thousands of ways to transform raw market data into more digestible forms for analysis. As these transformations have become more and more sophisticated, their connection with the underlying data has become tenuous. The vast majority of these transformations/filters/indicators are lagging signals—providing a summary of the training averages or volatilities.

There is nothing fundamentally wrong with indicators when viewed as data transformations for the sake of analysis. However, technical analysis tends to cross over into voodoo when *causality* is assigned to technical signals. Technical indicators are useful data transformations but do not *cause* the market to react or move in any way. When applying indicators to your strategy, try and keep an impartial, scientific mindset.

QuantConnect implements hundreds of technical indicators (qnt.co/book-supported-indicators), which are helpers covering most technical and basic financial mathematics analysis. Most technical indicators are just thinly disguised variants of mathematical or financial operations: averages and distributions.

Automatic Indicators

In QuantConnect, there are hundreds of helper functions to create indicators that are immediately ready to use (qnt.com/book-automatic-indicators) and registered for future data updates automatically. They are represented by the indicator acronym in the API:

```
# Create warmed-up indicator that automatically updates
auto_rsi = self.rsi("SPY", 10, MovingAverageType.SIMPLE)
```

Manual Indicators

Manual indicators are simple, standalone classes that implement the API behavior. Creating a manual indicator requires manually populating it with required data or registering the object for a data feed. Manually constructing indicators (qnt.co/book-manual-indicators) is harder than automatic ones, but it is helpful to give practitioners total control over the indicators' input data.

```python
# Create an indicator that needs manual update
manual_rsi = RelativeStrengthIndex(10, MovingAverageType.SIMPLE)

# Create 3-tradebar consolidator to control data feed for RSI.
consolidator = TradeBarConsolidator(3)

# Register consolidator for data and pipe those 3TB bars to indicator
self.register_indicator(symbol, manual_rsi, consolidator)
```

Indicator Warm Up

QuantConnect has built all its indicators around streaming data feeds to match live trading identically. *Warm up* is the process of streaming historical data into the indicator to prepare it for trading. This can be done automatically by QuantConnect by setting the following flag to true:

```python
self.settings.automatic_indicator_warmup = True
```

Storing Objects

You can use Python's duck-typing magic to conveniently store indicator objects on the security object. The following example shows how to create an automatically updated EMA object on Apple's security object. This new property can be accessed anywhere in the algorithm.

```python
aapl = self.add_equity("AAPL", Resolution.DAILY) # Create apple security
aapl.ema = self.ema("AAPL", 200) # Assign indicator to duck ema variable
```

Indicator Events

Once an indicator is updated, it fires an event you can use to refresh your algorithm's follow-on calculations. This is useful to control the sequence of events your strategy generates. The following example uses the indicator-updated event to plot the indicator on a chart:

```python
# After you create the indicator, attach an event handler
auto_rsi.updated += self.indicator_updated

def update_event_handler(self, indicator, indicator_data_point):
    if indicator.is_ready:
        self.plot("Indicator", "Value", indicator_data_point.value)
```

Sourcing Ideas

The scope of trading ideas a quant can explore is virtually limitless. The markets represent the sum of billions of individual contributing factors in a giant, infinitely complex puzzle! There are tens of thousands of assets, each with their own backgrounds and nuance.

There are two primary camps of idea generation: data-driven investing and hypothesis-driven investing. Both have large established funds following their general principles. We'll explore these two concepts next, as well as online references for how to generate ideas.

Hypothesis-driven Testing

Hypothesis-driven testing focuses on creating a test that you can accept or reject. We recommend that an algorithm hypothesis follow the pattern of cause and effect. Your aim should be to express your strategy in the following sentence:

A change in {cause} leads to an {effect}.

To seek inspiration, consider causes from your experience, intuition, or the media. Generally, causes of financial market movements fall into the following categories:

- Human psychology—mass hysteria or panic, typically the "why" behind momentum ("slow information dissemination" theory).
- World events—core global (political, technological) or local (corporate governance, product releases) events that change the core value of an asset.
- Market or company activity

Consider the examples in Figure 2.4.

Cause	leads to	Effect
Share class stocks are the same company, so any price divergence is irrational…	→	A perfect pairs trade. Since they are the same company, the price will revert.
New stock addition to the S&P500 Index causes fund managers to buy up stock…	→	An increase in the price of the new asset in the universe from buying pressure.
Increase in sunshine hours increases the production of oranges…	→	An increase in the supply of oranges and decreased price for orange juice futures.
Allegations of fraud by the CEO causes investor faith in the stock to fall…	→	A collapse of stock prices for the company as people panic.
FDA approval of a new drug for a pharmaceutical company…	→	A jump in stock prices for the company as the market opportunity expands.
News of a data breach potentially exposing the company to millions in liability…	→	A fall in price as investors weigh potential impact.

Figure 2.4 Cause-effect examples for trading strategy ideas.

Ideally, you should form a hypothesis at the start of your research and spend the remaining time exploring how to test your theory. If you find yourself deviating from your core theory or introducing code that isn't based on that hypothesis, you should stop and go back to thesis development as it risks becoming overfit.

Alvarez et al. (2014) illustrated the danger of creating your hypothesis based on test results. In their research, they examined the earnings yield factor in the technology sector over time. During 1998–1999, before the tech bubble burst, the factor was unprofitable. If you had seen the results and then decided to bet against the factor from 2000 to 2002, you would have lost a lot of money because the factor performed extremely well during that time.

There are millions of potential strategies to explore, limited only by your imagination and understanding of the markets. Once you have chosen a strategy to test, we recommend exploring it for a fixed, time-boxed period to reduce the chances of overfitting.

Data Driven Investing

Data driven investing searches for statistical anomalies and attempts to invest in them without an attempt to explain why they may be occurring.

Following this thesis, you believe explaining why an idea happens is largely a waste of time and likely incorrect. Humans are reasoning, pattern-matching machines and can assign reasons on backward-looking events for almost any data.

One of the strongest reasons to use hypothesis-driven investing is that you have a clear signal to stop trading a strategy when the cause of the hypothesis has ended. With data driven investing, funds can use statistically driven methods to remove alphas from the portfolio when they stop performing.

Quantpedia

As a source for inspiration, you can review multiple online sources for ideas. Quantpedia (qnt.co/book-quantpedia) comprehensively compiles and reviews academic research on trading strategies. Its primary goal is to bridge the gap between academic finance research and practical investment management. They analyze thousands of academic papers to extract actionable trading strategies, covering many asset classes, including equities, commodities, and fixed income.

The platform provides detailed descriptions, performance statistics, and implementation guidelines for each strategy, enabling investors to understand and potentially apply them in real-world scenarios. Strategies are categorized based on factors, such as momentum, value, volatility, and more, allowing users to explore different investment approaches systematically. You can find it at www.quantpedia.com.

QuantConnect Research and Strategy Explorer

The *QuantConnect Research* articles have roughly 100 paper publications with short write-ups on the how the paper was implemented on QuantConnect. These serve as an excellent source of ideas to apply to your own strategies. These can be found at qnt.co/book-research.

The *QuantConnect Explorer* hosts 50 live running strategies written by the core QuantConnect team, running in a public live-trading environment. Each strategy is built to be robust for in- and out-of-sample live trading—fully handling corporate actions and restoring algorithm state in case of restarts. This collection can be found at qnt.co/book-explore.

Part II

Foundations of AI and ML in Algorithmic Trading

Artificial intelligence (AI) refers to using advanced computational techniques and algorithms to perform complex tasks that typically require human intelligence. These tasks range from recognizing patterns in data and understanding natural language to making data-driven decisions.

While machine learning (ML) and AI are closely related fields, they are not synonymous: ML is a subset of AI that deals with developing algorithms and statistical models enabling computers to learn and make decisions without being explicitly programmed for specific tasks. AI includes other algorithms, such as rule-based systems and symbolic reasoning, which do not necessarily involve learning from data.

One of the critical applications of AI in finance is algorithmic trading, with AI analyzing vast amounts of historical data for profitable patterns, making predictions about future market movements with complex market dynamics models, and executing trades at the speed, scale, and efficiency superior to any human trader.

In addition, financial markets are inherently complex and unpredictable, and AI models must be carefully designed and trained, which includes selecting the right data sets, choosing the appropriate algorithms, and continuously monitoring and refining the models to improve their accuracy and reliability.

This part has been designed to provide a practical introduction to navigating this environment. We start with the outline of the step-by-step guide for AI-based financial forecasting, and then discuss each step in detail with hands-on examples illustrating the industry's best practices.

Step-by-step Guide for AI-based Algorithmic Trading

Step 1: Problem Definition
1. Define the problem and the objective; choose the variable you intend to predict or optimize.

Step 2: Dataset Preparation
1. Collect relevant data.
2. Carry out exploratory data analysis.
3. Preprocess the data.
   a. Clean the dataset of missing values.
   b. Clean the dataset of outliers.
   c. Carry out feature engineering.
   d. Consider normalization or standardization of certain features.
   e. Consider transforming time series features to be stationary.
   f. Consider identifying cointegrated time series with the Engle-Granger test.
4. Select the features, i.e., the independent variables with the strongest relationship to the dependent variable (the objective). Use the following:
   a. Correlation analysis
   b. Features importance analysis
   c. Auto-identification of features
   d. Dimensionality reduction/principal component analysis whenever possible
5. Split the dataset into a training and test dataset.

Step 3: Model Choice, Training, and Application
1. Select the most appropriate forecasting algorithm for the model.
2. Train the model typically, by adjusting the model parameters to best fit the historical training dataset, by minimizing the error between the predicted and actual values.
3. Evaluate the model on the test dataset using metrics, such as R-squared or mean square error (MSE). If needed, use cross-validation.
4. Deploy the model and keep retraining it for updated data sets.

Chapter 3

Step 1: Problem Definition

The problem definition step in algorithmic trading focuses on the identification of **the specific financial objective the algorithm aims to achieve,** such as predicting stock prices, optimizing trade execution, or managing risk through dynamic portfolio adjustments.

The chosen financial objective is then translated into **the target variable you intend to predict or optimize**—for example, a stock's future price, the next period's market volatility, or the expected return on a portfolio.

Once the target variable is identified, the next step is to specify **the scope and constraints of the problem**, such as defining the time frame for predictions (e.g., intraday, daily, weekly), the markets or assets to be included (e.g., equities, commodities, forex), any regulatory or operational constraints that must be considered, as well as the trading strategy's risk tolerance and performance benchmarks.

A well-defined problem also includes understanding the relationships between the target variable, **known as labels or dependent variables,** and potential predictor variables, **known as features or factors or independent variables.** These features can include historical price data, trading volumes, economic indicators, and even sentiment analysis from news articles or social media. Establishing **a clear hypothesis about how these features interact with the target variable** will inform the data collection and feature engineering processes.

Let's illustrate this step with three case studies.

Case Study 1: Forecasting Short-term Stock Market Trends

In this case study, the **financial objective** is to identify profitable trading opportunities within a daily time frame, with **the target variable** being the stock's closing price for the next trading day.

The **time frame** of the problem is daily predictions, and our **focus assets and markets** are equities from major stock exchanges, such as the NYSE and NASDAQ.

The **regulatory constraints** are compliance with relevant financial regulations, while the **operational constraints** are transaction costs and potential liquidity issues.

The **potential features** include the following:

- Historical Price Data: historical closing prices and high, low, and open prices.
- Trading Volumes: daily trading volumes.
- Technical Indicators: Moving Averages (MA), Relative Strength Index (RSI), and Bollinger Bands.
- Economic Indicators: economic data like interest rates and inflation rates.
- Sentiment Analysis: sentiment scores from financial news articles and social media.

We **hypothesize** that patterns in historical price, trading volumes, technical indicators, economic indicators, and sentiment analysis can provide varying degrees of predictive insights into the stock's future closing price.

Case Study 2: Mitigating Risk with Adaptive Portfolio Rebalancing

The problem definition step in this case study sets the **financial objective** of maximizing risk-adjustment returns while maintaining a desired risk profile. The **target variable** for this problem is the portfolio's risk-adjusted return, such as the Sharpe ratio.

The **portfolio constraints** are asset allocation limits and diversification rules.

The **time frame** is weekly portfolio adjustments, and we limit our **assets and markets** to US equities, bonds, and commodities.

The **regulatory constraints** include compliance with portfolio management regulations, and the **operational constraints** are transaction costs and rebalancing frequency.

The **potential features** include the following:

- Market Data: historical prices and returns of portfolio assets.
- Risk Metrics: volatility, value-at-risk (VaR), and asset correlations.
- Economic Indicators: macroeconomic data-impacting asset classes.
- Sentiment Analysis: market sentiment from news articles and social media.

We **hypothesize** that actively altering portfolio composition in response to market dynamics and risk assessments could improve the portfolio's returns when factoring in risk while adhering to a specified level of risk exposure.

Case Study 3: Enhancing Trade Execution with Reinforcement Learning Techniques

In this case study, our **financial objective** is to optimize trade execution to minimize transaction costs and market impact. The **target variable** for this problem is the execution price improvement compared to a benchmark price, such as the volume-weighted average price (VWAP).

The **time frame** is intraday trading; we focus on high-liquidity equities and exchange traded fund (ETF) **assets** in the US **markets**.

The **regulatory constraints** are compliance with market regulations and trading rules, and the **operational constraints** are order size, market impact, and liquidity.

The **potential features** include the following:

- Market Data: real-time order book data, trade prices, and volumes.
- Benchmarks: volume-weighted average price (VWAP) and time-weighted average price (TWAP).
- Order Execution Details: order size, type (market, limit), and execution time.
- Economic Indicators: relevant economic events and news that might impact market liquidity.
- Historical Execution Data: past execution performance and slippage data.

The **hypothesis** is that reinforcement learning algorithms applied to the trade execution process can reduce transaction costs and improve execution prices by better order placement and timing.

Chapter 4

Step 2: Dataset Preparation

Once the problem is defined, the next task is to gather and preprocess relevant historical data used to train and test the predictive model. The quality and comprehensiveness of the dataset directly impacts the model's performance and ability to generalize to unseen data.

Data Collection

The first phase of dataset preparation involves data collection, which includes gathering historical price data, trading volumes, and other relevant market data for the assets in question. Additionally, macroeconomic indicators, company financial statements, and even alternative data sources such as sentiment analysis from news articles or social media can provide valuable insights. It is crucial to ensure that the data is sourced from reliable providers to maintain accuracy and integrity.

Exploratory Data Analysis

After the data is collected, we need to understand the nature of the dataset and its features. **Exploratory Data Analysis (EDA)** analyzes and visualizes the dataset to uncover patterns, detect anomalies, and confirm assumptions using summary statistics and charts. It also assists in determining subsequent actions for data preprocessing and model formulation.

In Python, EDA can be efficiently performed using libraries such as pandas (see qnt.co/book-pandas) for data manipulation and tools like Sweetviz (see qnt.co/book-sweetviz) for automated EDA reporting.

To install Sweetviz, run this command

```
pip install sweetviz
```

Let's illustrate how to use Sweetviz in an example of a dataset of Age, Income, Gender, and City.

```python
import pandas as pd
import numpy as np
import sweetviz as sv

np.random.seed(42)

# Generate sample data
data = {
    'Age': np.random.randint(8, 90, size=100),
    'Income': np.random.randint(10000, 500000, size=100),
    'Gender': np.random.choice(['Male', 'Female'], size=100),
    'City': np.random.choice(['New York', 'Singapore', 'Paris', 'Rome', 'Tokyo'], size=100)
}

# Create a DataFrame
df = pd.DataFrame(data)

# Generate the general report
general_report = sv.analyze(df)
general_report.show_html('sweetviz_report.html')

# Generate report by gender
gender_report = sv.compare_intra(df, df['Gender'] == 'Male', ['Male', 'Female'])
gender_report.show_html('sweetviz_gender_comparison.html')
```

The code first generates an HTML file with a general interactive report on the dataset (Figure 4.1).

It also generates an HTML report by gender using Sweetviz's method `compare_intra`, allowing us to compare two subsets of a dataset (Figure 4.2).

Complete documentation is available at qnt.co/book-sweetviz-docs.

Data Preprocessing

Once we understand the nature of the input data, we move to the **preprocessing phase,** involving cleaning the dataset of data problems, such as missing values, the existence of outliers, removing duplicates, and correcting any errors or inconsistencies. These data problems can arise for various reasons, such as data entry errors, technical issues, market anomalies, or sudden unusual events. Furthermore, **normalization or**

Figure 4.1 Sweetviz dashboard with no comparison target.

standardization of features may be necessary, mainly when dealing with variables that have different scales. For instance, transforming all features to a standard scale can improve the performance and convergence of specific machine-learning algorithms. Additionally, **transforming time series features to be stationary** is often required for enhanced accuracy and reliability of models in time series analysis to ensure that the statistical properties of the series remain constant over time. Finally, the **Engle-Granger test** is used to identify cointegrated pairs of time series, essential for developing mean-reverting pairs trading strategies.

Handling Missing Data

Dealing with missing data is essential to the data preprocessing pipeline, especially for financial AI applications. Incomplete datasets can cause skewed outcomes, lower model accuracy, and erroneous financial forecasts.

Figure 4.2 Sweetviz dashboard with gender as the comparison target.

Identifying Missing Data

Before handling missing data, it is essential to identify where and how much data is missing. This can be achieved using pandas in Python:

```python
import pandas as pd
import numpy as np

# Set random seed for reproducibility
np.random.seed(42)

# Generate synthetic financial data
n_samples = 1000
data = {
    'Date': pd.date_range(start='1/1/2023', periods=n_samples, freq='D'),
    'Open': np.random.uniform(100, 500, size=n_samples),
    'High': np.random.uniform(100, 500, size=n_samples),
    'Low': np.random.uniform(100, 500, size=n_samples),
    'Close': np.random.uniform(100, 500, size=n_samples),
    'Volume': np.random.randint(1000, 100000, size=n_samples)
}
```

```python
# Convert Volume to float
data['Volume'] = data['Volume'].astype(float)

# Introduce some missing values for demonstration
data['Volume'][np.random.choice(n_samples, size=50, replace=False)] = np.nan
data['Close'][np.random.choice(n_samples, size=20, replace=False)] = np.nan

# Create a DataFrame
df = pd.DataFrame(data)

# Check for missing values
missing_data = df.isnull().sum()
print(missing_data)
```

Strategies for Handling Missing Data

1. **Removing Missing Values:** This approach is straightforward but can lead to significant data loss.

    ```python
    # Drop rows with missing values
    df_cleaned = df.dropna()


    # Drop columns with missing values
    df_cleaned = df.dropna(axis=1)
    ```

2. **Imputation:** involves filling in the missing values using statistical methods or machine learning models. We need to remove the Date columns from the imputation in all the examples since imputation works only on numerical columns.

    a. **Mean/Median/Mode Imputation:** Simple imputation can be done using the column's mean, median, or mode.

    ```python
    from sklearn.impute import SimpleImputer
    # Using mean for imputation
    imputer = SimpleImputer(strategy='mean')
    df.iloc[:, 1:] = imputer.fit_transform(df.iloc[:, 1:])
    ```

    b. **K-Nearest Neighbors (KNN) Imputation:** KNN imputation replaces missing values using the k-nearest neighbors' values.

    ```python
    from sklearn.impute import KNNImputer
    imputer = KNNImputer(n_neighbors=5)
    df.iloc[:, 1:] = imputer.fit_transform(df.iloc[:, 1:])
    ```

    c. **Multivariate Imputation by Chained Equations (MICE):** MICE performs multiple imputations by chaining together regression models.

    ```python
    from sklearn.experimental import enable_iterative_imputer
    from sklearn.impute import IterativeImputer
    imputer = IterativeImputer()
    df.iloc[:, 1:] = imputer.fit_transform(df.iloc[:, 1:])
    ```

Evaluating Imputation

After handling the missing data, we should evaluate the imputation's impact on the dataset with either visualizations or statistical measures to compare the original and imputed datasets.

Handling Outliers

Outliers in financial data can significantly skew the results of predictive models and lead to erroneous conclusions.

Identifying Outliers

The first step in handling outliers is to identify them. Standard techniques for identifying outliers include visualizations like box plots and scatterplots and statistical methods, such as the z-score and the interquartile range (IQR).

Using Box Plot to Identify Outliers A box plot (Figure 4.3) provides a visual summary of the distribution of a dataset and highlights the presence of outliers.

```
import pandas as pd
import matplotlib.pyplot as plt
# Sample financial data
data = {'Price': [100, 95, 96, 101, 103, 98, 99, 500, 103, 110]}
df = pd.DataFrame(data)

# Box plot
plt.figure(figsize=(10, 6))
plt.boxplot(df['Price'])
plt.title('Box Plot for Price')
plt.ylabel('Price')
plt.show()
```

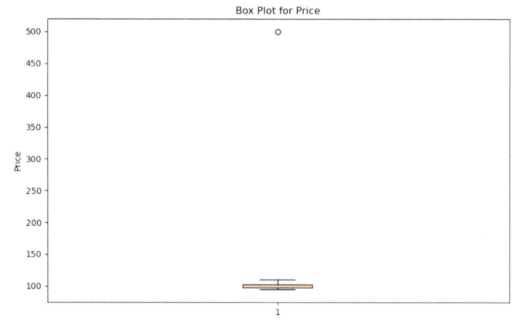

Figure 4.3 Box plot to identify outliers.

Figure 4.3 identifies an outlier of 500.

Using Z-score to Identify Outliers The z-score indicates how many standard deviations an element is from the mean. Typically, a z-score greater than two or less than −2, sometimes greater than three or less than −3, is considered an outlier.

```
import pandas as pd
import numpy as np

# Sample financial data
data = {'Price': [100, 95, 96, 101, 103, 98, 99, 500, 103, 110]}
df = pd.DataFrame(data)

# Calculate Z-scores
df['Z_score'] = (df['Price'] - df['Price'].mean()) / df['Price'].std()
# Identify outliers
outliers = df[np.abs(df['Z_score']) > 2]
print("Outliers using Z-score method:")
print(outliers)
```

With the output

```
Outliers using the Z-score method:
   Price   Z_score
7    500  2.844444
```

Using Interquartile Range (IQR) to Identify Outliers The IQR ranges between the first quartile (25th percentile) and the third quartile (75th percentile). Outliers are often defined as data points that lie beyond 1.5 times the IQR above the third quartile or below the first quartile.

```
import pandas as pd

# Sample financial data
data = {'Price': [100, 95, 96, 101, 103, 98, 99, 500, 103, 110]}
df = pd.DataFrame(data)

# Calculate IQR
Q1 = df['Price'].quantile(0.25)
Q3 = df['Price'].quantile(0.75)
IQR = Q3 - Q1

# Identify outliers
outliers = df[(df['Price'] < (Q1 - 1.5 * IQR)) | (df['Price'] > (Q3 + 1.5 * IQR))]
print("Outliers using IQR method:")
print(outliers)
```

With the output

```
Outliers using IQR method:
   Price
7    500
```

Handling Outliers

Once outliers are identified, there are several strategies to handle them. These include removing the outliers, transforming them, or capping/flooring their values.

1. **Removing Outliers:** removing outliers can be a straightforward approach, especially if the outliers are due to data entry errors.

```python
import pandas as pd
import numpy as np

# Sample financial data
data = {'Price': [100, 95, 96, 101, 103, 98, 99, 500, 103, 110]}
df = pd.DataFrame(data)

# Calculate Z-scores
df['Z_score'] = (df['Price'] - df['Price'].mean()) / df['Price'].std()

# Remove outliers using the Z-score method
df_cleaned = df[np.abs(df['Z_score']) <= 2]
print("Data after removing outliers:")
print(df_cleaned)
```

With the output

```
Data after removing outliers:
   Price   Z_score
0    100  -0.320445
1     95  -0.360006
2     96  -0.352094
3    101  -0.312533
4    103  -0.296708
5     98  -0.336269
6     99  -0.328357
8    103  -0.296708
9    110  -0.241323
```

2. **Transforming Outliers:** transforming outliers can be helpful when the outliers are legitimate observations that represent essential market events. In this case, we log transform the entire dataset.

```python
import pandas as pd
import numpy as np

# Sample financial data
data = {'Price': [100, 95, 96, 101, 103, 98, 99, 500, 103, 110]}
df = pd.DataFrame(data)

# Log transformation to reduce the impact of outliers
df['Price_log'] = np.log(df['Price'])
print("Data after log transformation:")
print(df)
```

With the output

```
Data after log transformation:
   Price  Price_log
0    100   4.605170
1     95   4.553877
2     96   4.564348
3    101   4.615121
4    103   4.634729
5     98   4.584967
6     99   4.595120
7    500   6.214608
8    103   4.634729
9    110   4.700480
```

3. Capping/Flooring Outliers: capping or flooring involves setting a threshold beyond which values are capped to reduce their influence.

```python
import pandas as pd
import numpy as np

# Sample financial data
data = {'Price': [100, 95, 96, 101, 103, 98, 99, 500, 103, 110]}
df = pd.DataFrame(data)

# Calculate IQR
Q1 = df['Price'].quantile(0.25)
Q3 = df['Price'].quantile(0.75)
IQR = Q3 - Q1

# Capping outliers using IQR method
lower_bound = Q1 - 1.5 * IQR
upper_bound = Q3 + 1.5 * IQR
df['Price_capped'] = np.where(df['Price'] > upper_bound, upper_bound,
np.where(df['Price'] < lower_bound, lower_bound, df['Price']))
print("Data after capping outliers:")
print(df)
```

With the output

```
Data after capping outliers:
   Price  Price_capped
0    100       100.000
1     95        95.000
2     96        96.000
3    101       101.000
4    103       103.000
5     98        98.000
6     99        99.000
7    500       110.125
8    103       103.000
9    110       110.000
```

Feature Engineering

Feature engineering is used to modify or create new features that can improve the performance of machine-learning models by transforming raw data into new values that better represent the underlying problem to the algorithms, enhancing their predictive power.

Techniques in feature engineering include normalization, standardization, encoding categorical variables, handling missing values, and creating interaction terms.

Let's illustrate with an example of creating two new moving averages features:

```
import pandas as pd
import numpy as np

# Set random seed for reproducibility
np.random.seed(42)

# Generate synthetic financial data
n_samples = 1000
data = {
    'Date': pd.date_range(start='1/1/2023', periods=n_samples, freq='D'),
    'Open': np.random.uniform(100, 500, size=n_samples),
    'High': np.random.uniform(100, 500, size=n_samples),
    'Low': np.random.uniform(100, 500, size=n_samples),
    'Close': np.random.uniform(100, 500, size=n_samples),
    'Volume': np.random.randint(1000, 100000, size=n_samples)
}

# Create a DataFrame
df = pd.DataFrame(data)

# Calculate moving averages
df['MA5'] = df['Close'].rolling(window=5).mean()       # 5-day moving average
df['MA10'] = df['Close'].rolling(window=10).mean()     # 10-day moving average
```

Normalization and Standardization of Features

Normalization and standardization transform data to a standard scale, making it easier to compare and analyze. They are instrumental when working with features that have different units or scales, as they help improve the performance and convergence of specific machine-learning algorithms.

Normalization

Normalization, known as min-max scaling, transforms the data to a specific range, usually between 0 and 1, by subtracting the minimum value of the feature, and then dividing the result by the range (maximum value minus minimum value).

The formula for normalization is

$$X_{norm} = \frac{X - X_{min}}{X_{max} - X_{min}}.$$

Normalization is beneficial for modeling algorithms with no data distribution assumption, such as neural networks or k-nearest neighbors.

```
import numpy as np
import pandas as pd
from sklearn.preprocessing import MinMaxScaler

# Sample data
data = {
```

```
    'Feature1': [.4, .2, .1, .9, .6],
    'Feature2': [90, 101, 95, 94, 102],
    'Feature3': [9000, 10100, 9500, 9400, 10200]
}
df = pd.DataFrame(data)

# Initialize the MinMaxScaler
scaler = MinMaxScaler()

# Fit and transform the data
normalized_data = scaler.fit_transform(df)

# Convert the normalized data back to a DataFrame
normalized_df = pd.DataFrame(normalized_data, columns=df.columns)

# Display the normalized DataFrame
print("Normalized DataFrame:")
print(normalized_df)
```

With the output

```
Normalized DataFrame:
    Feature1  Feature2  Feature3
0      0.375  0.000000  0.000000
1      0.125  0.916667  0.916667
2      0.000  0.416667  0.416667
3      1.000  0.333333  0.333333
4      0.625  1.000000  1.000000
```

Standardization

In finance, datasets often contain features with varying scales and units. For example, stock prices can range from a few dollars to several thousand dollars, daily returns in percentages are very low, and trading quantities can be in the range of millions. Such disparities can negatively impact the performance of specific machine-learning algorithms sensitive to the scale of the input data, such as support vector machines, which would assign disproportionate influence on features with large scale.

The primary goal of standardization, also known as z-score normalization, is to ensure that each feature contributes equally to the model by scaling the features to have a mean of zero and a standard deviation of one.

The mathematical formula for standardization is

$$Z = \frac{X - \mu}{\sigma}$$

Where:

- Z is the standardized value.
- X is the original value of the feature.
- μ is the mean of the feature, defined as

$$\mu = \frac{1}{N}\sum_{i=1}^{N} X_i$$

N is the number of data points, and X_i is the feature value for the ith data point.

- σ is the standard deviation of the feature defined as

$$\sigma = \sqrt{\frac{1}{N}\sum_{i=1}^{N}(X_i - \mu)^2}.$$

```python
import pandas as pd
from sklearn.preprocessing import StandardScaler

# Sample data
data = {
    'Feature1': [.4, .2, .1, .9, .6],
    'Feature2': [90, 101, 95, 94, 102],
    'Feature3': [9000, 10100, 9500, 9400, 10200]
}
df = pd.DataFrame(data)

# Initialize the StandardScaler
scaler = StandardScaler()

# Fit and transform the data
standardized_data = scaler.fit_transform(df)

# Convert the standardized data back to a DataFrame
standardized_df = pd.DataFrame(standardized_data, columns=df.columns)

# Display the standardized DataFrame
print("Standardized DataFrame:")
print(standardized_df)
```

With the output

```
Standardized DataFrame:
    Feature1   Feature2   Feature3
0  -0.139347  -1.422574  -1.422574
1  -0.836080   1.022475   1.022475
2  -1.184446  -0.311188  -0.311188
3   1.602486  -0.533465  -0.533465
4   0.557386   1.244752   1.244752
```

Transforming Time Series Features to Stationary

One of the aims of time series analysis is to ensure that the features have consistent statistical properties throughout time. A time series is called stationary when its statistical properties, such as mean, variance, and autocorrelation remain constant over time. A time series model may have difficulty finding patterns and making reliable predictions when the time series is non-stationary.

Standard techniques to achieve stationarity include differencing, detrending, and log transformation.

The Augmented Dickey-Fuller (ADF) test is a widely used method to test for stationarity. The ADF test helps determine if a time series has a unit root, indicating non-stationarity. If the test statistic is less than the critical value, the null hypothesis of a unit root is rejected, suggesting that the series is stationary.

Following is a Python example demonstrating the use of the ADF test with differencing:

```python
import pandas as pd
import numpy as np
from statsmodels.tsa.stattools import adfuller
import matplotlib.pyplot as plt

# Generate sample non-stationary data
np.random.seed(42)
time_series = np.random.randn(100).cumsum()

# Perform ADF test
result = adfuller(time_series)
print('ADF Statistic:', result[0])
print('p-value:', result[1])
for key, value in result[4].items():
    print('Critical Values:')
    print(f'    {key}, {value}')

# Plot the time series
plt.figure(figsize=(10, 6))
plt.plot(time_series, label='Original Time Series')
plt.title('Non-Stationary Time Series')
plt.legend()
plt.show()

# Differencing to make the series stationary
diff_series = np.diff(time_series, n=1)

# Perform ADF test on differenced series
result_diff = adfuller(diff_series)
print('ADF Statistic (Differenced):', result_diff[0])
print('p-value (Differenced):', result_diff[1])
for key, value in result_diff[4].items():
    print('Critical Values (Differenced):')
    print(f'    {key}, {value}')

# Plot the differenced time series
plt.figure(figsize=(10, 6))
plt.plot(diff_series, label='Differenced Time Series')
plt.title('Stationary Time Series After Differencing')
plt.legend()
plt.show()
```

With the output (Figures 4.4 and 4.5)

```
ADF Statistic: -1.3583317659818992
p-value: 0.6020814791099098
Critical Values:
    1%, -3.498198082189098
Critical Values:
    5%, -2.891208211860468
Critical Values:
    10%, -2.5825959973472097
ADF Statistic (Differenced): -10.008881137130237
p-value (Differenced): 1.800687720719554e-17
Critical Values (Differenced):
    1%, -3.4989097606014496
```

```
Critical Values (Differenced):
  5%, -2.891516256916761
Critical Values (Differenced):
  10%, -2.5827604414827157
```

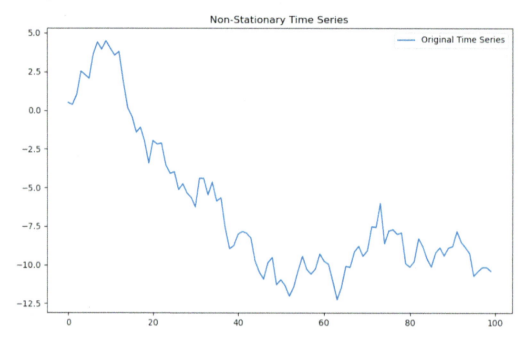

Figure 4.4 Example of a non-stationary time series.

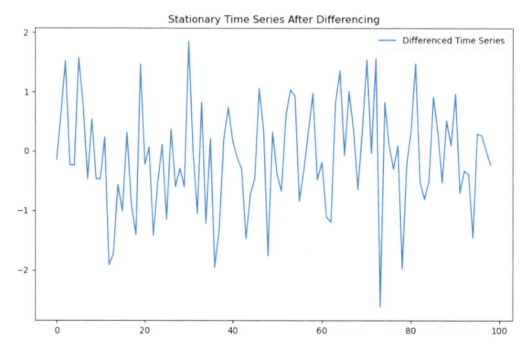

Figure 4.5 Example of a stationary time series that results from differentiating a non-stationary time series.

In finance, the recommended differentiating method is the fractional differentiation technique introduced by Lopez de Prado (2018, pp. 79–84), designed to avoid over-differentiating of the factors and to find a trade-off between stationarity and signal memory.

Let's redo the Python example demonstrating the use of the ADF test with fractional differentiation technique:

```python
import pandas as pd
import numpy as np
from statsmodels.tsa.stattools import adfuller
import matplotlib.pyplot as plt

def get_weights_ffd(d, thres):
    '''
    Computing the weights for differentiating the series with fixed window size

        Parameters:
            d (float): differentiating factor
            thres (float): threshold for cutting off weights

        Returns:
            w (np.ndarray): array containing weights
    '''
    w, k = [1.0], 1
    while True:
        w_ = -w[-1] / k * (d - k + 1)
        if abs(w_) < thres:
            break
        w.append(w_)
        k += 1
    w = np.array(w[::-1]).reshape(-1, 1)
    return w

def frac_diff_ffd(series, d, thres=1e-5):
    '''
    Fractional differentiation with constant width window
    Note 1: thres determines the cut-off weight for the window
    Note 2: d can be any positive fractional, not necessarily bounded
    [0,1]

        Parameters:
            series (pd.DataFrame): dataframe with time series
            d (float): differentiating factor
            thres (float): threshold for cutting off weights

        Returns:
            df (pd.DataFrame): dataframe with differentiated series
    '''
    w = get_weights_ffd(d, thres)
    width = len(w) - 1

    df = {}
    for name in series.columns:
        series_f = series[[name]].ffill().dropna()
        df_ = pd.Series(index=np.arange(series.shape[0]), dtype=object)
        for iloc1 in range(width, series_f.shape[0]):
            loc0, loc1 = series_f.index[iloc1 - width], series_f.index[iloc1]
            if not np.isfinite(series.loc[loc1, name]):
                continue    # exclude NAs
```

```python
            df_[loc1] = np.dot(w.T, series_f.loc[loc0:loc1])[0, 0]
        df[name] = df_.dropna().copy(deep=True)
    df = pd.concat(df, axis=1)
    return df

def ffd(process, thres=0.01):
    '''
    Finding the minimum differentiating factor that passes the ADF test

        Parameters:
            process (np.ndarray): array with random process values
            apply_constant_width (bool): flag that shows whether to use
             constant width window (if True) or increasing width window
             (if False)
            thres (float): threshold for cutting off weights
    '''
    for d in np.linspace(0, 1, 11):
        process_diff = frac_diff_ffd(pd.DataFrame(process), d, thres)
        test_results = adfuller(
            process_diff[process.name], maxlag=1, regression='c', autolag=None
        )
        if test_results[1] <= 0.05:
            break
    return process_diff[process.name]

# Generate sample non-stationary data
np.random.seed(42)
time_series = np.random.randn(100).cumsum()

# Perform ADF test
result = adfuller(time_series)
print('ADF Statistic:', result[0])
print('p-value:', result[1])
for key, value in result[4].items():
    print('Critical Values:')
    print(f'    {key}, {value}')

# Plot the time series
plt.figure(figsize=(10, 6))
plt.plot(time_series, label='Original Time Series')
plt.title('Non-Stationary Time Series')
plt.legend()
plt.show()

# Differencing to make the series stationary
diff_series = ffd(pd.Series(time_series, name='time_series'))

# Perform ADF test on differenced series
result_diff = adfuller(diff_series)
print('ADF Statistic (Differenced):', result_diff[0])
print('p-value (Differenced):', result_diff[1])
for key, value in result_diff[4].items():
    print('Critical Values (Differenced):')
    print(f'    {key}, {value}')

# Plot the differenced time series
plt.figure(figsize=(10, 6))
plt.plot(diff_series, label='Differenced Time Series')
plt.title('Stationary Time Series After Differencing')
plt.legend()
plt.show()
```

With the output

```
ADF Statistic: -1.3583317659818992
p-value: 0.6020814791099098
Critical Values:
    1%, -3.498198082189098
Critical Values:
    5%, -2.891208211860468
Critical Values:
    10%, -2.5825959973472097
ADF Statistic (Differenced): -3.614042461855659
p-value (Differenced): 0.0054981717565326035
Critical Values (Differenced):
    1%, -3.506057133647011
Critical Values (Differenced):
    5%, -2.8946066061911946
Critical Values (Differenced):
    10%, -2.5844100201994697
```

Given the ADF Statistic (Differenced): −3.614042461855659, let's consider typical critical values at the 1%, 5%, and 10% significance levels:

- 1%: −3.496
- 5%: −2.890
- 10%: −2.582

Since the value −3.614 is less than all critical values above, the differenced time series passes the ADF test at all 1%, 5%, and 10%, respectively, meaning it's stationary (Figures 4.6 and 4.7).

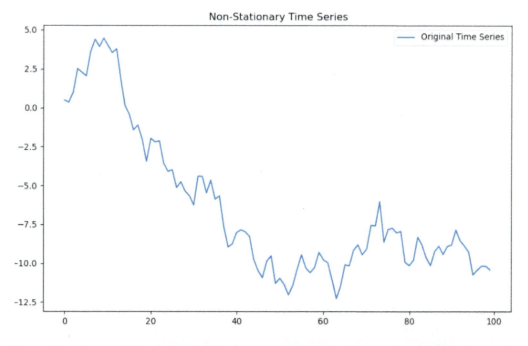

Figure 4.6 The original non-stationary time series before performing fractional differentiation.

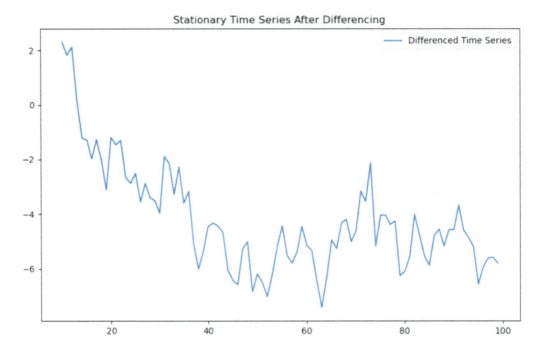

Figure 4.7 The stationary time series that results from performing fractional differentiation on the original non-stationary time series.

Identification of Cointegrated Time Series with Engle-Granger Test

Two or more non-stationary time series are cointegrated if the series have a stationary linear combination, indicating a stable long-term equilibrium relationship.

The Engle-Granger test is a widely used method to test for cointegration, allowing traders to identify pairs of assets that exhibit mean-reverting behavior, and then bet on the relative movement of two assets rather than their absolute prices.

Let us illustrate this with an example of two cointegrated non-stationary series (Figure 4.8).

```
import numpy as np
import pandas as pd
from statsmodels.tsa.stattools import adfuller, coint
import matplotlib.pyplot as plt

# Generate synthetic time series data
np.random.seed(42)
n = 100
time = np.arange(n)
# Simulate two non-stationary series (random walks)
asset1 = np.cumsum(np.random.randn(n)) + 41
asset2 = asset1 + np.random.randn(n)

# Create a DataFrame
data = pd.DataFrame({'asset1': asset1, 'asset2': asset2})
```

```python
# Function to perform ADF test
def adf_test(series, name):
    result = adfuller(series)
    print(f'ADF Statistic for {name}: {result[0]}')
    print(f'p-value for {name}: {result[1]}')
    for key, value in result[4].items():
        print(f'Critical Value {key}: {value}')
    print('\n')

# Step 1: Test each series for stationarity
print("ADF Test for asset1:")
adf_test(data['asset1'], 'asset1')
print("ADF Test for asset2:")
adf_test(data['asset2'], 'asset2')

# Step 2: Perform the Engle-Granger cointegration test
score, pvalue, _ = coint(data['asset1'], data['asset2'])

print(f'Engle-Granger Cointegration Test score: {score}')
print(f'Engle-Granger Cointegration Test p-value: {pvalue}\n')

# Step 3: Visualize the series and their spread
data['spread'] = data['asset1'] - data['asset2']

plt.figure(figsize=(14, 7))
plt.subplot(2, 1, 1)
plt.plot(data['asset1'], label='Asset 1')
plt.plot(data['asset2'], label='Asset 2')
plt.legend()
plt.title('Non-Stationary Time Series')

plt.subplot(2, 1, 2)
plt.plot(data['spread'], label='Spread (Asset 1 - Asset 2)')
plt.legend()
plt.title('Spread (Should be Stationary)')
plt.tight_layout()
plt.show()

# Step 4: Test the spread for stationarity
print("ADF Test for spread:")
adf_test(data['spread'], 'spread')
```

With the output (Figure 4.8)
And

```
ADF Test for asset1:
ADF Statistic for asset1: -1.3583317659819
p-value for asset1: 0.6020814791099095
Critical Value 1%: -3.498198082189098
Critical Value 5%: -2.891208211860468
Critical Value 10%: -2.5825959973472097


ADF Test for asset2:
ADF Statistic for asset2: -1.642378142665797
p-value for asset2: 0.4610184160167067
Critical Value 1%: -3.5019123847798657
Critical Value 5%: -2.892815255482889
Critical Value 10%: -2.583453861475781
```

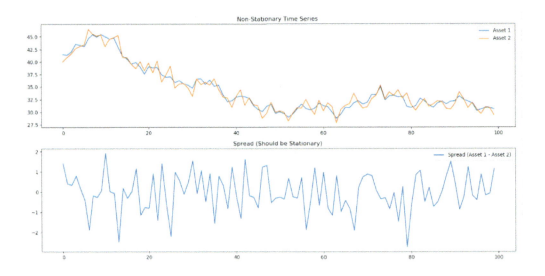

Figure 4.8 Two non-stationary assets that are cointegrated have a stationary spread.

```
Engle-Granger Cointegration Test score: -10.546923889518597
Engle-Granger Cointegration Test p-value: 1.0672395686754609e-17

ADF Test for spread:
ADF Statistic for spread: -10.875458876565842
p-value for spread: 1.3352313844030579e-19
Critical Value 1%: -3.498198082189098
Critical Value 5%: -2.891208211860468
Critical Value 10%: -2.5825959973472097
```

To determine whether the time series is stationary based on the Augmented Dickey-Fuller (ADF) test statistic, we need to compare the ADF statistic to the critical values and check the p-value.

The critical values are the following:

- Critical Value 1%: −3.4996365338407074
- Critical Value 5%: −2.8918307730370025
- Critical Value 10%: −2.5829283377617176

Suppose the ADF statistic is less than the critical value. In that case, we reject the null hypothesis (the null hypothesis is that two series are not cointegrated) and conclude the time series are cointegrated.

For the asset1, the ADF statistic is −1.3583317659819 (> all critical values 1%, 5%, and 10%), meaning certainly non-stationary; for the asset2, the ADF statistic is −1.642378142665797 (> all critical values 1%, 5% and 10%) indicating again non-stationary, whereas the ADF statistic for the spread is −10.875458876565842 indicating the series are cointegrated. In sum, while the individual assets are non-stationary, their spread is stationary, and they are suitable for pairs trading.

Let us explain the concept of **p-value** on the p-value of the spread of 1.3352313844030579e-19. Assuming the null hypothesis is true, the p-value is the probability of obtaining the results at least as extreme as the observed results. A p-value lower than 0.05 indicates strong evidence against the null hypothesis, so we reject the null hypothesis. In this example, the data suggests that the series is cointegrated. If the p-value is more significant than 0.05, we fail to reject the null hypothesis; for cointegration, it would mean that the time series are not cointegrated.

Furthermore, the **Hurst coefficient**, a measure ranging from 0 to 1 of the nature of the long-term memory of a time series, can provide further insights into the nature of the cointegrated time series:

- $H < 0.5$: the time series exhibits mean-reverting behavior; that is, while time series can oscillate, they eventually return to their long-term average.
- $H = 0.5$: the time series exhibits no long-term memory and behaves like a random walk.
- $H > 0.5$: the time series follows a strong trend in the same direction.

A Hurst coefficient of the spread significantly less than 0.5 suggests a robust mean reversion ideal for pairs trading (a market-neutral strategy of two cointegrated securities, with a long position in the underperforming asset and a short position in the outperforming asset, expecting profit from their convergence to the equilibrium).

Let's illustrate the Hurst coefficient on a simple example of two cointegrated time series—notice that we have removed all non-positive values for calculating the Hurst exponent values—this is necessary since the calculation of the exponent depends on logarithms (Figure 4.9).

```python
import numpy as np
import pandas as pd
from statsmodels.tsa.stattools import adfuller, coint
import matplotlib.pyplot as plt
from hurst import compute_Hc

# Generate synthetic cointegrated time series data
np.random.seed(42)
n = 1000  # Number of data points
time = np.arange(n)

# Generate a common stochastic trend
trend = np.cumsum(np.random.randn(n))

# Create two cointegrated series with added noise
asset1 = trend + 0.3 * np.random.randn(n)
asset2 = trend + 0.1 * np.random.randn(n)

# Create a DataFrame
data = pd.DataFrame({'asset1': asset1, 'asset2': asset2})

# Function to perform ADF test
def adf_test(series, name):
    result = adfuller(series)
```

```python
    print(f'ADF Statistic for {name}: {result[0]}')
    print(f'p-value for {name}: {result[1]}')
    for key, value in result[4].items():
        print(f'Critical Value {key}: {value}')
    print('\n')

# Test each series for stationarity
print("ADF Test for asset1:")
adf_test(data['asset1'], 'asset1')
print("ADF Test for asset2:")
adf_test(data['asset2'], 'asset2')

# Perform the Engle-Granger cointegration test
score, pvalue, _ = coint(data['asset1'], data['asset2'])

print(f'Engle-Granger Cointegration Test score: {score}')
print(f'Engle-Granger Cointegration Test p-value: {pvalue}\n')

# Calculate the spread
data['spread'] = data['asset1'] - data['asset2']

# Step 4: Test the spread for stationarity
print("ADF Test for spread:")
adf_test(data['spread'], 'spread')

# Remove zero and negative values in the spread for Hurst calculation
spread_non_zero = data['spread'][data['spread'] > 0]
if len(spread_non_zero) < len(data['spread']):
    print("Warning: Non-positive values in spread were removed for Hurst
calculation.")

# Ensure spread_non_zero is not empty and does not contain invalid values
if len(spread_non_zero) > 0 and (spread_non_zero <= 0).sum() == 0:
    # Calculate the Hurst exponent of the spread
    H, c, data_hurst = compute_Hc(spread_non_zero, kind='price', simplified=True)
    print(f'Hurst Exponent for spread: {H}')

    # Visualize the series and their spread
    plt.figure(figsize=(14, 7))
    plt.subplot(2, 1, 1)
    plt.plot(data['asset1'], label='Asset 1')
    plt.plot(data['asset2'], label='Asset 2')
    plt.legend()
    plt.title('Cointegrated Time Series')

    plt.subplot(2, 1, 2)
    plt.plot(data['spread'], label='Spread (Asset 1 - Asset 2)')
    plt.legend()
    plt.title('Spread (Should be Stationary)')
    plt.tight_layout()
    plt.show()
else:
    print("Error: Spread contains invalid values or is empty after removing
non-positive values.")
```

With the outputs (Figure 4.9)

Chapter 4. Step 2: Dataset Preparation

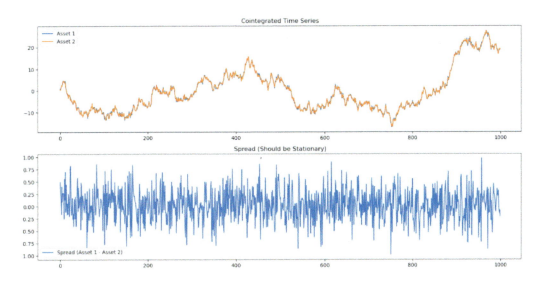

Figure 4.9 Two cointegrated assets and their stationary spread.

And

```
ADF Test for asset1:
ADF Statistic for asset1: -0.9841906190427494
p-value for asset1: 0.7589866498633684
Critical Value 1%: -3.4369193380671
Critical Value 5%: -2.864440383452517
Critical Value 10%: -2.56831430323573


ADF Test for asset2:
ADF Statistic for asset2: -1.0039798833431093
p-value for asset2: 0.7518099637843659
Critical Value 1%: -3.4369127451400474
Critical Value 5%: -2.864437475834273
Critical Value 10%: -2.568312754566378


Engle-Granger Cointegration Test score: -31.604955223815125
Engle-Granger Cointegration Test p-value: 0.0

ADF Test for spread:
ADF Statistic for spread: -31.570817098575255
p-value for spread: 0.0
Critical Value 1%: -3.4369127451400474
Critical Value 5%: -2.864437475834273
Critical Value 10%: -2.568312754566378


Warning: Non-positive values in spread were removed for Hurst calculation.
Hurst Exponent for spread: 0.3099860341085018
```

The Hurst exponent of 0.3 indicates that the assets would be ideal for pairs trading.

Feature Selection

The main goal of feature selection is to identify the most relevant features that contribute to the predictive power of a model by eliminating irrelevant features, which also helps reduce overfitting and improve the model's interpretability.

Let's explore four critical methods of feature selection: correlation analysis, feature importance analysis, auto-identification of features, and dimensionality reduction with principal component analysis (PCA).

Correlation Analysis

Correlation analysis helps identify features that are highly correlated with the target variable and features that are highly correlated with each other.

```python
import pandas as pd
import numpy as np
import seaborn as sns
import matplotlib.pyplot as plt

# Generate random sample data with correlations
np.random.seed(42)
size = 100
feature1 = np.random.randn(size)
feature2 = feature1 + np.random.randn(size) * 0.1  # Highly correlated with feature1
feature3 = np.random.randn(size)
target = feature1 * 0.5 + np.random.randn(size) * 0.1  # Highly correlated with target

data = {
    'Feature1': feature1,
    'Feature2': feature2,
    'Feature3': feature3,
    'Target': target
}
df = pd.DataFrame(data)

# Calculate correlation matrix
corr_matrix = df.corr()

# Display correlation matrix
print(corr_matrix)

# Plot heatmap
sns.heatmap(corr_matrix, annot=True, cmap='coolwarm')
plt.title('Correlation Matrix')
plt.show()
```

With the output (Figure 4.10)

```
          Feature1  Feature2  Feature3    Target
Feature1  1.000000  0.994477  0.190840  0.980875
Feature2  0.994477  1.000000  0.188663  0.974603
Feature3  0.190840  0.188663  1.000000  0.193556
Target    0.980875  0.974603  0.193556  1.000000
```

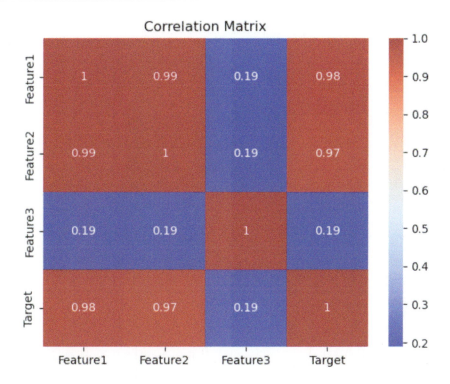

Figure 4.10 Correlation matrix of the target and factors.

Feature Importance Analysis

Tree-based machine-learning models, such as random forests, are frequently used for feature importance analysis as they naturally determine the importance of each feature in predicting the target variable.

To avoid selecting highly correlated features, we will first remove highly correlated features (correlation coefficient > 0.9) before running the feature importance analysis.

```
import pandas as pd
import numpy as np
from sklearn.ensemble import RandomForestRegressor
import matplotlib.pyplot as plt

# Generate random sample data with correlations
np.random.seed(42)
size = 100
feature1 = np.random.randn(size)
feature2 = feature1 + np.random.randn(size) * 0.1  # Highly correlated with
feature1
feature3 = np.random.randn(size)
target = feature1 * 0.5 + np.random.randn(size) * 0.1   # Highly correlated
with target

data = {
    'Feature1': feature1,
    'Feature2': feature2,
```

```python
    'Feature3': feature3,
    'Target': target
}
df = pd.DataFrame(data)
X = df.drop('Target', axis=1)
y = df['Target']

# Remove highly correlated features
corr_matrix = X.corr().abs()
upper = corr_matrix.where(np.triu(np.ones(corr_matrix.shape),
k=1).astype(bool))
to_drop = [column for column in upper.columns if any(upper[column] > 0.9)]
X_reduced = X.drop(columns=to_drop)

# Train a Random Forest model
model = RandomForestRegressor()
model.fit(X_reduced, y)

# Get feature importance
importances = model.feature_importances_
feature_names = X_reduced.columns
importance_df = pd.DataFrame({'Feature': feature_names, 'Importance':
importances})

# Display feature importance
print(importance_df)

# Plot feature importance
importance_df.sort_values(by='Importance', ascending=False).plot(kind='bar',
x='Feature', y='Importance')
plt.title('Feature Importance')
plt.show()
```

With the output (Figure 4.11)

```
    Feature    Importance
0   Feature1   0.984778
1   Feature3   0.015222
```

Auto-identification of Features

Auto-identification of features involves using algorithms and statistical methods to automatically select the most relevant features for a given predictive model. Techniques such as recursive feature elimination (RFE) and sklearn's `SelectFromModel` are commonly used.

When features are highly correlated, RFE, which iteratively removes the least important features and refits the model, might select multiple correlated features because they all seem essential in isolation. Therefore, we remove such features.

```python
import pandas as pd
import numpy as np
from sklearn.feature_selection import RFE
from sklearn.ensemble import RandomForestRegressor
import matplotlib.pyplot as plt

# Generate random sample data with correlations
np.random.seed(42)
```

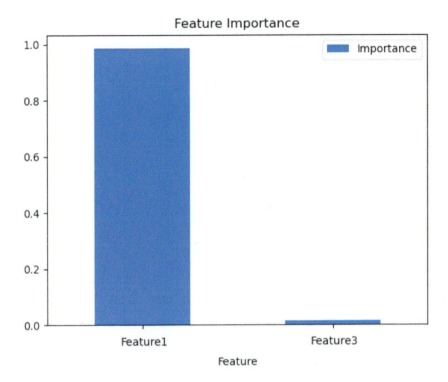

Figure 4.11 Feature importance plot of features 1 and 3. Feature 3 could be discarded to simplify the model and reduce the dataset dimensions.

```
size = 100
feature1 = np.random.randn(size)
feature2 = feature1 + np.random.randn(size) * 0.1   # Highly correlated with
feature1
feature3 = np.random.randn(size)
target = feature1 * 0.5 + np.random.randn(size) * 0.1   # Highly correlated
with targetfeature1

data = {
    'Feature1': feature1,
    'Feature2': feature2,
    'Feature3': feature3,
    'Target': target
}
df = pd.DataFrame(data)
X = df.drop('Target', axis=1)
y = df['Target']

# Remove highly correlated features
corr_matrix = X.corr().abs()
upper = corr_matrix.where(np.triu(np.ones(corr_matrix.shape),
k=1).astype(bool))
to_drop = [column for column in upper.columns if any(upper[column] > 0.9)]
X_reduced = X.drop(columns=to_drop)

# Apply Recursive Feature Elimination
model = RandomForestRegressor()
rfe = RFE(estimator=model, n_features_to_select=2)
rfe.fit(X_reduced, y)
```

```
# Get selected features
selected_features = X_reduced.columns[rfe.support_]
print(f'Selected Features: {selected_features}')

# Plot selected features
importance_df = pd.DataFrame({'Feature': X_reduced.columns, 'Importance':
rfe.support_.astype(int)})
importance_df.plot(kind='bar', x='Feature', y='Importance')
plt.title('Auto-Identification of Features')

# Adjust the bottom margin to add more space for x-axis labels
plt.subplots_adjust(bottom=0.2)

plt.show()
```

With the output (Figure 4.12)

```
Selected Features: Index(['Feature1', 'Feature3'], dtype='object')
```

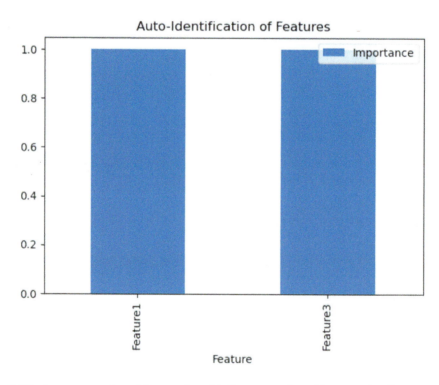

Figure 4.12 Importance plot of features 1 and 3 that were selected by recursive feature elimination.

Dimensionality Reduction/Principal Component Analysis

Dimensionality refers to the number of features in a dataset. The higher the number of features there is in a dataset, the more computationally intensive the models are, the more memory is required, the more difficult is to find any sensible patterns within the dataset, and the more likely the model is to overfit.

Principal component analysis (PCA) is a statistical technique that simplifies the analysis of complex data sets with many features by identifying a new smaller set of features that capture most of the underlying data's variation.

The newly identified features are called the **principal components**. They are a linear combination of the original features and are uncorrelated. They are ordered in descending order, so that the first principal component captures the most variance.

Standardization is crucial for PCA to ensure that each feature contributes equally to the principal components.

In finance, PCA is used for risk management, portfolio optimization, and reducing the complexity of large datasets while retaining important information.

These are the general steps to implement the PCA:

1. Calculate the covariance matrix by calculating the covariance between each pair of features.
2. Calculate the eigenvectors (they represent the direction of principal components) and eigenvalues (they represent the amount of variance explained by each principal component) of the covariance matrix.
3. Determine the number of principal components of interest; this is usually done by sorting the eigenvalues by the **explained variance ratio** (the proportion of the dataset's total variance captured by each principal component) in descending order and choosing the top K eigenvectors, which in aggregate explain the desired percentage of the total variance, e.g., 90%.
4. Create a feature matrix consisting of the selected top K eigenvectors as columns.
5. Project the original standardized data onto the selected principal components by multiplying the original data with the feature vector matrix.

In Python, the sklearn library provides PCA implementation.

```python
import pandas as pd
import numpy as np
from sklearn.decomposition import PCA
from sklearn.preprocessing import StandardScaler
import matplotlib.pyplot as plt

# Generate random sample data with correlations
np.random.seed(42)
size = 100
feature1 = np.random.randn(size)
feature2 = feature1 + np.random.randn(size) * 0.1  # Highly correlated with feature1
feature3 = np.random.randn(size)
target = feature1 * 0.5 + np.random.randn(size) * 0.1  # Highly correlated with feature1

data = {
    'Feature1': feature1,
    'Feature2': feature2,
    'Feature3': feature3,
    'Target': target
}
```

```python
df = pd.DataFrame(data)
X = df.drop('Target', axis=1)

# Standardize the data
scaler = StandardScaler()
X_standardized = scaler.fit_transform(X)

# Apply PCA
pca = PCA(n_components=2)
principal_components = pca.fit_transform(X_standardized)

# Create a DataFrame with the principal components
pca_df = pd.DataFrame(data=principal_components, columns=['Principal
Component 1', 'Principal Component 2'])

# Display the explained variance ratio
print(f'Explained variance ratio: {pca.explained_variance_ratio_}')

# Plot the principal components
plt.scatter(pca_df['Principal Component 1'], pca_df['Principal Component 2'])
plt.xlabel('Principal Component 1')
plt.ylabel('Principal Component 2')
plt.title('Principal Component Analysis')
plt.show()
```

With the output (Figure 4.13)

```
Explained variance ratio: [0.68742233 0.3107374]
```

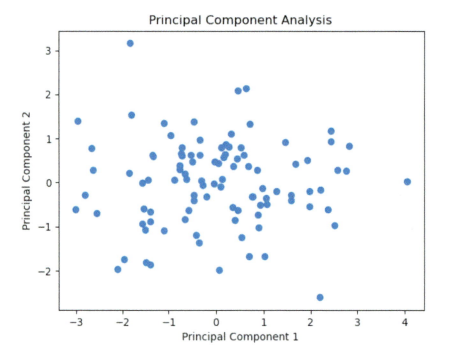

Figure 4.13 PCA transformed the feature matrix from three dimensions to two new dimensions that maximize the variance in the dataset.

In the scatterplot, each point represents a sample from the original dataset projected onto the plane defined by the first two components. The spread of the points along the axes of the principal components indicates how much variance is captured by each component.

Splitting of Dataset into Training, Testing, and Possibly Validation Sets

In general, it is recommended to separate your dataset into training, testing, and possibly validation sets when developing and evaluating machine learning models:

1. **Training Set:** this subset of the data is used to train your model. The model learns the patterns and relationships from this data.
2. **Testing Set:** after training, the model is evaluated on this set to assess its performance and generalization to unseen data. It helps identify any overfitting or underfitting issues. Overfitting is a modeling error where a model becomes too complex because it memorizes the training data, including its data noise and outliers, too well, resulting in poor generalization of new, unseen data.
   On the other hand, underfitting is a modeling error where a model is too simple to capture the underlying patterns in the data, resulting in poor performance on the training and new, unseen data.
3. **Validation Set (Optional):** this set is used during training to tune hyperparameters. Hyperparameters are machine-learning settings that are preset before the learning starts controlling the learning process itself. Unlike model parameters learned from the training dataset, the hyperparameters are predefined—the Validation Sets help prevent overfitting by providing an additional check during the training phase.

How to Split Your Data

1. Training and Testing Split
   - A common approach is to split the data into 70–80% for training, and 20–30% for testing.
   - Use functions like `train_test_split` from libraries such as sklearn to perform this split.
2. Training, Validation, and Testing Split
   - If you use a validation set, a typical approach is to split the data into 60% for training, 20% for validation, and 20% for testing.

Here's an example of how you might split your data using sklearn:

```
import pandas as pd
import numpy as np
from sklearn.model_selection import train_test_split
```

```python
# Generate random sample data
np.random.seed(42)
size = 100
feature1 = np.random.randn(size)
feature2 = feature1 + np.random.randn(size) * 0.1  # Highly correlated with
feature1
feature3 = np.random.randn(size)
target = feature1 * 0.5 + np.random.randn(size) * 0.1  # Highly correlated
with feature1

data = {
    'Feature1': feature1,
    'Feature2': feature2,
    'Feature3': feature3,
    'Target': target
}
df = pd.DataFrame(data)

# Split the data into training and testing sets
X = df.drop('Target', axis=1)
y = df['Target']
X_train, X_test, y_train, y_test = train_test_split(X, y, test_size=0.2,
random_state=42)

# Print the shapes of the training and testing sets
print(f'Training features shape: {X_train.shape}')
print(f'Training target shape: {y_train.shape}')
print(f'Testing features shape: {X_test.shape}')
print(f'Testing target shape: {y_test.shape}')
```

With the output

```
Training features shape: (80, 3)
Training target shape: (80,)
Testing features shape: (20, 3)
Testing target shape: (20,)
```

The sklearn's train_test_split function

```
sklearn.model_selection.train_test_split(*arrays, test_size=None,
train_size=None, random_state=None, shuffle=True, stratify=None)
```

has these parameters:

1. **arrays**
   - The input data (features and labels) you want to split. Typically, these are your feature matrix X and target vector y.
2. **test_size**
   - Determines the proportion of the dataset to include in the test split. It can be a float (between 0.0 and 1.0), an integer (number of test samples), or None. If None, it will be set to the complement of the train_size.
3. **train_size**
   - Determines the proportion of the dataset to include in the train split. It can be a float (between 0.0 and 1.0), an integer (number of train samples), or None. If None, it will be set to the complement of the test_size.

4. `random_state`
   - Controls the shuffling applied to the data before applying the split. Pass an integer for reproducible output across multiple function calls.
5. `shuffle`
   - Whether or not to shuffle the data before splitting. The default is `True`.
6. `stratify`
   - If this is not `None`, data is divided proportionally, using this as the class label. This helps with classification problems to keep the balance of the target variable in the train and test sets.

If your dataset is small or imbalanced (in a classification problem, one class of dataset significantly outnumbers the others) or you are looking for a more robust assessment of the model robustness, you should use **cross-validation**. Cross-validation is a statistical method based upon splitting the dataset into multiple subsets ("folds"), and then iteratively training and testing the model on different combinations of these folds.

The most common form of cross-validation is **k-fold cross-validation,** where the dataset is split into k-equally sized folds with the model trained on k-1 folds and tested on the remaining fold. This process is repeated k-times with each fold serving once the role of the test set. The model performance metric is then defined as the average of the performance metrics for each of the k runs.

The clear benefit of cross-validation is the more reliable estimation of the model performance than with a single test set. However, cross-validation is more computationally intensive than using a single test set.

Let's compare the performance of the test-train approach with the k-fold cross-validation in an example of classifying the Wine dataset from the UCI Machine Learning Repository. The dataset is composed of the chemical analysis of three different types of wine grapes grown in Italy.

```python
import numpy as np
from sklearn.datasets import load_wine
from sklearn.model_selection import cross_val_score, train_test_split
from sklearn.ensemble import RandomForestClassifier
from sklearn.metrics import accuracy_score

# Load dataset
data = load_wine()
X, y = data.data, data.target

# Initialize the model
model = RandomForestClassifier(random_state=42)

# Perform 5-fold cross-validation
cv_scores = cross_val_score(model, X, y, cv=5)
print("Cross-validation scores:", cv_scores)
print("Mean cross-validation score:", cv_scores.mean())

# Perform a typical train-test split
X_train, X_test, y_train, y_test = train_test_split(X, y, test_size=0.2, random_state=42)
```

```python
# Train the model
model.fit(X_train, y_train)

# Test the model
y_pred = model.predict(X_test)
test_accuracy = accuracy_score(y_test, y_pred)
print("Train-test split accuracy:", test_accuracy)

# Compare the results
print("\nComparison of Results:")
print(f"Mean cross-validation score: {cv_scores.mean():.4f}")
print(f"Train-test split accuracy: {test_accuracy:.4f}")
```

With the output

```
Cross-validation scores: [0.97222222 0.94444444 0.97222222 0.97142857 1.]
Mean cross-validation score: 0.9720634920634922
Train-test split accuracy: 1.0

Comparison of Results:
Mean cross-validation score: 0.9721
Train-test split accuracy: 1.0000
```

The results indicate that the model performs well on the given dataset; however, the perfect score on the train-test split indicates potential overfitting.

Chapter 5

Step 3: Model Choice, Training, and Application

In the rapidly evolving world of financial trading, leveraging advanced artificial intelligence (AI) methods can significantly enhance predictive accuracy and strategic decision-making.

In AI, a **model** is a mathematical construct trained on a dataset to recognize patterns, make predictions, provide recommendations, or perform other tasks. It represents the learned relationships and structures within the training dataset to be used on the dataset itself, or to make predictions on data the model has not seen.

The two primary types of machine-learning techniques for analyzing data are supervised and unsupervised learning. **Supervised learning** involves training a model on labeled data, where the input features and corresponding output labels are known. It is commonly used for tasks such as classification and regression, where the goal is to predict labels (classification) or continuous values (regression) for new, unseen data. The typical algorithms are linear regression, decision trees, support vector machines, and supervised ranking algorithms. On the other hand, **unsupervised learning** deals with unlabeled data, focusing on discovering hidden patterns or structures within the dataset. Clustering and dimensionality reduction are typical applications of unsupervised learning, utilizing algorithms such as k-means clustering, and principal component analysis (PCA).

Large language models rely on both supervised and unsupervised learning techniques and are thus sometimes called **semi-supervised learning**. First, the model is trained on vast amounts of text data without explicit labels, aiming at predicting the next word in a sentence. Second, the model is usually fine-tuned by training it on a curated set of documents with specific labels.

Reinforcement learning (outlined in a separate chapter) is an individual concept from supervised and unsupervised learning. It is a paradigm where an agent learns to make decisions by taking actions in an environment to maximize cumulative rewards through trial and error. An example of this model application is the self-driving car.

This chapter introduces various regression techniques and machine-learning algorithms that have become essential tools for modern financial analysts and traders.

We begin with **linear regression**, a fundamental method for modeling the relationship between a dependent variable and one or more independent variables, which is crucial for predicting asset prices based on historical data. **Polynomial regression** extends this by fitting a non-linear relationship, allowing for more complex trend capturing. **Least absolute shrinkage and selection operator (LASSO) regression** introduces regularization to prevent overfitting, effectively handling datasets with numerous predictors. **Ridge regression** similarly adds a penalty term to improve model generalization. **Markov switching dynamic regression** models time series data that switch between different regimes, reflecting market conditions more accurately. **Decision tree regression** provides a non-parametric approach, splitting the data into branches to make predictions based on decision rules. **Support vector machines (SVM) regression with wavelet forecasting** combines the strengths of SVMs and wavelet transformations for precise predictions in noisy environments. A **multiclass random forest model**, which extends the random forest algorithm to handle multiple classes, is effective for classification problems involving more than two categories. **Logistic regression** is pivotal for classification tasks, such as predicting the likelihood of a market event. Moving beyond regression, **hidden Markov models** offer robust frameworks for modeling time series data with hidden states, capturing market regime transitions. **Gaussian Naive Bayes** applies probabilistic methods to classification, which is particularly useful in high-dimensional datasets. Lastly, **convolutional neural networks (CNN)**, traditionally used in image processing, are adapted for financial time series, capturing intricate patterns and trends.

The **LGBRanker** excels in ordering items based on their relevance or importance. **OPTICS clustering**, known for its ability to identify clusters of varying densities, is ideal for discovering structures in large datasets. The **OpenAI language model**, with its advanced natural language understanding capabilities, is adept at performing complex language tasks. **Amazon Chronos**, designed for time series forecasting, leverages machine learning to provide accurate and scalable predictions. **FinBERT** specializes in financial sentiment analysis and interprets financial texts to gauge market sentiment and inform trading strategies.

Each method is illustrated with a Python example, showcasing its practical applications in financial trading and assessing each model's performance.

Regression

Regression is a statistical method of finding how variables relate to each other. It tries to fit a mathematical model to the dataset to show how a dependent variable depends on independent variables.

Linear Regression

Description	Linear regression is a fundamental method for modeling the relationship between a dependent variable and one or more independent variables.
Key Use Cases in Finance	Trend analysis, risk management, and forecasting future values of financial metrics, such as stock prices, returns, interest rates, company valuation, or economic indicators.
Feature Normalization/ Standardization Required	Not required but recommended.
Python Libraries Setup	`pip install numpy pandas matplotlib scikit-learn`

Linear regression is a fundamental statistical method used to model the relationship between a dependent variable and one or more independent variables.

The key advantages of the method are that it is computationally fast and straightforward to implement and interpret, making it a good starting point for predictive modeling. However, it may not perform well if the relationship is non-linear or if the data has significant outliers.

In finance, it is often used for trend analysis, risk management, and forecasting future values of financial metrics, such as stock prices, returns, interest rates, company valuation, or economic indicators.

Normalization or standardization is not strictly required for linear regression but can improve the performance and interpretability of the model, especially when the features have different scales.

Python Example

```python
import numpy as np
import pandas as pd
import matplotlib.pyplot as plt
from sklearn.model_selection import train_test_split
from sklearn.linear_model import LinearRegression
from sklearn.metrics import mean_squared_error, r2_score

# Generate Sample Data
# Assuming we have a simple dataset with a linear relationship
np.random.seed(0)
X = np.random.rand(100, 1) * 10  # Feature: Random values between 0 and 10
y = 2.5 * X + np.random.randn(100, 1) * 2  # Target: Linear relationship
with noise

# Split the data into training and test datasets
X_train, X_test, y_train, y_test = train_test_split(X, y, test_size=0.2,
random_state=0)

# Use the Linear Regression method
model = LinearRegression()
model.fit(X_train, y_train)
```

```python
# Plot the sample chart with the training and test data and the fitted model
plt.figure(figsize=(10, 6))
plt.scatter(X_train, y_train, color='blue', label='Training data')
plt.scatter(X_test, y_test, color='green', label='Test data')
plt.plot(X_test, model.predict(X_test), color='red', linewidth=2,
label='Fitted line')
plt.xlabel('Feature')
plt.ylabel('Target')
plt.title('Linear Regression')
plt.legend()
plt.show()

# Retrieve model fit statistics
y_pred = model.predict(X_test)
mse = mean_squared_error(y_test, y_pred)
r2 = r2_score(y_test, y_pred)
print(f'Mean Squared Error: {mse}')
print(f'R^2 Score: {r2}')

# Interpretation of the results
# A lower MSE and an R^2 score close to 1 indicate a good fit. You can tweak
the model by adding more features, transforming existing features, or using
regularization techniques
```

Output (Figure 5.1):

```
Mean Squared Error: 4.173733526278071
R^2 Score: 0.9295849975491168
```

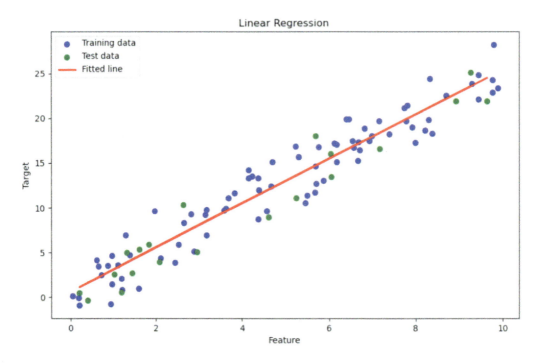

Figure 5.1 Example of linear regression.

Polynomial Regression

Description	Polynomial regression extends linear regression by fitting a non-linear relationship between the independent and dependent variables, allowing for more complex trend capturing in the data.
Key Use Cases in Finance	Modeling the cyclical behavior of financial markets, forecasting interest rates, improving the fit of economic growth models, and analyzing the performance of financial assets.
Feature Normalization/ Standardization Required	Not required but recommended.
Python Libraries Setup	`pip install numpy pandas matplotlib scikit-learn`

Polynomial regression is a generalization of linear regression that allows for a curved relationship between the dependent and independent variables. Use polynomial regression when the variables have a non-linear relationship that can be modeled with polynomial terms.

Be careful of overfitting, especially with polynomials of high degree. Regularization techniques are used to prevent overfitting, which works by adding a penalty term to the loss function, which discourages substantial coefficients in the polynomial equation. Two common types of regularization are L1 regularization, which adds the absolute values of the coefficients (leading to lasso regression explained later), and L2 regularization, which adds the squared values of the coefficients (leading to ridge regression explained later). Regularization helps improve the model's performance on unseen data, by avoiding the issue where the model fits the training data too closely, capturing noise instead of the actual underlying patterns.

In finance, polynomial regression helps model more complex relationships in time series data, capturing the cyclical behavior of economic indicators, and improving the fit of models predicting stock prices.

Normalization or standardization can be beneficial, particularly when polynomial terms significantly increase the range of feature values.

Python Example

```python
import numpy as np
import pandas as pd
import matplotlib.pyplot as plt
from sklearn.model_selection import train_test_split
from sklearn.preprocessing import PolynomialFeatures
from sklearn.linear_model import LinearRegression
from sklearn.metrics import mean_squared_error, r2_score

# Generate Sample Data
np.random.seed(0)
X = np.random.rand(100, 1) * 10  # Feature: Random values between 0 and 10
y = 2.5 * X**2 + np.random.randn(100, 1) * 10  # Target: Quadratic relationship with noise

# Split the data into training and test datasets
X_train, X_test, y_train, y_test = train_test_split(X, y, test_size=0.2, random_state=0)
```

```python
# Use Polynomial Features and Linear Regression
poly = PolynomialFeatures(degree=2)
X_train_poly = poly.fit_transform(X_train)
X_test_poly = poly.transform(X_test)

model = LinearRegression()
model.fit(X_train_poly, y_train)

# Plot the sample chart with the training and test data and the fitted model
plt.figure(figsize=(10, 6))
plt.scatter(X_train, y_train, color='blue', label='Training data')
plt.scatter(X_test, y_test, color='green', label='Test data')
X_plot = np.linspace(0, 10, 100).reshape(-1, 1)
y_plot = model.predict(poly.transform(X_plot))
plt.plot(X_plot, y_plot, color='red', linewidth=2, label='Fitted curve')
plt.xlabel('Feature')
plt.ylabel('Target')
plt.title('Polynomial Regression')
plt.legend()
plt.show()

# Retrieve model fit statistics
y_pred = model.predict(X_test_poly)
mse = mean_squared_error(y_test, y_pred)
r2 = r2_score(y_test, y_pred)
print(f'Mean Squared Error: {mse}')
print(f'R^2 Score: {r2}')

# Interpretation of the results
# Lower MSE and higher R^2 indicate a good fit. Watch for overfitting by examining
the performance on test data.
```

With the output (Figure 5.2)

```
Mean Squared Error: 102.85467801527334
R^2 Score: 0.981491014534497
```

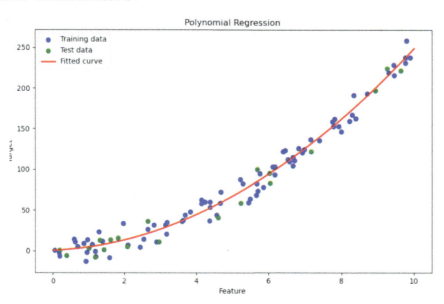

Figure 5.2 Example of polynomial regression.

LASSO Regression

Description	LASSO regression introduces regularization to linear regression to prevent overfitting, effectively handling datasets with numerous predictors.
Key Use Cases in Finance	Feature selection for financial models, predicting credit risk, identifying significant factors affecting stock prices, enhancing portfolio optimization models.
Feature Normalization/ Standardization Required	Essential.
Python Libraries Setup	`pip install numpy pandas matplotlib scikit-learn`

Least absolute shrinkage and selection operator (LASSO) regression is a type of linear regression that includes a regularization term to shrink the coefficients of less important features to zero. LASSO regression is a good choice when you have many features and think that only some of them are relevant for the prediction of the target variable. It avoids overfitting and enhances model generalization. However, it may not perform well if all features are essential, or if you require an exact model with all features included (Figure 5.3).

In LASSO regression, the parameter alpha controls the regularization strength. The higher the alpha, the stronger the regularization and the coefficients of less essential features shrink toward zero, effectively performing feature selection.

Formally, the loss function is modified to include a penalty term defined as the sum of the absolute values of the coefficients:

$$Loss = RSS + \alpha \sum_{i=1}^{n} |w_i|$$

The residual sum of squares (RSS) is defined as the sum of the squared differences between the observed and predicted values, w_i are the model coefficients, and α is the regularization parameter. The LASSO regression aims to minimize the loss function; hence, the higher the α, the lower the coefficients.

In finance, LASSO regression can help identify the most significant predictors of financial outcomes, such as asset returns or credit risk.

Normalization or standardization is essential for LASSO regression to ensure the regularization term is applied uniformly across all features.

Python Example

```python
import numpy as np
import pandas as pd
import matplotlib.pyplot as plt
from sklearn.model_selection import train_test_split
from sklearn.linear_model import Lasso
from sklearn.preprocessing import StandardScaler
from sklearn.metrics import mean_squared_error, r2_score

# Generate Sample Data
np.random.seed(0)
```

```python
X = np.random.rand(100, 10)  # Features: Random values with 10 features
true_coeffs = np.array([22.5, -1.5, 0, 100, 3, 0, 45, 0, 1, 0])
y = X @ true_coeffs + np.random.randn(100) * 2  # Target: Linear combination
with noise

# Split the data into training and test datasets
X_train, X_test, y_train, y_test = train_test_split(X, y, test_size=0.2,
random_state=0)

# Standardize the features
scaler = StandardScaler()
X_train_scaled = scaler.fit_transform(X_train)
X_test_scaled = scaler.transform(X_test)

# Use Lasso Regression
model = Lasso(alpha=0.01)  # Adjusted alpha for better fit
model.fit(X_train_scaled, y_train)

# Plot the sample chart with the training and test data and the fitted model
plt.figure(figsize=(10, 6))
y_pred_train = model.predict(X_train_scaled)
plt.scatter(y_train, y_pred_train, color='blue', alpha=0.5, label='Training data')
y_pred_test = model.predict(X_test_scaled)
plt.scatter(y_test, y_pred_test, color='green', alpha=0.5, label='Test data')
plt.plot([y.min(), y.max()], [y.min(), y.max()], 'k--', lw=2, label='Ideal fit')
plt.xlabel('Actual values')
plt.ylabel('Predicted values')
plt.title('Lasso Regression: Predicted vs. Actual')
plt.legend()
plt.show()

# Plot the coefficients
plt.figure(figsize=(10, 6))
plt.plot(model.coef_, marker='o', linestyle='none', label='Lasso coefficients')
plt.xlabel('Feature index')
plt.ylabel('Coefficient value')
plt.title('Lasso Regression Coefficients')
plt.legend()
plt.show()

# Retrieve model fit statistics
mse = mean_squared_error(y_test, y_pred_test)
r2 = r2_score(y_test, y_pred_test)
print(f'Mean Squared Error: {mse}')
print(f'R^2 Score: {r2}')

# Interpretation of the results
# Lasso regression coefficients help identify important features. Lower MSE and
higher R^2 indicate a good fit.
# The regularization parameter (alpha) can be tweaked to adjust the amount of
shrinkage.
```

With the outputs (Figures 5.3 and 5.4)

```
Mean Squared Error: 2.885180122300261
R^2 Score: 0.9961485834952417
```

Chapter 5. Step 3: Model Choice, Training, and Application 95

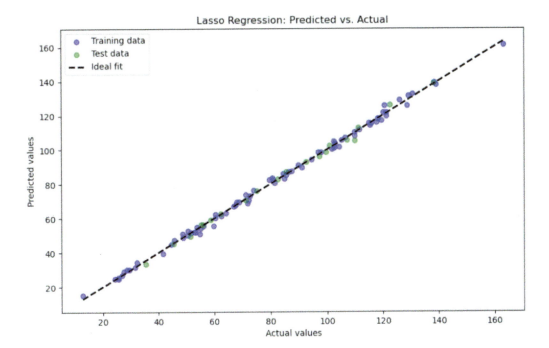

Figure 5.3 Example of LASSO regression.

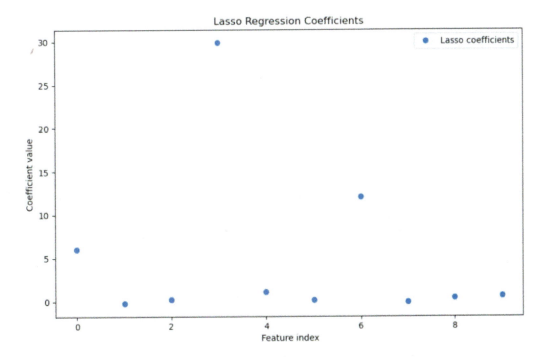

Figure 5.4 Example of LASSO regression coefficients.

Notice that most of the features have close to zero coefficient values.

Ridge Regression

Description	Ridge regression extends linear regression by adding a penalty to the loss function proportional to the sum of the squared coefficients, helping to prevent overfitting by shrinking the coefficients towards zero while maintaining all features in the model.
Key Use Cases in Finance	Forecasting economic indicators, predicting stock returns, reducing model complexity in portfolio optimization, and handling multicollinearity in financial data.
Feature Normalization/ Standardization Required	Essential.
Python Libraries Setup	`pip install numpy pandas matplotlib scikit-learn`

Ridge regression is a technique used to analyze multiple regression data that suffers from multicollinearity, a situation when independent variables are highly correlated, making it difficult to isolate the individual effect of each variable on the dependent variable and leading to unreliable coefficient estimates. By adding a degree of bias to the regression estimates, ridge regression can improve the model's prediction accuracy and interpretability.

In ridge regression, the parameter alpha (the regularization parameter or penalty term) controls the amount of regularization applied to the model. It balances the trade-off between fitting the training data well and keeping the model coefficients small to prevent overfitting. The formula for the ridge regression loss function is

$$Loss = RSS + \alpha \sum_{i=1}^{n} w_i^2$$

Where:

- RSS measures the sum of the squared differences between the observed and predicted values.
- α is the regularization parameter. It becomes the ordinary linear regression with no regularization when equal to zero. The higher the α, the more the coefficients are shrunk, at the potential cost of underfitting for its enormous value.
- w_i are the coefficients of the model.

In finance, it is often used for forecasting and reducing model complexity while maintaining predictive performance.

Normalization or standardization is essential to ensure the regularization term is applied uniformly across all features.

Python Example

```
import numpy as np
import pandas as pd
import matplotlib.pyplot as plt
from sklearn.model_selection import train_test_split
```

```python
from sklearn.linear_model import Ridge
from sklearn.preprocessing import StandardScaler
from sklearn.metrics import mean_squared_error, r2_score

# Generate Sample Data
np.random.seed(0)
X = np.random.rand(100, 10)  # Features: Random values with 10 features
true_coeffs = np.array([20.5, -1.5, 0, 45, 3, 0, 0, 0, 1, 0])
y = X @ true_coeffs + np.random.randn(100) * 2   # Target: Linear combination with noise

# Split the data into training and test datasets
X_train, X_test, y_train, y_test = train_test_split(X, y, test_size=0.2, random_state=0)

# Standardize the features
scaler = StandardScaler()
X_train_scaled = scaler.fit_transform(X_train)
X_test_scaled = scaler.transform(X_test)

# Use Ridge Regression
model = Ridge(alpha=1.0)
model.fit(X_train_scaled, y_train)

# Plot the sample chart with the training and test data and the fitted model
plt.figure(figsize=(10, 6))
y_pred_train = model.predict(X_train_scaled)
plt.scatter(y_train, y_pred_train, color='blue', alpha=0.5, label='Training data')
y_pred_test = model.predict(X_test_scaled)
plt.scatter(y_test, y_pred_test, color='green', alpha=0.5, label='Test data')
plt.plot([y.min(), y.max()], [y.min(), y.max()], 'k--', lw=2, label='Ideal fit')
plt.xlabel('Actual values')
plt.ylabel('Predicted values')
plt.title('Ridge Regression: Predicted vs. Actual')
plt.legend()
plt.show()


# Plot the sample chart with the training and test data and the fitted model
# For high-dimensional data, we focus on coefficients
plt.figure(figsize=(10, 6))
plt.plot(model.coef_, marker='o', linestyle='none', label='Ridge coefficients')
plt.xlabel('Feature index')
plt.ylabel('Coefficient value')
plt.title('Ridge Regression Coefficients')
plt.legend()
plt.show()

# Retrieve model fit statistics
y_pred = model.predict(X_test_scaled)
mse = mean_squared_error(y_test, y_pred)
r2 = r2_score(y_test, y_pred)
print(f'Mean Squared Error: {mse}')
print(f'R^2 Score: {r2}')

# Interpretation of the results
# Ridge regression coefficients show the impact of regularization. Lower MSE and higher R^2 indicate a good fit.
# The regularization parameter (alpha) can be adjusted to control the amount of shrinkage.
```

With the outputs (Figures 5.5 and 5.6)

```
Mean Squared Error: 2.9934174282331862
R^2 Score: 0.982163488280449
```

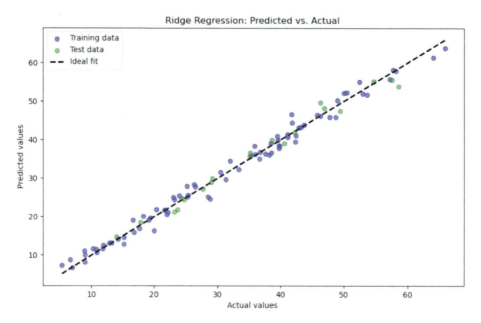

Figure 5.5 Example of ridge regression.

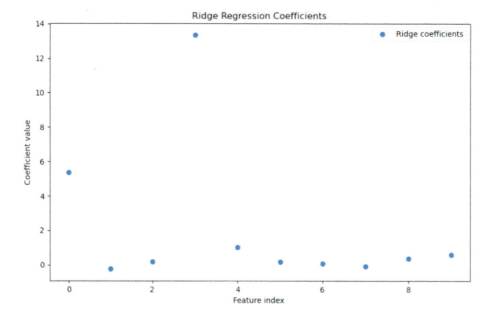

Figure 5.6 Example of ridge regression coefficients.

Notice most of the features' coefficients are essentially zeros.

Markov Switching Dynamic Regression

Description	Markov Switching Dynamic Regression models time series data that switches between different regimes, reflecting market conditions more accurately.
Key Use Cases in Finance	Modeling business cycles and economic growth, detecting bull and bear market regimes, forecasting with structural breaks, enhancing risk management models.
Feature Normalization/ Standardization Required	Not required but recommended.
Python Libraries Setup	`pip install numpy pandas matplotlib statsmodels`

Markov (or Markov-switching) regression models are useful for modeling complicated patterns in time series data, where the effect of variables may vary depending on hidden, often unobservable, states. In these models, there are multiple potential states ("regimes"), each with its own sets of regression parameters (e.g., different parameters during the rising and falling markets). A random process drives the switch between the states and depends on only each state (i.e., there is no history dependency).

In these models, there are multiple potential states ("regimes"), each with its own sets of regression parameters (e.g., different parameters during the rising and falling markets). The switch between the states is driven by a random process and depends on only each state (i.e., there is no history dependency).

Markov switching dynamic regression (MSDR) models capture regime changes in time series data. They allow the parameters of a regression model to switch between different states according to a Markov process. They are unsuitable for small datasets or when the regime changes are infrequent or random.

In finance, MSDR models are valuable for modeling economic cycles, detecting market regimes, and improving forecasts by accounting for structural breaks and regime shifts.

Normalization or standardization is recommended to improve convergence and interpretability, especially when dealing with multiple features.

Python Example

```python
import numpy as np
import pandas as pd
import matplotlib.pyplot as plt
import statsmodels.api as sm
from statsmodels.tsa.regime_switching.markov_regression import MarkovRegression
```

```python
# Generate Sample Data with Different Volatilities
np.random.seed(0)
n = 200
X = np.linspace(0, 20, n)
regime_1 = 2.5 * X[:n//2] + np.random.randn(n//2) * 5  # Higher volatility in regime 1
regime_2 = -1.5 * X[n//2:] + 30 + np.random.randn(n//2) * 1  # Lower volatility in regime 2
y = np.concatenate([regime_1, regime_2])

# Create a DataFrame
data = pd.DataFrame({'X': X, 'y': y})

# Fit Markov Switching Dynamic Regression
model = MarkovRegression(data['y'], k_regimes=2, trend='c', switching_variance=True)
result = model.fit()

# Plot the observed data and fitted regimes
plt.figure(figsize=(12, 8))

# Plot observed data
plt.plot(data['X'], data['y'], label='Observed', color='blue')

# Extract smoothed probabilities
smoothed_probs = result.smoothed_marginal_probabilities

# Plot the observed data and regime probabilities
for t in range(len(smoothed_probs)):
    if smoothed_probs.iloc[t, 0] > 0.5:
        plt.plot(data['X'].iloc[t], data['y'].iloc[t], 'ro', alpha=0.5)
    else:
        plt.plot(data['X'].iloc[t], data['y'].iloc[t], 'go', alpha=0.5)

# Highlight regime changes
regime_changes = np.argmax(smoothed_probs.values, axis=1)
for i in range(1, len(regime_changes)):
    if regime_changes[i] != regime_changes[i - 1]:
        plt.axvline(x=data['X'].iloc[i], color='gray', linestyle='--', linewidth=1)

plt.xlabel('Feature (X)')
plt.ylabel('Target (y)')
plt.title('Markov Switching Dynamic Regression with Two Regimes')
plt.legend(['Observed', 'Regime 1', 'Regime 2'])
plt.show()

# Plot the regime probabilities
plt.figure(figsize=(12, 6))
plt.plot(data['X'], smoothed_probs[0], label='Regime 1 Probability', color='red')
plt.plot(data['X'], smoothed_probs[1], label='Regime 2 Probability', color='green')
plt.xlabel('Feature (X)')
plt.ylabel('Probability')
plt.title('Smoothed Regime Probabilities')
plt.legend()
plt.show()
```

Chapter 5. Step 3: Model Choice, Training, and Application

```
# Retrieve model fit statistics
print(result.summary())

# Interpretation of the results
# The summary provides detailed statistics on the fitted model, including
transition probabilities and regime-specific parameters.
# These statistics help understand the regime changes and their impact on the
dependent variable.
```

With the outputs (Figures 5.7 and 5.8)

```
                        Markov Switching Model Results
==============================================================================
Dep. Variable:                      y   No. Observations:                  200
Model:                MarkovRegression   Log Likelihood                -610.192
Date:                Wed, 31 Jul 2024   AIC                           1232.384
Time:                        13:02:59   BIC                           1252.174
Sample:                             0   HQIC                          1240.393
                                - 200
Covariance Type:               approx
                             Regime 0 parameters
==============================================================================
                 coef    std err          z      P>|z|      [0.025      0.975]
------------------------------------------------------------------------------
const          6.2026      0.488     12.714      0.000       5.246       7.159
sigma2        19.6916      2.580      7.631      0.000      14.634      24.749
                             Regime 1 parameters
==============================================================================
                 coef    std err          z      P>|z|      [0.025      0.975]
------------------------------------------------------------------------------
const         17.2055      0.928     18.547      0.000      15.387      19.024
sigma2        35.9522      6.107      5.887      0.000      23.983      47.922
                         Regime transition parameters
==============================================================================
                 coef    std err          z      P>|z|      [0.025      0.975]
------------------------------------------------------------------------------
p[0->0]        0.9937      0.007    150.494      0.000       0.981       1.007
p[1->0]        0.0182      0.015      1.183      0.237      -0.012       0.048
==============================================================================

Warnings:
[1] Covariance matrix calculated using numerical (complex-step) differentiation.
```

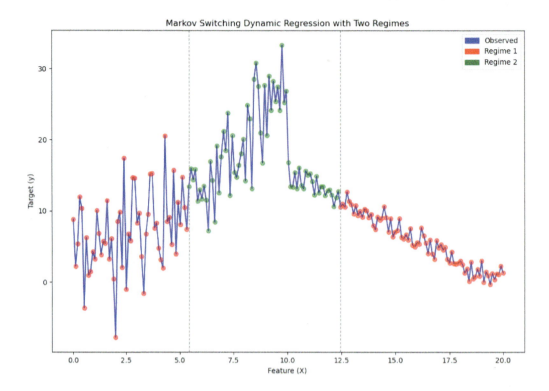

Figure 5.7 Example of Markov switching dynamic regression.

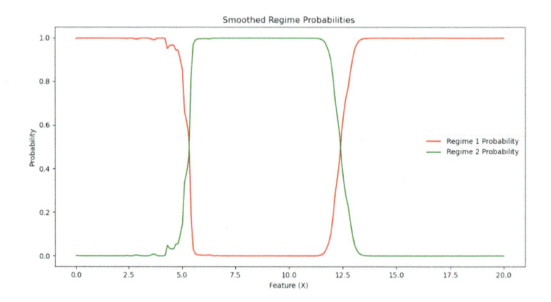

Figure 5.8 Smoothed regime probabilities of the Markov switching dynamic regression.

Decision Tree Regression

Description	Decision tree regression provides a non-parametric approach, splitting the data into branches to make predictions based on decision rules.
Key Use Cases in Finance	Modeling credit risk, forecasting financial distress, identifying key drivers of stock price movements, and predicting loan defaults.
Feature Normalization/ Standardization Required	Not required.
Python Libraries Setup	`pip install numpy pandas matplotlib scikit-learn`

Decision tree regression is a non-linear predictive modeling technique that partitions the data into subsets based on feature values, resulting in a tree-like structure. Use decision tree regression when you need an interpretable model to capture non-linear relationships without requiring extensive feature engineering. It is prone to overfitting, so pruning techniques or ensemble methods (like random forests) are often used to improve generalization.

In finance, decision tree regression can model complex relationships in data, identify critical determinants of financial outcomes, and provide intuitive visualizations of decision-making processes.

Normalization or standardization is not required for decision tree regression since it is based on splitting rules invariant to feature scaling.

Python Example

```python
import numpy as np
import pandas as pd
import matplotlib.pyplot as plt
from sklearn.model_selection import train_test_split
from sklearn.tree import DecisionTreeRegressor, plot_tree
from sklearn.metrics import mean_squared_error, r2_score

# Generate Sample Data
np.random.seed(0)
X = np.random.rand(100, 1) * 10  # Feature: Random values between 0 and 10
y = 2.5 * np.sin(X).ravel() + np.random.randn(100) * 0.5  # Target: Non-linear relationship with noise

# Split the data into training and test datasets
X_train, X_test, y_train, y_test = train_test_split(X, y, test_size=0.2, random_state=0)

# Use Decision Tree Regression
model = DecisionTreeRegressor(max_depth=3)
model.fit(X_train, y_train)

# Plot the sample chart with the training and test data and the fitted model
plt.figure(figsize=(10, 6))
plt.scatter(X_train, y_train, color='blue', label='Training data')
plt.scatter(X_test, y_test, color='green', label='Test data')
X_plot = np.linspace(0, 10, 100).reshape(-1, 1)
y_plot = model.predict(X_plot)
```

```python
plt.plot(X_plot, y_plot, color='red', linewidth=2, label='Fitted model')
plt.xlabel('Feature')
plt.ylabel('Target')
plt.title('Decision Tree Regression')
plt.legend()
plt.show()

# Display the generated trees
plt.figure(figsize=(12, 8))
plot_tree(model, filled=True)
plt.title('Decision Tree Structure')
plt.show()

# Retrieve model fit statistics
y_pred = model.predict(X_test)
mse = mean_squared_error(y_test, y_pred)
r2 = r2_score(y_test, y_pred)
print(f'Mean Squared Error: {mse}')
print(f'R^2 Score: {r2}')

# Interpretation of the results
# Decision tree regression results include the structure of the tree, showing
splits and leaf values.
# Lower MSE and higher R^2 indicate a good fit. Pruning can help improve model
generalization.
```

With the output (Figures 5.9 and 5.10)

```
Mean Squared Error: 0.573935429046908
R^2 Score: 0.8041605163184924
```

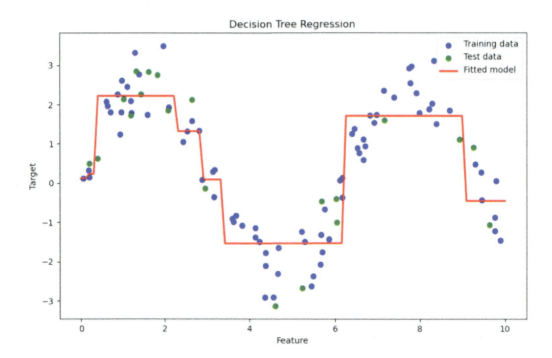

Figure 5.9 Example of decision tree regression.

Chapter 5. Step 3: Model Choice, Training, and Application

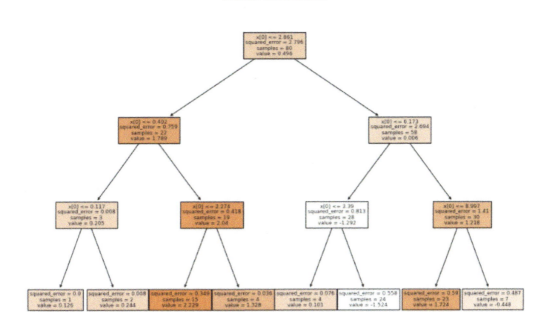

Figure 5.10 Decision tree structure.

Support Vector Machines Regression with Wavelet Forecasting

Description	Support vector machines (SVM) regression with wavelet forecasting combines the strengths of SVMs and wavelet transformations for precise predictions in noisy environments.
Key Use Cases in Finance	Stock price forecasting, volatility prediction, high-frequency trading, analyzing cyclical financial data.
Feature Normalization/Standardization Required	Essential.
Python Libraries Setup	`pip install numpy pandas matplotlib scikit-learn pywavelets`

SVM regression, combined with wavelet transforms, is a powerful method for forecasting time series with trends and seasonal patterns.

SVMs are supervised learning models that can perform classification and regression:

- They are effective for classification problems because they can discover the best boundary that separates the data into different groups. For classification problems, SVMs find a hyperplane that optimally divides the data into classes.
- Support vector regression (SVR) aims to find a function that is as smooth as possible and that contains the maximum number of data points within a given margin boundary.

SVM regression captures complex relationships, while wavelet transforms decompose time series data into different frequency components. It may be computationally intensive and less interpretable than simpler models.

It is helpful in finance for financial forecasting; SVR's ability to handle non-linear patterns in financial data makes it ideal for financial and economic forecasting.

Normalization or standardization is essential for SVM to ensure proper convergence and performance, especially when dealing with different scales.

SVM regression has these parameters:

1. **Kernel type:** linear/polynomial/RBF, depending on the nature of data and problem complexity; the default one used by sklearn is RBF.
2. **Regularization parameter (C):** controls the trade-off between a low training error and minimizing the model complexity. A more significant C value might lead to a smaller margin but fewer misclassifications, while a smaller C value creates a more significant margin but more misclassifications.
3. **Epsilon:** the smaller the value, the more precise fit to the training set and the more likely the case of overfitting.
4. **Gamma:** defines how far the influence of a single training example reaches. The default value is auto, but you might try scale or specific numerical values.

Wavelet forecasting is a method in time series analysis that applies wavelets to break down data into different frequency components, revealing patterns hidden in the overall data. This method helps examine non-stationary data where statistical properties vary over time. It separates these components, models them individually, and then uses the outcomes to reassemble and enhance the precision of forecasts. Wavelet forecasting is frequently used in economics, finance, and environmental science.

In finance, wavelet forecasting's ability to effectively handle non-stationary and volatile data enables it to capture short-term and long-term trends and seasonal cycles present in asset prices or economic indicators time series.

In Python, the PyWavelets library performs wavelet decomposition and reconstruction on a signal. It operates in two steps:

Step 1: Wavelet decomposition (`pywt.wavedec`)

Wavelet decomposition is a method of breaking down a signal into its component wavelets at various levels of detail, which allows the simultaneous examination of the signal in both the time and frequency domains.

```
coeffs = pywt.wavedec(y, 'db1', level=2)
```

This function performs a multi-level wavelet decomposition on the signal y, where `'db1'` refers to the Daubechies wavelet with one vanishing moment and `level=2` refers to the target output of 2 decomposition levels.

The output is a list of arrays containing the wavelet coefficients.

Step 2: Wavelet reconstruction (`pywt.wavedec`)

Reconstructing the original signal from its wavelet coefficients is called wavelet reconstruction and can help with signal denoising, compression, and other signal-processing tasks.

```
y_wavelet = pywt.waverec(coeffs, 'db1')
```

Chapter 5. Step 3: Model Choice, Training, and Application

This function reconstructs the signal from the coefficients `coeffs` with the `db1` wavelet type.

The output `y_wavelet` is the reconstructed signal.

Python Example

```python
import numpy as np
import pandas as pd
import matplotlib.pyplot as plt
from sklearn.metrics import mean_squared_error, r2_score
from sklearn.model_selection import train_test_split
from sklearn.svm import SVR
from sklearn.preprocessing import StandardScaler
import pywt

# Generate Sample Data
np.random.seed(0)
n = 200
X = np.linspace(0, 20, n).reshape(-1, 1)
y = 2.5 * np.sin(X).ravel() + np.random.randn(n) * 0.5  # Target: Non-linear relationship with noise

# Apply Wavelet Transform
coeffs = pywt.wavedec(y, 'db1', level=2)
y_wavelet = pywt.waverec(coeffs, 'db1')

# Split the data into training and test datasets
X_train, X_test, y_train, y_test = train_test_split(X, y_wavelet, test_size=0.2, random_state=0)

# Standardize the features
scaler = StandardScaler()
X_train_scaled = scaler.fit_transform(X_train)
X_test_scaled = scaler.transform(X_test)

# Use SVM Regression
model = SVR(kernel='rbf', C=100, epsilon=0.01)
model.fit(X_train_scaled, y_train)

# Plot the sample chart with the training and test data and the fitted model
plt.figure(figsize=(10, 6))
plt.scatter(X_train, y_train, color='blue', label='Training data')
plt.scatter(X_test, y_test, color='green', label='Test data')
X_plot = np.linspace(0, 20, 200).reshape(-1, 1)
X_plot_scaled = scaler.transform(X_plot)
y_plot = model.predict(X_plot_scaled)
plt.plot(X_plot, y_plot, color='red', linewidth=2, label='Fitted model')
plt.xlabel('Feature')
plt.ylabel('Target')
plt.title('SVM Regression with Wavelet Forecasting')
plt.legend()
plt.show()

# Retrieve model fit statistics
y_pred = model.predict(X_test_scaled)
mse = mean_squared_error(y_test, y_pred)
r2 = r2_score(y_test, y_pred)
print(f'Mean Squared Error: {mse}')
print(f'R^2 Score: {r2}')
```

```
# Interpretation of the results
# SVM regression with wavelet forecasting results provides insights into the
model's predictive accuracy.
# Lower MSE and higher R^2 indicate a good fit. Adjust the wavelet function and
SVM parameters to optimize performance.
```

With the outputs (Figure 5.11)

```
Mean Squared Error: 0.36018129235244006
R^2 Score: 0.8918512062597711
```

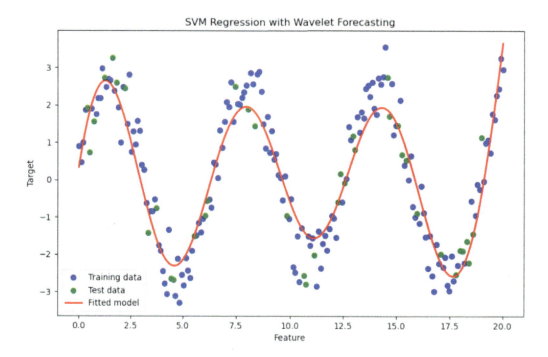

Figure 5.11 Example of SVM regression.

One of the most effective methods of finding the correct values of the SVR method's hyperparameters is by a grid search:

```
import numpy as np
from sklearn.metrics import mean_squared_error, r2_score
from sklearn.model_selection import train_test_split, GridSearchCV
from sklearn.svm import SVR
from sklearn.preprocessing import StandardScaler
import pywt

# Generate Sample Data
np.random.seed(0)
n = 200
```

```python
X = np.linspace(0, 20, n).reshape(-1, 1)
y = 2.5 * np.sin(X).ravel() + np.random.randn(n) * 0.5  # Target: Non-linear
relationship with noise

# Apply Wavelet Transform
coeffs = pywt.wavedec(y, 'db1', level=2)
y_wavelet = pywt.waverec(coeffs, 'db1')

# Split the data into training and test datasets
X_train, X_test, y_train, y_test = train_test_split(X, y_wavelet, test_size=0.2,
random_state=0)

# Standardize the features
scaler = StandardScaler()
X_train_scaled = scaler.fit_transform(X_train)
X_test_scaled = scaler.transform(X_test)

# Use SVM Regression
model = SVR(kernel='rbf')
param_grid = {
    'C': [0.1, 1, 10, 100],
    'epsilon': [0.01, 0.1, 0.5, 1],
    'gamma': ['scale', 'auto', 0.01, 0.1, 1, 10]
}

grid_search = GridSearchCV(estimator=model, param_grid=param_grid, cv=5,
scoring='r2')

# Fit the model
grid_search.fit(X_train_scaled, y_train)

# Retrieve the best parameters and best score
best_params = grid_search.best_params_
best_score = grid_search.best_score_

print(f'Best parameters: {best_params}')
print(f'Best R² score: {best_score}')

# Use the best model
best_model = grid_search.best_estimator_

# Evaluate the best model on the test set
y_pred = best_model.predict(X_test_scaled)
mse = mean_squared_error(y_test, y_pred)
r2 = r2_score(y_test, y_pred)

print(f'Test Mean Squared Error: {mse}')
print(f'Test R² Score: {r2}')
```

With the outputs

```
Best parameters: {'C': 10, 'epsilon': 0.5, 'gamma': 10}
Best R² score: 0.9192064453967035
Test Mean Squared Error: 0.2655530910167665
Test R² Score: 0.9202644693735217
```

Classification

Multiclass Random Forest Model

Description	An ensemble learning method that constructs multiple decision trees to classify data into more than two categories.
Key Use Cases in Finance	Fraud detection, customer segmentation, and credit risk assessment.
Feature Normalization/ Standardization Required	Not required.
Python Libraries Setup	`pip install numpy lightgbm scikit-learn matplotlib seaborn`

The multiclass random forest model is an ensemble learning method that builds multiple decision trees to classify data into more than two categories. By aggregating the predictions of several decision trees, as compared to using single decision trees, the model improves accuracy and reduces overfitting.

Key Concepts
- Ensemble Learning: ensemble learning is a technique that combines the predictions of multiple machine-learning models to produce a single, more accurate prediction with the motivation that by integrating the strengths of various models, the ensemble can outperform any individual model. Standard ensemble methods include bagging, boosting, and stacking.
- Decision Tree: a decision tree is a simple yet powerful predictive model that splits the data into subsets based on the value of input features. Each node in the tree represents a feature, each branch represents a decision rule, and each leaf node represents a class label. Decision trees are easy to interpret and can handle both numerical and categorical data but are prone to overfitting.
- Random Forest: a random forest is an ensemble learning method that constructs multiple decision trees during training and merges their predictions to improve accuracy and control overfitting. It uses techniques like bootstrapping (random sampling with replacement) and feature randomness to ensure that the trees are diverse and uncorrelated, resulting in a more robust model that's better generalized to unseen data.
- Bagging: bagging, short for bootstrap aggregating, is an ensemble learning technique that trains multiple models on different random subsets of the data and then averages their predictions.

Python Example
We have chosen the LightGBM Python library for its excellent performance in large dataset classification. Its hyperparameters include the following:

- `boosting_type`: the boosting algorithm to use. In this example, we use the 'rf' boosting type (random forest), which is a LightGBM model configured for multi-class classification using multiple trees combined to enhance model performance by minimizing the multiclass logarithmic loss.
- `num_leaves`: the maximum number of leaves in one tree. The larger the number, the more likely the model overfits.
- `learning_rate`: the reduction of the step size used in changing weights. The smaller the number, the more robust the model and the more trees required.
- `feature_fraction`: the fraction of features to consider at each split in tree-building.
- `bagging_fraction`: the fraction of data to be used for each boosting iteration.
- `bagging_freq`: the iteration frequency with which bagging is performed.

We generate sample data using sklearn's `make_classification` method. We use `GridSearchCV` to find the best hyperparameter values.

```python
import numpy as np
import lightgbm as lgb
from sklearn.datasets import make_classification
from sklearn.model_selection import train_test_split, GridSearchCV
from sklearn.metrics import accuracy_score, classification_report, confusion_matrix
import matplotlib.pyplot as plt
import seaborn as sns

# Generate sensible sample data using make_classification
n_samples = 1000
n_features = 5
n_classes = 3

X, y = make_classification(n_samples=n_samples, n_features=n_features,
n_informative=int(n_features * 0.6), n_redundant=n_features - int(n_features *
0.6), n_classes=n_classes, random_state=0)

# Split the data into training and test datasets
X_train, X_test, y_train, y_test = train_test_split(X, y, test_size=0.2,
random_state=42)

# Visualize the distribution of the classes in the dataset
plt.figure(figsize=(10, 6))
sns.countplot(x=y)
plt.title("Distribution of Classes in the Dataset")
plt.xlabel("Class")
plt.ylabel("Frequency")
plt.show()

# Define the parameter grid for hyperparameter tuning
param_grid = {
    'num_leaves': [30, 50, 70],
    'learning_rate': [0.01, 0.05, 0.1, 0.2],
    'feature_fraction': [0.5, 0.6, 0.7, 0.8, 0.9],
    'bagging_fraction': [0.5, 0.6, 0.7, 0.8, 0.9],
    'bagging_freq': [1, 5, 10]
}
```

```python
# Create a LightGBM model
lgb_estimator = lgb.LGBMClassifier(boosting_type='rf', objective='multiclass',
num_class=n_classes, metric='multi_logloss')

# Perform Grid Search
grid_search = GridSearchCV(estimator=lgb_estimator, param_grid=param_grid,
scoring='accuracy', cv=3, verbose=1)
grid_search.fit(X_train, y_train)

# Get the best parameters and accuracy from the grid search
best_params = grid_search.best_params_
best_accuracy = grid_search.best_score_
print("Best Parameters:", best_params)
print("Best Accuracy:", best_accuracy)

# Train the model with the best parameters
model = lgb.LGBMClassifier(boosting_type='rf', objective='multiclass',
num_class=n_classes, **best_params)
model.fit(X_train, y_train, eval_set=[(X_test, y_test)])

# Predict and evaluate the model
y_pred = model.predict(X_test)
accuracy = accuracy_score(y_test, y_pred)
print("Accuracy after tuning:", accuracy)
print("Classification Report:\n", classification_report(y_test, y_pred))

# Confusion Matrix
conf_matrix = confusion_matrix(y_test, y_pred)
plt.figure(figsize=(10, 6))
sns.heatmap(conf_matrix, annot=True, fmt="d", cmap="Blues",
xticklabels=range(n_classes), yticklabels=range(n_classes))
plt.title("Confusion Matrix")
plt.xlabel("Predicted Class")
plt.ylabel("True Class")
plt.show()

# Plot feature importance
plt.figure(figsize=(10, 6))
lgb.plot_importance(model, max_num_features=10, importance_type="gain")
plt.title("Feature Importance")
plt.show()
```

With outputs (Figures 5.12, 5.13, and 5.14)

```
Accuracy after tuning: 0.875
Classification Report:
              precision    recall  f1-score   support

           0       0.88      0.89      0.88        56
           1       0.90      0.81      0.85        74
           2       0.86      0.93      0.89        70

    accuracy                           0.88       200
   macro avg       0.88      0.88      0.88       200
weighted avg       0.88      0.88      0.87       200
```

Notice the classification classes are approximately balanced.

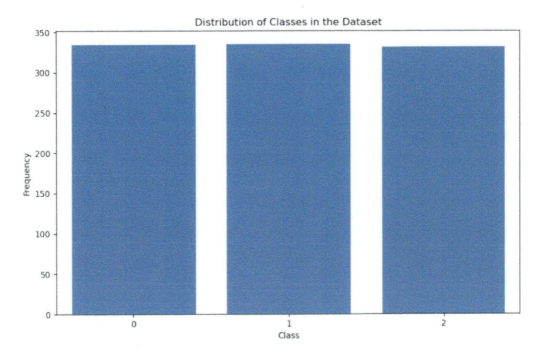

Figure 5.12 Example of class distribution in a dataset.

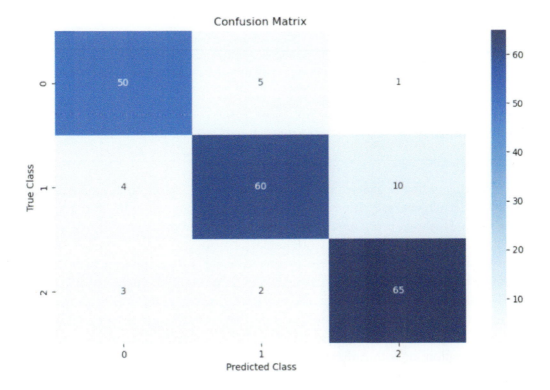

Figure 5.13 Example of confusion matrix.

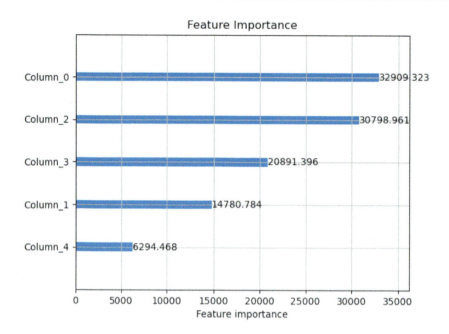

Figure 5.14 Example of feature importance.

Logistic Regression

Description	Logistic Regression is pivotal for classification tasks, such as predicting the likelihood of a market event.
Key Use Cases in Finance	Predicting credit default, fraud detection, loan approval decisions, buy/sell recommendations.
Feature Normalization/ Standardization Required	Recommended.
Python Libraries Setup	`pip install numpy pandas matplotlib scikit-learn`

Logistic regression is widely used in finance for binary classification problems (e.g., default/no default, buy/sell). It provides probabilities and can be extended to multiclass classification. However, it assumes a linear relationship between the predictors and the log odds of the outcome, which may not hold in all cases.

In finance, logistic regression can predict whether a loan applicant will default, whether a transaction is fraudulent, or whether a customer will buy a financial product. By estimating the odds of different outcomes, logistic regression helps financial institutions make informed decisions, manage risk, and develop targeted marketing strategies.

Normalization or standardization is recommended, especially when predictors have different scales, to ensure the model converges appropriately and to improve interpretability.

Python Example

```python
import numpy as np
import pandas as pd
import matplotlib.pyplot as plt
from sklearn.model_selection import train_test_split
from sklearn.linear_model import LogisticRegression
from sklearn.preprocessing import StandardScaler
from sklearn.metrics import confusion_matrix, classification_report,
roc_curve, auc

# Generate Sample Data
np.random.seed(0)
X = np.random.rand(100, 10)  # Features: Random values with 10 features
true_coeffs = np.array([2.5, -1.5, 0, 0, 3, 0, 0, 0, 1, 0])
logits = X @ true_coeffs + np.random.randn(100) * 2
y = (logits > np.median(logits)).astype(int)  # Target: Binary outcome
based on logits

# Split the data into training and test datasets
X_train, X_test, y_train, y_test = train_test_split(X, y, test_size=0.2,
random_state=0)

# Standardize the features
scaler = StandardScaler()
X_train_scaled = scaler.fit_transform(X_train)
X_test_scaled = scaler.transform(X_test)

# Use Logistic Regression
model = LogisticRegression()
model.fit(X_train_scaled, y_train)

# Plot the sample chart with the training and test data and the fitted model
# For binary classification, we plot the ROC curve
y_pred_prob = model.predict_proba(X_test_scaled)[:, 1]
fpr, tpr, _ = roc_curve(y_test, y_pred_prob)
roc_auc = auc(fpr, tpr)

plt.figure(figsize=(10, 6))
plt.plot(fpr, tpr, color='blue', label=f'ROC curve (area = {roc_auc:.2f})')
plt.plot([0, 1], [0, 1], color='red', linestyle='--')
plt.xlabel('False Positive Rate')
plt.ylabel('True Positive Rate')
plt.title('ROC Curve')
plt.legend()
plt.show()

# Retrieve model fit statistics
print("Classification Report")
print(classification_report(y_test, model.predict(X_test_scaled)))
print("Confusion Matrix")
print(confusion_matrix(y_test, model.predict(X_test_scaled)))

# Interpretation of the results
# The classification report and confusion matrix provide detailed metrics on the
model's performance.
# A higher AUC indicates better model performance. Adjust regularization
parameters to control overfitting.
```

With the outputs (Figure 5.15)

```
Classification Report
              precision    recall  f1-score   support

           0       0.55      0.75      0.63         8
           1       0.78      0.58      0.67        12

    accuracy                           0.65        20
   macro avg       0.66      0.67      0.65        20
weighted avg       0.68      0.65      0.65        20

Confusion Matrix
[[6 2]
 [5 7]]
```

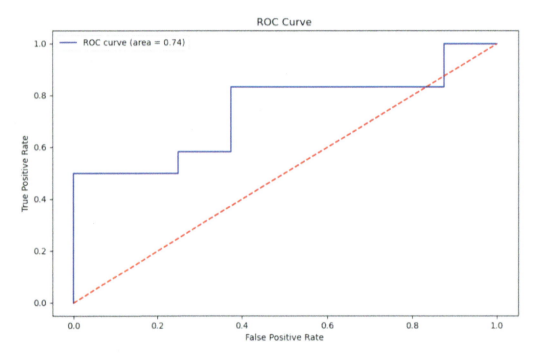

Figure 5.15 Example of ROC curve.

For classification models, a **confusion matrix** is a table used to describe the performance of a model by comparing the predicted labels with the actual labels. It is a 2 × 2 matrix for binary classification:

- True Positive (TP): the number of instances correctly predicted as the positive class.
- True Negative (TN): the number of instances correctly predicted as the negative class.
- False Positive (FP): the number of instances incorrectly predicted as the positive class (Type I error).
- False Negative (FN): the number of instances incorrectly predicted as the negative class (Type II error).

The confusion matrix looks like this:

	Predicted Positive	**Predicted Negative**
Actual Positive	TP	FN
Actual Negative	FP	TN

The following key metrics are derived from the confusion matrix:

1. **Accuracy:** the ratio of correctly predicted instances (both positive and negative) to the total cases.

$$Accuracy = \frac{TP + TN}{TP + TN + FP + FN}$$

2. **Precision (Positive Predictive Value):** the ratio of correctly predicted positive instances to the total predicted positives.

$$Precision = \frac{TP}{TP + FP}$$

3. **Recall (Sensitivity or True Positive Rate):** the ratio of correctly predicted positive instances to the total actual positives.

$$Recall = \frac{TP}{TP + FN}$$

4. **F1 Score:** the harmonic mean of precision and recall, providing a balance between the two.

$$F1\ Score = \frac{2 \times Precision \times Recall}{Precision + Recall}$$

The **receiver operating characteristics (ROC) curve** plots the actual positive rate (sensitivity) against the false positive rate (1 − specificity) at various threshold levels, allowing you to assess the model's ability to distinguish between positive and negative classes; a higher area under the curve (AUC) value indicates better overall model performance, with values closer to 1 representing excellent performance.

Hidden Markov Models

Description	Hidden Markov models offer robust frameworks for modeling time series data with hidden states, capturing market regime transitions.
Key Use Cases in Finance	Modeling market regimes, pattern recognition in time series data, predicting economic cycles, and improving trading strategies.
Feature Normalization/ Standardization Required	Not required but recommended.
Python Libraries Setup	`pip install numpy pandas matplotlib hmmlearn`

Hidden Markov models (HMMs) are statistical models that represent systems with hidden states and provide probabilistic state predictions. However, they can be complex to train and require careful parameter estimation.

In finance, HMMs are used to model market regimes, detect patterns in time series data, and improve forecasting by capturing the probabilistic transitions between states.

Normalization or standardization can improve model convergence and interpretability, especially when dealing with multiple features.

HMMs take the number of states ("regimes") as input. To find the correct number of states, start with two and increase depending on the result.

Python Example
```python
import numpy as np
import pandas as pd
import matplotlib.pyplot as plt
from hmmlearn import hmm

# Generate Sample Data
np.random.seed(0)
n = 200
X = np.linspace(0, 20, n)
state_1 = 2.5 * np.sin(X[:n//2]) + np.random.randn(n//2) * 0.5
state_2 = -1.5 * np.sin(X[n//2:]) + 2 + np.random.randn(n//2) * 0.5
y = np.concatenate([state_1, state_2])

# Fit Hidden Markov Model
model = hmm.GaussianHMM(n_components=2, covariance_type="full", n_iter=100)
model.fit(y.reshape(-1, 1))

# Predict hidden states
hidden_states = model.predict(y.reshape(-1, 1))

# Plot the sample chart with the hidden states
plt.figure(figsize=(10, 6))
plt.plot(X, y, label='Observed', color='blue')
plt.plot(X[hidden_states == 0], y[hidden_states == 0], 'ro', label='State 1')
plt.plot(X[hidden_states == 1], y[hidden_states == 1], 'go', label='State 2')
plt.xlabel('Feature')
plt.ylabel('Target')
plt.title('Hidden Markov Model')
plt.legend()
plt.show()

# Retrieve model fit statistics
print('Transition Matrix')
print(model.transmat_)
print('Means and Variances of Each State')
print(model.means_)
print(model.covars_)

# Interpretation of the results
# The transition matrix shows the probabilities of moving from one state
to another.
# The means and variances provide insights into the characteristics of each
hidden state.
```

With the outputs (Figure 5.16)

```
Transition Matrix
[[0.98722454 0.01277546]
 [0.05087947 0.94912053]]
Means and Variances of Each State
[[ 2.05014575]
 [-1.43768284]]
[[[1.13209908]]
 [[1.05456691]]]
```

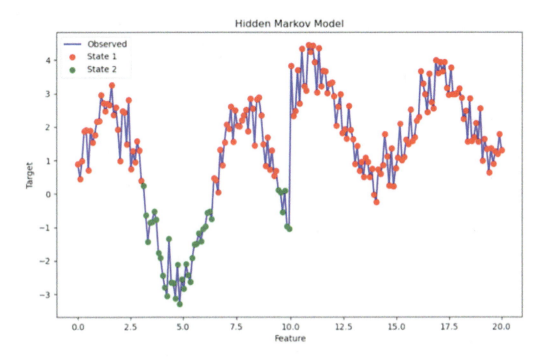

Figure 5.16 Example of hidden Markov model.

Gaussian Naive Bayes

Description	Gaussian Naive Bayes applies probabilistic methods to classification, which is particularly useful in high-dimensional datasets.
Key Use Cases in Finance	Classifying credit risk, predicting market trends, anomaly detection in trading data, fraud detection.
Feature Normalization/ Standardization Required	Not required but recommended.
Python Libraries Setup	`pip install numpy pandas matplotlib scikit-learn`

The Gaussian Naive Bayes algorithm is a classification method that detects spam, diagnoses diseases, or is used for fraud detection. The technique uses Bayes' Theorem, assuming features have a normal (Gaussian) shape. It learns the mean and variance of features from the training data and uses them to estimate the probabilities for each class. Then, it chooses the class with the highest probability for the new data.

Gaussian Naive Bayes is effective for classification tasks with normally distributed features. It is simple to implement and interpret but may underperform if the feature distribution deviates significantly from normality or the feature independence assumption does not hold.

It is helpful in finance for classifying financial risks, predicting market movements, and detecting anomalies in trading patterns.

Normalization or standardization can improve model performance, especially when features have different scales or are not normally distributed.

Python Example

```python
import numpy as np
import pandas as pd
import matplotlib.pyplot as plt
from sklearn.model_selection import train_test_split
from sklearn.naive_bayes import GaussianNB
from sklearn.preprocessing import StandardScaler
from sklearn.metrics import confusion_matrix, classification_report, roc_curve, auc

# Generate Sample Data
np.random.seed(0)
X = np.random.rand(100, 10)   # Features: Random values with 10 features
true_coeffs = np.array([2.5, -1.5, 0, 0, 3, 0, 0, 0, 1, 0])
logits = X @ true_coeffs + np.random.randn(100) * 2
y = (logits > np.median(logits)).astype(int)   # Target: Binary outcome based on logits

# Split the data into training and test datasets
X_train, X_test, y_train, y_test = train_test_split(X, y, test_size=0.2, random_state=0)

# Standardize the features
scaler = StandardScaler()
X_train_scaled = scaler.fit_transform(X_train)
X_test_scaled = scaler.transform(X_test)

# Use Gaussian Naive Bayes
model = GaussianNB()
model.fit(X_train_scaled, y_train)

# Plot the sample chart with the training and test data and the fitted model
# For binary classification, we plot the ROC curve
y_pred_prob = model.predict_proba(X_test_scaled)[:, 1]
fpr, tpr, _ = roc_curve(y_test, y_pred_prob)
roc_auc = auc(fpr, tpr)

plt.figure(figsize=(10, 6))
plt.plot(fpr, tpr, color='blue', label=f'ROC curve (area = {roc_auc:.2f})')
plt.plot([0, 1], [0, 1], color='red', linestyle='--')
plt.xlabel('False Positive Rate')
plt.ylabel('True Positive Rate')
plt.title('ROC Curve')
plt.legend()
plt.show()
```

Chapter 5. Step 3: Model Choice, Training, and Application

```
# Retrieve model fit statistics
print("Classification Report:")
print(classification_report(y_test, model.predict(X_test_scaled)))
print("Confusion Matrix:")
print(confusion_matrix(y_test, model.predict(X_test_scaled)))

# Interpretation of the results
# The classification report and confusion matrix provide detailed metrics on the
model's performance. A higher AUC indicates better model performance. Adjust
feature engineering and preprocessing to improve results.
```

With outputs (Figure 5.17)

```
Classification Report:
              precision    recall  f1-score   support

           0       0.64      0.88      0.74         8
           1       0.89      0.67      0.76        12

    accuracy                           0.75        20
   macro avg       0.76      0.77      0.75        20
weighted avg       0.79      0.75      0.75        20

Confusion Matrix:
[[7 1]
 [4 8]]
```

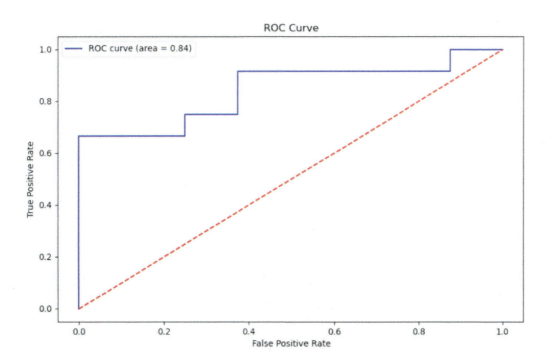

Figure 5.17 ROC curve of Gaussian Naive Bayes.

Convolutional Neural Networks

Description	Convolutional neural networks (CNN), traditionally used in image processing, are adapted here for financial time series, capturing intricate patterns and trends.
Key Use Cases in Finance	Stock price prediction, anomaly detection in financial data, high-frequency trading, sentiment analysis from financial news.
Feature Normalization/ Standardization Required	Essential.
Python Libraries Setup	`pip install numpy pandas matplotlib scikit-learn tensorflow`

Machine-learning models trying to imitate how the human brain works are called neural networks. These models have interconnected layers of nodes or "neurons." Using a mathematical function, they transform the input data to produce output. Training involves learning from data by changing their connections (or weights) to predict the correct output.

CNNs are deep learning models initially designed for image processing but have been adapted for various applications, including time series forecasting in finance. CNNs can capture complex patterns and dependencies in data that simpler models cannot. CNNs require extensive computational resources and tuning but offer high predictive power and flexibility. They may be unsuitable for small datasets or where model interpretability is crucial.

In finance, CNNs help predict stock prices, detect anomalies, and analyze financial time series data.

Normalization or standardization is essential to ensure faster convergence and better performance.

To build an effective neural network model, the first step is to choose the appropriate model architecture and determine the number of layers. Key model architectures include feedforward neural networks for simple pattern recognition, CNN for recognizing complex patterns or features, recurrent neural networks (RNN) for time series data and understanding context, and transformer models for natural language processing.

Once the architecture is selected, the next step is to architect the model. This step involves deciding on the size of the input layer, determining the number and connections between the hidden layers, and defining the size of the output layer.

Choosing the model's hyperparameters and methods to avoid overfitting is crucial for optimal performance. Key hyperparameters include the loss function, which measures the quality of the model's performance, and the optimizer, which updates model weights based on the loss function values. Overfitting avoidance methods, such as regularization, dropout, early stopping, and data augmentation, are essential to ensure the model generalizes well to unseen data.

Python Example

In the following example, we construct this neural network:

- The Keras/TensorFlow framework has been chosen due to its simplicity and ease of use, as well as the high-speed performance provided by TensorFlow.
- We use
  - convolutional layers for their ability to capture effectively complex patterns;
  - long short-term memory (LSTM) layers, which are designed to learn from sequential data by maintaining long-term dependencies; and
  - a dropout layer, a regularization technique preventing overfitting by randomly setting a fraction of the input units to zero during training.

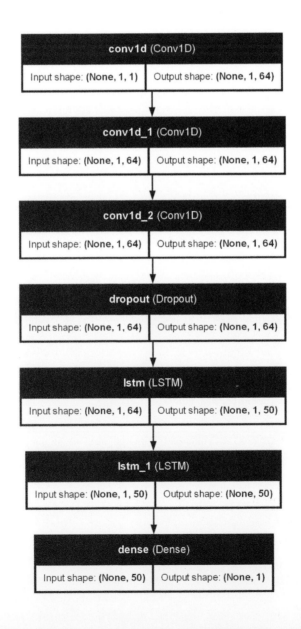

- We train the neural network with the Adam (adaptive moment estimation) optimization algorithm because it has low memory requirements, is computationally efficient, and works well with large datasets.

```python
import numpy as np
import pandas as pd
import matplotlib.pyplot as plt
from sklearn.metrics import mean_squared_error, r2_score
from sklearn.model_selection import train_test_split
from sklearn.preprocessing import StandardScaler
from tensorflow.keras.models import Sequential
from tensorflow.keras.layers import Conv1D, Dense, Flatten, Dropout, LSTM
import tensorflow as tf

# Enable logging
tf.get_logger().setLevel('INFO')

# Generate Sample Data
np.random.seed(0)
n = 1000
X = np.linspace(0, 1000, n)
y = np.sin(X/100)  # Target: Long sinusoidal wave

# Plot the sine wave
plt.figure(figsize=(10, 6))
plt.plot(X, y, label='sin(x)')
plt.xlabel('X')
plt.ylabel('sin(X)')
plt.title('Sine Wave')
plt.legend()
plt.grid(True)
plt.show()

# Reshape data for CNN
X = X.reshape(-1, 1)
y = y.reshape(-1, 1)

# Split the data into training and test datasets
X_train, X_test, y_train, y_test = train_test_split(X, y, test_size=0.2, random_state=0)

# Standardize the features
scaler = StandardScaler()
X_train_scaled = scaler.fit_transform(X_train)
X_test_scaled = scaler.transform(X_test)

# Reshape for CNN input
X_train_scaled = X_train_scaled.reshape((X_train_scaled.shape[0], 1, 1))
X_test_scaled = X_test_scaled.reshape((X_test_scaled.shape[0], 1, 1))

# Use CNN-LSTM for Regression
model = Sequential()
model.add(Conv1D(filters=64, kernel_size=1, activation='relu', input_shape=(1, 1)))
```

```python
model.add(Conv1D(filters=64, kernel_size=1, activation='relu'))
model.add(Conv1D(filters=64, kernel_size=1, activation='relu'))
model.add(Dropout(0.5))
model.add(LSTM(50, return_sequences=True))
model.add(LSTM(50))
model.add(Dense(1))
model.compile(optimizer='adam', loss='mse')

# Fit the model with logging
history = model.fit(X_train_scaled, y_train, epochs=300, batch_size=32, verbose=1,
validation_split=0.2)

# Plot the sample chart with the training and test data and the fitted model
y_pred = model.predict(X_test_scaled)

plt.figure(figsize=(10, 6))
plt.scatter(X_test, y_test, color='green', label='Test data')
plt.scatter(X_test, y_pred, color='red', label='Fitted model')
plt.xlabel('Feature')
plt.ylabel('Target')
plt.title('CNN-LSTM Neural Network Regression')
plt.legend()
plt.show()

# Retrieve model fit statistics
mse = mean_squared_error(y_test, y_pred)
r2 = r2_score(y_test, y_pred)
print(f'Mean Squared Error: {mse}')
print(f'R^2 Score: {r2}')

# Plot training & validation loss values
plt.figure(figsize=(10, 6))
plt.plot(history.history['loss'], label='Train loss')
plt.plot(history.history['val_loss'], label='Validation loss')
plt.title('Model loss')
plt.xlabel('Epoch')
plt.ylabel('Loss')
plt.legend(loc='upper right')
plt.show()

# Interpretation of the results
# CNN-LSTM regression results provide insights into the model's ability to capture
complex patterns.
# Lower MSE and higher R^2 indicate a good fit. Adjust the network architecture
and parameters to optimize performance.
```

With the outputs (Figures 5.18 and 5.19)

```
Epoch 1/300
20/20 _____ 2s 13ms/step - loss: 0.4776 - val_loss: 0.3855
...
Epoch 300/300
20/20 _____ 0s 3ms/step - loss: 0.0018 - val_loss: 0.0759
7/7 _____ 0s 27ms/step
Mean Squared Error: 0.08142697718792646
R^2 Score: 0.8100884046552388
```

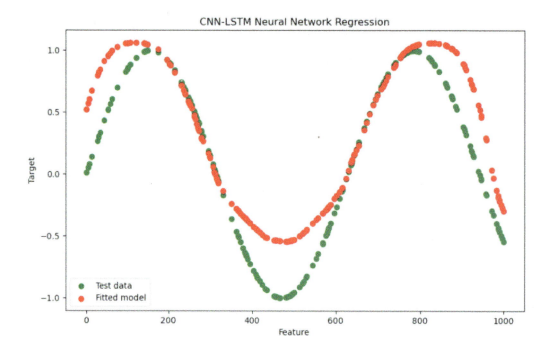

Figure 5.18 Example of neural network regression.

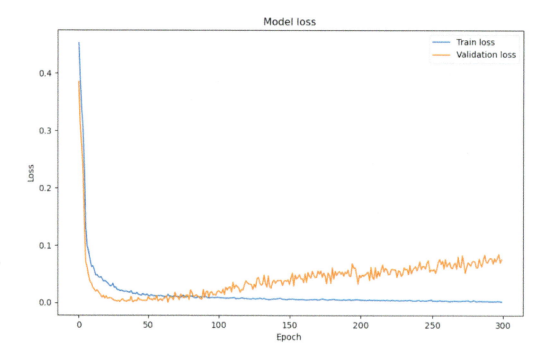

Figure 5.19 Example of model loss.

Chapter 5. Step 3: Model Choice, Training, and Application

The model loss chart indicates the following:

- The training loss is consistently decreasing, indicating the model is effectively learning from the training data.
- However, the validation loss is increasing, meaning the model is overfitting, where the model is learning noise and details from the training data, and does not effectively generalize to the new data.

Ranking

LGBRanker Ranking

Description	LGBRanker is a ranking algorithm from the LightGBM library designed to optimize ranking-specific objectives.
Key Use Cases in Finance	Credit risk modeling (ranking customers by default risk), recommendation systems (prioritizing financial products for customers), customer ranking (ranking clients by potential value or risk), and portfolio optimization (ranking assets for investment decisions).
Feature Normalization/ Standardization Required	Not required but recommended.
Python Libraries Setup	`pip install numpy lightgbm matplotlib scikit-learn`

LGBRanker is an algorithm from the LightGBM library designed for ranking tasks, optimizing ranking-specific objectives to produce highly accurate ordered lists in large-scale, complex datasets.

LGBRanker is a ranking algorithm that utilizes LambdaRank (see qnt.co/book-lambdarank) as its underlying optimization method.

> "Learning-to-rank is the application of machine learning in the construction of ranking models for information retrieval systems. In learning-to-rank, training data consists of lists of items with some partial order specified between items in each list, and **the ranking model's purpose is to rank, i.e., produce a permutation of items in new, unseen lists.**"
>
> —Xindi Wang

The critical applications in finance are credit risk modeling, where LambdaRank can rank borrowers based on the likelihood of defaulting on loans; recommendation systems with LamdaRank providing banking products based upon a client's transaction history and other behavioral data; customer ranking, where the clients are ranked upon their potential value to the financial institution, or portfolio optimization with LambdaRank helping ranking assets based upon their expected returns and risk profiles.

As a tree-based algorithm, LGBRanker does not require normalization or standardization, but it can enhance its performance, especially when processing features on vastly different scales.

Python Example

Let us demonstrate using the library LGBMRanker model to rank stocks based on synthetic data (i.e., historical returns, volatility, and momentum). We introduce a target ranking based on a weighted combination of the features. We split the stocks into 10 groups, each containing 10 stocks. Each group is a distinct subset of the data for which rankings are generated and evaluated independently. An example of the grouping could be daily stock rankings: each day could be a group, and the model ranks stocks within each day. Alternatively, different portfolio market segments are groups, and the model ranks the assets within each segment.

```python
import numpy as np
from lightgbm import LGBMRanker
import matplotlib.pyplot as plt
from sklearn.model_selection import train_test_split
from sklearn.preprocessing import StandardScaler
from sklearn.metrics import ndcg_score

# Step 1: Generate Synthetic Stock Data
np.random.seed(42)
n_stocks = 100
n_groups = 10

# Features: historical returns, volatility, and momentum
historical_returns = np.random.rand(n_stocks, 1)
volatility = np.random.rand(n_stocks, 1)
momentum = np.random.rand(n_stocks, 1)

# Create a feature matrix
X = np.hstack((historical_returns, volatility, momentum))

# Generate synthetic target ranking based on a combination of features
true_rank = historical_returns * 0.5 + volatility * 0.3 + momentum * 0.2
y = np.argsort(np.argsort(true_rank.flatten()))  # Rank stocks

# Ensure the labels are within the expected range for LightGBM
y = np.digitize(y, bins=np.linspace(0, n_stocks, 32)) - 1

# Assume each group consists of n_stocks // n_groups stocks for ranking
groups = np.repeat(np.arange(n_groups), n_stocks // n_groups)

# Step 2: Split Data into Training and Testing Sets
X_train, X_test, y_train, y_test, group_train, group_test = train_test_split(
    X, y, groups, test_size=0.2, random_state=42, stratify=groups)
```

```python
# Define group sizes
train_group_sizes = np.bincount(group_train)
test_group_sizes = np.bincount(group_test)

# Remove zero entries in group sizes
train_group_sizes = train_group_sizes[train_group_sizes != 0]
test_group_sizes = test_group_sizes[test_group_sizes != 0]

# Step 3: Initialize and Train LGBMRanker
model = LGBMRanker(
    objective="lambdarank",
    metric= "ndc"",
    boosting_type ""gb"t",
    learning_rate=0.05,
    num_leaves=31,
    ndcg_eval_at=[1, 3, 5]
)

# Fit the model
model.fit(X_train, y_train, group=train_group_sizes, eval_set=[(X_test, y_test)],
eval_group=[test_group_sizes])

# Step 4: Predict and Evaluate
y_pred = model.predict(X_test)

# Filter out groups with fewer than 2 documents
unique_groups = np.unique(group_test)
valid_groups = [g for g in unique_groups if np.sum(group_test == g) > 1]

# Calculate NDCG score for each valid group and average them
ndcg_scores = [ndcg_score([y_test[group_test == g]], [y_pred[group_test == g]],
k=5) for g in valid_groups]
mean_ndcg = np.mean(ndcg_scores)
print(f'Mean NDCG Score @5: {mean_ndcg}')

# Visualization of results

# Scatter Plot of True vs. Predicted Rankings for Multiple Groups
plt.figure(figsize=(12, 8))
for group in valid_groups:
    plt.scatter(y_test[group_test == group], y_pred[group_test == group],
alpha=0.6, label=f'Group {group}')

plt.xlabel('True Rankings')
plt.ylabel('Predicted Rankings')
plt.title('True vs. Predicted Rankings for Multiple Groups')
plt.legend()
plt.show()
```

With the output

```
Mean NDCG Score @5: 0.9859718699852197
```

Normalized discounted cumulative gain (NDCG) is a benchmark performance metric for evaluating the quality of a ranking. The NDCG score ranges from 0 to 1, where 1 indicates a perfect ranking. The @5 in the name of the score refers to evaluating the top five items in the ranked list.

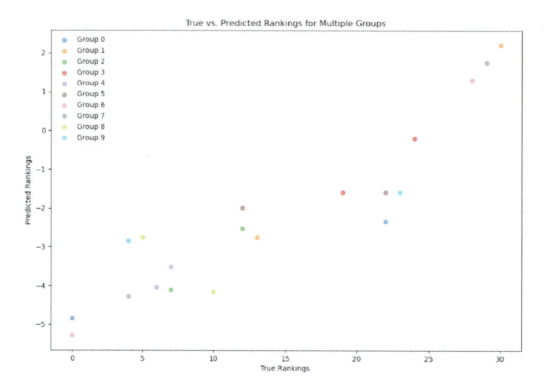

Figure 5.20 Example of true versus predicted ranking for multiple groups.

Figure 5.20 communicates a similar story to the NDCG Score @5—most points are close to the diagonal line where the model's predicted rankings match the accurate rankings, indicating the model's performance is very good.

Clustering

OPTICS Clustering

Description	A density-based clustering algorithm that identifies clusters of varying densities in noisy data with an unknown number of clusters.
Key Use Cases in Finance	Detecting anomalies in transaction data, segmenting clients based on transaction patterns, and identifying market regimes.
Feature Normalization/ Standardization Required	Recommended.
Python Libraries Setup	`pip install numpy matplotlib scikit-learn`

Clustering is a technique used to identify insights and patterns in complex datasets. OPTICS (**O**rdering **P**oints **T**o **I**dentify the **C**lustering **S**tructure) is one of the most frequently used algorithms for noisy data with an unknown number of clusters. Unlike traditional clustering methods like k-means, which require specifying the number of clusters beforehand, OPTICS processes data points based on their density reachability and core distance, allowing it to discover the underlying clustering structure without needing a predefined number of clusters.

Key applications in finance include detecting anomalies in transaction data, segmenting clients based on behavioral patterns, and identifying different market regimes.

For optimal performance, feature normalization is recommended to ensure that all features contribute equally to the clustering process.

Python Example

Let's illustrate how to use the OPTICS algorithm in Python to generate synthetic data using the `sklearn.datasets.make_blobs` method.

```python
import numpy as np
import matplotlib.pyplot as plt
from sklearn.cluster import OPTICS
from sklearn.datasets import make_blobs
from sklearn.preprocessing import StandardScaler
from sklearn.metrics import silhouette_score, davies_bouldin_score

# Generate synthetic data
X, _ = make_blobs(n_samples=300, centers=4, cluster_std=0.6, random_state=42)

# Standardize features (feature normalization)
scaler = StandardScaler()
X_scaled = scaler.fit_transform(X)

# Apply OPTICS clustering
optics = OPTICS(min_samples=10, xi=0.05, min_cluster_size=0.1)
optics.fit(X_scaled)

# Extract labels and core sample indices
labels = optics.labels_
core_samples = np.zeros_like(labels, dtype=bool)

# Print numerical performance metrics
# Filter out noise points (-1) for metrics calculation
mask = labels != -1
print("Silhouette Score:", silhouette_score(X_scaled[mask], labels[mask]))
print("Davies-Bouldin Index:", davies_bouldin_score(X_scaled[mask], labels[mask]))

# Plot the clustering results
plt.figure(figsize=(10, 6))
unique_labels = set(labels)
colors = [plt.cm.Spectral(each) for each in np.linspace(0, 1, len(unique_labels))]

for k, col in zip(unique_labels, colors):
    if k == -1:
        # Black used for noise.
        col = [0, 0, 0, 1]

    class_member_mask = (labels == k)
    xy = X_scaled[class_member_mask & core_samples]
    plt.plot(xy[:, 0], xy[:, 1], 'o', markerfacecolor=tuple(col),
markeredgecolor='k', markersize=14)
```

```
    xy = X_scaled[class_member_mask & ~core_samples]
    plt.plot(xy[:, 0], xy[:, 1], 'o', markerfacecolor=tuple(col),
markeredgecolor='k', markersize=6)

plt.title('OPTICS Clustering')
plt.xlabel('Feature 1')
plt.ylabel('Feature 2')
plt.show()
```

With the output

```
Silhouette Score: 0.9007128264042205
Davies-Bouldin Index: 0.13502085379361267
```

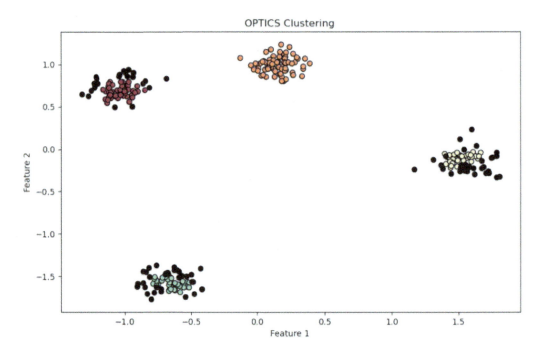

Figure 5.21 Example of OPTICS clustering.

Silhouette score (the higher, the better clustering) measures how similar each point is to its cluster compared to others. Davies-Bouldin index (the lower, the better clustering) measures the average similarity ratio of each cluster compared to its most similar cluster.

The black color is used in Figure 5.21 to indicate noise.

Language Models

OpenAI Language Model

Description	Large language models (LLMs) are models capable of understanding and generating human-like text, making them valuable for processing and analyzing large volumes of financial data.
Key Use Cases in Finance	Market analysis and research, regulatory compliance, and reporting.

Feature Normalization/ Standardization Required	Not required.
Python Libraries Setup	`pip install openai json`

Large language models (LLMs) like OpenAI's GPT series are developed using vast textual datasets. They are engineered to process and produce text that resembles human writing and performing tasks, such as summarizing documents, translating languages, responding to queries, composing text, and evaluating sentiment.

LLMs are advanced AI systems designed to understand and generate human-like text based on vast amounts of data. Their key advantages are their ability to analyze and interpret complex language patterns, develop coherent and contextually relevant text, and provide insights from unstructured data. However, LLMs can be computationally intensive and require substantial data for training to achieve high performance.

In finance, LLMs are utilized for sentiment analysis, automated report generation, predictive analytics, and risk management.

Normalization is generally unnecessary for textual data used in LLMs, but normalizing these features can enhance the model's performance and consistency when numerical features accompany the text.

Python Example

```python
import openai
import json

# Set up your OpenAI API key
openai.api_key = 'YOUR_API_KEY_HERE'

def analyze_sentiment(text):
    response = openai.chat.completions.create(
        model="gpt-4",
        messages=[
            {"role": "user", "content": f "Analyze the sentiment of the following text and provide a sentiment score from 0 to 10 in JSON in the property called sentiment_score:\n\n{text}\n\""}
        ]
    )
    return json.loads(response.choices[0].message.content)['sentiment_score']

def test_analyze_sentiment():
    test_sentences = [
        """I absolutely love this new phone!It's fantastic and exceeds all my expectations""",
        """This is the worst experience I have ever had with a company. Totally unacceptable""",
        """Meh, the movie was just okay. Not too good, not too bad""",
        """I am thrilled with my new job. The team is great and the work is fulfilling""",
        """The food was terrible, and the service was even worse. I am never coming back here""",
        """Wow, what a beautiful day! The sun is shining and everything feels perfect""",
        """This product is a complete waste of money. It broke after one use""",
```

```
            """I am feeling pretty neutral about this situation, neither happy nor
sad""",
            """The concert last night was amazing! Best performance I've ever seen""",
            """Ugh, what a horrible traffic jam. Made me late for work and ruined
my day"""
    ]

    for i, sentence in enumerate(test_sentences):
        try:
            sentiment_score = analyze_sentiment(sentence)
            print(f"Test {i+1}: Sentence: \"{sentence}\"")
            print(f"Sentiment Score: {sentiment_score}\n")
        except Exception as e:
            print(f"Test {i+1}: Sentence: \"{sentence}\"")
            print(f"Error: {e}\n")

# Run the test method
test_analyze_sentiment()
```

With the outputs

```
Test 1: Sentence: "I absolutely love this new phone! It's fantastic and exceeds
all my expectations."
Sentiment Score: 9.5

Test 2: Sentence: "This is the worst experience I have ever had with a company.
Totally unacceptable!"
Sentiment Score: 0

Test 3: Sentence: "Meh, the movie was just okay. Not too good, not too bad."
Sentiment Score: 5

Test 4: Sentence: "I am thrilled with my new job. The team is great and the work
is fulfilling!"
Sentiment Score: 9.5

Test 5: Sentence: "The food was terrible, and the service was even worse. I am
never coming back here."
Sentiment Score: 1

Test 6: Sentence: "Wow, what a beautiful day! The sun is shining and everything
feels perfect."
Sentiment Score: 9

Test 7: Sentence: "This product is a complete waste of money. It broke after
one use."
Sentiment Score: 1.5

Test 8: Sentence: "I am feeling pretty neutral about this situation, neither
happy nor sad."
Sentiment Score: 5

Test 9: Sentence: "The concert last night was amazing! Best performance I've
ever seen."
Sentiment Score: 9.5

Test 10: Sentence: "Ugh, what a horrible traffic jam. Made me late for work and
ruined my day."
Sentiment Score: 2
```

Amazon Chronos Model

Description	The Chronos model is a pretrained time series forecasting model.
Key Use Cases in Finance	Asset prices/trends prediction.
Feature Normalization/ Standardization Required	Required.
Python Libraries Setup	`pip install git+https://github.com/amazon-science/chronos-forecasting.git`
	`pip install torch pandas numpy matplotlib sklearn`

Chronos (see qnt.co/book-amazon-chronos-tiny and qnt.co/book-amazon-chronos-large) is a collection of ready-to-use time series forecasting models based on language model architectures. A time series is converted into a sequence of tokens by scaling and quantizing, and a language model is trained on these tokens using the cross-entropy loss. Chronos models have been trained on a large corpus of public time series data and artificial data created using Gaussian processes.

In finance, the Chronos model is suitable for time series forecasting to predict future asset prices, trends, or market movements, aiding in portfolio optimization and risk management.

Normalization or standardization is essential to ensure faster convergence and better performance.

For production use, the pretrained models, such as the Chronos models, are fine-tuned to the task-specific dataset to obtain enhanced performance. Later examples in the book illustrate this process.

Python Example

Let us create a synthetic time series and apply the Chronos model to forecast 30 days.

Notice the following line:

```
forecast_values = np.median(forecast, axis=0)
```

The predicted output is an array with rows of several predicted samples and columns of the predicted values for each of the 30 forecasted days. This line produces a single time series of medians of the expected values.

Instead, we could consider generating the 10%, 50%, and 90% quantiles, providing us with the range of likely values:

```
low, median, high = np.quantile(forecast, [0.1, 0.5, 0.9], axis=0)
```

The complete source code follows:

```python
import torch
import pandas as pd
import numpy as np
import matplotlib.pyplot as plt
from chronos import ChronosPipeline
from sklearn.preprocessing import StandardScaler
from sklearn.metrics import mean_squared_error, mean_absolute_error
```

```python
# Load the pre-trained Chronos model
model = ChronosPipeline.from_pretrained(
    "amazon/chronos-t5-tiny",
    device_map="cuda" if torch.cuda.is_available() else "cpu",
    torch_dtype=torch.bfloat16,
)

# Generate a representative time series (e.g., sine wave with noise)
np.random.seed(0)
dates = pd.date_range(start='2022-01-01', periods=200, freq='D')
series = np.sin(np.linspace(0, 20, 200)) + np.random.normal(0, 0.5, 200)
data = {'date': dates, 'close': series}
df = pd.DataFrame(data)

# Normalize the data
scaler = StandardScaler()
normalized_data = scaler.fit_transform(df[['close']])

# Convert normalized data to a PyTorch tensor
tensor_data = torch.tensor(normalized_data)

# Forecast future prices for the next 30 days
prediction_length = 30
forecast = model.predict(tensor_data, prediction_length)

# Convert forecast back to original scale
forecast = scaler.inverse_transform(forecast[0].numpy())

# Combine original and forecasted data for visualization
forecast_dates = pd.date_range(start=dates[-1] + pd.Timedelta(days=1), periods=prediction_length, freq='D')

forecast_values = np.median(forecast, axis=0)

forecast_df = pd.DataFrame({'date': forecast_dates, 'forecast': forecast_values})
combined_df = pd.concat([df[['date', 'close']], forecast_df], axis=0)

# Plot the original and forecasted data
plt.figure(figsize=(12, 6))
plt.plot(df['date'], df['close'], label='Original')
plt.plot(forecast_df['date'], forecast_df['forecast'], label='Forecast', linestyle='--')
plt.xlabel('Date')
plt.ylabel('Close Price')
plt.title('Original vs Forecasted Closing Prices')
plt.legend()
plt.show()

# Calculate and print performance metrics
# For simplicity, compare last 30 days of original data with forecast
actual = df['close'].values[-prediction_length:]
predicted = forecast.flatten()[:len(actual)]

mse = mean_squared_error(actual, predicted)
mae = mean_absolute_error(actual, predicted)

print(f"Mean Squared Error (MSE): {mse:.4f}")
print(f"Mean Absolute Error (MAE): {mae:.4f}")
```

With the output (Figure 5.22)

```
Mean Squared Error (MSE): 6.4039
Mean Absolute Error (MAE): 2.4492
```

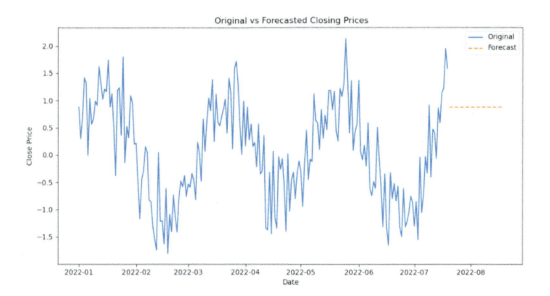

Figure 5.22 Example of Amazon Chronos prediction.

FinBERT Model

Description	The FinBERT model is a pretrained financial sentiment analysis model designed to classify the sentiment of financial texts using the BERT architecture. It has been optimized to understand the language used in the financial domain.
Key Use Cases in Finance	Sentiment analysis of financial texts, market prediction, risk management, portfolio management, customer feedback analysis, and assessing the impact of events to inform investment decisions and understand market and investor reactions.
Feature Normalization/ Standardization Required	Required.
Python Libraries Setup	`pip install tensorflow transformers tf-keras`

FinBERT (qnt.co/book-finbert) is a pretrained natural language processing (NLP) model designed to analyze the sentiment of financial texts. It is developed by further training the BERT language model on a large corpus of financial data, fine-tuning it specifically for financial sentiment classification.

The FinBERT model is used in finance for sentiment analysis of financial texts, such as news, reports, and social media, to understand market sentiment and investor mood. It aids in predicting market movements, managing risks, and informing portfolio management strategies by correlating sentiment trends with stock price movements. Finally, FinBERT is used to analyze customer feedback for improving financial products and services and to assess the impact of specific events, such as earnings reports or mergers, on market sentiment.

Normalization or standardization is essential to ensure faster convergence and better performance.

For production use, the pretrained models, such as the FinBERT models, are fine-tuned to the task-specific dataset to obtain enhanced performance. A later example in the book illustrates this process.

Python Example

Let us illustrate how to use the FinBERT model's sentiment analysis on a set of synthetic financial texts. The texts are first preprocessed to generate tokenized inputs; an attention mask is created to ensure the model focuses on relevant parts. Sentiment predictions are then obtained, and the results are printed with corresponding sentiment labels ("negative," "positive").

```python
import random
import numpy as np
import tensorflow as tf
from transformers import BertTokenizer, TFBertForSequenceClassification, BertConfig

random.seed(42)
np.random.seed(42)
tf.random.set_seed(42)

# Load the tokenizer and the model
model_path = "ProsusAI/finbert"
tokenizer = BertTokenizer.from_pretrained(model_path)
model = TFBertForSequenceClassification.from_pretrained(
    model_path,
    config=BertConfig.from_pretrained(model_path, num_labels=2)
)

# Create longer synthetic financial data
texts = [
    "The purchase price will be paid in cash and stock upon the closure of the transaction, scheduled for April 1, 2025",
    "With this, the company will exit the contract manufacturing service segment and enter the more profitable software and services market",
    "Commission income fell to SGD 2.1 mn from SGD 5.1 mn in the corresponding period in 2021",
    "Finnish media group Talentum has issued a profit warning followed by no dividend payment for 2023 and entering bankruptcy protection",
    "The loss for the second quarter of 2024 was EUR 0.1 mn smaller than the loss of the first quarter of 2024 indicating strong positive upturn in the business"
]
```

```python
# Preprocess the texts
inputs = tokenizer(
    texts,
    return_tensors='tf',
    padding=True,
    truncation=True,
    max_length=512,
    add_special_tokens=True
)

# Ensure model focuses on relevant parts using attention mask
inputs['attention_mask'] = tf.cast(inputs['attention_mask'], dtype=tf.float32)

# Get sentiment predictions
outputs = model(**inputs)
predictions = tf.nn.softmax(outputs.logits, axis=-1).numpy()

# Define the sentiment labels
labels = ['negative', 'positive']

# Print the results
for i, text in enumerate(texts):
    sentiment = labels[tf.argmax(predictions[i]).numpy()]
    confidence = tf.reduce_max(predictions[i]).numpy()
    print(f"Text: {text}\nSentiment: {sentiment} (Confidence: {confidence:.2f}); Predictions: {predictions[i]}\n")
```

With the output

```
Text: The purchase price will be paid in cash and stock upon the closure of the
transaction, scheduled for April 1, 2025
Sentiment: negative (Confidence: 0.59); Predictions: [0.5932849 0.4067151]

Text: With this, the company will exit the contract manufacturing service segment
and enter the more profitable software and services market
Sentiment: negative (Confidence: 0.53); Predictions: [0.52938175 0.47061822]

Text: Commission income fell to SGD 2.1 mn from SGD 5.1 mn in the corresponding
period in 2021
Sentiment: negative (Confidence: 0.52); Predictions: [0.52257305 0.47742692]

Text: Finnish media group Talentum has issued a profit warning followed by no
dividend payment for 2023 and entering bankruptcy protection
Sentiment: negative (Confidence: 0.53); Predictions: [0.5345768  0.46542326]

Text: The loss for the second quarter of 2024 was EUR 0.1 mn smaller than the loss
of the first quarter of 2024 indicating strong positive upturn in the business
Sentiment: positive (Confidence: 0.59); Predictions: [0.4091295  0.59087044]
```

Part III

Advanced Applications of AI in Trading and Risk Management

In this part of the book, we dive deeper into the practical application of AI and machine-learning techniques you've learned in previous chapters. We have identified and illustrated the fundamental building blocks of modern algorithmic trading strategies in practical simplified examples. The examples have been designed to provide you with enough experience and confidence to create and manage your trading algorithms.

Getting Started with Source Code

All the source code for the examples and exercises in this part is available on our GitHub repository. Follow these steps to access and use the code:

1. **Read the instructions:** Follow the instructions on how to make the most of the source code at https://github.com/QuantConnect/HandsOnAITradingBook.
2. **Clone the repository:** Open your terminal or command prompt and run the following command to clone the repository to your local machine:

```
git clone https://github.com/QuantConnect/HandsOnAITradingBook.git
```

3. **Explore the code:** Inside the repository are folders organized by chapters and topics. Each folder contains Jupyter notebooks or Python scripts with detailed code examples and explanations.
4. **Deploy the models on QuantConnect:** After you log into your QuantConnect account, head to the Learning Center and clone the source code for the book into the new projects on your account, which will allow you to instantly see the effects of your code changes on the results of the trading strategies.

Chapter 6

Applied Machine Learning

 Example 1—ML Trend Scanning with MLFinlab

Predicting	Price direction
Technology	Regression/classification
Asset Class	Crypto
Difficulty	Easy
Type	Research notebook
Source Code	qnt.co/book-example1

Summary

Applying the trend scanning package from the MLFinLab library to detect price trends (down-trend/no-trend/up-trend) to invest in the primary trend.

Motivation

Accurate trend prediction is essential for algorithmic trading strategies for these use cases:

1. <u>Strategy selection</u>—accurate trend identification helps select the most suitable trading strategy for the current market conditions, as different market phases benefit different strategies.

2. <u>Optimal trade entry/exit</u>—identifying the market trends enables traders to determine the most profitable moment for entering or exiting a trade.
3. <u>Trend following</u>—traders can ride market waves by accurately identifying and following trends.
4. <u>Contrarian strategies</u>—identifying overextended trends and positioning for expected reversals can help profit from market corrections.

Model

Model Features	A time series of the close prices of BTCUSD.
Predicted Label	−1, 0, 1 for downward trend, no trend, or upward trend.
Model	`trend_scanning_labels` method from the MLFinLab's trend scanning packages.

We use the `trend_scanning_labels` method, a component of the MLFinLab's trend_scanning package open-sourced for this book, introduced by Marcos Lopez de Prado (see qnt.co/book-trend-scanning).

```
def trend_scanning_labels(price_series: pd.Series, t_events: list = None,
observation_window: int = 20,  metric: str = 't_value', look_forward: bool =
True, min_sample_length: int = 5, step: int = 1) -> pd.DataFrame
```

The method is valuable for the classification of market regimes (downtrend, no-trend, and uptrend):

- It maps a vector of observations (in our case, close prices) to −1 for a downward trend, 0 for no trend, and 1 for an upward trend.
- It works by creating a set of linear regression models over different lookback periods:
  - The independent variable is `1, 1=0, ..., L-1` where `L` is the length of the observation window of choice – in our case, `L = 20`, that is, we're looking for the trailing 20 data points to determine the trend.
  - The dependent variable is the closing price `1` steps into the future.
  - For each model, we calculate the t-value associated with the estimated regressor coefficient (beta) and select the model with the largest t-value in absolute value; it's the most statistically significant model. In linear regression, the t-value determines the significance of the individual regression coefficient. The larger the value, the more significant the coefficient is.
  - The trend label is then the sign of the largest t-value.
- The method returns a data frame with several columns, the following most importantly:
  - `Index`—(pd.Timestamp) TimeIndex of the labels.
  - `t1`—(pd.Timestamp) Label end-time where the observed trend has the highest `t-value`, i.e., the end of a strong upward trend (for look forward) and the start of a solid downward trend (for look backward).

- `t-value`—(float) Sign of `t-value` represents the direction of the trend. A positive `t-value` represents an upward trend.
- `ret`—(float) Price change percentage from index time to label end time.
- `bin`— (int) Binary label value based on the sign of price change.

Let us illustrate with an example of analyzing a time series of closing prices with a chart (Figure 6.1) showing the closing prices time series in blue and the most significant t-values time series in red. The green markers indicate an upward trend (label 1), the yellow markers indicate no trend (label 0), and the red markers indicate a downward trend (label −1).

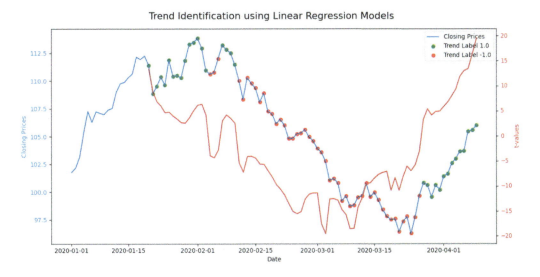

Figure 6.1 Example of trend identification using linear regression models.

```
import numpy as np
import pandas as pd
import matplotlib.pyplot as plt
from sklearn.linear_model import LinearRegression
from trend_scanning_labels import trend_scanning_labels

# Generate sample data for demonstration (closing prices)
np.random.seed(0)
dates = pd.date_range(start='2020-01-01', periods=100)
closes = pd.Series(np.random.randn(100).cumsum() + 100, index=dates)

# Parameters
L = 20

# Get trend labels using the trend_scanning_labels function
trend_labels_df = trend_scanning_labels(closes, closes.index,
look_forward=False, observation_window=L, min_sample_length=5)

# Extract t-values and trend labels
t_values = trend_labels_df['t_value'].dropna()
trend_labels = trend_labels_df['bin'].dropna()
```

```python
# Plotting
fig, ax1 = plt.subplots(figsize=(12, 6))

# Plot closing prices
color = 'tab:blue'
ax1.set_xlabel('Date')
ax1.set_ylabel('Closing Prices', color=color)
ax1.plot(closes.index, closes, color=color, label='Closing Prices')
ax1.tick_params(axis='y', labelcolor=color)

# Create a second y-axis for the t-values
ax2 = ax1.twinx()
color = 'tab:red'
ax2.set_ylabel('t-values', color=color)
ax2.plot(t_values.index, t_values, color=color, label='t-values')
ax2.tick_params(axis='y', labelcolor=color)

# Add trend labels
colors = {1: 'green', 0: 'yellow', -1: 'red'}
for i in range(len(trend_labels)):
    label = trend_labels.iloc[i]
    date = trend_labels.index[i]
    ax1.scatter(date, closes.loc[date], color=colors[label], s=30,
label=f'Trend Label {label}')

# Handle legend for trend labels to avoid duplicates
handles, labels = ax1.get_legend_handles_labels()
unique_labels = dict(zip(labels, handles))
ax1.legend(unique_labels.values(), unique_labels.keys())

# Add title
fig.suptitle('Trend Identification using Linear Regression Models',
fontsize=16)
fig.tight_layout()
```

Trading Universe

We consider trading only Bitcoin (BTCUSD).

Portfolio Construction

Model Training Time	Once a day.
Portfolio Rebalancing Time	Once a day.
Portfolio Weights	100% invested in Bitcoin whenever the trend is upward and 0% otherwise.

The portfolio weight of Bitcoin is

- 100% whenever the trend is upward, or
- 0% otherwise.

Trading Logic

While being simple, this strategy of holding 100% of the portfolio in BTCUSD whenever the trend is upward, and 100% in USD otherwise, does yield better results than the simple buy and hold bitcoin strategy (Figure 6.2):

```python
from trend_scanning_labels import trend_scanning_labels
from backtestlib import rough_daily_backtest

trend = trend_scanning_labels(
    closes, closes.index, observation_window=20, look_forward=False,
    min_sample_length=5
)['bin'].dropna()
portfolio_weights = pd.DataFrame(trend.where(trend != -1, 0))
portfolio_weights.columns = [symbol]
rough_daily_backtest(qb, portfolio_weights)
```

Where `closes` are the close prices of BTCUSD stored in a data frame.

```python
qb = QuantBook()
symbol = qb.add_crypto("BTCUSD", Resolution.DAILY).symbol
history = qb.history(symbol, datetime(2016, 1, 1), datetime(2024, 1, 1))
closes = history.loc[symbol]['close']
```

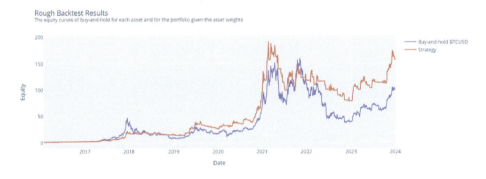

Figure 6.2 Equity curves of the strategy and selected benchmark.

Implementation Insights

We implement this strategy in QuantConnect's research notebook.

Let us assess the accuracy of the predictions, which is defined as the number of correct predictions divided by the total number of predictions.

```python
accuracy = sum(correct_predictions) / len(correct_predictions)
```

To calculate the `correct_predictions`, we calculate the percentage change in the closing price between consecutive days, shift the result by one day back since we're predicting the *future* sign of change, align the result with the expected values, ignore the last value since it's a NaN due to the shift, convert the results to the values $-1, 0$, or 1 depending on the results' sign, and compare it with the sign of the predicted value.

```python
correct_predictions = np.sign(
    closes.pct_change().shift(-1).loc[trend.index].iloc[:-1]
) == np.sign(trend.iloc[:-1])
```

For this setup, the accuracy is 51.2%, meaning the predictions are slightly better than random guesses. Despite this, the trading strategy is far more profitable than just holding the BTCUSD (Figure 6.3).

Figure 6.3 Predictions and observed log price.

Example 2—Factor Preprocessing Techniques for Regime Detection

Predicting	Future return
Technology	Classification and PCA
Asset Class	US index
Difficulty	Easy
Type	Research notebook
Source Code	qnt.co/book-example2

Summary

This example illustrates the significant impact of different transformations on factor values before training an ML model.

Motivation

Raw financial markets data is often noisy, skewed, and can encompass a variety of distributions and scales, making it challenging to find the proper relationship between the variables. By applying appropriate preprocessing techniques, the machine-learning models are trained on a more suitable representation of the underlying data, which usually results in substantial improvements in the model's predictive power.

Model

Model Features	Random factors.
Predicted Label	The label is one if the future weekly return for the SPY market index from open to open is positive; otherwise, the label is 0.
Model	Multiclass random forest model.

We explore the effects of various factor-preprocessing techniques on the model's performance, with out-of-sample (OOS) accuracy as our benchmark. The OOS accuracy is the proportion of correctly classified instances in the test set.

The model we build is a multiclass random forest classification model predicting the probability of the input factors being associated with each of two classes:

- Class label 1 indicates that the weekly return from the market open to the next week's market open is positive.
- The class label is 0 otherwise.

We study the following factor preprocessing techniques:

- Raw factors.
- Turning factors into stationary factors.
- Standardization of the factors.
- PCA factorization.

Trading Universe

We consider the ETF SPY's daily data from January 1, 2000, to January 1, 2024.

Implementation Insights

Step 1: Build the label.

The label is calculated from the history data frame as follows (see also Figure 6.4):

```
label = history.loc[symbol]['open'].pct_change(5).shift(-5).dropna().apply(
    lambda x: int(x > 0)
)
```

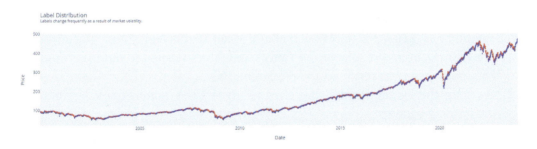

Figure 6.4 Scatter plot that colors each closing price based on the direction of future returns.

The label's distribution indicates that label one is more frequent in the dataset in Figure 6.5.

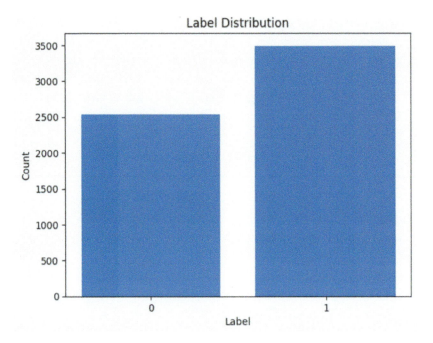

Figure 6.5 A bar chart showing the count of each label.

Step 2: Define the factors used to predict the label.
Next, we must define the factors to input into the model to predict the label.

For simplicity, we introduce random factors and make one of the factors non-stationary.

```
np.random.seed(2)
num_factors = 4
num_samples = len(label)
factors = np.random.rand(num_samples, num_factors)
# Make one of the factors non-stationary.
factors[:, -1] = factors[:, -1].cumsum()
```

Step 3: Define the performance benchmark for evaluating different factors.
The method `oss_accuracy` tests how well the given factors explain the given labels:
1. We create a train-test split of the factors and labels where we train the model on 75% of the data and test it on the remaining 25%.
2. We train the lightgbm multiclass classifier model (see qnt.co/book-lightgbm) on the training dataset.
3. We evaluate how well the trained model performs on the test dataset and print the resulting OOS accuracy, defined as the proportion of correctly classified instances in the test set.

```
import lightgbm as lgb
from sklearn.model_selection import train_test_split
from sklearn.metrics import accuracy_score
```

```python
def oos_accuracy(factors, label):
    X_train, X_test, y_train, y_test = train_test_split(
        factors, label, test_size=0.25, shuffle=False
    )
    model = lgb.train(
        {
            'seed': 1234,
            'verbose': -1,
            'boosting_type': 'rf',
            'feature_fraction': 0.8,
            'objective': 'multiclass',
            'num_class': 2,
            'bagging_freq': 5,
            'bagging_fraction': 0.8,
            'is_unbalanced': True
        },
        train_set=lgb.Dataset(
            data=X_train, label=y_train, free_raw_data=True
        ).construct()
    )
    predictions = model.predict(X_test)
    x = list(range(len(predictions)))
    go.Figure(
        [
            go.Scatter(x=x, y=predictions[:, 0], name=0),
            go.Scatter(x=x, y=predictions[:, 1], name=1)
        ],
        dict(
            title="Probability of Each Label<br><sup>Class 1 gets a greater"
                + "probability because the SPY has an upward bias</sup>",
            xaxis_title="Date", yaxis_title="Probability"
        )
    ).show()
    y_hat = predictions.argmax(axis=1)
    print(f"Accuracy: {round(accuracy_score(y_hat, y_test), 4)}")
```

Step 4: Evaluate the model's performance on the raw factors.
The first test is using just the raw factor values. The OOS accuracy is 0.6101 (Figure 6.6).

```
oss_accuracy(factors, label)
```

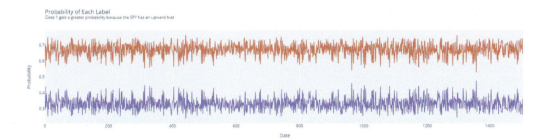

Figure 6.6 Time series plots that show the probability of each label from the model's predictions.

Step 5: Test model accuracy using stationary factors.
Lopez De Prado (2018) explains that *"supervised learning algorithms typically require stationary features."*

Let us test if our features are stationary using the augmented Dickey-Fuller test for stationarity.

```
from statsmodels.tsa.stattools import adfuller

for factor_idx in range(num_factors):
    factor = factors[:, factor_idx]
    test_results = adfuller(factor, maxlag=1, regression='c', autolag=None)
    # Check the p-value.
    output = "Stationary" if test_results[1] <= 0.05 else "Not stationary"
    print(f"Factor {factor_idx}: {output}")
```

The outputs confirm all factors but one, in our case, is already stationary as we designed them to be.

```
Factor 0: Stationary
Factor 1: Stationary
Factor 2: Stationary
Factor 3: Not stationary
```

Step 6: Make factors stationary, if necessary.
If the raw factors aren't stationary, we can transform them to make them stationary.

In our case, using the fractional differentiated factors gives us an OOS accuracy of 0.5849 (Figure 6.7).

```
oss_accuracy(stationary_factors.values, label)
```

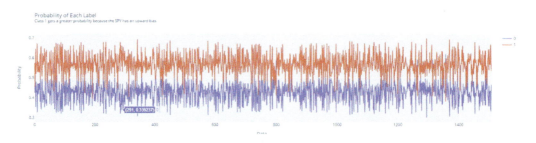

Figure 6.7 Time series plots that show the probability of each label from the model's predictions with stationary factors.

Step 7: Introduce standardization of factors.
Next, we test standardization, transforming the factor values into a mean of zero and a standard deviation of one. Standardized variables are necessary to assess their contribution to a model—using different units or scales would make the comparison difficult. Furthermore, standardizing the factors is an essential preprocessing step before applying PCA.

Chapter 6. Applied Machine Learning

```
from sklearn.preprocessing import StandardScaler

scaler = StandardScaler()
standardized_factors = scaler.fit_transform(stationary_factors)
```

Using the standardized factors gives us an OOS accuracy of 0.5882 (Figure 6.8).

```
oss_accuracy(standardized_factors, label)
```

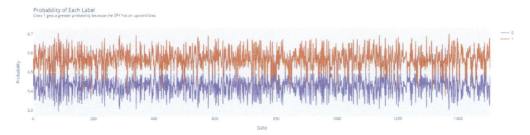

Figure 6.8 Time series plots that show the probability of each label from the model's predictions with standardized factors.

Step 8: Introduce PCA factorization.
Next, we test using PCA.

```
from sklearn.decomposition import PCA

pca = PCA(random_state=0)
principal_components = pca.fit_transform(standardized_factors[1:, :])
principal_components
```

Using the transformed data points in the reduced-dimensional space to train and test the ML model gives us an OOS accuracy of 0.5962 (Figure 6.9).

```
oss_accuracy(principal_components, label)
```

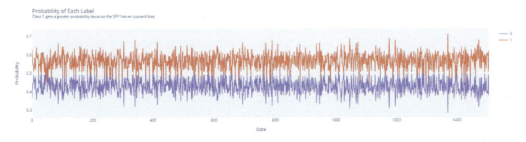

Figure 6.9 Time series plots that show the probability of each label from the model's predictions with the principal components.

Step 9: Compare the OSS accuracies.
In this particular use case, none of the factor preprocessing techniques lead to any significant improvement over raw data due to the factors being random numbers. Choosing

the best factor preprocessing technique to deliver the best OSS is naturally case-specific.

Factor Preprocessing Technique	OSS Accuracy
Raw Data	**0.6101**
Stationary Factors	0.5849
Standardized Factors	0.5882
PCA Factors	0.5962

Example 3—Reversion vs. Trending: Strategy Selection by Classification

Predicting	Volatility
Technology	Neural networks
Asset Class	US equities
Difficulty	Easy
Type	Research notebook
Source Code	qnt.co/book-example3

Summary

We are applying neural networks to forecast whether the next trading day will favor momentum or reversion risk exposure by categorizing periods of reversion vs. trending, and then using different strategies (we switch between holding the SPY index and TLT bonds) based on the current volatility regime (using volatility, VIX, ATR, RSI).

Motivation

Momentum strategies capitalize on the tendency of stock prices to continue moving in the same direction for a certain period. In the context of this strategy, holding the SPY index tracking the S&P 500 allows the traders to gain exposure to broader market momentum. When the market is trending, the SPY index is expected to continue in its direction.

On the other hand, the reversion risk strategies, sometimes called mean reversion strategies, are based on the belief that the asset prices will revert to their historical mean levels after deviating from them for a certain period. TLT, which tracks the long-term US Treasury bonds, is often used in a reversion risk strategy since bonds tend to perform well during market reversion. When the markets show the first sign of reversion, holding TLT bonds provides a reasonable hedge against market declines.

In highly dynamic financial markets, the ability to forecast whether the next trading day will favor momentum or reversion risk exposure allows investors to adjust their portfolios dynamically. This strategy ensures that investors are better positioned to capitalize on momentum gains during trends and mitigate losses during reversion periods.

Model

Model Features	• Relative strength index.
	• Average true range.
	• The standard deviation of daily returns.
	• Value of the VIX index.
Predicted Label	Label 1 = Momentum regime; Label 0 = reversion regime.
Model	Sequential neural network.

We create the label of 1 when the next day favors the momentum factor exposure and 0 otherwise by using the momentum and short-term reversal factor time series from Kenneth R. French's website (see qnt.co/book-french-data-library).

```
# Label 1 = Momentum regime; Label 0 = Reversion regime.
label = (momentum > reversion.reindex(momentum.index)).dropna().astype(int)
# The label is the regime of the following day, not day that just passed
label = label.shift(-1).dropna()
```

We introduce a matrix of these factors/indicators as a proxy for the current volatility regime:

1. Relative strength index (RSI) of the SPY over the last 21 days (a month).
2. Average true range (ATR) of the SPY over the previous 21 days (a month), normalized by 21-day SMA of price.
3. The standard deviation of daily returns of SPY over the last 21 days (a month).
4. Chicago Board Options Exchange's (CBOE's) Volatility Index (VIX index).

Before inputting the factors into the neural network training, we standardize them and split them into the training and test datasets.

We create a simple **sequential neural network** with two dense layers using the Keras library:

- The network has four inputs, one for each factor.
- The first layer has eight neurons/nodes.
- The outer layer has one neuron and a sigmoid activation function, which returns a value between 0 and 1, representing the probability of the positive class (momentum-friendly regime).

```
import tensorflow as tf
from tensorflow import keras
from tensorflow.keras import layers
from keras.utils import set_random_seed
from sklearn.metrics import accuracy_score

set_random_seed(0)

model = keras.Sequential(
    [
        layers.Input(shape=(X.shape[1],)),
        layers.Dense(8, activation='relu'),
```

```
        layers.Dense(1, activation='sigmoid')
    ]
)
```

We use the adam optimizer and binary_crossentropy as the loss function.

```
model.compile(
    optimizer='adam', loss='binary_crossentropy', metrics=['accuracy']
)
```

The <u>optimizer</u> minimizes the value of the loss function by updating the neural network (NN) weights. The Adam optimizer (an extension to stochastic gradient descent) is an adaptive learning rate optimization algorithm used widely due to its efficiency and low memory requirements.

<u>The loss function</u> evaluates how well the neural network fits the dataset—the further the predictions are from the actual results, the higher its value is. The goal of the training is to make the predictions as accurate as possible, that is, to minimize the loss function's value.

The loss function `binary_crossentropy` is a loss function used in binary classification problems.

Metrics are used to evaluate the model's performance; for classification problems, the most common metric is accuracy.

We <u>train</u> the model across 100 epochs using just the training dataset.

```
model.fit(X_train, y_train, epochs=100, verbose=0)
```

The epochs parameter specifies the number of times the network is trained on the training dataset. One hundred epochs is a reasonable number of iterations for this minor model, chosen by experience.

We predict <u>the model's accuracy</u> using the testing dataset (the data the model has not seen yet).

```
y_hat = (model.predict(X_train, verbose=0) > 0.5).astype(int)
print(f"In-sample accuracy: {accuracy_score(y_hat, y_train)}")

y_hat = (model.predict(X_test, verbose=0) > 0.5).astype(int)
print(f"Out-of-sample accuracy: {accuracy_score(y_hat, y_test)}")
print(f"OOS Label counts: {np.unique(y_hat, return_counts=True)[1]}")
```

With the results

```
In-sample accuracy: 0.554843141744905
Out-of-sample accuracy: 0.5276615527661552
OOS label counts: [ 592 1559]
```

We chose a benchmark for this strategy to the percentage of up-days of the SPY ETF, which over a 10-year period 2014–2024 had 54.4% up-days. The model results showed an in-sample accuracy of 55.48%—better than the underlying benchmark or random-guessing (with an accuracy of 50%). The out-of-sample accuracy (tested on not data not seen by the model) of 52.77% is lower than in-sample accuracy, which is usual and confirms that the model is only slightly better than random guesses, and thus suggests better input data may be required, along with enhancing the NN with more layers and/or factors and other tweaks.

Trading Universe

We consider only two assets, either SPY or TLT.

Portfolio Construction

Model Training Time	Once before we start backtesting.
Portfolio Rebalancing Time	Once a day at the market open.
Portfolio Weights	100% in SPY, if the model predicts the current regime favors momentum, and otherwise 100% in TLT.

The strategy rules are as follows:

- If the model predicts the current regime favors momentum over reversion, long SPY. Otherwise, long TLT.
- Rebalance at market open.

Trading Logic

The portfolio is rebalanced daily at market open—we predict if today's market is likely to benefit momentum (i.e., predictions == 1), and then set the portfolio weights as such.

```
portfolio_weights = pd.DataFrame({
    spy_symbol: predictions,
    qb.add_equity("TLT", Resolution.DAILY).symbol: abs(predictions-1)
})
```

Implementation Insights

The RSI and ATR features are implemented using the standard QuantConnect Indicators. For the STD factor, we set up a custom indicator.

```
spy_symbol = qb.add_equity("SPY", Resolution.DAILY).symbol

# Define the parameters.
period = 21
start_date = datetime(1990, 1, 1)
end_date = datetime(2024, 1, 1)
```

```python
# Get the RSI indicator data.
rsi = qb.Indicator(
    RelativeStrengthIndex(period), spy_symbol, start_date, end_date
)['relativestrengthindex']

# Get the ATR indicator (normalized by SMA of price) data.
atr = qb.Indicator(
    AverageTrueRange(period, MovingAverageType.SIMPLE),
    spy_symbol, start_date, end_date
)['averagetruerange']
atr /= qb.Indicator(
    SimpleMovingAverage(period), spy_symbol, start_date, end_date
)['simplemovingaverage']

# Get the STD indicator (STD of daily returns) data.
roc = RateOfChange(1)
std = IndicatorExtensions.of(StandardDeviation(period), roc)
history = qb.history[TradeBar](spy_symbol, start_date, end_date)
window = {column: [] for column in ['time', 'std_of_roc']}
def update_window(sender, updated):
    if not sender.is_ready:
        return
    window['time'].append(updated.end_time)
    window["std_of_roc"].append(updated.value)
std.updated += update_window
for bar in history:
    roc.update(bar.end_time, bar.close)
std = pd.DataFrame(window).set_index('time')['std_of_roc']

# Get the VIX factor data.
vix_symbol = qb.add_data(CBOE, "VIX", Resolution.DAILY).symbol
vix = qb.history(vix_symbol, start_date, end_date).loc[vix_symbol]['close']
vix.name = "vix"

# Combine factors into a matrix
factors = pd.concat([rsi, atr, std, vix], axis=1).dropna()
```

Example 4—Alpha by Hidden Markov Models

Predicting	Volatility regime
Technology	Hidden Markov models (HMM) clustering
Asset Class	US equities, equity options, and index options
Difficulty	Easy-medium
Type	Full strategy
Source Code	qnt.co/book-example4

Summary

We use a Markov regression model to predict the market volatility regime (a low-volatility or a high-volatility environment) and allocate our funds accordingly. We offer three different portfolio allocation algorithms; we start with investing in two ETFs, SPY/TLT, then expand to invest in an SPY straddle option, and finally, we use an index option.

Motivation

Volatility, often defined as the rate and magnitude of price changes in a market, directly influences the risk and return profiles of assets.

Anticipating volatility regimes is a critical part of any effective trading strategy.

Volatility regimes can be broadly categorized into low- and high-volatility environments:

- In **a low-volatility regime**, market prices tend to be more stable with smaller, more predictable price movements and bullish trends, where growth-oriented assets like equities perform well.
- Conversely, **a high-volatility regime** is characterized by more significant, erratic price swings, often indicative of market uncertainty or bearish trends. During such periods, defensive assets like bonds or strategies that benefit from volatility, such as options trading, become more attractive.

Predicting these regimes allows traders to adjust their asset allocation dynamically (Figure 6.10).

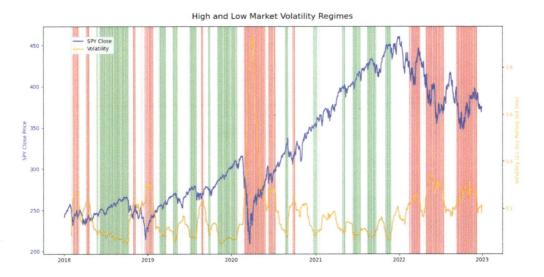

Figure 6.10 The price and volatility of SPY, along with highlighted zones of low/high volatility regimes.

This visualization of SPY close price and volatility (the annualized, rolling 21-day standard deviation of daily SPY close price returns) helps understand how market volatility fluctuates. It highlights high (periods where volatility exceeds the 75th percentile threshold [red shading]) and low (periods where volatility is below the 25th percentile threshold [green shading]) volatility.

With the **Markov regression model**, we can accurately predict high and low market volatility environments and allocate our funds strategically to optimize returns and manage risk.

Model

Model Features	Daily returns of SPY.
Predicted Label	The current market regime: label 0 for a low volatility one and label 1 for the high volatility.
Model	Markov-switching regression.

We implement a Markov-switching regression model (qnt.co/book-markov-regression) to detect two distinct volatility regimes:

- Low-volatility regime.
- High-volatility regime.

To train the model, we use the trailing 3 years of daily returns of the S&P 500 market index.

Trading Universe

In this example, we implement three distinct portfolio allocation algorithms.

We begin with a straightforward investment in two ETFs: SPY, representing the S&P 500, for capitalizing on market gains, and TLT, representing long-term US Treasury bonds, for stability during market downturns.

We then incorporate an SPY straddle option, which profits from increased volatility regardless of market direction, adding potential profitability during turbulent times (Figure 6.11).

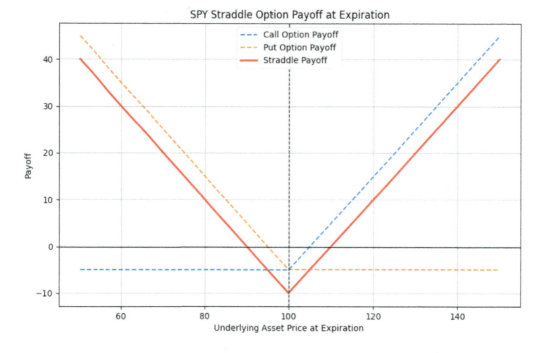

Figure 6.11 Payoffs of a call option, put option, and an option straddle.

The Straddle options strategy involves buying both a call option and a put option with the same strike price and expiration date. The combined payoff of the straddle strategy in red shows profitability when the underlying asset price moves significantly away from the strike price in either direction, benefiting from increased volatility. This combined payoff curve is a combination of the following:

- Call Option Payoff (dashed line): The payoff for the call option increases as the underlying asset price rises above the strike price minus the premium paid.
- Put Option Payoff (dashed line): The payoff for the put option increases as the underlying asset price falls below the strike price minus the premium paid.

Finally, we integrate an index option, leveraging its ability to provide amplified returns. Instead of using SPY as the underlying asset, this algorithm uses the SPX index, a more accurate representation of the S&P 500.

Portfolio Construction

Model Training Time	Every day, 1 minute after the market opens.
Portfolio Rebalancing Time	After the model training.
Portfolio Weights	See following description.

We provide three different trading strategies, each exploiting the identified volatility regimes with varying instruments of the market:

	A low-volatility environment	A high-volatility environment
Algorithm 1	We allocate 100% of the portfolio to a risk-on investment: the SPDR S&P 500 ETF Trust, SPY.	We allocate 100% of the portfolio to a risk-off investment: the iShares 20 Plus Year Treasury Bond ETF, TLT.
Algorithm 2	We short one SPY option straddle.	We long one SPY option straddle.
Algorithm 3	We short one SPX Index option straddle.	We long one SPX Index option straddle.

Trading Logic

We train the model at the beginning of each day, and the algorithm only rebalances when the regime switches low → high or high → low volatility; we aim at anticipating market downturns and remain invested during periods of market growth.

The trading logic is based on the predicted regime value.

```
# Create the markov model.
# `k_regimes` defines the number of regimes. In this case,
# we want 2 regimes (high and low volatility).
# `switching_variance` defines whether or not each regime
# can have its own variance.
```

```
model = MarkovRegression(
    self._daily_returns, k_regimes=2, switching_variance=True
)

# Get the current market regime (0 => low volatility; 1 => high
# volatility).
regime = model.fit().smoothed_marginal_probabilities.values\
    .argmax(axis=1)[-1]
```

Tearsheet

<u>Algorithm 1</u>

The results show the following:

- A lookback period of 4 years achieves the most significant Sharpe ratio.
- The Sharpe ratio is susceptible to changes in the lookback period.
- A lookback period of 1 year leads to a negative Sharpe ratio.
- See Figures 6.12 and 6.13.

Backtest parameters:

- `lookback_years`: 3

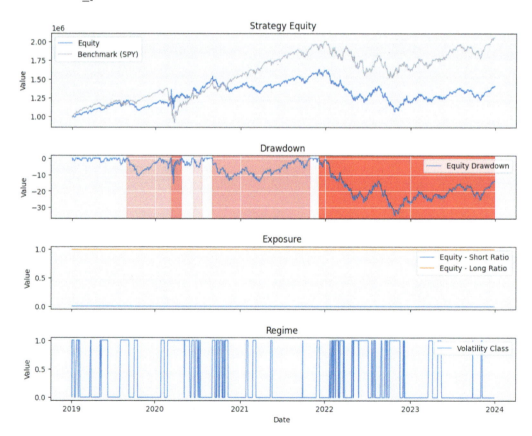

Figure 6.12 Equity curve, performance plots, and custom plots for Example 4.1.

Chapter 6. Applied Machine Learning 163

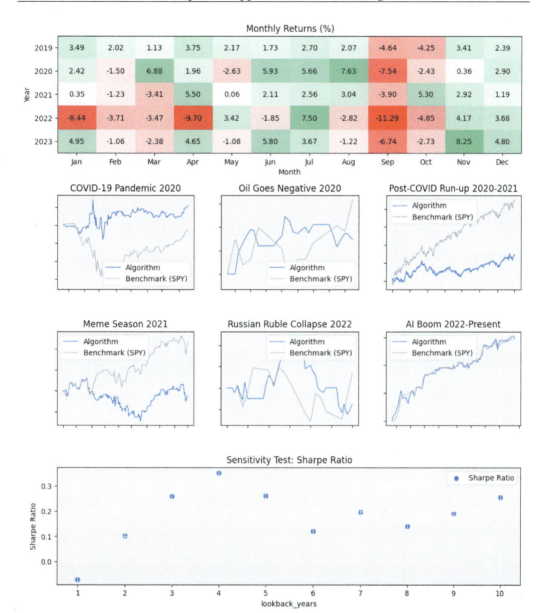

Figure 6.13 Monthly returns, crisis events, and sensitivity tests for Example 4.1.

Algorithm 2

See Figures 6.14 and 6.15.

Backtest parameters:

- `lookback_years`: 3
- `min_expiry`: 90
- `max_expiry`: 365
- `min_hold_period`: 7

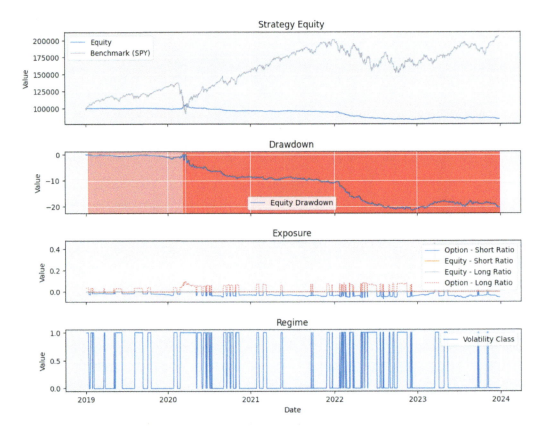

Figure 6.14 Equity curve, performance plots, and custom plots for Example 4.2.

Algorithm 3

See Figures 6.16 and 6.17.
   Backtest parameters:

- `lookback_years`: 3
- `min_expiry`: 0
- `max_expiry`: 180
- `min_hold_period`: 0

Implementation Insights

Algorithm 1

When the model detects a high volatility regime, the algorithm allocates 100% of the portfolio to TLT. When the model detects a low volatility regime, the algorithm allocates 100% of the portfolio to SPY. We retrain the model every day, 1 minute after the market opens. If the identified volatility regime changes, we rebalance the portfolio.

Chapter 6. Applied Machine Learning 165

Figure 6.15 Monthly returns and crisis events for Example 4.2.

```python
def _trade(self):
    # Create the markov model.
    # `k_regimes` defines the number of regimes. In this case,
    # we want 2 regimes (high and low volatility).
    # `switching_variance` defines whether or not each regime
    # can have its own variance.
    model = MarkovRegression(
        self._daily_returns, k_regimes=2, switching_variance=True
    )
    # Get the current market regime (0 => low volatility; 1 => high
    # volatility).
    regime = model.fit().smoothed_marginal_probabilities.values\
        .argmax(axis=1)[-1]
    self.plot('Regime', 'Volatility Class', regime)

    # Rebalance when the regime changes.
    if regime != self._previous_regime:
        self.set_holdings(
            [
                PortfolioTarget(self._tlt, regime),
                PortfolioTarget(self._spy, int(not regime))
            ]
        )
    self._previous_regime = regime
```

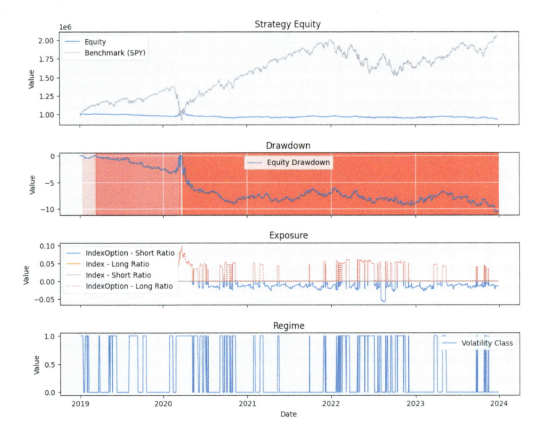

Figure 6.16 Equity curve, performance plots, and custom plots for Example 4.3.

Algorithm 2

This algorithm extends the previous algorithm; however, instead of rotating between SPY and TLT, we open straddles with SPY option contracts.

The rebalance logic changes as follows:

- When in a low volatility regime, we open a short straddle.
- When in a high volatility regime, we open a long straddle.

We pick the contracts with the closest expiration and are at the money to form the straddles. Since we are trading American-style options and selling a contract when we open a straddle, the buyer can exercise the option before it expires. In this case, we liquidate the remaining leg of the straddle and open a new straddle at the next market opening.

When we trade equity options, we need to adjust our data structures storing options trade information each time a split occurs.

The trading algorithm is just replacing resulting action based upon the predicted volatility regime change. The position sizing is not performed to keep the algorithm simple.

Chapter 6. Applied Machine Learning 167

Figure 6.17 Monthly returns and crisis events for Example 4.3.

```python
def _trade(self):
    # Create the markov model.
    # `k_regimes` defines the number of regimes. In this case,
    # we want 2 regimes (high and low volatility).
    # `switching_variance` defines whether or not each regime
    # can have its own variance.
    model = MarkovRegression(
        self._daily_returns, k_regimes=2, switching_variance=True
    )

    # Get the current market regime (0 => low volatility; 1 => high
    # volatility).
    regime = model.fit().smoothed_marginal_probabilities.values\
        .argmax(axis=1)[-1]
    self.plot('Regime', 'Volatility Class', regime)

    # Rebalance when the regime changes or when we aren't invested.
    if regime != self._previous_regime or not self.portfolio.invested:
        # Close the previous straddle if there is one.
        for symbol in self._equity.hedge_contracts:
            self.liquidate(symbol)
        self._equity.hedge_contracts = []

        # Get the option chain.
        option_chains = self.current_slice.option_chains
        if self._option_symbol not in option_chains:
            return
```

```python
        chain = option_chains[self._option_symbol]
        min_expiry_date = self.time + self._min_expiry + self._min_hold_period
        expiries = [
            contract.expiry
            for contract in chain
            if contract.expiry >= min_expiry_date
        ]

        # Define the straddle type. Low volatility regime => short
        # straddle; High volatility regime => long straddle.
        if regime == 0:
            option_type = OptionStrategies.short_straddle
            expiry = min(expiries)
        else:
            option_type = OptionStrategies.straddle
            expiry = max(expiries)

        # Get the ATM strike price.
        strike = sorted(
            [contract for contract in chain if contract.expiry == expiry],
            key=lambda contract: abs(
                chain.underlying.price - contract.strike
            )
        )[0].strike

        # Create the strategy. Low volatility regime => short
        # straddle; High volatility regime => long straddle.
        option_strategy = option_type(
            self._option_symbol, strike, expiry
        )

        # Open the straddle trade.
        tickets = self.buy(option_strategy, 1)

        # Save a reference to each of the contracts.
        self._equity.hedge_contracts = [t.symbol for t in tickets]
    self._previous_regime = regime

def on_order_event(self, order_event):
    # When one of the straddle legs are assigned/exercised
    # and we now have a position in the underlying Equity,
    # liquidate everything and remove the hedges.
    if (order_event.status == OrderStatus.FILLED and
        self._equity.invested and
        self._equity.hedge_contracts):
        self.liquidate(self._equity.symbol)
        for symbol in self._equity.hedge_contracts:
            self.liquidate(symbol)
        self._equity.hedge_contracts = []
```

Algorithm 3

This algorithm is an extension of the previous one:

- Instead of using equity options, we use a European-style index options to prevent early exercise of the contracts.
- Instead of using SPY as the underlying asset, this algorithm uses the SPX index, a more accurate representation of the S&P 500.

The algorithm code remains the same, except the buyer of the contracts we sell can only exercise the contract on the expiry day. Thus, we remove the logic that liquidates the remaining legs in the straddle.

```python
def _trade(self):
    # Create the markov model.
    # `k_regimes` defines the number of regimes. In this case,
    # we want 2 regimes (high and low volatility).
    # `switching_variance` defines whether or not each regime
    # can have its own variance.
    model = MarkovRegression(
        self._daily_returns, k_regimes=2, switching_variance=True
    )

    # Get the current market regime (0 => low volatility; 1 => high
    # volatility).
    regime = model.fit().smoothed_marginal_probabilities.values\
        .argmax(axis=1)[-1]
    self.plot('Regime', 'Volatility Class', regime)

    # Rebalance when the regime changes, when we aren't invested,
    # or when we need to rollover the contracts.
    if (regime != self._previous_regime or
        not self.portfolio.invested or
        self._expiry - self.time < self._min_expiry):
        # Close the previous straddle if there is one.
        self.liquidate()

        # Get the option chain.
        option_chains = self.current_slice.option_chains
        if self._option_symbol not in option_chains:
            return
        chain = option_chains[self._option_symbol]
        min_expiry_date = self.time + self._min_expiry + self._min_hold_period
        expiries = [
            contract.expiry
            for contract in chain
                if contract.expiry >= min_expiry_date
        ]
        if not expiries:
            return

        # Define the straddle type. Low volatility regime => short
        # straddle; High volaility regime => long straddle.
        if regime == 0:
            option_type = OptionStrategies.short_straddle
            expiry = min(expiries)
        else:
            option_type = OptionStrategies.straddle
            expiry = max(expiries)

        # Get the ATM strike price.
        strike = sorted(
            [contract for contract in chain if contract.expiry == expiry],
            key=lambda contract: abs(
                chain.underlying.price - contract.strike
            )
        )[0].strike
```

```
    # Create the strategy. Low volatility regime => short
    # straddle; High volaility regime => long straddle.
    option_strategy = option_type(
        self._option_symbol, strike, expiry
    )

    # Open the straddle trade.
    tickets = self.buy(option_strategy, 1)

    self._index.hedge_contracts = [t.symbol for t in tickets]
    self._expiry = expiry
self._previous_regime = regime

def on_order_event(self, order_event):
    # When one of the straddle legs are assigned/exercised,
    # the other leg is automatically liquidated so let's
    # remove the reference to each leg.
    if (order_event.status == OrderStatus.FILLED and
        order_event.is_assignment):
        self._index.hedge_contracts = []
        self._expiry = datetime.min
```

 ## Example 5—FX SVM Wavelet Forecasting

Predicting	Price
Technology	Support vector machines regression
Asset Class	Forex
Difficulty	Medium
Type	Full strategy
Source Code	qnt.co/book-example5

Summary

The algorithm uses support vector machines (SVMs) and wavelets to predict the future price of forex pairs. It first breaks down the past closing prices of each pair into components using wavelet decomposition. Then, it uses the SVM to make a one-step-ahead forecast for each element. Finally, it combines the components to get the overall estimates of the SVM-wavelet model.

Motivation

Various factors influence forex markets, including economic indicators, market sentiment, and geopolitical events with multiple frequencies and patterns. In addition, forex markets are inherently non-stationary (their statistical properties change over time), and forex data is very noisy, making it challenging to identify the underlying patterns.

Wavelet decomposition is particularly valuable in this context since it naturally captures complex dynamics (it decomposes dynamics into individual components), enhances predictive accuracy by isolating the significant time series components, ignoring the noise, and quickly adapts to market changes by capturing both short-term fluctuations and long-term trends.

SVM has been chosen to model the wavelet-decomposed components because of its robustness in handling non-linear relationships. SVM produces forecasts for each decomposed component, which are then used to reconstruct the predicted components.

Model

Model Features	Closing FX prices.
Predicted Label	Forecasted FX price one day ahead.
Model	SVM runs on decomposed wavelets.

We implement a class SVMWavelet with only one public method, forecast:

1. We use the pywt Python package to work with wavelets.

   ```
   import pywt
   ```

2. Wavelet choice: To break down the time series into different frequency components, we use the Symlet 10 wavelets ("sym10"), a family of wavelets used for their smoothing properties.

   ```
   w = pywt.Wavelet('sym10')
   ```

3. To determine the size of the input vector, we use the formula and solve for len(data):

   $$\log_2\left(\frac{len\ (data)}{wave\ length\ -\ 1}\right) = levels$$

   where
   a. We intend to decompose the time series into the three levels of components.
   b. The length of a Symlet 10 wavelet is 20, and we focus on implementing three levels of components.
   Which results in len(data) == 152.

4. We set a threshold scaling factor for denoising the wavelet coefficients to 0.5. The factor itself can be any number between 0 and 1.

   ```
   threshold = 0.5
   ```

5. We decompose the input array into several arrays of coefficients using the chosen wavelet.

   ```
   coeffs = pywt.wavedec(data, w)
   ```

6. We denoise all the coefficients except the first approximation ones, apply the SVR to predict the net value of the current coefficients, and store the forecasted value at the end of the coefficients array.

   ```
   for i in range(len(coeffs)):
       if i > 0:
           # Don't threshold the approximation coefficients.
           coeffs[i] = pywt.threshold(coeffs[i], threshold*max(coeffs[i]))
       forecasted = self._svm_forecast(coeffs[i])
       coeffs[i] = np.roll(coeffs[i], -1)
       coeffs[i][-1] = forecasted
   ```

7. Finally, we reconstruct the data from the updated wavelet coefficients using the inverse wavelet transformation and return the last value, the forecasted future value.

```
datarec = pywt.waverec(coeffs, w)
return datarec[-1]
```

Trading Universe

We adopt EURUSD as the benchmark. We trade these currency pairs: EUR/JPY, GBP/USD, AUD/CAD, and NZD/CHF.

Portfolio Construction

Model Training Time	Upon receipt of new daily FX data.
Portfolio Rebalancing Time	After model training.
Portfolio Weights	See following description.

We set the weights as follows:

- The ideal weight is the expected return forecasted FX value over yesterday's close as long as it's above `self._weight_threshold` with its default value of 0.005.
- We always hold the weight times the `self._leverage` with its default value of 20.

```
prices = np.array(list(security.window))[::-1]
forecasted_value = self._wavelet.forecast(prices)
weight = (forecasted_value / bar.close) -1
if abs(weight) > self._weight_threshold:
    self.set_holdings(security.symbol, weight * self._leverage)
```

Trading Logic

We place orders in this algorithm in the consolidation handler, which receives daily data and predicts the next close value. If the potential return from investing today (i.e., forecast value/current price − 1) is more significant than a specified threshold, we invest in the currency pair under defined leverage.

Tearsheet

Parameter `period`:

- The minimum is 63 because it's 3 months of trading days.
- The maximum is 189 because it's 9 months of trading days.
- The step size is 21 because it's 1 month of trading days.

The results show the following:

- The Sharpe ratio is maximized with a `period` of 8 months, but results are volatile between each consecutive period (high sensitivity).

- The Sharpe ratio is typically greater with `weight_threshold` > 0.004 rather than <= 0.004.
- See Figures 6.18 and 6.19.

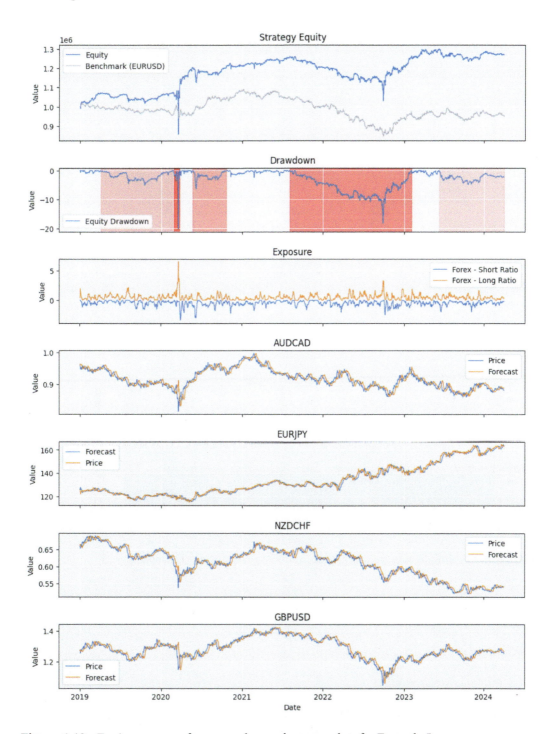

Figure 6.18 Equity curve, performance plots, and custom plots for Example 5.

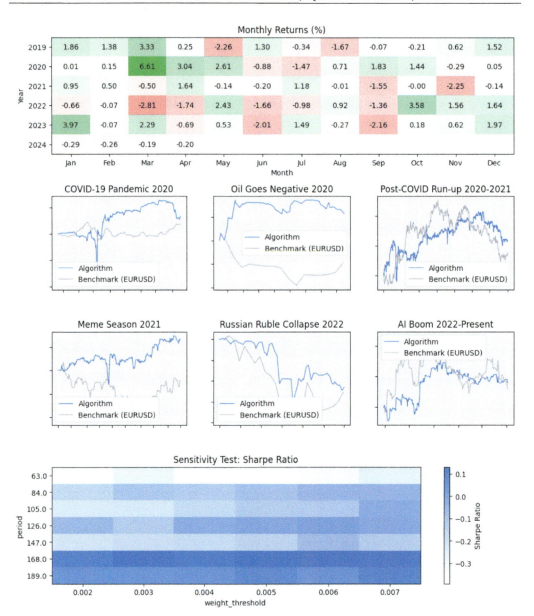

Figure 6.19 Monthly returns, crisis events, and sensitivity tests for Example 5.

Backtest parameters:

- `period`: 152.
- `leverage`: 20.
- `weight_threshold`: 0.005.

Implementation Insights

The training code is significant for two reasons: how it builds the training dataset and how it finds the optimal values of SVR hyperparameters.

In detail, the SVR method proceeds as follows:

1. We first partition the data into chunks of the size of 10.

    ```
    X, y = self._partition_array(data, size=sample_size)
    ```

    To illustrate how this method works, let's consider the following example:

    ```
    data = np.array([1, 2, 3, 4, 5, 6, 7, 8, 9, 10])
    sample_size = 3 # Call the method with sample data and a sample size X
    y = example._partition_array(data, size=sample_size)
    ```

    which returns

    ```
    Partitions (X): [[1 2 3] [2 3 4] [3 4 5] [4 5 6] [5 6 7] [6 7 8] [7 8 9]]
    One-step ahead values (y): [ 4  5  6  7  8  9 10]
    ```

    In other words, it prepares the features and labels for the SVR training.

2. We execute a grid search to find the optimal range of SVR's hyperparameters C and epsilon.

    ```
    gsc = GridSearchCV(
        SVR(),{
            'C': [.05, .1, .5, 1, 5, 10],
            'epsilon': [0.001, 0.005, 0.01, 0.05, 0.1]
        },
        scoring='neg_mean_squared_error'
    )

    model = gsc.fit(X, y).best_estimator_
    ```

3. We return the forecasted value for the next step.

    ```
    model.predict(data[np.newaxis, -sample_size:])[0]
    ```

    In sum, the _svm_forecast method is defined as follows:

```
def _svm_forecast(self, data, sample_size=10):
    '''
    Partitions `data` and fits an SVM model to this data, then
    forecasts the value one time-step into the future
    '''
    X, y = self._partition_array(data, size=sample_size)

    gsc = GridSearchCV(
        SVR(),
        {
            'C': [.05, .1, .5, 1, 5, 10],
            'epsilon': [0.001, 0.005, 0.01, 0.05, 0.1]
        },
        scoring='neg_mean_squared_error'
    )

    model = gsc.fit(X, y).best_estimator_
    return model.predict(data[np.newaxis, -sample_size:])[0]
```

Example 6—Dividend Harvesting Selection of High-Yield Assets

Predicting	Dividend rank
Technology	Regression models
Asset Class	US equities
Difficulty	Medium-hard
Type	Full strategy
Source Code	qnt.co/book-example6

Summary

We build a portfolio of the assets with the highest predicted dividend yield. We use a decision tree regression model to predict future dividend yields based on several financial ratios: PE ratio, revenue growth, free cash flow to operating cash flow ratio, dividend payout ratio, and current ratio.

Motivation

One of the most effective strategies to maximize returns while minimizing risks is dividend harvesting, where an investor invests in assets with the highest dividend yields (defined as dividend per share divided by the price per share). This results in a steady income stream and provides additional stability to the portfolio: companies paying regular dividends are usually financially stable.

Model

Model Features	• PE ratio: It is calculated by dividing the current market price of a stock by its earnings per share (EPS). • Revenue growth: Growth in revenue between the last two financial reports. • Free cash flow to operating cash flow ratio: The ratio of free cash flow to operating cash flow in the last financial report. • Dividend payout ratio: The ratio of dividends paid to net income during the last quarter. • Current ratio: Current assets divided by current liabilities.
Predicted Label	Dividend yield.
Model	Decision tree regressor.

This example demonstrates how to concentrate the portfolio on the assets likely to produce the most significant dividend yield from their next dividend payment.

Due to the complexities of the relationships between these factors, we decided to implement the model using the decision tree regression model (see qnt.co/book-decision-tree).

Trading Universe

The universe of the assets is the top 100 constituents of the QQQ ETF, with the most significant weights selected at the beginning of each month.

Portfolio Construction

Model Training Time	On the first trading date of every month, 30 minutes before the market opens.
Portfolio Rebalancing Time	Immediately after training the model.
Portfolio Weights	Each asset's weight is computed as its predicted dividend yield divided by the total sum of predicted yields.

Trading Logic

The trading method itself rebalances the portfolio, so the weight of each asset is proportional to the expected dividend yield (assign greater weight to assets we think will produce larger dividend yields).

```python
def _trade(self):
    r_squared_values = []
    prediction_by_symbol = {}
    for symbol in self._universe.selected:
        symbol_data = self._symbol_data_by_symbol[symbol]
        r_squared = symbol_data.train()
        if r_squared is None:
            continue
        r_squared_values.append(r_squared)
        prediction_by_symbol[symbol] = symbol_data.predict()

    prediction_sum = sum(prediction_by_symbol.values())
    portfolio_targets = [
        PortfolioTarget(symbol, prediction / prediction_sum)
        for symbol, prediction in prediction_by_symbol.items()
    ]
    self.set_holdings(portfolio_targets, True)
    self.plot("Portfolio Size", "Count", len(portfolio_targets))
```

Tearsheet

The results show the following:

- The Sharpe ratio only ranges from 0.476 to 0.617.
- The Sharpe ratio is typically more significant with a larger universe.
- The results are more sensitive to changes in `universe_size` than `lookback_years`.
- All parameter combinations lead to a positive Sharpe ratio.
- See Figures 6.20 and 6.21.

178 HANDS-ON AI TRADING WITH PYTHON, QUANTCONNECT, AND AWS

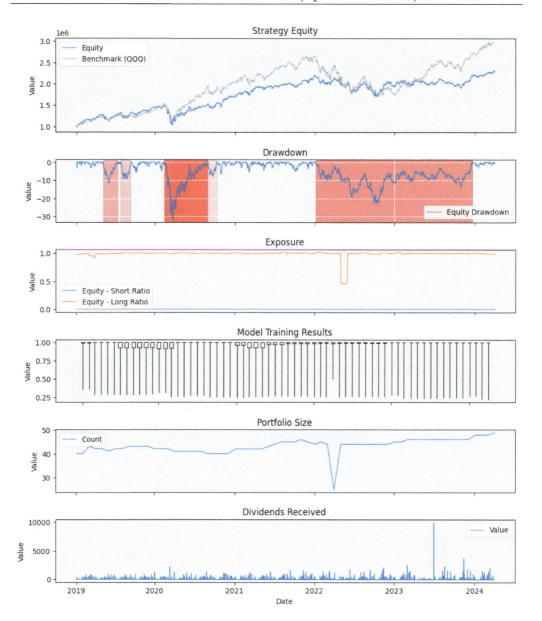

Figure 6.20 Equity curve, performance plots, and custom plots for Example 6.

Parameter `universe_size`:

- The minimum is 20, so at least one asset will have a dividend payment.
- The maximum is 100 to select all assets in the QQQ ETF (the universe).
- The step size is 20 because it leads to round numbers.

Chapter 6. Applied Machine Learning

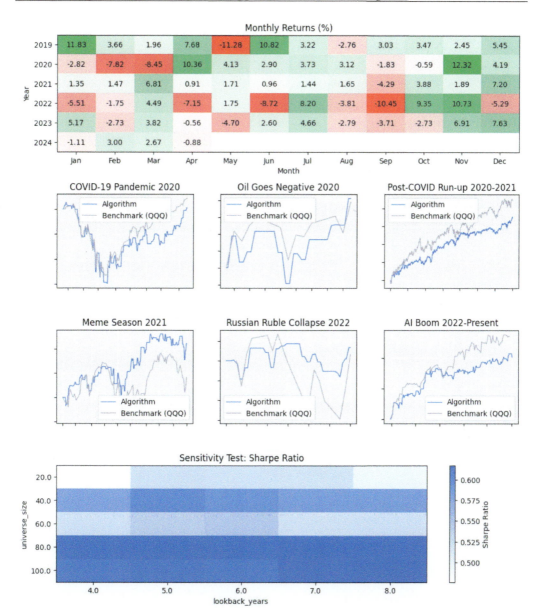

Figure 6.21 Monthly returns, crisis events, and sensitivity tests for Example 6.

Parameter `lookback_years`:

- The minimum is 4 because dividend payments don't happen very frequently.
- The maximum is 8 because anything further into the past may no longer be relevant.
- The step size is 1 because it's the smallest possible step size.

Backtest parameters:

- `universe_size`: 100.
- `lookback_years`: 5.

Implementation Insights

During the selection of the trading universe, we create for each constituent of the ETF an instance of the class `SymbolData`, which encapsulates each ETF constituent:

- Five years of history of all fundamental factors, 5 years of history of the label (i.e., the dividend yield), along with the class methods to build the history.
- An instance of the sklearn's `DecisionTreeRegressor`.
- The training method is mainly technical; it constructs the training dataset for the regression of current period factors and the next dividend yield.
- The prediction method just applies the latest values of the factors and uses the trained model to return the next period's expected dividend yield.

The trading algorithm also logs the total dividends received:

- On each new market data received (`on_data` method), it updates the Dividends Received chart with the new dividends received.
- At the end of the backtesting of the algorithm (`on_end_of_algorithm`), we log all the dividend payments received throughout the backtesting.

```python
def on_data(self, data):
    dividends_received = 0
    for symbol, dividend in data.dividends.items():
        security_holding = self.portfolio[symbol]
        if security_holding.invested:
            dividends_received += (
                dividend.distribution * security_holding.quantity
            )
    self.plot("Dividends Received", "Value", dividends_received)

def on_end_of_algorithm(self):
    self.log("Dividends received:")
    dividend_by_symbol = {
        security.symbol: security.holdings.total_dividends
        for security in self.securities.total
        if security.holdings.total_dividends
    }
    sorted_by_dividends_earned = sorted(
        dividend_by_symbol.items(), key=lambda x: x[1], reverse=True
    )
    for symbol, total_dividends in sorted_by_dividends_earned:
        self.log(f"- ${total_dividends} ({symbol.value})")
    self.log("----------------")
    self.log(f"Total: ${sum(dividend_by_symbol.values())}")
```

Example 7—Effect of Positive-Negative Splits

Predicting	Returns (equities)
Technology	Regression
Asset Class	US equities
Difficulty	Easy-medium
Type	Full strategy
Source Code	qnt.co/book-example7

Summary

This algorithm tries to profit from the expected volatility of stock splits. It uses a multiple linear regression model to estimate the future return when a stock split is imminent. It trades in the same direction, and then liquidates the position after 1 week.

Motivation

Due to innovative products, the investments they attract and dynamic business models, tech companies often experience more rapid growth than firms in traditional industries, leading to substantial increases in their stock prices.

When the stock prices reach levels perceived as too high, companies often resort to stock splits. A stock split increases the number of shares while proportionally decreasing the share price, enhancing liquidity and making the stock more accessible to a broader base of investors.

Historically, stocks tend to perform well after a stock split announcement as the perceived lower price and increased accessibility draw in more investors, driving up demand and, hence, the stock price. In addition, the market views stock splits as a positive signal, indicating that the company's management is confident in its prospects.

This strategy leverages historical data and market psychology surrounding stock splits to capitalize on the upcoming volatility caused by stock splits. It creates a linear regression model on the split factors (split direction) announced at the event of a split warning, the trailing 1-month return of the tech sector ETF (sector momentum), and the future price return after the intended holding duration.

Model

Model Features	• The reported split factor for each stock split. • The sector monthly return using the ETF XLK.
Predicted Label	The look-ahead future return of holding the corresponding stock for 3 days as of the day of the split announcement.
Model	Linear regression.

Trading Universe

We consider the fundamental universe of all the Morningstar technology classified assets.

Portfolio Construction

Model Training Time	At midnight of the first trading day of each month.
Portfolio Rebalancing Time	After each reported split.
Portfolio Weights	We limit the number of open trades; we aim at placing up to four simultaneous open positions and allocate for each position 25% of the total allocated cash.

Trading Logic

The trading algorithm monitors the split events; each split triggers the event handler `on_splits`, which receives all split events for subscribed stocks.

The method procceds as follows:

Step 1: We filter out any split event of the tech sector ETF since we do not intend to trade it.

Step 2: Depending on the type of split, we act as follows:

- For all split warnings, we first check if we can open another trade. (We limit the number of open trades—we aim at placing up to four simultaneous open positions and allocate 25% of the total allocated cash for each position.) If we can, we predict the expected return given the split factor and the current value of the rate of change sector indicator. Suppose the predicted return is positive, and the optimal number of trades is positive. In that case, we place the corresponding trade by creating an instance of the class `trade`, which we append to the list of active trades of any given symbol in the dictionary `_trades_by_symbol`.
- For all splits that occurred, we update the instance of the corresponding trade object with the actual split parameters.

The results show that the algorithm dramatically outperforms the XLK benchmark.

Tearsheet

The results show the following:

- A `hold_duration` of 3 days generates the most significant Sharpe ratio.
- All the Sharpe ratios are $>= 0.7$.
- See Figures 6.22 and 6.23.

    Backtest parameters:

- `max_open_trades`: 4.
- `hold_duration`: 3.
- `training_lookback_years`: 4.

Chapter 6. Applied Machine Learning 183

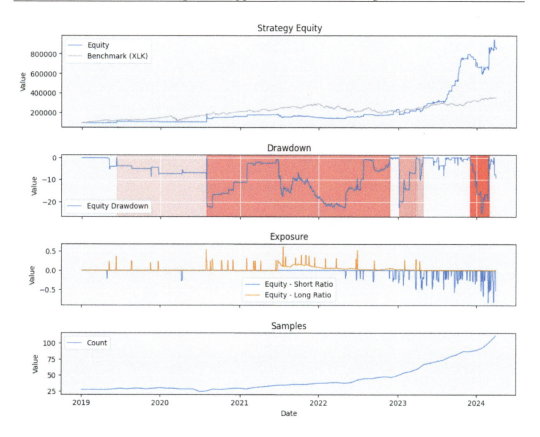

Figure 6.22 Equity curve, performance plots, and custom plots for Example 7.

Parameter `hold_duration`:

- The minimum is 1 because it's the smallest positive integer.
- The maximum is 5 because it equals one trading week.
- The step size is one because it's the smallest possible step size.

Parameter `training_lookback_years`:

- The minimum is 3 because split payments don't happen very frequently.
- The maximum is 6 because anything further into the past may no longer be relevant.
- The step size is 1 because it's the smallest possible step size.

Implementation Insights

We hold a record of all trades in the global dictionary `_trades_by_symbol`; for a symbol, it stores the list of active trades in instances of the class `trade`. This class places the trade for each selected split, adjusting the quantity of the stocks bought by the actual `split_factor` when the split happens and closing the trade after the hold period elapses.

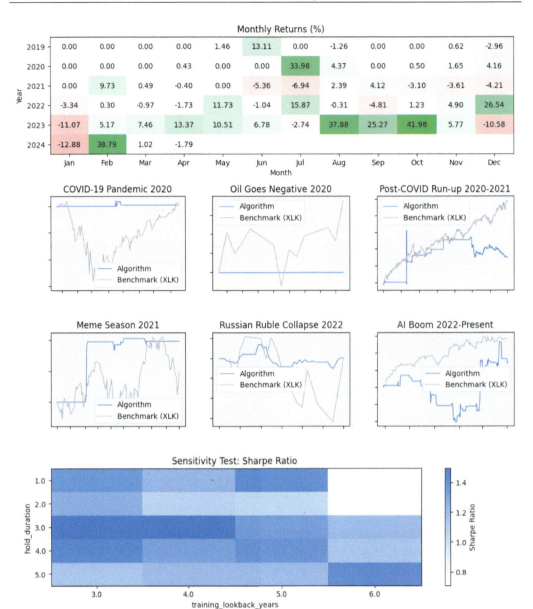

Figure 6.23 Monthly returns, crisis events, and sensitivity tests for Example 7.

```
class Trade:
    def __init__(self, algorithm, symbol, hold_duration, quantity):
        self.closed = False
        self._symbol = symbol
        self._close_time = algorithm.time + hold_duration
        self._quantity = quantity
        algorithm.market_on_open_order(symbol, quantity)

    def on_split_occurred(self, split):
        self._quantity = int(self._quantity / split.split_factor)
```

```
def scan(self, algorithm):
    if not self.closed and self._close_time <= algorithm.time:
        algorithm.market_on_open_order(self._symbol , -self._quantity)
        self.closed = True
```

We utilize Scheduled Events to run a function at midnight every day to retrain the models, update the future return, and exit trades:

The `_train` method proceeds as follows:

1. First, it retrieves the history of splits for the monitored stocks within the monitored lookback period.
2. Then, it retrieves the historical pricing of the monitored stocks with splits.
3. Next, it builds row-by-row the training numpy array with the three columns—the reported split factor, sector return, and the look-ahead return.
4. Finally, we train the linear regression model to predict the future return using the reported split factor and sector return.

Example 8—Stop Loss Based on Historical Volatility and Drawdown Recovery

Predicting	Downside volatility for stop loss
Technology	Regression/forecasting
Asset Class	US equities and US options
Difficulty	Medium-hard
Type	Full strategy
Source Code	qnt.co/book-example8

Summary

We employ regression models to safeguard a portfolio against downside risks. *We start with* a simple model featuring a fixed percentage-based stop-loss order as a benchmark. We then progress to a more complex model, dynamically adjusting the stop-loss distance using LASSO regression. In the final model, we substitute the stop market order with a put option, with parameters optimized through LASSO regression.

Motivation

Market volatility and unforeseen economic and company-specific news can lead to significant losses if appropriate risk management strategies are not in place.

Traditional risk management techniques often involve stop-loss orders, which automatically sell a security when its price falls to a predetermined level.

While simple and widely used, fixed percentage-based stop-loss orders have limitations. They do not account for the dynamic nature of market conditions. They can lead to premature exits during temporary market dips, potentially resulting in missed recovery opportunities and increased trading costs.

Recognizing these limitations, we employ a series of increasingly sophisticated regression models to enhance the effectiveness of stop-loss strategies and better protect a portfolio against downside risks:

1. Fixed Percentage-based Stop-loss Order: We use a simple model with a fixed percentage-based stop-loss order as a starting point. This model serves as a benchmark for our strategy, providing a baseline measure of protection against downside risks. While straightforward, this approach does not adapt to changing market conditions, which can lead to suboptimal performance.
2. Dynamic Stop-loss Distance Using LASSO Regression: To address the rigidity of fixed stop-loss orders, we advance to a more complex model that dynamically adjusts the stop-loss distance. By employing LASSO regression, we identify key factors influencing price movements and determine the optimal stop-loss levels based on these factors. This adaptive approach helps balance protecting against significant losses and avoiding unnecessary exits during short-term volatility.
3. Put Option Substitution with LASSO Regression Optimization: In the final model, we seek to enhance our risk management strategy by replacing the stop market order with a put option. Put options provide a guaranteed floor price for the underlying asset, offering a more robust form of protection. The parameters of the put option, including strike price and expiration date, are optimized using LASSO regression, which allows us to tailor the option strategy to current market conditions and ensure that the portfolio is effectively shielded from downside risks while minimizing costs.

Advanced regression models ensure that our strategies are data-driven and adaptive, providing superior protection compared to traditional methods.

Model

The first trading algorithm places a fixed price percentage stop-loss order.

The second and the third trading algorithms share the same model. It was not changed between experiments, so the performance of the second and third algorithms could be compared better.

Model Features	• VIX.
	• Average true range of the last n months.
	• The standard deviation of the previous n months.
Predicted Label	• Weekly low return: the return from the opening price of the week to the minimum low price over the following 5 trading days (1 week).
Model	LASSO regression model.

LASSO regression is optimal for this trading strategy because it effectively selects the most relevant features, reduces noise by excluding less essential variables, and prevents overfitting through regularization. Additionally, LASSO regression handles multicollinearity, ensuring robust performance with correlated predictors. These result in more stable and generalizable models that adapt dynamically to changing market conditions.

Trading Universe

We trade KO stock, and in algorithm three, we include KO put options.

Portfolio Construction

Model Training Time	Two minutes after the market opens on the first trading day of each week.
Portfolio Rebalancing Time	Immediately after the model is trained.
Portfolio Weights	100% of the portfolio is held in the KO stock.

Trading Logic

Each of the three algorithms buys 100,000 USD worth of shares of KO stocks at the beginning of each week and liquidates the position within a week:

- Algorithm 1: A benchmark algorithm buying and selling the same number of shares with a stop-loss order at 95% of the original purchase price at 9:32 am at the start of each week, and then liquidating the remaining shares, if any, the following week at 9 am before the market opens.
- Algorithm 2: An identical algorithm where we replace the 95% stop-loss order with a stop-loss order $0.01 below the LASSO regression predicted low price of the stock.
- Algorithm 3: An identical algorithm where we replace the stop-loss order with a put option placed below the LASSO regression predicted low price of the stock.

Tearsheet

Algorithm 1: Benchmark—Fixed Percentage Stop Loss

The results show the following:

- The Sharpe ratio collapses when the stop loss is too tight (>= 0.985).
- 17/20 of the stop-loss distances tested outperform buy-and-hold (0.263 Sharpe).
- See Figures 6.24 and 6.25.

    Backtest parameters:

- `stop_loss_percent`: 0.95.

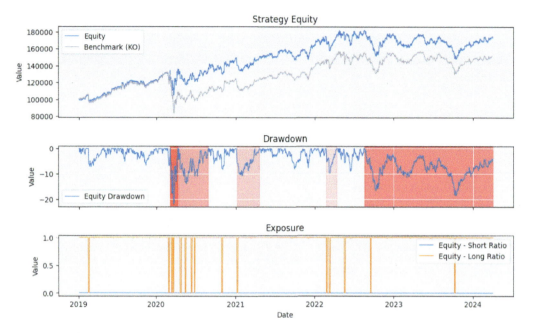

Figure 6.24 Equity curve and performance plots for Example 8.1.

Parameter `stop_loss_percent`:

- The minimum is 0.9 because KO isn't very volatile. It only dropped >20% once during the backtest period.
- The maximum is 0.995 because anything tighter than a 0.5% stop loss will likely trigger the stop loss in every trade.
- The step size is 0.005 because it gives us 20 different parameter values to test with just one decimal place.

Algorithm 2: ML Placed Stop Loss

The results show the following:

- The Sharpe ratio generally increases with a larger `stop_loss_buffer` over our tested range.
- 28/30 parameter combinations tested outperform buy-and-hold (0.263 Sharpe).
- All parameter combinations lead to a positive Sharpe ratio.
- See Figures 6.26 and 6.27.

Backtest parameters:

- `indicator_lookback_months`: 3
- `stop_loss_buffer`: 0.01
- `alpha_exponent`: 4

Chapter 6. Applied Machine Learning 189

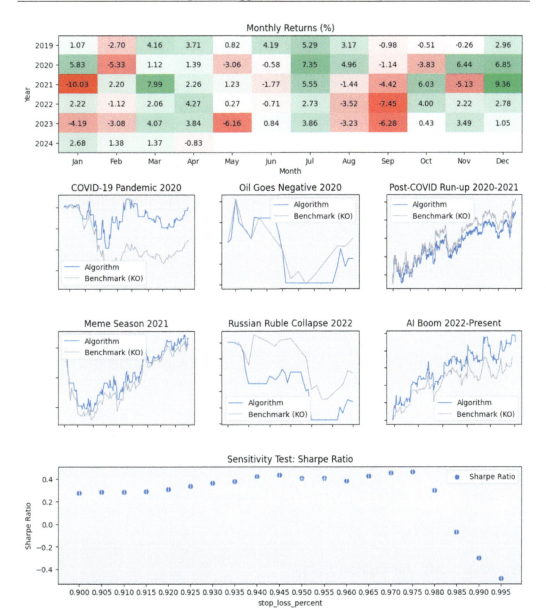

Figure 6.25 Monthly returns, crisis events, and sensitivity tests for Example 8.1.

Parameter `indicator_lookback_months`:

- The minimum is 1 because it's the smallest integer to choose.
- The maximum is 6 because it's half a year.
- The step size is 1 because it's the smallest integer to choose.

Parameter `stop_loss_buffer`:

- The minimum is 0.01 because it's the minimum price variation of the asset.

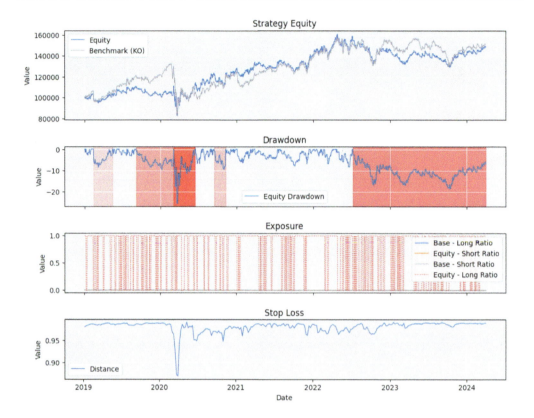

Figure 6.26 Equity curve, performance plots, and custom plots for Example 8.2.

- The maximum is 1.01 because it's almost exactly $1, and anything more significant will place the stop relatively far away from the model's prediction.
- The step size is 0.25 because it equals one quarter and gives us several samples between the minimum and maximum.

Algorithm 3: ML Put Option Hedge

See Figures 6.28 and 6.29.
  Backtest parameters:

- `alpha_exponent`: 4.

Implementation Insights

Algorithm 1: Benchmark—Fixed Percentage Stop Loss

We place a market order for 100,000 USD worth of KO stocks at the beginning of each week, 2 minutes after the market opens at 9:30 am. At the same time, we place a sell-stop market order for the identical quantity of stocks whenever the price drops to a given percentage (`self._stop_loss_percent` defined as 95%) of the purchase price.

Chapter 6. Applied Machine Learning

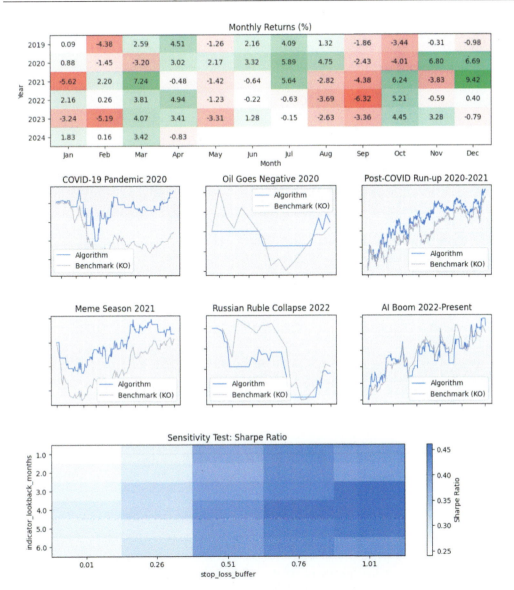

Figure 6.27 Monthly returns, crisis events, and sensitivity tests for Example 8.2.

If the stop-loss order is not executed during the week, we liquidate the position with a Market on Open at the beginning of the following week; see the method liquidate.

Algorithm 2: ML Placed Stop Loss

The input factors for our model are as follows:

- VIX.
- Average True Range of the last 22 daily closing prices of the KO stock.
- The standard deviation of the last 22 daily closing prices of the KO stock.

Figure 6.28 Equity curve, performance plots, and custom plots for Example 8.3.

```
def initialize(self):
    ...
    self._security = self.add_equity(
        "KO", data_normalization_mode=DataNormalizationMode.RAW
    )
    self._symbol = self._security.symbol

    period = 22 * self.get_parameter('indicator_lookback_months', 1)
    self._vix = self.add_data(CBOE, "VIX", Resolution.DAILY).symbol
    self._atr = AverageTrueRange(period, MovingAverageType.SIMPLE)
    self._std = StandardDeviation(period)
```

This version of the algorithm uses a LASSO regression model to adjust the stop-loss distance to improve performance dynamically.

The regression model is run on the data frame _samples containing 3 years of samples.

```
def initialize(self):
    # ...
    # Create a DataFrame to store the factors and labels.
    self._samples = pd.DataFrame(
        columns=['vix', 'atr', 'std', 'weekly_low_return'],
        dtype=float
    )
    self._samples_lookback = timedelta(3 * 365)
```

Chapter 6. Applied Machine Learning 193

Figure 6.29 Monthly returns and crisis events for Example 8.3.

The columns of the model data frame are as follows:

- `vix`—the CBOE VIX daily values.
- `atr`—average true range of the APPL stock over the last 22 days.
- `std`—standard deviation of the AAPL stock over the previous 22 days.
- `weekly_low_return`—the label we train the model to predict; the rate of change from today's open price to the low price over the upcoming 5 trading days (1 week).

The code populating `_samples` data frame is highly technical, and we set up consolidators to produce the daily bars from the minute bars the algorithm receives. In addition, we repopulate the entire data frame whenever there is a stock split so that our indicators reflect the new adjusted prices. Finally, we update the training data frame with updated VIX values whenever they arrive.

The algorithm is ready to trade once we have populated the training dataset stored in the `_samples` data frame. It works as follows—at the beginning of each week:

1. We buy the KO stock.
2. We predict the low price of the week.

3. We place a stop market order with a stop price of $0.01 (the `self._stop_loss_buffer`) below the predicted weekly low price; the stop loss is only hit if the market is more volatile than we expected. If the stop loss isn't hit throughout the week, we cancel it and liquidate the long position in the underlying with a Market On Open order.

```python
def initialize(self):
    # …
    self._stop_loss_buffer = self.get_parameter('stop_loss_buffer', 0.01)

    date_rule = self.date_rules.week_start(self._symbol)
    self.schedule.on(
        date_rule,
        self.time_rules.after_market_open(self._symbol, 2),
        self._enter
    )
    self.schedule.on(
        date_rule,
        self.time_rules.after_market_open(self._symbol, -30),
        self.liquidate
    )

    self._model = Lasso(alpha=10**(-self.get_parameter('alpha_exponent', 4)))

def _enter(self):
    # Train a model to predict the return from today's open to the
    # low price of the upcoming week.
    training_samples = self._samples.dropna()
    self._model.fit(
        training_samples.iloc[:, :-1],
        training_samples.iloc[:, -1]
    )

    prediction = self._model.predict(
        [self._samples.iloc[:, :-1].dropna().iloc[-1]]
    )[0]
    predicted_low_price = self._security.open * (1 + prediction)
    self.plot("Stop Loss", "Distance", 1 + prediction)

    # Place the entry order.
    quantity = self.calculate_order_quantity(self._symbol, 1)
    self.market_order(self._symbol, quantity)
    # Place the stop loss $0.0x below the predicted low price, so
    # that the stop loss is only hit if the market is more volatile
    # than we expected.
    self.stop_market_order(
        self._symbol, -quantity,
        round(predicted_low_price - self._stop_loss_buffer, 2)
    )
```

Algorithm 3: ML Put Option Hedge

This strategy builds on the previous version by substituting the stop market order with a put option. Both methods protect against downside price movements, each with its pros and cons:

- With a stop market order, we can accurately specify the stop price. However, with a stop market order, we don't know the fill price. If the market is volatile or there is a big overnight gap in price, the stop market order may be filled below our chosen stop price. In addition, when the stop market order is activated, it executes as a market order, exposing us to spread costs and market impact.
- The key drawback to using a put option is that we must pay extra to buy the option contract. With a put option hedge, we cannot choose an exact strike price. We can only select a strike price nearest our preferred stop-loss level. However, we know precisely what price our "stop loss" will fill with a put option hedge because it's the strike price of the option we select. With a put option hedge, we are not vulnerable to gaps, spread costs, or market impact because if the underlying price falls below the strike price, we can always exercise the option to sell the shares.

Fees are included by default in LEAN trading algorithms. This example, however, demonstrates how to change the fee model, even though the `InteractiveBrokers FeeModel` is the default fee model.

```python
class CaseOfTheMondaysAlgorithm(QCAlgorithm):

    def initialize(self):
        # ...
        self.set_security_initializer(
            IBFeesSecurityInitializer(
                self.brokerage_model,
                FuncSecuritySeeder(self.get_last_known_prices)
            )
        )

class IBFeesSecurityInitializer(BrokerageModelSecurityInitializer):

    def __init__(self, brokerage_model, security_seeder):
        super().__init__(brokerage_model, security_seeder)

    def initialize(self, security):
        super().initialize(security)
        security.set_fee_model(InteractiveBrokersFeeModel())
```

We create identical factors and training data frames as in Algorithm 2.

The trading algorithm works as follows:

- At 9:32 am, at the start of every week, we buy KO shares and calculate the share's week's low price as in Part II.
- However, instead of using a stop market order this time, we select the first put contract with a strike price below the `predicted_low_price + contract.ask_price`. We add the `contract.ask_price` to the prediction because the contract costs money, so we tighten up the stop loss to pay for it.
- The contracts expire on Friday. If they expire ITM, they exercise automatically and close our long position in the underlying stock. If they expire OTM, they expire worthless, and we liquidate the underlying stock with a market on an open order.

```python
class CaseOfTheMondaysAlgorithm(QCAlgorithm):

    def initialize(self):
        # ...

        date_rule = self.date_rules.week_start(self._symbol)
        self.schedule.on(
            date_rule,
            self.time_rules.after_market_open(self._symbol, 2),
            self._enter
        )
        self.schedule.on(
            date_rule,
            self.time_rules.after_market_open(self._symbol, -30),
            self._liquidate_if_possible
        )

        self._model = Lasso(alpha=10**(-self.get_parameter('alpha_exponent', 4)))

    def _liquidate_if_possible(self):
        self.liquidate(self._symbol)
        for symbol, security_holding in self.portfolio.items():
            # If it's an Option contract and we have no open orders for
            # it, liquidate it.
            if (security_holding.type == SecurityType.OPTION and
                not list(self.transactions.get_open_order_tickets(symbol))):
                self.liquidate(symbol)

    def _enter(self):
        # Train a model to predict the return from today's open to the
        # low price of the upcoming week.
        training_samples = self._samples.dropna()
        self._model.fit(
            training_samples.iloc[:, :-1],
            training_samples.iloc[:, -1]
        )

        prediction = self._model.predict(
            [self._samples.iloc[:, :3].dropna().iloc[-1]]
        )[0]
        predicted_low_price = self._security.open * (1 + prediction)
        self.plot("Stop Loss", "Distance", 1 + prediction)

        for chain in self.current_slice.option_chains.values():
            # Buy the underlying Equity.
            quantity = self.calculate_order_quantity(self._symbol, 1)
            self.market_order(self._symbol, quantity)

            # Select the put Contract.
            puts = [
                contract
                for contract in chain
                if contract.strike < predicted_low_price + contract.ask_price
            ]
            contract=sorted(puts, key=lambda contract: contract.strike)[-1]

            # Buy the put Contract.
            tag=f"Predicted week low price: {round(predicted_low_price, 2)}"
            self.market_order(contract.symbol, quantity // 100, tag=tag)
```

Discussion of the Performance of Algorithm 1, Algorithm 2, and Algorithm 3
All three algorithm versions trade in isolation, and we can easily compare their relative performances.

The results show that the put Option hedge underperforms a stop market order usage. Algorithm 1: Fixed Percentage Stop Loss produced superior results. There are plenty of ways to improve the strategies, and these implementations should be used as a springboard for your research.

Example 9—ML Trading Pairs Selection

Predicting	Preprocessing likely pairs clusters
Technology	PCA, clustering for pairs
Asset Class	US equities
Difficulty	Medium-hard
Type	Research rotebook
Source Code	qnt.co/book-example9

Summary

We use the PCA to transform the standardized returns of assets into their principal components. Then, we cluster assets with OPTICS, run a cointegration test, and calculate the Hurst exponent for mean reversion. Finally, we calculate the pair's half-life and the number of spread-crosses in 12 months.

Motivation

In finance, **PCA** is crucial for identifying the underlying factors that drive asset price movements. The first three principal components (PCs) in the context of stock returns can be interpreted as follows:

1. First Principal Component (PC1)—Market Factor: The first principal component captures the most significant variance in the stock returns data. Since most stocks tend to move with the broader market, this principal component is usually interpreted as the market factor reflecting the general market trend.
2. Second Principal Component (PC2)—Sector/Industry Factor: The second principal component captures the most significant variance, often interpreted as reflecting sector or industry-specific factors.
3. Third Principal Component (PC3)—Style/Size Factor: The third principal component explains the variance not captured by the first two principal components and can be interpreted as a style/size factor capturing variations due to the differences in investment style (growth vs. value stocks) or company size (small-cap vs. large cap stocks).

Once the assets are transformed into their principal components, we employ the **OPTICS clustering algorithm** to group assets with similar characteristics. By grouping similar assets, we can identify potential pairs or groups that exhibit comparable behaviors, which is valuable for pairs trading.

Testing for **cointegration** is critical for identifying pairs of assets that share a long-term equilibrium relationship despite short-term price deviations. **The Hurst exponent** measures the tendency of a time series to revert to its mean or to exhibit trending behavior. By combining cointegration and the Hurst exponent, we can rigorously test and confirm the mean-reverting properties of asset pairs.

Finally, we calculate the pair's **half-life** and the **number of spread-crosses** over 12 months. The half-life of a pair measures how quickly the spread between two cointegrated assets reverts to its mean. A shorter half-life indicates a faster mean reversion, which is desirable for trading as it allows for more frequent and reliable profit opportunities. The number of spread crosses indicates how often the spread between the pair crosses its mean. A higher number of spread-crosses suggests more frequent trading opportunities, making the pair attractive for a mean-reversion strategy.

Implementation Insights

In this example, based upon the MLFinLab blog post (qnt.co/book-hudson-pairs), we use ML to help us discover candidate pairs of stocks for a pairs trading strategy.

Step 1: Calculate daily returns of assets under consideration.
We first select all assets trading on a single day (January 3, 2024). We gather 3 years of historical closing prices for all the assets (roughly January 2022–2024). We drop assets with NaN values in the historical data, leaving 927 assets in total. From the series of closing prices, we calculate the daily returns of each asset.

```
qb = QuantBook()
end_date = datetime(2024, 1, 3)

universe_history = qb.universe_history(
    qb.universe.etf('IWB'), end_date - timedelta(1), end_date
)
symbols = [fundamental.symbol for fundamental in universe_history.iloc[0]]

prices = qb.history(
    symbols, end_date - timedelta(3 * 365), end_date, Resolution.DAILY
)['close'].unstack(0).dropna(axis=1)
daily_returns = prices.pct_change().dropna()
```

Step 2: Standardize the daily returns.
We then standardize the daily returns in preparation for principal component analysis.

```
from sklearn.preprocessing import StandardScaler
standardized_returns = StandardScaler().fit_transform(daily_returns)
```

Step 3: Run PCA.
We apply the PCA to reduce the dimensionality of the dataset to three principal components.

```
from sklearn.decomposition import PCA
pca = PCA(n_components=3, random_state=0)
pca.fit(standardized_returns)
```

Step 4: Load Principal Components into a Data Frame.
We load the principal components into a data frame to show the exposure of each asset to each principal component.

```
factor_exposures = pd.DataFrame(
    index=[f"component_{i}" for i in range(pca.components_.shape[0])],
    columns=daily_returns.columns,
    data=pca.components_).T
```

Let's display the results (Figures 6.30 and 6.31):

```
go.Figure(
    [
        go.Scatter3d(
            x=[row['component_0']],
            y=[row['component_1']],
            z=[row['component_2']],
            mode='markers',
            marker=dict(size=3, color='blue'),
            text=symbol,
            showlegend=False
        )
        for symbol, row in factor_exposures.iterrows()
    ],
    dict(
        scene=dict(
            xaxis_title='X', yaxis_title='Y', zaxis_title='Z',
            camera=dict(
                eye=dict(x=2, y=1.5, z=1.5)
            )
        ),
        title='3D Representation of Assets<br><sup>The coordinates represent '
            + 'the contribution the asset has to each component</sup>',
height=600, width=900
    )
).show()

# Each row of pca.components_ corresponds to a principal component, and
# the values within each row indicate the contribution of the original
# features to that principal component.
factor_exposures
```

Step 5: Organize the assets into clusters using the OPTICS algorithm.
Using the OPTICS clustering algorithm, we organize the assets into clusters based on their 3D-factor exposures (Figure 6.32).

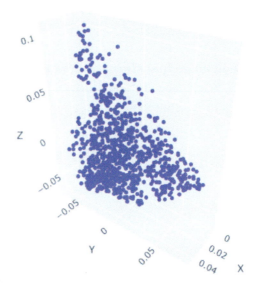

Figure 6.30 Asset representations in 3D space.

	component_0	component_1	component_2
Symbol			
A RPTMYV3VC57P	0.036965	0.031454	0.030914
AA R735QTJ8XC9X	0.040697	−0.023039	−0.035844
AA WF7IHVI76I5H	0.031304	−0.017483	−0.042513
AAL VM9RIYHM8ACL	0.034789	0.006323	−0.047596
AAP SA48O8J43YAT	0.027324	−0.013965	−0.000761
...	...	...	...
ZION R735QTJ8XC9X	0.036183	−0.039567	−0.046786
ZM X3RPXTZRW09X	0.027722	0.076046	0.003985
ZMH S6ZZPKTVDY05	0.033683	−0.000613	0.010533
ZS WSVUOMELFQED	0.028628	0.081103	0.001394
ZTS VDRJHVQ4FNFP	0.033949	0.030440	0.049610

927 rows × 3 columns

Figure 6.31 Asset coordinates in 3D space.

```
from sklearn.cluster import OPTICS

clustering = OPTICS().fit(factor_exposures)

# Display the results.
group_by_cluster_id = {
    cluster_id: factor_exposures.iloc[
```

Chapter 6. Applied Machine Learning

```
            [i for i, x in enumerate(clustering.labels_) if x == cluster_id]
        ]
        for cluster_id in sorted(set(clustering.labels_))
}
go.Figure(
    [
        go.Scatter3d(
            x=group['component_0'], y=group['component_1'],
            z=group['component_2'], mode='markers',
            marker=dict(size=3), text=group.index,
            name=f"Group {cluster_id}" if cluster_id >= 0 else "Noisy group",
            visible=True if cluster_id >= 0 else 'legendonly'
        )
        for cluster_id, group in group_by_cluster_id.items()
    ],
    dict(
        scene=dict(
            xaxis_title='X', yaxis_title='Y', zaxis_title='Z',
            camera=dict(eye=dict(x=1.752, y=1.25, z=1.25))
        ),
        title='3D Representation of Assets<br><sup>The coordinates represent '
            + 'the contribution the asset has to each component</sup>',
height=600, width=900
    )
).show()

# Drop noisy samples.
labels = clustering.labels_[clustering.labels_ != -1]
print(
    f"Out of {len(clustering.labels_)} assets, OPTICS found {len(labels)}",
    f"non-noisy samples and organized them into {len(set(labels))} groups."
)
```

Out of 927 assets, OPTICS found 347 non-noisy samples and organized them into 44 groups.

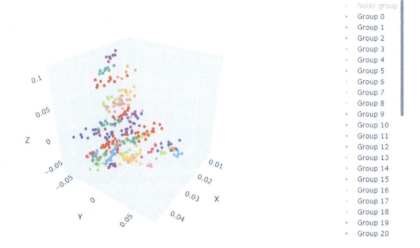

Figure 6.32 Asset representations in 3D space, color coded by group clusters.

Step 6: Identify potential trading pairs.

With the assets separated into distinct groups, we now look for candidate pairs within each group. Within each group, we analyze every possible combination of its assets. (Each pair has two assets from the same group.)

We select a pair if it meets the following four tests:
1. The pair's constituents are cointegrated.
2. The pair's spread's Hurst exponent exhibits a mean-reverting characteristic.
3. The pair's spread diverges and converges within a reasonable time frame.
4. The pair's spread reverts to the mean frequently enough.

Let's discuss each test in detail.

Test 6.1: The pair's constituents are cointegrated.
To accomplish this, we perform Engle-Granger tests (swapping the independent variable for each test) and select the test result with the lowest (i.e., most significant) test statistic with its p-value <= 1%.

```python
from arch.unitroot.cointegration import engle_granger
# …
        cointegration_test_results = [
            engle_granger(prices[symbol_a], prices[symbol_b]),
            engle_granger(prices[symbol_b], prices[symbol_a])
        ]

        cointegration_test_result = sorted(cointegration_test_results,
key=lambda x: x.stat)[0]

        if cointegration_test_result.pvalue > 0.01:
            test_results.loc[test_results_index[0], 'count'] += 1
            continue # Test failed: This pair is not cointegrated
```

Engle-Granger test is an econometric method used to test cointegration between two non-stationary time series.

"If two or more series are individually integrated (in the time series sense) but some linear combination of them has a lower order of integration, then the series are said to be cointegrated."

—*Wikipedia*

The test follows two key steps. First, assuming the two non-stationary variables are integrated of order 1, we estimate their long-run linear relationship. Second, the residuals from the first step's regression are tested for stationarity; if so, the relationship between the two time series is stable and long term.

Test 6.2: The pair's spread's Hurst exponent exhibits a mean-reverting characteristic.
To accomplish this, we calculate the spread using the hedge ratio from the preceding regression test, calculate the Hurst exponent, and ensure it is < 0.5.

```
spread = prices[cointegration_test_result.cointegrating_vector.index[0]] +
cointegration_test_result.cointegrating_vector.values[1] *
prices[cointegration_test_result.cointegrating_vector.index[1]]
H, _, _ = compute_Hc(spread, kind='price', simplified=False)
if H >= 0.5:
    test_results.loc[test_results_index[1], 'count'] += 1
    continue # Test failed: The spread doesn't lean towards mean-reverting
```

Hurst exponent ("H") is a statistical measure of long-term time series memory (i.e., the degree of mean-reversion of a time series):

- H < 0.5: the time series tends to return to its average value after moving up or down (mean reversion).
- H == 0.5: the future time series values will tend to be independent of the past trajectory.
- H > 0.5: the future time series values will boost the trend in the time series—the time series is strongly monotonous—an increasing time series will remain increasing, and a decreasing time series will tend to decrease.

Test 6.3: The pair's spread diverges and converges within a reasonable time frame.
To accomplish this, we calculate the half-life of the spread (i.e., the expected time for the spread to mean-revert) and ensure that "1 day < half-life < 1 year."

```
lagged_spread = np.roll(spread, 1)
lagged_spread[0] = 0
spread_delta = spread - lagged_spread
spread_delta.iloc[0] = 0
# run OLS regression to find the regression coefficient
model = OLS(spread_delta, add_constant(lagged_spread))
beta = model.fit().params.iloc[1]
half_life = -np.log(2) / beta
if not (1 < half_life < 252):
    test_results.loc[test_results_index[2], 'count'] += 1
    continue # Test failed: Half-life not between 1 day and 1 year
```

Test 6.4: The pair's spread reverts to the mean frequently enough.
To accomplish this, we check if the spread crosses the mean at least, on average, 12 times per year or 36 times in total.

```
mean_value = spread.mean()
crossings = (spread > mean_value) & (spread.shift(1) <= mean_value) |
(spread < mean_value) & (spread.shift(1) >= mean_value)
num_crossings = crossings.sum()
if num_crossings < 3*12: # 36 months in 3 years
    test_results.loc[test_results_index[3], 'count'] += 1
    continue # Test failed: Spread didn't cross the mean at least 12
times per year
```

Once all these conditions have been met, we plot the results, showing the number of pairs tested, the results of the four tests, and the pairs detected at the end (Figure 6.33).
Pairs tested: 1357.

	count	percent_of_tested	cumulative_percent_of_tested
Failed at cointegration test	1315	0.9690	0.9690
Failed at Hurst test	12	0.0088	0.9778
Failed at half-life test	0	0.0000	0.9778
Failed at crossing the mean	0	0.0000	0.9778

Figure 6.33 Output of pairs detection process.

Pairs detected: 30.

We then plot the price of each pair and their spread. This helps to visually confirm they're good pairs for trading (Figure 6.34).

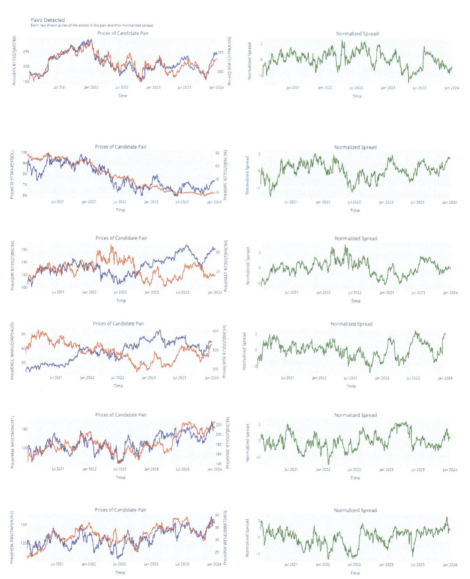

Chapter 6. Applied Machine Learning 205

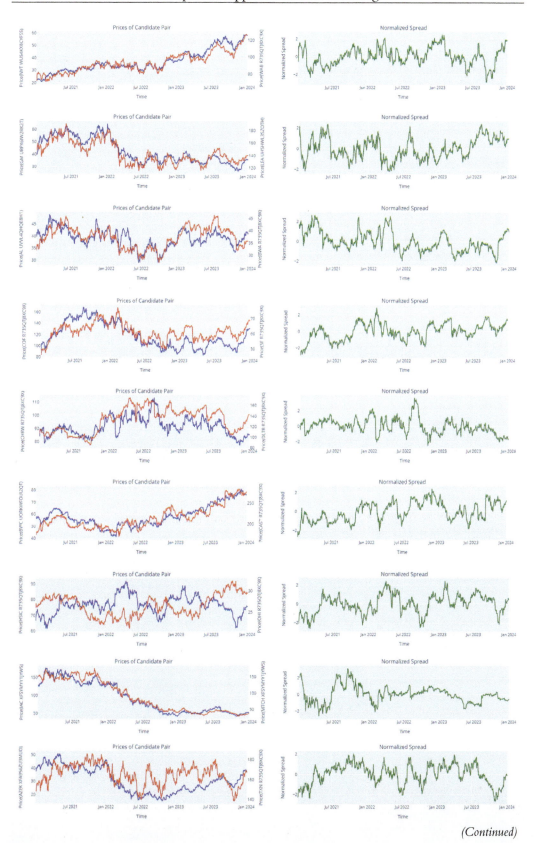

(Continued)

Figure 6.34 *(Continued)*

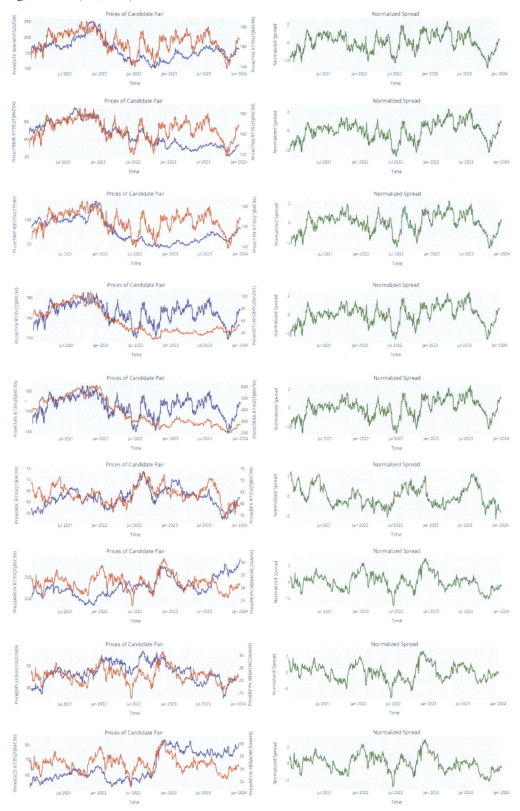

Chapter 6. Applied Machine Learning   207

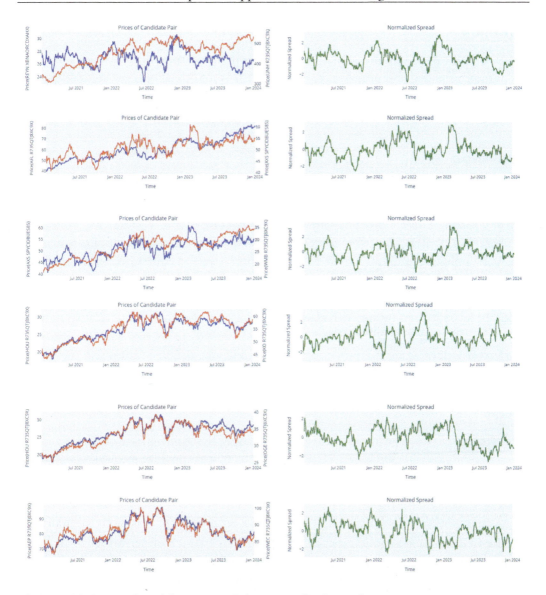

Figure 6.34 Prices of candidate pairs and their normalized spread.

Example 10—Stock Selection through Clustering Fundamental Data

Predicting	Performance rank
Technology	PCA, learning to rank algorithm
Asset Class	US equities
Difficulty	Hard
Type	Full strategy
Source Code	qnt.co/book-example10

Summary

We apply principal component analysis (PCA) to reduce hundreds of fundamental factors to their principal components. We then use the resulting vectors to predict the rank of stock relative performance. We use a "learning-to-rank algorithm" to form a portfolio of the subset of stocks that we expect to have the most significant future returns.

Motivation

By applying Principal Component Analysis (PCA), we reduce hundreds of fundamental factors into their principal components, capturing the critical drivers of stock returns and minimizing noise. Utilizing these principal component vectors, we employ a learning-to-rank algorithm to predict the relative performance of stocks. Learning-to-rank, a technique commonly used in information retrieval and machine learning, is designed to order items such that the most relevant ones appear at the top. This example enables us to rank stocks based on their predicted future returns. This approach is compelling because it predicts individual stocks' absolute performance and relative performance. By forming a portfolio from the highest-ranked stocks, we aim to maximize future returns, leveraging the power of PCA for effective data reduction and the precision of learning-to-rank algorithms for optimal stock selection.

Model

Model Features	The first five PCA principal components from standardized 100 fundamental factors for 100 most liquid stocks in the market.
Predicted Label	Rank based upon the return from holding the stock for 22 full trading days.
Model	LGBMRanker.

The LGBMRanker model has been chosen for its balance of performance, flexibility, and efficiency. Compared to simpler models like linear regression, which are easy to interpret but limited in capturing complex relationships, LGBMRanker excels in modeling non-linear interactions between features. It outperforms traditional methods like SVM and random forests in terms of speed and memory efficiency while being less resource-intensive than neural networks. Although it requires careful tuning of hyperparameters, LGBMRanker offers robust performance and effective handling of large datasets.

Trading Universe

The algorithm does fundamental universe selection at the start of each month. First, we select the top 100 most liquid equities from all assets with available fundamental data. Second, we reduce the set of assets to just the 10 equities that are ranked the highest for future returns.

Portfolio Construction

Model Training Time	At the start of each month, after the algorithm selects the 10 stocks to trade.
Portfolio Rebalancing Time	At the start of each month, 1 minute after the market opens.
Portfolio Weights	We form an equal-weighted portfolio of 10 stocks, i.e., each stock weighs 1/10.

Tearsheet

The results show the following:

- The most significant Sharpe ratio was achieved using the smallest value for both parameter `final_universe_size` and `components`.
- All the Sharpe ratios are $>= 0$.
- The performance can be sensitive to small changes in the `components` parameter. Changing it from 3 to 4 when the universe size is 5 drops the Sharpe ratio from 0.45 to 0.09.
- See Figures 6.35 and 6.36.

Figure 6.35 Equity curve, performance plots, and custom plots for Example 10.

Figure 6.36 Monthly returns, crisis events, and sensitivity tests for Example 10.

Parameter `final_universe_size`:

- The minimum is 5 because anything smaller will concentrate the portfolio on a few assets.
- The maximum is 25 because it makes the universe select the top quartile of assets, a common approach in practice.
- The step size is 5 because it leads to round numbers that traders would likely choose.

Parameter `components`:

- The minimum is 3 because the first three components typically explain >= 80% of the variation in the data.
- The maximum is 7 because each additional component explains less of the variation in the data.
- The step size is 1 because it's the smallest possible step size.

Backtest parameters:

- `liquid_universe_size`: 100.
- `final_universe_size`: 10.
- `lookback_period`: 365.
- `components`: 5.

Implementation Insights

Notice we infer the trading calendar by using an auxiliary symbol object, SPY.

```
schedule_symbol = Symbol.create("SPY", SecurityType.EQUITY, Market.USA)
date_rule = self.date_rules.month_start(schedule_symbol)
```

We store the factors' history in a dictionary indexed by the symbol, with the corresponding value being a pandas' data frame, with the column being each factor of interest and rows including the historical values of each factor:

```
factors_by_symbol = {
    symbol: pd.DataFrame(columns=self._factors)
    for symbol in liquid_symbols
}
history = self.history[Fundamental](
    liquid_symbols, self._lookback_period + timedelta(2)
)
for fundamental_dict in history:
    for symbol, asset_fundamentals in fundamental_dict.items():
        factor_values = []
        for factor in self._factors:
            factor_values.append(eval(f"asset_fundamentals.{factor}"))
        t = asset_fundamentals.end_time
        factors_by_symbol[symbol].loc[t] = factor_values
```

To apply the PCA, we cannot have any `NaN` values, and we discard any asset that has fewer than 20 factors remaining. The result of this step is the lists `tradable_symbols` and `factors_to_use`.

```
all_non_nan_factors = []
tradable_symbols = []
min_accepted_non_nan_factors = len(self._factors)
for symbol, factor_df in factors_by_symbol.items():
    non_nan_factors = set(factor_df.dropna(axis=1).columns)
    if len(non_nan_factors) < 20:
```

```
        # Let's say an asset needs at least 20 factors (otherwise
        # the `intersection` operation will remove almost all
        # factors).
        continue
    min_accepted_non_nan_factors = min(
        min_accepted_non_nan_factors, len(non_nan_factors)
    )
    tradable_symbols.append(symbol)
    all_non_nan_factors.append(non_nan_factors)
if not all_non_nan_factors:
    return []
factors_to_use = all_non_nan_factors[0]
for x in all_non_nan_factors[1:]:
    factors_to_use = factors_to_use.intersection(x)
factors_to_use = sorted(list(factors_to_use))
```

Our model aims to predict the rank of the future return of holding each asset for one month (i.e., 22 trading days). Let's calculate the future holding return:

```
history = self.history(
    tradable_symbols,
    self._lookback_period + timedelta(1),
    Resolution.DAILY
)
label_by_symbol = {}
for symbol in tradable_symbols[:]:
    # Remove the asset if there is not data for it.
    if symbol not in history.index:
        tradable_symbols.remove(symbol)
        continue
    open_prices = history.loc[symbol]['open'].shift(-1)
    # `shift(-1)` so that the open price here represents the
    # fill of a MOO order immediately after this universe
    # selection.

    # Calculate the future return of holding for 22 full
    # trading days (1 month).
    label_by_symbol[symbol] = open_prices.pct_change(
        self._prediction_period
    ).shift(-self._prediction_period).dropna()
```

The `prediction_period` is defined in the algorithm's `initialize` method as:

```
self._prediction_period = 22
```

Notice this line:

```
label_by_symbol[symbol] = open_prices.pct_change(self.prediction_period).
shift(-self.prediction_period).dropna()
```

We calculate the percentage change between the current row and `prediction_period` away from the prior row. We shift the data backward (i.e., future data will become historical data), and finally, we remove rows with `NaN` values.

After potentially eliminating some factors and assets, we must create a single data frame for the factor matrix and the label vector for training.

Chapter 6. Applied Machine Learning

```python
X_train = pd.DataFrame()
y_train = pd.DataFrame()
for symbol in tradable_symbols:
    labels = label_by_symbol[symbol]
    factors = factors_by_symbol[symbol][factors_to_use].reindex(
        labels.index).ffill()
    X_train = pd.concat([X_train, factors])
    y_train[symbol] = labels
X_train = X_train.sort_index()
```

Now that we have a matrix of factor values, we apply PCA to reduce the dimensionality of the factor matrix to just five factors, and then transform the original data into the space defined by the five principal components.

```python
def initialize(self):
    # ...
    self._components = self.get_parameter('components', 5)
    self._scaler = StandardScaler()
    self._pca = PCA(n_components=self._components, random_state=0)
```

And then in `_select_assets`:

```python
def _select_assets(self, fundamental):
    # ...
    X_train_pca = self._pca.fit_transform(
        self._scaler.fit_transform(X_train)
    )
```

Before using the LGBRanker algorithm, we must convert the label vector into a ranked one. The ranking algorithm starts with a rank of 1, which we need to convert to 0. In addition, we need to remove `NaN` values.

```python
y_train = y_train.rank(axis=1, method='first').values.flatten() - 1
y_train = y_train[~np.isnan(y_train)]
```

Notice this line:

```python
y_train.rank(axis=1, method='first').values.flatten()-1
```

- `y_train.rank(axis=1, method='first')`: This assigns each element along each row (axis=1) a rank in the data frame. If some elements have an identical value, the `method='first'` argument will give ranks based on their order (whoever comes first gets a lower rank). The output is another data frame with the same shape as `y_train` but with the original values changed by their ranks.
- `.values`: This converts the data frame into a NumPy array, which is required for the subsequent processing.
- `.flatten()`: This collapses the NumPy array into one dimension. If the original array was 2D (like a data frame), the resulting array is a 1D array with concatenated rows.
- −1: This subtracts one from all the elements in the array so that the ranks are zero-based.

Next, we train a learning-to-rank LGBMRanker model with the factors and labels. We train the algorithm to rank "assets" for a given "rebalance date." Therefore, before training, we count the possible assets for every rebalance date and provide it to the `fit` method. We are using the LambdaRank objective.

```
model = LGBMRanker(
    objective="lambdarank",
    label_gain=list(range(len(tradable_symbols)))
)
# The `group` is a mapping from rebalance time to the number of
# assets at that time.
group = X_train.reset_index().groupby("time")["time"].count()
model.fit(X_train_pca, y_train, group=group)
```

Now, we can predict the ranking of assets over the upcoming month:

```
X = pd.DataFrame()
for symbol in tradable_symbols:
    X = pd.concat(
        [X, factors_by_symbol[symbol][factors_to_use].iloc[-1:]]
    )
prediction_by_symbol = {
    tradable_symbols[i]: prediction
    for i, prediction in enumerate(
        model.predict(self._pca.transform(self._scaler.transform(X)))
    )
}
```

Let's select the highest-ranking assets:

```
sorted_predictions = sorted(
    prediction_by_symbol.items(), key=lambda x: x[1]
)
```

We select just the best 10 assets with the greatest prediction labels:

```
return [x[0] for x in sorted_predictions[-self._final_universe_size:]]
```

Where `final_universe_size` is defined as 10 in the algorithm's initialize method:

```
self._final_universe_size = self.get_parameter(
    'final_universe_size', 10
```

Example 11—Inverse Volatility Rank and Allocate to Future Contracts

Predicting	Volatility
Technology	Ridge regression
Asset Class	Futures
Difficulty	Hard
Type	Full strategy
Source Code	qnt.co/book-example11

Chapter 6. Applied Machine Learning

Summary

We construct a portfolio of futures contracts weighted by the inverse of the corresponding expected opening price volatility over the next week. The expected opening price volatility over the next week is predicted using a ridge regression model on the past closing price volatility, average true range (ATR), standard deviation, and open interest.

Motivation

The strategy leverages the inverse volatility ranking method, assuming lower volatility assets tend to have more stable and predictable returns.

By weighing assets inversely proportionally to their expected volatility, the strategy inherently allocates more capital to less volatile investments, which tends to reduce the overall risk of the portfolio, and at the same time, this tends to improve the Sharpe ratio of the portfolio.

The trading universe has been chosen to be widely diversified to limit the impact of any single asset's performance on the overall portfolio.

Model

Model Features	• <u>Volatility (standard deviation of daily returns) over the last 3 months.</u> We monitor both the opening and closing price volatility—the future opening volatility will be predicted using the historical closing price volatility. • <u>ATR over the last 3 months</u>: 　• The true range is the greatest of the following: 　　• The difference between the current high and the current low. 　　• The *absolute* difference between the current low and the previous close. 　　• The *absolute* difference between the current high and the previous close. 　• The average true range is then an exponential moving average of the true range. • <u>Open interest</u>: Open interest is the total number of derivative contracts that are still active and not settled. The contract is considered "open" from when the buyer or seller starts it until the other party ends it.
Predicted Label	Open prices volatility.
Model	Ridge regression.

Ridge regression was chosen for the following reasons:

1. Ridge regression effectively handles **multicollinearity** (when model features could be correlated).
2. Ridge regression **includes a regularization term** (a penalty on the size of coefficients: the coefficients of unimportant factors shrink more than the coefficients of essential factors), which prevents overfitting and makes them more stable and less sensitive to minor changes in data.
3. Ridge regression is simple and computationally efficient.

Trading Universe

We limit ourselves to the universe of the *front-month* contracts of these futures contracts:

- Indices
  - VIX
  - S&P 500 E-Mini
  - Nasdaq 100 E-Mini
  - DOW 30 E-Mini
- Energy
  - Brent crude
  - Gasoline
  - Heating oil
  - Natural gas
- Grains
  - Corn
  - Oats
  - Soybeans
  - Wheat

Portfolio Construction

Model Training Time	On the first day of every week, 2 minutes after the market open.
Portfolio Rebalancing Time	Immediately after training the model.
Portfolio Weights	The asset weights are a function of their respective volatilities: weight = 3/sigma/sum(sigma)/Futures Contract Multiplier This weighting function is designed to give greater weight to less volatile assets. The numerator 3 scales the positions to achieve the desired position size: • If it is set to 1, the algorithm only trades a few of the futures in the universe because of the `minimum_order_margin_portfolio_percentage` setting. • If it is set too high, we run into margin calls. • Three was the middle ground where the algorithm trades most futures without setting `minimum_order_margin_portfolio_percentage` to zero.

Tearsheet

The results show the following:

- The Sharpe ratio is typically highest when at least one of the indicators uses a 6-month lookback.
- The Sharpe ratio is typically lowest when at least one of the indicators uses a 3-month lookback.

Chapter 6. Applied Machine Learning

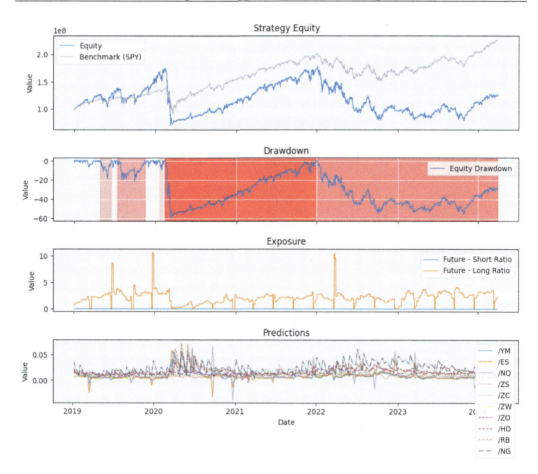

Figure 6.37 Equity curve, performance plots, and custom plots for Example 11.

- All parameter combinations are profitable.
- See Figures 6.37 and 6.38.

  Parameter `std_months`:

- The minimum is 1 because it is the smallest possible integer.
- The maximum is 6 because it is half a year.
- The step size is one because it is the smallest possible step size.

  Parameter `atr_months`:

- The minimum is 1 because it is the smallest possible integer.
- The maximum is 6 because it is half a year.
- The step size is 1 because it is the smallest possible step size.

  Used backtest parameters:

- `std_months`: 3
- `atr_months`: 3
- `training_set_duration`: 365

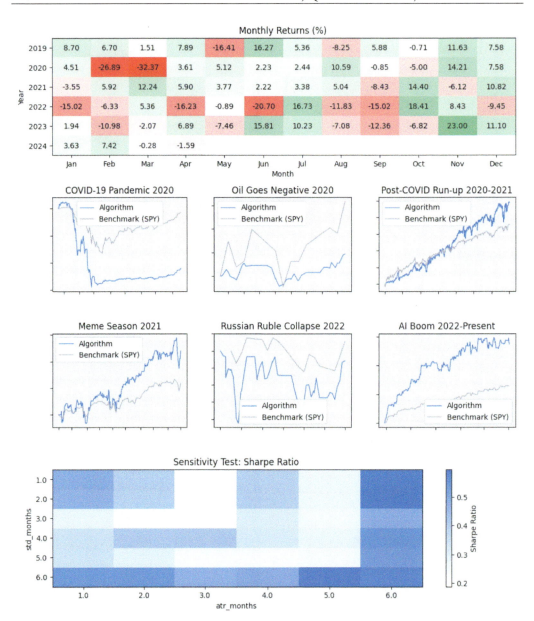

Figure 6.38 Monthly returns, crisis events, and sensitivity tests for Example 11.

Implementation Insights

We implement the **volatility model features** via the chaining of indicators:

Step 1: We create an indicator for daily closing and opening price returns.

```
security.close_roc = RateOfChange(1)
security.open_roc = RateOfChange(1)
```

Chapter 6. Applied Machine Learning 219

Step 2: We create an indicator for the standard deviation of daily closing and opening price returns.

```
security.std_of_close_returns = IndicatorExtensions.of(
    StandardDeviation(self._std_period),
    security.close_roc
)

security.std_of_open_returns = IndicatorExtensions.of(
    StandardDeviation(self._future_std_period), security.open_roc
)
```

We implement the **ATR model feature** via an indicator:

```
security.atr = AverageTrueRange(self._atr_period)
```

Where we defined `self._atr_period` in the algorithm's initialize method to be by default about the number of days in 3 months (3 * 26):

```
def initialize(self):
    # …
    self._atr_period = self.get_parameter('atr_months', 3) * 26
```

We **populate the indicator data** by consolidating the model's features (`indicator_history`) and the dependent variable (`label_history`) into daily bins.

```
security.indicator_history = pd.DataFrame()
security.label_history = pd.Series()

security.consolidator = self.consolidate(
    security.symbol, Resolution.DAILY, self._consolidation_handler
)
```

For each security, the `indicator_history` will store the daily values of the features `atr`, `std_of_close_returns`. The `label_history` is a series that contains the future volatility of the upcoming week.

```
def _consolidation_handler(self, consolidated_bar):
    security = self.securities[consolidated_bar.symbol]
    t = consolidated_bar.end_time
    if security.atr.update(consolidated_bar):
        security.indicator_history.loc[t, 'atr'] = \
            security.atr.current.value
    security.close_roc.update(t, consolidated_bar.close)
    if security.std_of_close_returns.is_ready:
        security.indicator_history.loc[t, 'std_of_close_returns'] = \
            security.std_of_close_returns.current.value
    security.open_roc.update(t, consolidated_bar.open)

    if (security.std_of_open_returns.is_ready and
        len(security.indicator_history.index) > self._future_std_period):
        security.label_history.loc[
            security.indicator_history.index[-self._future_std_period - 1]
        ] = security.std_of_open_returns.current.value
```

```
security.indicator_history = security.indicator_history[
    (security.indicator_history.index >=
     self.time - self._training_set_duration)
]
security.label_history = security.label_history[
    (security.label_history.index >=
     self.time - self._training_set_duration)
]
```

Notice the following:

- The indicator's `update()` method returns `True` if the indicator is ready; in this case, we store the successful value in the `indicator_history`.
- There is a special handling for `close_roc` and `open_roc`. For `open_roc`, we proceed differently:
  - We do not check the return value of the `open_roc.update()` because we are interested in the success of the dependent indicator `std_of_open_returns`.
  - We are only interested in predicting the volatility over the upcoming `_future_std_period` trading days (1 week).
  - We shift the future indices into the past in preparation for regression predicting the future opening price volatility.
- Finally, we filter out older data that are not interesting for the training; see `_training_set_duration`.

To train the model, we first retrieve the Open Interest data for all active futures contracts in the portfolio.

```
open_interest = self.history(
    OpenInterest, [c.symbol for c in self._contracts],
    self._training_set_duration, fill_forward=False
)
open_interest.index = open_interest.index.droplevel(0)
```

Notice the data frame's index is a multi-index with three levels (expiry, symbol, time) and we drop the expiry index level.

Then, we construct the factors data frame column-wise (`axis=1`), appending the `open_interest` data frame for the given symbol to the data frame of `indicator_history`.

```
factors = pd.concat(
    [security.indicator_history, open_interest.loc[symbol]],
    axis=1
).ffill().loc[security.indicator_history.index].dropna()
```

We also forward populate missing data (`ffill`) and align the concatenated data frame's index to the index of the `indicator_history`'s `index`, and remove any rows that contain `NaN` (`dropna`).

We also create the labels data structures:

```
label = security.label_history
idx = sorted(
    list(set(factors.index).intersection(set(label.index)))
)
```

```
if len(idx) < 20:
    continue
```

We are interested only in the labels associated with the feature dates and only if there are at least 20 values; otherwise, the training process would not have enough data.

Now, we are ready to train the model and store the predictions in the dictionary `expected_volatility_by_security`:

```
model = Ridge()
model.fit(factors.loc[idx], label.loc[idx])

prediction = model.predict([factors.iloc[-1]])[0]
if prediction > 0:
    expected_volatility_by_security[security] = prediction
```

Once we establish the expected volatility, we can place orders to rebalance the portfolio.

Example 12—Trading Costs Optimization

Predicting	Trading costs
Technology	Decision tree regression
Asset Class	Crypto
Difficulty	Hard
Type	Full strategy
Source Code	qnt.co/book-example12

Summary

This algorithm demonstrates using machine learning to reduce trading costs. We build a `DecisionTreeRegressor` model to predict the trading costs with these factors:

- Absolute order quantity.
- Average true range.
- Average daily volume.
- Spread percentage ((ask − bid)/bid).
- Top of book size (in dollars).

Then, we place an order only if the predicted costs per invested dollar are lower than the average trading cost over the last 10 trading days. We store extensive details for further analysis in the research Jupyter Notebook.

Motivation

In financial trading, minimizing costs is crucial for maximizing returns. This trading algorithm leverages machine learning to reduce trading costs by building a `DecisionTreeRegressor` model.

Modeling trading costs involves predicting the expenses associated with executing trades, which various market factors can influence. The algorithm considers the following:

- Absolute order quantity, which is the size of the trade order, directly impacts the cost due to potential market impact and liquidity constraints.
- The ATR is included as it measures market volatility, indicating the potential cost variations based on price movements.
- Average daily volume is critical, as higher trading volumes imply better liquidity and lower costs. In comparison, lower volumes can lead to higher costs due to slippage and market impact.
- Spread percentage ((ask − bid)/bid) is another essential component, representing the difference between the bid and ask prices. A more extensive spread indicates higher costs for executing trades.
- Lastly, the top-of-book size (in dollars) is considered, which reflects the available liquidity at the best bid and ask prices and helps gauge the immediate cost implications for the order size being executed.

Model

Model Features	- Absolute order quantity. - Average true range. - Average daily volume. - Spread percent ((ask − bid)/bid). - Top of book size (in dollars).
Predicted Label	Actual trading costs
Model	`DecisionTreeRegressor`

Trading Universe

We trade only one asset, BTCUSD.

Portfolio Construction

Model Training Time	At midnight on the first day of each month.
Portfolio Rebalancing Time	At midnight of every day, and then with every new market data.
Portfolio Weights	We buy 10 BTC in each entry order.

Trading Logic

The trading algorithm runs in two modes:
   Mode 1 (Benchmark Run):

- First, we run a benchmark algorithm (set `self._benchmark = True`), which buys 10 Bitcoin at midnight and liquidates the position at 1 am daily.
- As the benchmark algorithm runs, it records the orders' fill price, quantity, and cost.

- At the end of the algorithm, all captured data is saved in QuantConnect's Object Store for further analysis in the Jupyter Notebook.

Mode 2 (Candidate Algorithm—Trading Costs Optimization):

- After the benchmark algorithm finishes, we can run the candidate algorithm (set `self._benchmark = False`).
- The candidate algorithm buys 10 Bitcoin at midnight but liquidates it at some point between 1 am and 11:59 pm when it predicts that the liquidation costs are lower than usual.
- If it gets to 11:59 pm and has not liquidated the position yet, it liquidates the position regardless of the predicted costs; we tag such an order with "Hit time limit."

In other words, the Mode 1 algorithm liquidates the position every day with no intelligence and is used to measure the value of the machine-language (ML) model in Mode 2. The Mode 2 algorithm incorporates some sophistication in finding the ideal time to liquidate the position.

Implementation Insights

We defined a `SpreadSlippageModel` to simulate the impact of market spread on the execution price of trades. We are using the spread as a proxy for a high-cost environment for market orders.

```
class SpreadSlippageModel:
    def get_slippage_approximation(self, asset, order):
        return asset.ask_price - asset.bid_price
```

The Mode 2 (Candidate Algorithm—Trading Costs Optimization) algorithm places the same trades as the Mode 1 (Benchmark Run) version at the beginning of the trading window; once it has gained enough samples to train the ML model, it finally starts delaying trades to reduce costs.

The Candidate algorithm uses a `DecisionTreeRegressor` model to predict the costs of placing a trade.

- We train the model to predict the costs of an order (commission + slippage), and we capture these in `_costs`.
- We convert the predicted cost of an order to the "predicted cost per dollar traded."
- The model only trades when the "predicted cost per dollar traded" is lower than the trailing average cost of filled trades.

We capture all orders in a data frame `_order_fills` with the following columns:

- `fill_price`.
- `quantity`.
- `cost`.
- `tag`—used to add comments on the order (e.g., if the trade was executed due to the time limit).

We persist the orders into a CSV file at the end of the algorithm to allow detailed trade analysis. For Mode 1, the file is called `benchmark_order_fills`, while for Mode 2 it is `candidate_order_fills`.

```
def on_end_of_algorithm(self):
    key = ("benchmark" if self._benchmark else "candidate") + "_order_fills"
    self._order_fills.to_csv(self.object_store.get_file_path(key))
```

Running QuantConnect's backtest of the trading algorithm illustrates in the charts "Costs" and "Costs per Dollar" how the algorithm work; see Figure 6.39.

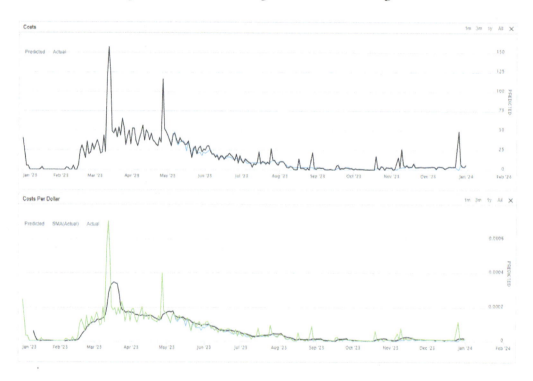

Figure 6.39 Plots of trading costs. Trading costs begin to decrease after the model has gathered a sufficient number of samples.

The Research Jupyter Notebook has been designed to analyze the costs of both backtest modes.

Step 1: Load the orders csv files.

```
qb = QuantBook()
def get_order_fills(key):
    return pd.read_csv(
        qb.object_store.get_file_path(f"{key}_order_fills"),
        index_col=0, parse_dates=True
    )
benchmark_orders = get_order_fills("benchmark")
candidate_orders = get_order_fills("candidate")
```

Step 2: Calculate summary statistics.

```python
same_index = candidate_orders.index == benchmark_orders.index
matching_fill_times = candidate_orders[same_index].index
different_fill_times_for_candidate = candidate_orders[~same_index].index
different_fill_times_for_benchmark = benchmark_orders[~same_index].index

print(f"Number of trades: {len(benchmark_orders)}")
print("Number of trades with the same fill times:",
len(matching_fill_times))
print(
    "Number of trades with different fill times:",
    len(different_fill_times_for_candidate)
)
costs_saved = sum(
    benchmark_orders['cost'].values - candidate_orders['cost'].values
)
print("Costs saved by delaying orders:", f"${round(costs_saved, 2)}")

# For all pairs of orders between the two algorithms, ensure the
# quantities match.
candidate_quantities = candidate_orders['quantity'].values
benchmark_quantities = benchmark_orders['quantity'].values
if not all(candidate_quantities == benchmark_quantities):
    raise Exception('Error: The algorithms traded different quantities')

# For the orders that fill at the same time for both algorithms, ensure
# the fill price and costs also match.
candidate_info = candidate_orders.loc[matching_fill_times].drop('tag', axis=1)
benchmark_info = benchmark_orders.loc[matching_fill_times].drop('tag', axis=1)
if not all(candidate_info == benchmark_info):
    raise Exception(
        'Error: Fill prices and costs of identical orders do not match'
    )
```

With the output:

```
Number of trades: 1827
Number of trades with the same fill times: 798
Number of trades with different fill times: 1029
Costs saved by delaying orders: $36429.7
```

Step 3: Analyze the delayed orders that filled before the time limit.

Let us compare the costs of executing the delayed orders and benchmark orders (see Figure 6.40):

```python
from collections import Counter
import plotly.graph_objects as go

# Calculate number of orders that the algorithm delayed (and didn't hit
# the time limit).
index_numbers_of_time_limited_orders = []
index_numbers_of_delayed_orders = []
for i in range(len(benchmark_orders.index)):
    # Skip orders that filled at the same time.
    if benchmark_orders.index[i] == candidate_orders.index[i]:
        continue
```

```python
        # Skip orders that hit the time limit.
        if "Hit time limit" in candidate_orders.iloc[i]['tag']:
            index_numbers_of_time_limited_orders.append(i)
            continue
        index_numbers_of_delayed_orders.append(i)

def display_order_results(title, index_numbers):
    cost_deltas = (
        benchmark_orders.iloc[index_numbers]['cost'].values
        - candidate_orders.iloc[index_numbers]['cost'].values
    )
    candidate_dollar_volume = (
        abs(candidate_orders.iloc[index_numbers]['quantity'])
        * candidate_orders.iloc[index_numbers]['fill_price']
    ).values
    cost_deltas_per_dollar_volume = cost_deltas / candidate_dollar_volume

    fig = go.Figure(data=[go.Histogram(x=cost_deltas_per_dollar_volume, nbinsx=100)])
    fig.update_layout(
        title="Distribution of Costs Saved<br><sup>Costs saved for "
            + f"Delayed Orders that {title}</sup>",
        xaxis_title="Costs Saved Per Dollar Volume (>0 => Candidate Saved Money)",
        yaxis_title="Count"
    )
    fig.show()

    print("Number of orders:", len(index_numbers))
    pct_of_cheaper_orders = (
        len(cost_deltas[cost_deltas > 0])
        / len(candidate_orders) * 100
    )
    print(
        "Number of orders that lowered costs:",
        len(cost_deltas[cost_deltas > 0]),
        f"({round(pct_of_cheaper_orders, 2)}% of all orders)"
    )
    pct_of_no_change = (
        len(cost_deltas[cost_deltas == 0])
        / len(candidate_orders) * 100
    )
    print(
        "Number of orders that didn't change costs:",
        len(cost_deltas[cost_deltas == 0]),
        f"({round(pct_of_no_change, 2)}% of all orders)"
    )
    pct_of_raised_orders = (
        len(cost_deltas[cost_deltas < 0])
        / len(candidate_orders) * 100
    )
    print(
        "Number of orders that raised costs:",
        len(cost_deltas[cost_deltas < 0]),
        f"({round(pct_of_raised_orders, 2)}% of all orders)"
    )
    print(f"Total costs saved: ${round(sum(cost_deltas), 2)}")

display_order_results(
    "Filled Before the Time Limit", index_numbers_of_delayed_orders
)
```

```
minutes_delayed = (
    candidate_orders.iloc[index_numbers_of_delayed_orders].index
    - benchmark_orders.iloc[index_numbers_of_delayed_orders].index
)
num_orders_by_delay_duration = pd.Series(
    Counter([x.total_seconds() / 60 for x in minutes_delayed])
).sort_index()

fig = go.Figure(
    go.Scatter(
        x=num_orders_by_delay_duration.index,
        y=num_orders_by_delay_duration.values, mode='lines'
    )
)
fig.update_layout(
    title="Number of Orders Filled Per Delay Duration<br><sup>Most order fill "
        + "within 90 minutes</sup>",
    xaxis_title="Minutes Delayed",
    yaxis_title="Number of Orders Filled"
)
fig.show()
```

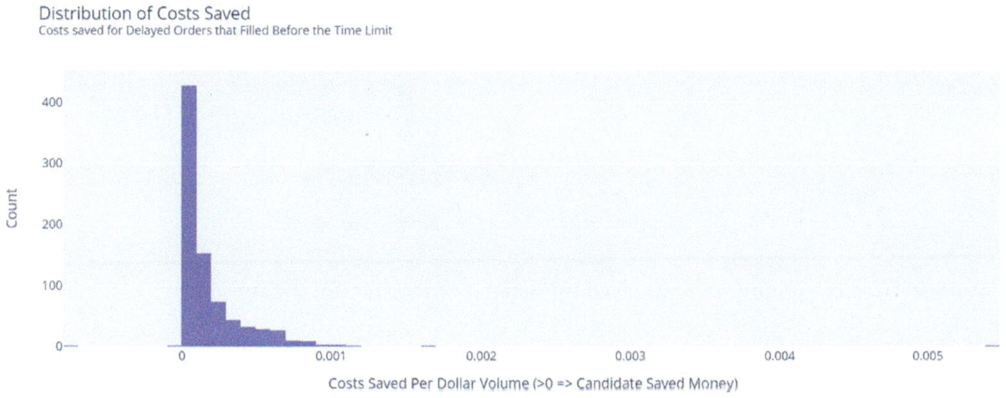

Figure 6.40 Distribution of costs saved for delayed orders that filled before the time limit.

We can see that by delaying the orders, we saved $36,260.20.

```
Number of orders: 815
Number of orders that lowered costs: 774 (42.36% of all orders)
Number of orders that did not change costs: 28 (1.53% of all orders)
Number of orders that raised costs: 13 (0.71% of all orders)
Total costs saved: $36260.2
```

Figure 6.41 shows how long the orders were delayed:

Step 4: Analyze the delayed orders that hit the time limit.
Let us also compare these orders' execution costs versus the execution costs of the benchmark (Figure 6.42):

```
display_order_results(
    "Hit the Time Limit", index_numbers_of_time_limited_orders
)
```

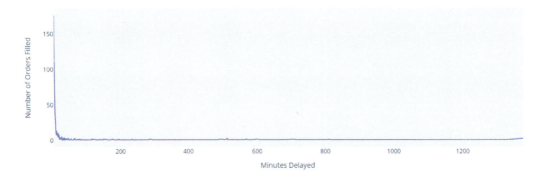

Figure 6.41 Distribution that shows the number of orders that filled at each delay time.

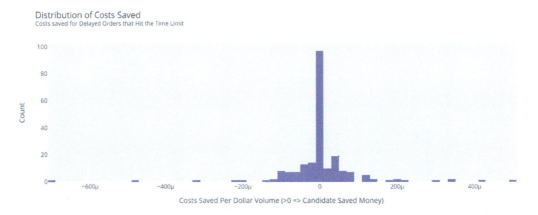

Figure 6.42 Distribution of costs saved for delayed orders that hit the time limit.

```
Number of orders: 214
Number of orders that lowered costs: 90 (4.93% of all orders)
Number of orders that did not change costs: 43 (2.35% of all orders)
Number of orders that raised costs: 81 (4.43% of all orders)
Total costs saved: $169.5
```

 # Example 13—PC A Statistical Arbitrage Mean Reversion

Predicting	Price
Technology	PCA
Asset Class	US equities
Difficulty	Hard
Type	Full strategy
Source Code	qnt.co/book-example13

Summary

This algorithm describes using principal component analysis and linear regression for statistical arbitrage. Statistical arbitrage strategies use mean-reversion models to exploit price differences between related securities.

Motivation

This algorithm leverages principal component analysis (PCA) and linear regression to implement an effective statistical arbitrage strategy.

The first three PCA's principal components represent the underlying factors driving the price movements of the securities, making them crucial for accurate modeling and prediction. The linear regression model then uses the principal components and historical prices to predict each security's price. By comparing the actual prices to these predictions, the algorithm identifies deviations, which are the regression model's residuals.

Mean-reversion, the central principle of this strategy, posits that prices will revert to their long-term average over time. Therefore, when a security's price deviates significantly from its expected value, as indicated by a large residual, it is likely to revert.

Based on these deviations, the algorithm assigns weights to each stock in the portfolio, positioning itself to profit when the prices move back toward their mean. This systematic approach ensures that the portfolio is dynamically adjusted to capitalize on temporary mispricings, enhancing the potential for profitable trades.

Model

Model Features	The first three PCA's principal components of standardized log returns.
Predicted Label	Standardized log return.
Model	Linear regression.

We chose linear regression since it is simple, easily interpretable, and computationally efficient. However, depending on the specific dataset, we should consider alternatives, such as ridge regression, LASSO regression, random forest regression, SVM regression, or NN, to enhance the model's performance.

Trading Universe

At the start of each month, we select the trading universe defined as the 100 most liquid stocks in the market with their price above 5 USD.

Portfolio Construction

Model Training Time	One minute after the market opens on the first trading day of a month.
Portfolio Rebalancing Time	After model training.
Portfolio Weights	We select only the assets with residuals significantly below the mean residual (their z-score is less than -1.5, corresponding to approximately 93.32nd percentile).
	The z-score of its residuals weighs each selected stock in the portfolio.

We choose the assets with their most recent z-scores of the residuals much smaller than -1.5, that is, the assets with residuals significantly below the mean. In other words, we select the assets with log returns much lower than the model predicted. Assuming mean reversion, this indicates the assets with the most likely appreciation.

Trading Logic

At the start of every month, 1 minute after the market has opened, we get the historical price data and run the principal component analysis to transform the trailing prices of all the stocks in the universe to the first three component factors. Then, we fit an ordinary least squares (OLS) model for each stock using the principal components, choose the stocks with statistically significant residuals, and adjust their portfolio weight (see qnt.co/book-stat-arb-us-equities).

Tearsheet

The results show the following:

- The Sharpe ratio is maximized when `num_components=3` and `lookback_days=126` (6 months).
- The Sharpe ratio is typically the lowest when using 3/4 months for `lookback_days`.
- All parameter combinations are profitable.
- See Figures 6.43 and 6.44.

Figure 6.43 Equity curve, performance plots, and custom plots for Example 13.

Chapter 6. Applied Machine Learning   231

Figure 6.44 Monthly returns, crisis events, and sensitivity tests for Example 13.

Parameter `num_components`:

- The minimum is 2 because it is the minimum number to perform multiple linear regression.
- The maximum is 6 because each consecutive component explains less of the variance in the data. The first three components already explain more than 90% of the variance, and each additional component explains less than the previous component.
- The step size is 1 because it is the smallest possible step size.

Parameter `lookback_days`:

- The minimum is 21 because it is 1 month of trading days.
- The maximum is 126 because it is 6 months of trading days.
- The step size is 21 because it is the smallest step possible.

Backtest parameters:

- `num_components`: 3
- `lookback_days`: 63
- `z_score_threshold`: 1.5
- `universe_size`: 100

Implementation Insights

The trading algorithm consists of three steps:

Step 1: Get the historical price data.

```python
tradeable_assets = [
    symbol
    for symbol in self._universe.selected
    if (self.securities[symbol].price and
        symbol in self.current_slice.quote_bars)

history = self.history(
    tradeable_assets, self._lookback, Resolution.DAILY,
    data_normalization_mode=DataNormalizationMode.SCALED_RAW
).close.unstack(level=0)
```

Notice the `data_normalization_mode` chosen; we require the historical pricing data to be adjusted for splits and dividends.

Step 2: Run PCA and select the assets and their weights according to their level of deviation of the residuals from the linear regression after PCA for each symbol.

```python
def _get_weights(self, history):
    # Get sample data for PCA (smooth it using np.log function).
    sample = np.log(history.dropna(axis=1))
    sample -= sample.mean()  # Center it column-wise

    # Fit the PCA model for sample data.
    model = PCA().fit(sample)

    # Get the first n_components factors.
    factors = np.dot(sample, model.components_.T)[:,:self._num_components]

    # Add 1's to fit the linear regression (intercept).
    factors = sm.add_constant(factors)

    # Train Ordinary Least Squares linear model for each stock.
    model_by_ticker = {
```

```
        ticker: sm.OLS(sample[ticker], factors).fit()
        for ticker in sample.columns
}

# Get the residuals from the linear regression after PCA for each stock.
resids = pd.DataFrame(
    {ticker: model.resid for ticker, model in model_by_ticker.items()}
)

# Get the Z scores by standarizing the given pandas dataframe.
# This is the residual of the most recent day.
zscores = ((resids - resids.mean()) / resids.std()).iloc[-1]

# Get the stocks far from their mean (for mean reversion).
selected = zscores[zscores < -self._z_score_threshold]

# Return the weights for each selected stock.
weights = selected * (1 / selected.abs().sum())
return weights.sort_values()
```

Step 3: Enter the position.
For each selected stock, if the standardized residual deviates from the zero, we enter the position oppositely, expecting mean reversion.

```
self.set_holdings(
    [
        PortfolioTarget(symbol, -weight)
        for symbol, weight in weights.items()
    ],
    True
)
```

Example 14—Temporal CNN Prediction

Predicting	Price direction
Technology	Convolutional neural networks (CNN)
Asset Class	US equities
Difficulty	Hard
Type	Full strategy
Source Code	qnt.co/book-example14

Summary

We apply a temporal CNN to predict the direction of future stock prices (up, down, stationary) based on trailing open/high/low/close/volume (OHLCV) stock data.

Motivation

Predicting whether stock prices will increase or decrease allows traders to make informed decisions on buying, selling, or holding securities. By entering and exiting positions at the correct times, they can maximize their returns on investment.

This trading algorithm employs a temporal CNN utilizing trailing OHLCV data to forecast whether stock prices will move up, down, or remain stationary.

Temporal CNNs have been chosen for the following reasons:

- Temporal patterns—designed to handle sequential time series data, allowing them to recognize patterns over different time frames.
- Feature extraction—CNNs automatically extract relevant significant features from the raw OHLCV data.
- Non-linear relationships—CNNs can model complex, non-linear relationships in stock price movements.
- Robustness to noise—CNNs filter out noise from the data by focusing only on significant patterns.

CNN provides superior performance for this use case to other models:

- Linear regression would not be suitable due to the non-linear relationships in the stock price data.
- Decision trees or random forests frequently overfit the data and cannot capture temporal patterns.
- Support vector machines can handle non-linear relationships and classification well but provide no natural support for sequential data.

Model

Model Features	For each stock, we use five factors: • Open • High • Low • Close • Volume
Predicted Label	Up/down/stationary
Model	Temporal CNN

We build a temporal CNN to model the price movements of a single stock:

- Temporal CNNs are called temporal since they operate on data that varies over time ("temporal").
- Temporal CNNs are called convolutional since they implement convolutional layers to extract features.

For each security, as inputs, we use five factors:

```
factor_names = ['open', 'high', 'low', 'close', 'volume']
```

We model three price moment labels as integers:

```
class Direction:
    UP = 0
    DOWN = 1
    STATIONARY = 2
```

Chapter 6. Applied Machine Learning

We chose the Keras deep learning library for this model.

Input Layer

The input layer shall accept the 15 days of history for each of the factors OHLCV, meaning a shape of the 15 * 5.

```
inputs = Input(shape=(15, 5))
```

We then feed the input layer into the convolutional layer used to extract the features; we split the layer into three temporal regions based on time: long-term, mid-term, and short-term.

```
long_term = Lambda(
    lambda x: tf.split(x, num_or_size_splits=3, axis=1)[0]
)(feature_extraction)
mid_term = Lambda(
    lambda x: tf.split(x, num_or_size_splits=3, axis=1)[1]
)(feature_extraction)
short_term = Lambda(
    lambda x: tf.split(x, num_or_size_splits=3, axis=1)[2]
)(feature_extraction)

long_term_conv = Conv1D(1, 1, activation='relu')(long_term)
mid_term_conv = Conv1D(1, 1, activation='relu')(mid_term)
short_term_conv = Conv1D(1, 1, activation='relu')(short_term)
```

Next, we combine these three layers and flatten them as we work with 2D matrices.

```
# Combine the three layers back into one.
combined = Concatenate(axis=1)(
    [long_term_conv, mid_term_conv, short_term_conv]
)
flattened = Flatten()(combined)
```

Finally, we define the output layer as having three outputs: up, stationary, and down.

```
outputs = Dense(3, activation='softmax')(flattened)
```

The entire model can be depicted as shown in Figure 6.45.

```
def _create_model(self):
    """Creates the neural network model."""
    inputs = Input(shape=(self._n_tsteps, len(factor_names)))

    # Extract features using a Convolutional layers ("CNN").
    feature_extraction = Conv1D(30, 4, activation='relu')(inputs)

    # Split layer into three regions based on time, ("Temporal").
    long_term = Lambda(
        lambda x: tf.split(x, num_or_size_splits=3, axis=1)[0]
    )(feature_extraction)
    mid_term = Lambda(
        lambda x: tf.split(x, num_or_size_splits=3, axis=1)[1]
```

```python
)(feature_extraction)
short_term = Lambda(
    lambda x: tf.split(x, num_or_size_splits=3, axis=1)[2]
)(feature_extraction)

long_term_conv = Conv1D(1, 1, activation='relu')(long_term)
mid_term_conv = Conv1D(1, 1, activation='relu')(mid_term)
short_term_conv = Conv1D(1, 1, activation='relu')(short_term)

# Combine the three layers back into one.
combined = Concatenate(axis=1)(
    [long_term_conv, mid_term_conv, short_term_conv]
)

# Flattening is required since our input is a 2D matrix.
flattened = Flatten()(combined)

# 1 output neuron for each class (Up, Stationary, Down).
# See the Direction class.
outputs = Dense(3, activation='softmax')(flattened)

# Specify the input and output layers of the model.
self._cnn = Model(inputs=inputs, outputs=outputs)

# Compile the model.
self._cnn.compile(
    optimizer='adam',
    loss=CategoricalCrossentropy(from_logits=True)
)
```

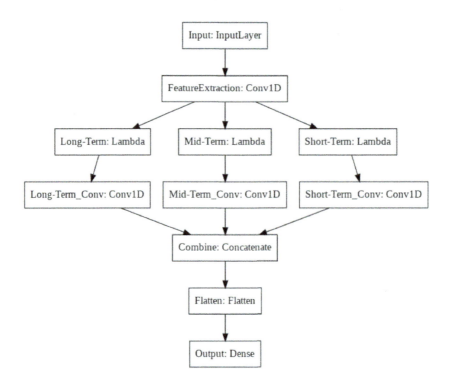

Figure 6.45 Architecture of the temporal CNN model.

Notice we are using the `CategoricalCrossentropy` function designed for multi-class classification problems with one-hot encoded target labels. (We will use the `utils.to_categorical` function for this.)

Trading Universe

At the start of each week, we choose the three components of the QQQ ETF with the most significant weight.

Portfolio Construction

Model Training Time	On the first trading day of each week at 9 am.
Portfolio Rebalancing Time	On the first trading day of each week, 2 minutes after the market opens.
Portfolio Weights	The weights are set by assigning each security a value based on the predicted direction (up or down) and the confidence level of the prediction, adjusting for overall portfolio balance to ensure the total weight absolute sum is lower than or equal to 1.

Trading Logic

We trade at the start of each week 2 minutes after the market opens.

```python
def initialize(self):
    #...

    self.schedule.on(
        date_rule, self.time_rules.after_market_open(etf, 2), self._trade
    )

def _trade(self):
    # Get predictions for all the assets.
    weight_by_symbol = {}
    for symbol in self._universe.selected:
        security = self.securities[symbol]
        symbol_df = security.history.tail(15)
        prediction, confidence = security.cnn.predict(symbol_df)
        if (prediction != Direction.STATIONARY and
            not math.isnan(confidence) and
            confidence > .55):
            factor = (-1 if prediction == Direction.DOWN else 1)
            weight_by_symbol[security.symbol] = factor * confidence
        self.plot("Confidence", str(security.symbol.id), confidence)

    # Calculate portfolio weights and rebalance.
    weight_sum = sum([abs(x) for x in weight_by_symbol.values()])
    weight_factor = 1 if weight_sum <= 1 else 1 / weight_sum
    portfolio_targets = [
        PortfolioTarget(symbol, weight * weight_factor)
        for symbol, weight in weight_by_symbol.items()
    ]
    self.set_holdings(portfolio_targets, True)
```

The following occurs for each selected security:

- The `trade` method retrieves the OHLCV stock data for the last 15 trading days.
- Then, it calls our model's prediction method.
- If the predicted direction is not `STATIONARY` and has a confidence more significant than 55%, we assign each security a weight of `confidence` for the predicted `UP` direction and `-confidence` for the predicted `DOWN` prediction.
- Finally, we normalize the target weights of each selected security; the weighting ensures that the target weights are proportional to the confidence measure and that they have an absolute sum of 1.

In addition, this trading strategy provides an example of handling of stock splits.

```
def on_splits(self, splits):
    for symbol, split in splits.items():
        if split.type == SplitType.SPLIT_OCCURRED:
            self._initialize_security(self.securities[symbol])
```

Tearsheet

The results show the following:

- The Sharpe ratio typically increases as we increase the number of training samples.
- Most parameter combinations are unprofitable.
- See Figures 6.46 and 6.47.

  Parameter `training_samples`:

- The minimum is 300 because it is slightly longer than the number of trading days per year.
- The maximum is 700 because it is large but not too large to cause the model training to be too slow.
- The step size is 100 because it generates excellent round numbers.

  Parameter `universe_size`:

- The minimum is 2 because we want the algorithm to be always invested. If only one asset and the model predicts a stationary direction, the algorithm will be uninvested for some rebalances.
- The maximum is 10 because the algorithm would take longer than an hour to backtest if we use more than 10.
- The step size is 2 because it gives us five different values of `universe_size` between 2 and 10.

Chapter 6. Applied Machine Learning

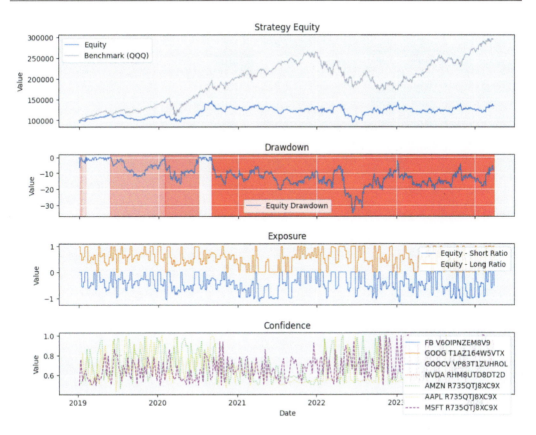

Figure 6.46 Equity curve, performance plots, and custom plots for Example 14.

Backtest parameters:

- `training_samples`: 500.
- `universe_size`: 3.

Implementation Insights

We call the `_create_model()` method in the constructor of the model class.

For the model training, we need to encode the time series data into the format accepted by the model:

- We construct the labels to be predicted.
  - We calculate a 5-day rolling average price—we chose five 5-day rolling averages since they are more stable than actual prices.
  - We calculate the return of the rolling average close prices and shift the time series backward as we build a prediction model that predicts the move UP/DOWN in the future based upon older data.
  - Then, if they are above/below the stationarity threshold, we label them as UP/DOWN.

240 HANDS-ON AI TRADING WITH PYTHON, QUANTCONNECT, AND AWS

Figure 6.47 Monthly returns, crisis events, and sensitivity tests for Example 14.

- We create an input 2D matrix of the actual market data, rescale it using the `StandardScaler` to ensure convergence of the training algorithm, and return the result.

```
def _prepare_data(
      self, data, rolling_avg_window_size=5, stationary_threshold=.0001):
   df = data[factor_names]
   shift = -(rolling_avg_window_size - 1)

   def label_data(row):
      if row['close_avg_change_pct'] > stationary_threshold:
```

```python
        return Direction.UP
    elif row['close_avg_change_pct'] < -stationary_threshold:
        return Direction.DOWN
    else:
        return Direction.STATIONARY

df['close_avg'] = df['close'].rolling(
    window=rolling_avg_window_size
).mean().shift(shift)
df['close_avg_change_pct'] = \
    (df['close_avg'] - df['close']) / df['close']

df['movement_labels'] = df.apply(label_data, axis=1)

data = []
labels = []
for i in range(len(df)-self._n_tsteps+1+shift):
    label = df['movement_labels'].iloc[i + self._n_tsteps - 1]
    data.append(df[factor_names].iloc[i:i + self._n_tsteps].values)
    labels.append(label)
data = np.array(data)

dim1, dim2, dim3 = data.shape
data = data.reshape(dim1 * dim2, dim3)

data = self._scaler.fit_transform(data)

data = data.reshape(dim1, dim2, dim3)

return data, utils.to_categorical(labels, num_classes=3)
```

Notice that sci-kit's `StandardScaler` works only in 2D, so we must convert the data into 2D temporarily and then back:

```
dim1, dim2, dim3 = data.shape
data = data.reshape(dim1 * dim2, dim3)
data = self._scaler.fit_transform(data)
data = data.reshape(dim1, dim2, dim3)
```

The training code then is simply the preparation of the data and fitting the prepared data into the model created in the constructor of the class.

```python
def train(self, data):
    data, labels = self._prepare_data(data)
    self._cnn.fit(data, labels, epochs=20)
```

We chose 20 epochs for demonstration purposes.

Finally, the prediction code is straightforward:

- We standardize the market data by filling up missing data forward (`ffill`)—meaning we propagate the last known value forward.
- We then use the Keras' `prediction` method to return the predicted label and confidence.

```python
def predict(self, input_data):
    input_data = self._scaler.transform(
        input_data.fillna(method='ffill').values
    )
    prediction = self._cnn.predict(input_data[np.newaxis, :])[0]
    direction = np.argmax(prediction)
    confidence = prediction[direction]
    return direction, confidence
```

 ## Example 15—Gaussian Classifier for Direction Prediction

Predicting	Returns direction
Technology	Gaussian Naive Bayes classifier
Asset Class	US equities
Difficulty	Hard
Type	Full strategy
Source Code	qnt.co/book-example15

Summary

We apply Gaussian Naive Bayes (GNB) classifiers to predict the daily returns of the technology stocks class (positive, negative, or flat).

Motivation

This example solves the same problem as the previous example. However, instead of using CNNs, this trading algorithm employs GNB classifiers to forecast the daily returns of technology stocks, categorizing them as positive, negative, or flat.

GNB is particularly well-suited for this task due to its simplicity, efficiency, and effectiveness in handling high-dimensional data.

Unlike CNN, GNB models are simple, computationally efficient, and highly interpretable due to the GNB's assumption that the features are typically distributed and independent. In addition, GNB relies on manual feature engineering and preprocessing, while CNNs automatically extract the relevant features from raw data.

The choice between GNB and CNN depends on the trading strategy's specific requirements, including the data's nature and whether it meets GNB's assumptions, computational resources, and the importance of interpretability versus predictive power.

Model

Model Features	Four daily returns (open to close).
Predicted Label	The signs ($-1, 0, 1$) of the return in 22 *trading* days into the future (we intend to hold each stock for 30 *calendar* days).
Model	GNB classifier.

The model has been inspired by this paper (see qnt.co/book-stock-market-index-direction).

Trading Universe

At the beginning of each week, we choose the 10 largest stocks from the technology sector as defined by Morningstar.

Portfolio Construction

Model Training Time	On the first trading day of each week at 9 am.
Portfolio Rebalancing Time	On the first trading day of each week, 2 minutes after the market opens.
Portfolio Weights	Equally weighted portfolio of all stocks the model identifies as expecting positive return (the sign of +1).

Tearsheet

The results show the following:

- The Sharpe ratio is most significant with a small universe size (5). It is probably because the number of independent variables in the ML model grows as the universe grows, potentially overwhelming the model with noise and not allowing it to learn.
- All parameter combinations are profitable.
- See Figures 6.48 and 6.49.

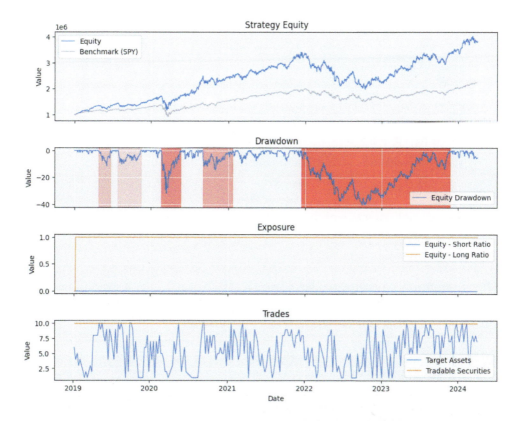

Figure 6.48 Equity curve, performance plots, and custom plots for Example 15.

Figure 6.49 Monthly returns, crisis events, and sensitivity tests for Example 15.

Parameter `days_per_sample`:

- The minimum is 2 because we have two factors for each asset instead of just one.
- The maximum is 8 because anything more significant may cause the number of factors to be so large that it floods the model with noise.
- The step size is 1 because it is the smallest possible step size.

Parameter `universe_size`:

- The minimum is 5 because anything smaller may cause the algorithm to resort to just cash during one of the rebalances.

Chapter 6. Applied Machine Learning   245

- The maximum is 25 because including too many assets in the universe will cause the number of independent variables in the ML model to grow very large.
- The step size is 5 because it leads to excellent round numbers between the minimum and maximum.

Backtest parameters:

- `days_per_sample`: 4
- `samples`: 100
- `universe_size`: 10

Implementation Insights

This algorithm illustrates the difference between its backtesting and live modes. For the live mode, the algorithm's field `live_mode` is `True`, and we utilize a pickle file to store the trained models; we load them in the `initialize()` method, update them in the `_train` method, and then save them in the `on_end_of_algorithm` method:

```python
def initialize(self):
    # ...
    if self.live_mode:
        self._models_by_symbol = {}
        self._key = 'gnb_models.pkl'
        if self.object_store.contains_key(self._key):
            self._models_by_symbol = pickle.loads(
                self.object_store.read_bytes(self._key)
            )
def _train(self):
    # ...
    for security in self._tradable_securities:
        symbol = security.symbol
        security.model = GaussianNB().fit(
            features.loc[idx], labels_by_symbol[symbol].loc[idx]
        )
        # If we're live trading, save the trained model in case the
        # algorithm is stopped and re-deployed before the
        # `_trade` method runs.
        if self.live_mode:
            key = str(symbol.id)
            self._models_by_symbol[key] = pickle.dumps(security.model)
def on_end_of_algorithm(self):
    if self.live_mode:
        self.object_store.save_bytes(
            self._key, pickle.dumps(self._models_by_symbol)
        )
```

In this example, we utilize customized features—open to close intraday return and the sign of the change of open price from one day to the next day—and for these, we need to consolidate the intraday price data ourselves.

Anytime we add new security to the trading universe, we set up for the security a daily consolidator of the market data and warm up the security's features (`security.features_by_day`) and labels history data structure (`security.labels_by_day`) used to train the model.

```python
def on_securities_changed(self, changes):
    for security in changes.added_securities:
        security.model = None
        self._set_up_consolidator(security)
        self._warm_up(security)

    for security in changes.removed_securities:
        self.subscription_manager.remove_consolidator(
            security.symbol, security.consolidator
        )
```

The consolidator's code is called on each market data record received and adjusts the security's data structure used for model training.

```python
def _set_up_consolidator(self, security):
    security.consolidator = self.consolidate(
        security.symbol, Resolution.DAILY, self._consolidation_handler
    )

def _consolidation_handler(self, bar):
    security = self.securities[bar.symbol]
    time = bar.end_time
    open_ = bar.open
    close = bar.close

    # Update the features.
    open_close_return = (close - open_) / open_
    if not self._update_features(security, time, open_close_return):
        return

    # Update the labels.
    open_days = security.previous_opens[
        (security.previous_opens.index <=
        time - timedelta(self._holding_period))
    ]
    if len(open_days) == 0:
        return
    open_day = open_days.index[-1]
    previous_open = security.previous_opens[open_day]
    open_open_return = (open_ - previous_open) / previous_open
    security.labels_by_day[open_day] = np.sign(open_open_return)
    security.labels_by_day = security.labels_by_day[-self._samples:]

    security.previous_opens.loc[time] = open_
    security.previous_opens = security.previous_opens[
        -self._holding_period:
    ]

def _update_features(self, security, day, open_close_return):
    """
    Updates the training data features.
```

```
Inputs
   - day
   Timestamp of when we're aware of the open_close_return
   - open_close_return
   Open to close intraday return

Returns T/F, showing if the features are in place to start
updating the training labels.
"""
security.roc_window = np.append(
    open_close_return, security.roc_window
)[:self._days_per_sample]

if len(security.roc_window) < self._days_per_sample:
    return False

security.features_by_day.loc[day] = security.roc_window
security.features_by_day = security.features_by_day[
    -(self._samples + self._holding_period + 2):
]
return True
```

The warm-up method sets up the critical data structures for training the model (`labels_by_day`, `features_by_day`) and helping data structures (`roc_window`, `previous_opens`). It prepopulates them with daily historical data, and then leaves them to be updated in real time using the consolidator explained earlier.

```
def _warm_up(self, security):
    security.roc_window = np.array([])
    security.previous_opens = pd.Series()
    security.labels_by_day = pd.Series()
    security.features_by_day = pd.DataFrame(
        {
            f'{security.symbol.id}_(t-{i})' : []
            for i in range(1, self._days_per_sample + 1)
        }
    )

    # Get historical prices.
    history = self.history(
        security.symbol, self._lookback, Resolution.DAILY,
        data_normalization_mode=DataNormalizationMode.SCALED_RAW
    )
    if history.empty or 'close' not in history:
        self.log(f"Not enough history for {security.symbol} yet")
        return

    # Calculate the features.
    history = history.loc[security.symbol]
    history['open_close_return'] = (
        (history.close - history.open) / history.open
    )

    # Calculate the labels.
    start = history.shift(-1).open
    end = history.shift(-22).open  # Trading days instead of calendar days.
    history['future_return'] = (end - start) / start
```

```
    for day, row in history.iterrows():
        security.previous_opens[day] = row.open

        # Update the features.
        if not self._update_features(security, day, row.open_close_return):
            continue

        # Update the labels.
        if not pd.isnull(row.future_return):
            security.labels_by_day[day] = np.sign(row.future_return)
            security.labels_by_day = security.labels_by_day[
                -self._samples:
            ]
    security.previous_opens = security.previous_opens[
        -self._holding_period:
    ]
```

Whenever there is a stock split, we must reinitiate the datasets:

```
def on_splits(self, splits):
    for symbol, split in splits.items():
        if split.type != SplitType.SPLIT_OCCURRED:
            continue
        security = self.securities[symbol]
        # Reset the consolidator and warm-up the factors
        # and labels.
        self.subscription_manager.remove_consolidator(
            symbol, security.consolidator
        )
        self._set_up_consolidator(security)
        self._warm_up(security)
```

We train the model every trading day at 9 am, and it is run if we have enough data points (`_is_ready` method).

```
def initialize(self):
    # …

    schedule_symbol = Symbol.create("SPY", SecurityType.EQUITY, Market.USA)
    date_rule = self.date_rules.week_start(schedule_symbol)
    self.train(date_rule, self.time_rules.at(9, 0), self._train)

def _is_ready(self, security):
    return (
        security.features_by_day.shape[0] ==
        self._samples + self._holding_period + 2
    )

def _train(self):
    """
    Trains the Gaussian Naive Bayes classifier model.
    """
    features = pd.DataFrame()
    labels_by_symbol = {}

    self._tradable_securities = []
    for symbol in self._universe.selected:
```

```python
        security = self.securities[symbol]
        if self._is_ready(security):
            self._tradable_securities.append(security)
            features = pd.concat(
                [features, security.features_by_day],
                axis=1
            )
            labels_by_symbol[symbol] = security.labels_by_day

# The first and last row can have NaNs because this `_train`
# method fires when the universe changes, which is before the
# consolidated bars close. Let's remove them.
features.dropna(inplace=True)

# Find the intersection of the indices for the features and
# labels.
idx = set([t for t in features.index])
for i, (symbol, labels) in enumerate(labels_by_symbol.items()):
    a = set([t for t in labels.index])
    idx &= a
idx = sorted(list(idx))

for security in self._tradable_securities:
    symbol = security.symbol
    security.model = GaussianNB().fit(
        features.loc[idx], labels_by_symbol[symbol].loc[idx]
    )
    # If we're live trading, save the trained model in case the
    # algorithm is stopped and re-deployed before the
    # `_trade` method runs.
    if self.live_mode:
        key = str(symbol.id)
        self._models_by_symbol[key] = pickle.dumps(security.model)
```

Trading

We trade on every trading day 2 minutes after the market opens.

```python
def initialize(self):
    # …
    schedule_symbol = Symbol.create("SPY", SecurityType.EQUITY, Market.USA)
    date_rule = self.date_rules.week_start(schedule_symbol)

    self.schedule.on(
        date_rule,
        self.time_rules.after_market_open(schedule_symbol, 2),
        self._trade
    )

def _trade(self):
    # Get the features.
    features = [[]]
    for security in self._tradable_securities:
        features[0].extend(security.features_by_day.iloc[-1].values)

    # Select the assets that the model predicts will have
    # positive returns.
    long_symbols = []
    for security in self._tradable_securities:
```

```
        # If the live algorithm hasn't called _train yet, load
        # the trained model from the Object Store.
        key = str(security.symbol.id)
        if (self.live_mode and
            not hasattr(security, 'model') and
            key in self._models_by_symbol):
            security.model = pickle.loads(self._models_by_symbol[key])
        # If the model predicts 1, save this asset to long.
        if security.model.predict(features) == 1:
            long_symbols.append(security.symbol)
if len(long_symbols) == 0:
    return
# Rebalance the portfolio.
weight = 1 / len(long_symbols)
self.set_holdings(
    [PortfolioTarget(symbol, weight) for symbol in long_symbols],
    True
)
```

Example 16—LLM Summarization of Tiingo News Articles

Predicting	News sentiment
Technology	Large language model (LLM)
Asset Class	US equities
Difficulty	Medium hard
Type	Research notebook
Source Code	qnt.co/book-example16

Summary

We build a rolling sentiment OpenAI GPT4 model on alternative news data linked to US tech companies and trade upon the sentiment trend.

Motivation

Traders seek out nontraditional data sources to obtain a competitive advantage by uncovering insights extending past conventional financial indicators.

Sentiment analysis applied to news data captures the market's emotional reaction to events and announcements. It offers early detection of upcoming market trends, including potential downturns, and helps quantify investors' psychological impact of the news.

Model

Model Features	News article
Predicted Label	A score from −10 to 10, where:
	• −10 represents extremely negative sentiment.
	• 0 represents neutral sentiment.
	• 10 represents extremely positive sentiment.
Model	gpt−4

Trading Universe

We are interested in trading only TSLA stock, either holding or shorting it.

Portfolio Construction

Model Training Time	On-demand recalculating in the research notebook.
Portfolio Rebalancing Time	Hourly.
Portfolio Weights	• 100% of the portfolio held in a long TSLA position if the sentiment score is increasing and we are not yet holding a long TSLA position. • 100% of the portfolio held in a short position if the sentiment is negative, is decreasing, and we are not yet short TSLA.

Trading Logic

The research notebook generates a CSV file for each date with three columns:

- `hour` (the index)—each row corresponds to a specific hour.
- `sentiment`—the column holds the aggregated sentiment score for all news articles reviewed during that hour. The sentiment score ranges from -10 (extremely negative) to $+10$ (extremely positive), with 0 indicating neutral sentiment.
- `volume`—the number of news articles reviewed during that hour.

The trading algorithm monitors the corresponding CSV file in the object store, and on each update, after the market opens, it checks the following:

- <u>If sentiment is flat/increasing and not already long, long.</u> We intentionally do not check if the sentiment is non-negative since, in case it is negative, given the sentiment trend, we expect the sentiment to reverse and then benefit from the upward price trend.
- <u>If the sentiment is negative, decreasing, and not already short, short.</u>

```
if self._roc.current.value >= 0 and not self._tsla.holdings.is_long:
    self.set_holdings(self._tsla.symbol, 1)
elif (sentiment < 0 and
    self._roc.current.value < 0 and
    not self._tsla.holdings.is_short):
    self.set_holdings(self._tsla.symbol, -1)
```

Tearsheet

This strategy outperforms the benchmark TSLA (buy and hold TSLA) in terms of risk-adjusted returns:

- The algorithm achieves a 1.695 Sharpe ratio.
- In contrast, the benchmark (buy and hold TSLA) achieves a -0.06 Sharpe ratio.
- See Figure 6.51.

252 HANDS-ON AI TRADING WITH PYTHON, QUANTCONNECT, AND AWS

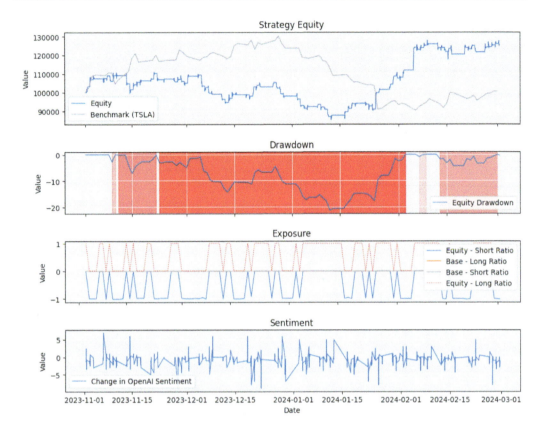

Figure 6.50 Equity curve, performance plots, and custom plots for Example 16.

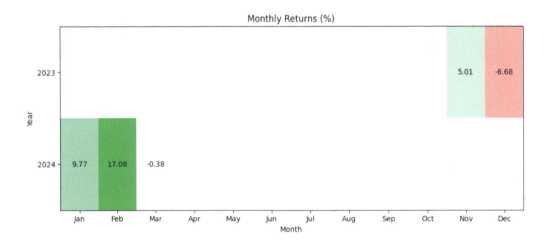

Figure 6.51 Monthly returns for Example 16.

Implementation Insights

We start in the **Research Environment (research.ipynb)** to gather the required data, train the model, and store its results in QuantConnect's object store.

Step 1: Subscribe to the news articles for the asset of interest.
We subscribe to the TiingoNews data of TSLA, i.e., news articles that feature TSLA, for the backtesting time window from November 1, 2023, to March 1, 2024.

```
qb = QuantBook()
symbol = qb.add_equity("TSLA").symbol

dataset_symbols = qb.add_data(TiingoNews, symbol).symbol

news_articles = qb.history[TiingoNews](
    dataset_symbols, datetime(2023, 11, 1), datetime(2024, 3, 1),
    Resolution.DAILY
)
```

Step 2: Group the articles by date, remove duplicate articles.
We aim to produce sentiment scores for each hour, and we start by grouping first by date, removing duplicate articles, and storing the results in the dictionary `deduplicated_articles_by_date`.

Step 3: Get hourly sentiment values from OpenAI.
We group the articles by hour for these reasons:
1. Hourly sensitivity scores are more stable.
2. There are fewer calls to OpenAI API.

We pass all the articles within each hour to ChatGPT and ask it to provide an hourly sentiment score with a prompt

```
Article <i> title: <title>
Article <i> description: <Description>
   . . .
Review the news titles and descriptions above and then create an aggregated
sentiment score which represents the emotional positivity towards TSLA after
seeing all of the news articles. -10 represents extreme negative sentiment,
+10 represents extreme positive sentiment, and 0 represents neutral
sentiment. Reply ONLY with the numerical value in JSON format. For example,
`{ "sentiment-score": 0 }`
```

Then, we save the scores into a CSV file in QuantConnect's object store:

```
from openai import OpenAI
client = OpenAI(api_key="<your_api_key>")

# Iterate through each day.
For date, articles in deduplicated_articles_by_date.items():
print(date)
# Group this day's articles into hourly buckets.
Articles_by_hour = {}
for article in articles:
        hour = article.end_time.hour
```

```
            if hour not in articles_by_hour:
                articles_by_hour[hour] = []
            articles_by_hour[hour].append(article)

# Create a series to hold the sentiment scores for the hours in this
# day.
Sentiment_by_hour = pd.DataFrame(dtype=float)
for hour, articles in articles_by_hour.items():
        # Create a prompt for OpenAI.
        Prompt = ""
        for I, article in enumerate(articles):
            prompt += (
                f"Article {i+1} title: {article.title}\n"
                + f"Article {i+1} description: {article.description}\n\n"
            )
        prompt += (
            "Review the news titles and descriptions above and then create an "
            + "aggregated sentiment score which represents the emotional "
            + "positivity towards TSLA after seeing all of the news articles. "
            + "-10 represents extreme negative sentiment, +10 represents "
            + "extreme positive sentiment, and 0 represents neutral sentiment."
            + " Reply ONLY with the numerical value in JSON format. For "
            + 'example, `{ "sentiment-score": 0 }`'
        )

        # Call the OpenAI API to get the sentiment.
        chat_completion = client.chat.completions.create(
            messages=[{"role": "user", "content": prompt}],
            model="gpt-4"
        )
        sentiment = json.loads(
            chat_completion.choices[0].message.content
        )['sentiment-score']

        # Save the factors.
        sentiment_by_hour.loc[hour, 'sentiment'] = sentiment
        sentiment_by_hour.loc[hour, 'volume'] = len(articles)

    # Save the dataset file to the Object Store.
    file_path = qb.object_store.get_file_path(
        f"tiingo-{date.strftime('%Y-%m-%d')}.csv"
    )
    sentiment_by_hour.to_csv(file_path)
```

We are ready to process the generated CSV files in QuantConnect's backtesting environment.

Step 4: Apply the trained results in a backtesting algorithm.

Now, we transition to the backtesting environment to build an algorithm that uses the sentiment values from ChatGPT. In the main.py file, we define a custom data class that reads the CSV data from the Object Store and injects it into the algorithm.

```
class TiingoNewsSentiment(PythonData):

    def get_source(self, config, date, is_live):
        return SubscriptionDataSource(
            f"tiingo-{date.strftime('%Y-%m-%d')}.csv",
```

```
            SubscriptionTransportMedium.OBJECT_STORE,
            FileFormat.CSV
        )

    def reader(self, config, line, date, is_live):
        # Skip the header line.
        if line[0] == ",":
            return None

        # Parse the CSV line into a list.
        data = line.split(',')

        # Construct the new sentiment data point.
        t = TiingoNewsSentiment()
        t.symbol = config.symbol
        t.time = date.replace(hour=int(data[0]), minute=0, second=0)
        t.end_time = t.time + timedelta(hours=1)
        t.value = float(data[1])
        t["sentiment"] = t.value
        t["volume"] = float(data[2])

        return t
```

We apply a `RateOfChange` indicator to the data set to observe the direction of sentiment changes.

```
    def initialize(self):
        self.set_start_date(2023, 11, 1)
        self.set_end_date(2024, 3, 1)
        self.set_cash(100_000)
        self._tsla = self.add_equity("TSLA")
        self._dataset_symbol = self.add_data(
            TiingoNewsSentiment, "TiingoNewsSentiment", Resolution.HOUR
        ).symbol
        self._roc = self.roc(self._dataset_symbol, 2)

        self.set_benchmark(self._tsla.symbol)
```

The trading logic is as follows:

- If sentiment is flat/increasing and we are not already long, we are long.
- If sentiment is negative and is decreasing and we are not already short, we are short.

```
def on_data(self, data):
    # Get the current sentiment.
    if self._dataset_symbol not in data:
        return
    sentiment = data[self._dataset_symbol].value

    # If the market isn't open right now, do nothing.
    if not self.is_market_open(self._tsla.symbol):
        return

    if self._roc.current.value >= 0 and not self._tsla.holdings.is_long:
        self.set_holdings(self._tsla.symbol, 1)
    elif (sentiment < 0 and
```

```
        self._roc.current.value < 0 and
    not self._tsla.holdings.is_short):
        self.set_holdings(self._tsla.symbol, -1)
```

 ## Example 17—Head Shoulders Pattern Matching with CNN

Predicting	Pattern matching
Technology	CNN
Asset Class	Forex
Difficulty	Hard
Type	Research notebook
Source Code	qnt.co/book-example17

Summary

This example introduces a one-dimensional CNN to detect a technical head-and-shoulder (H&S) trading pattern. We construct a synthetic training set, and then train a CNN to detect similar H&S patterns in a forex market.

Motivation

Technical analysis utilizes historical price and volume data to forecast future market movements. It reflects market psychology and the collective behavior of participants, providing rule-based criteria for trading decisions.

The head and shoulders pattern is a technical analysis chart formation used to predict upcoming bullish-to-bearish trend reversals. It is characterized by its distinctive shape, a head surrounded by two shoulders:

- Left shoulder—prices rise to a peak and then subsequently decline.
- Head—after forming the left shoulder, prices peak and then decline again.
- Right shoulder—prices rise but less than in the head and then fall back.
- The neckline acts as a level of support and is drawn, connecting the low points of the left and right shoulders.

The usual way to trade this pattern is to short the asset when the price closes below the neckline after the right shoulder, expecting the price to rise. See Figure 6.52.

Detecting and acting upon trading patterns can significantly enhance trading performance and profitability. This trading algorithm employs a one-dimensional CNN to detect the head and shoulders pattern. We chose CNNs since they excel at identifying complex patterns within data, automatically learning, extracting relevant features from raw price data, and filtering out noise.

By focusing on the forex market, where price movements are continuous and highly responsive to global events, this algorithm aims to capitalize on the pattern's frequent occurrence and high reliability.

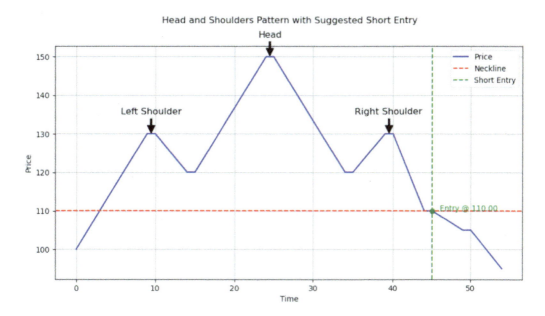

Figure 6.52 Head and shoulder pattern and the typical entry timing.

Model

Model Features	25 close pricing data points.
Predicted Label	The probability of each class:
	• class 0 = no pattern.
	• class 1 = the pattern is present.
Model	One-dimensional CNN.

The architecture of the sequential (we add layers one by one in sequence) CNN is as follows:

- Input layer accepts 25 data points (features), with each feature being treated as a unique channel.
- A one-dimensional convolutional layer (32 filters or kernels with a kernel size of 5) produces tensors of new features by sliding the filters over the filter. The relu activation feature helps the network learn complex, non-linear patterns in the data.
- Max pooling layer—we reduce the dimension of the outputs from the convolutional layer to 2 and take the max of each pool to make the recognition invariant to scale and reduce the computational complexity.
- Flatten layer that then connects to the output layer.
- The output layer uses the sigmoid activation function, the standard for binary classification problems.

We implement in Keras:

```
Model = Sequential()
model.add(Input(shape=(X_train.shape[1], 1)))
model.add(Conv1D(filters=32, kernel_size=5, activation='relu'))
```

```
model.add(MaxPooling1D(pool_size=2))
model.add(Flatten())
model.add(Dense(1, activation='sigmoid'))
```

Trading Universe

We are interested only in the USD/CAD currency pair.

Portfolio Construction

Model Training Time	We train the model only once on synthetic data in the research notebook.
Portfolio Rebalancing Time	When each monitored closing price arrived.
Portfolio Weights	We take the historical price path over 25–100 days (in steps of 10) and down-sample each one to 25 data points, then input it into the CNN. For each sample that the model is >=50% confident contains the heads and shoulder pattern, we short 10,000 USD of the forex pair.

Trading Logic

For backtesting, we gather daily closing prices of the USD/CAD pair from January 1, 2019, to January 1, 2024.

The trading algorithm responds to the new USD/CAD daily closing prices:

- At each point, we slice the history into various lookback window sizes; the minimum window size is 25 closing prices (the input size for the CNN), and the maximum is 100 closing prices. We increase the window size in step 10.

  While the trained CNN model accepts 25 data points as input, the H&S pattern can occur over a more extended period, and thus, we need to down-sample the input data to 25 data points while retaining the general shape of the price path. An analogy of the down-sampling process would be reducing a 1920 × 1080 image to a 1280 × 720 image. The visual of the down-sampled image is almost identical to the original photo but has fewer data points.

  This down-sampling process is used to search for the pattern's presence over several lookback window sizes. Once we down-sample each lookback window's data points to 25, we standardize them and feed them into CNN to get a prediction.
- The output of the model is the probability of each class (class 0 = no pattern; class 1 = the pattern is present).
- For each lookback window, when the model returns a probability of 50% or higher for class 1, we short 10,000 USD and hold the position for 10 days.

The trading code:

```python
def initialize(self):
    self.set_start_date(2019, 1, 1)
    self.set_end_date(2024, 4, 1)
```

```python
        self.set_cash(100_000)
        self._security = self.add_forex("USDCAD", Resolution.DAILY)
        self._symbol = self._security.symbol

        self._max_size = self.get_parameter('max_size', 100)
        self._step_size = self.get_parameter('step_size', 10)
        self._confidence_threshold = self.get_parameter(
            'confidence_threshold', 0.5
        ) # 0.5 => 50%
        self._holding_period = timedelta(
            self.get_parameter('holding_period', 10)
        )

        self._model = load_model(
            self.object_store.get_file_path("head-and-shoulders-model.keras")
        )
        self._trailing_prices = pd.Series()
        self._liquidation_quantities = []

    def on_data(self, data):
        t = self.time
        price = data[self._symbol].close

        # Update the trailing window.
        self._trailing_prices.loc[t] = price
        self._trailing_prices = self._trailing_prices.iloc[-self._max_size:]

        # Calculate the order quantity.
        quantity = 0

        for size in range(self._min_size, self._max_size + 1, self._step_size):
            # Ensure there are enough trailing data points to fill this
            # window size.
            if len(self._trailing_prices) < size:
                continue

            window_trailing_prices = self._trailing_prices.iloc[-size:]
            # Downsample the trailing prices in this window to be 25
            # data points.
            low_res_window = downsample(window_trailing_prices.values)
            # Standardize the downsampled trailing prices.
            factors = np.array(
                (
                    (low_res_window - low_res_window.mean())
                    / low_res_window.std()
                )
            ).reshape(1, self._min_size, 1)
            # Get the probability of the technical trading pattern in
            # the downsampled and standardized window.
            prediction = self._model.predict(factors, verbose=0)[0][0]
            if prediction > self._confidence_threshold:
                self.log(
                    f"{t}: Pattern detected between "
                    + f"{window_trailing_prices.index[0]} and "
                    + f"{window_trailing_prices.index[-1]} with "
                    + f"{round(prediction * 100, 1)}% confidence."
                )

                quantity -= 10_000
```

```python
    if quantity:
        self._cad_before_sell = self.portfolio.cash_book['CAD'].amount
        # Place the entry order.
        self.market_order(self._symbol, quantity)
        # Schedule the exit order.
        t_exit = t + self._holding_period
            self.schedule.on(
                self.date_rules.on(t_exit.year, t_exit.month, t_exit.day),
                self.time_rules.at(t_exit.hour, t_exit.minute),
                self._liquidate_position
            )

def _liquidate_position(self):
    quantity = round(
        self._liquidation_quantities.pop(0) / self._security.ask_price
    )
    if quantity:
        self.market_order(self._symbol, quantity)

def on_order_event(self, order_event):
    # When the entry order fills, record the amount of CAD
    # traded so that we can liquidate the correct amount later.
    if (order_event.status == OrderStatus.FILLED and
        order_event.direction == OrderDirection.SELL):
        self._liquidation_quantities.append(
            self.portfolio.cash_book['CAD'].amount - self._cad_before_sell
        )
```

Tearsheet

The results show the following:

- The Sharpe ratio increases with the holding period.
- The Sharpe ratio decreases with the confidence threshold (probably since there are so few trades).
- All parameter combinations are profitable.
- See Figures 6.53 and 6.54.

    Parameter `confidence_threshold`:

- The minimum is 0.3 because going lower than that means <30% confidence; we found the pattern, which is low/unlikely.
- The maximum is 0.9 because there are already only a few trades.
- The step size is 0.1 because it leads to excellent round values.

    Parameter `holding_period`:

- The minimum is 2 because it is the shortest holding period with daily data.
- The maximum is 10 because of our experience.
- The step size is 1 because it is the smallest possible step size.

Chapter 6. Applied Machine Learning

Figure 6.53 Equity curve, performance plots, and custom plots for Example 17.

Backtest parameters:

- `max_size`: 100
- `step_size`: 10
- `confidence_threshold`: 0.8
- `holding_period`: 10

Implementation Insights

We trained the neural network in the research notebook.

Step 1: Create a synthetic input dataset.
We start by creating 100,000 samples of the head and shoulders pattern. See Figure 6.55.

Each sample consists of 25 data points, but each sample has an element of randomness to make it unique in the training set. We standardize each sample in preparation for training the CNN.

Figure 6.54 Monthly returns, crisis events, and sensitivity tests for Example 17.

```python
from scipy.stats import norm, uniform

np.random.seed(1)
ref_count = 100_000
v1 = np.array([0] * ref_count) + 0.02 * norm.rvs(size=(ref_count,))
p1 = np.array([1] * ref_count) + 0.2 * norm.rvs(size=(ref_count,))
v2 = v1 + 0.2 * norm.rvs(size=(ref_count,))
v3 = v1 + 0.2 * norm.rvs(size=(ref_count,))
p3 = p1 + 0.02 * norm.rvs(size=(ref_count,))
p2 = 1.5 * np.maximum(p1, p3) + abs(uniform.rvs(size=(ref_count,)))
v4 = v1 + 0.02 * norm.rvs(size=(ref_count,))
ref = pd.DataFrame([
    v1,
    (v1*.75 + p1*.25) + 0.2 * norm.rvs(size=(ref_count,)),
```

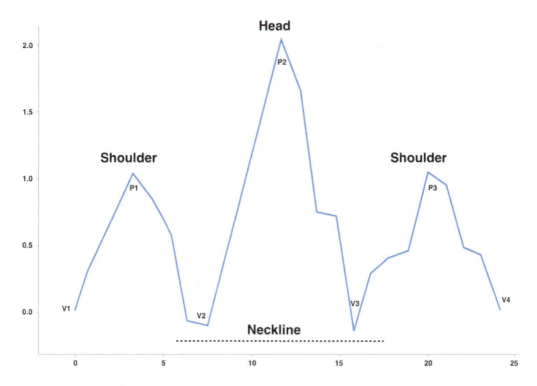

Figure 6.55 Line plot of our synthetic H&S pattern.

```
        (v1+p1)/2 + 0.2 * norm.rvs(size=(ref_count,)),
        (v1*.25 + p1*.75) + 0.2 * norm.rvs(size=(ref_count,)),
        p1,
        (v2*.25 + p1*.75) + 0.2 * norm.rvs(size=(ref_count,)),
        (v2+p1)/2 + 0.2 * norm.rvs(size=(ref_count,)),
        (v2*.75 + p1*.25) + 0.2 * norm.rvs(size=(ref_count,)),
        v2,
        (v2*.75 + p2*.25) + 0.2 * norm.rvs(size=(ref_count,)),
        (v2+p2)/2 + 0.2 * norm.rvs(size=(ref_count,)),
        (v2*.25 + p2*.75) + 0.2 * norm.rvs(size=(ref_count,)),
        p2,
        (v3*.25 + p2*.75) + 0.2 * norm.rvs(size=(ref_count,)),
        (v3+p2)/2 + 0.2 * norm.rvs(size=(ref_count,)),
        (v3*.75 + p2*.25) + 0.2 * norm.rvs(size=(ref_count,)),
        v3,
        (v3*.75 + p3*.25) + 0.2 * norm.rvs(size=(ref_count,)),
        (v3+p3)/2 + 0.2 * norm.rvs(size=(ref_count,)),
        (v3*.25 + p3*.75) + 0.2 * norm.rvs(size=(ref_count,)),
        p3,
        (v4*.25 + p3*.75) + 0.2 * norm.rvs(size=(ref_count,)),
        (v4+p3)/2 + 0.2 * norm.rvs(size=(ref_count,)),
        (v4*.75 + p3*.25) + 0.2 * norm.rvs(size=(ref_count,)),
        v4
])

ref = ((ref - ref.mean()) / ref.std()).T

positive_samples = []
for _, row in ref.iterrows():
    positive_samples.append(row.values)
```

We generate the vertical coordinates of the points v1, p1, v2, p2, v3, p3, and v4, and for each consecutive pair of the key points, we put in three points interpolating the line between them. In total, each sample has 25 data points.

For example, we put in three points between the points v1 and p1:

```
(v1*.75 + p1*.25) + 0.2 * norm.rvs(size=(ref_count,)),
(v1+p1)/2 + 0.2 * norm.rvs(size=(ref_count,)),
(v1*.25 + p1*.75) + 0.2 * norm.rvs(size=(ref_count,)),
```

Notice that we generate 100,000 such points with random noise from normal (Gaussian) distribution (norm.rvs).

Next, we create 100,000 samples of 25 price paths, which are random walks.

```
equity_curves = (
    np.random.randn(ref.shape[0], ref.shape[1]) / 1000 + 1
).cumprod(axis=1)
negative_samples = (
    (equity_curves - np.mean(equity_curves, axis=1, keepdims=True))
    / np.std(equity_curves, axis=1, keepdims=True)
)
```

We organize the training set to have one positive sample (the simulated H&S pattern), one negative sample, one positive sample, and so on...

```
X = np.array(
    [
        value
        for pair in zip(positive_samples, negative_samples)
        for value in pair
    ]
)
y = np.array([1 if i % 2 == 0 else 0 for i in range(len(X))])
```

Step 2: Split the input dataset into a training and testing dataset.

We split the 200,000 samples into training and testing sets (80%/20% split).

```
from sklearn.model_selection import train_test_split
from keras.models import Sequential
from keras.layers import Conv1D, MaxPooling1D, Flatten, Dense, Input
from keras.utils import set_random_seed

set_random_seed(0)

X_train, X_test, y_train, y_test = train_test_split(
    X, y, test_size=0.2, shuffle=False
)

X_train = np.reshape(X_train, (X_train.shape[0], X_train.shape[1], 1))
X_test = np.reshape(X_test, (X_test.shape[0], X_test.shape[1], 1))
```

Step 3: Create the neural network model.

We implement the sequential neural network model.

```
model = Sequential()
model.add(Input(shape=(X_train.shape[1], 1)))
model.add(Conv1D(filters=32, kernel_size=5, activation='relu'))
model.add(MaxPooling1D(pool_size=2))
model.add(Flatten())
model.add(Dense(1, activation='sigmoid'))
```

Step 4: Compile, train, and evaluate the model.

We compile, fit, and evaluate the model on the test set. On the test set, it achieves an accuracy of 99.9%.

```
# Compile the model.
model.compile(
    optimizer='adam', loss='binary_crossentropy', metrics=['accuracy']
)

# Train the model.
model.fit(
    X_train, y_train, epochs=10, batch_size=16,
    validation_data=(X_test, y_test)
)

# Evaluate the model.
test_loss, test_acc = model.evaluate(X_test, y_test)
print(f'Test Accuracy: {test_acc}')
```

Step 5: Save the model to the object store.

```
model.save(qb.object_store.get_file_path("head-and-shoulders-model.keras"))
```

Once we save the model, we can use it in a backtest.

Example 18—Amazon Chronos Model

Predicting	Future price path
Technology	Amazon Chronos
Asset Class	US equities
Difficulty	Hard
Type	Full strategy
Source Code	qnt.co/book-example18

Summary

This example demonstrates an application of a pre-trained HuggingFace "amazon/chronos-t5-tiny" model to forecast the future performance of the five most liquid assets in the market. Using these forecasts, the algorithm employs the SciPy package to optimize the portfolio weights to maximize the future risk-adjusted returns as measured by the Sharpe ratio. The portfolio is rebalanced every 3 months to align with the latest market predictions and conditions.

Motivation

This example builds upon two powerful components: the advanced forecasting capabilities of the Amazon Chronos model and the robust portfolio optimization using the Sharpe ratio.

The pre trained HuggingFace Amazon Chronos model, specifically the "amazon/chronos-t5-tiny," is utilized for its superior performance in time-series forecasting. By leveraging a pre trained model, the algorithm saves considerable time and resources that would otherwise be spent on training, allowing for quick deployment and immediate application. The model's scalability enables it to handle large datasets on powerful hardware such as graphics processing units (GPUs). Compared to traditional models like ARIMA or other AI solutions like long short-term memory (LSTM) networks, Amazon Chronos specializes in financial market predictions.

The algorithm employs the Sharpe ratio for portfolio optimization to maximize risk-adjusted returns, ensuring that the portfolio is optimized for both returns and risk and aligning with modern portfolio theory's best practices. However, the Sharpe ratio assumes normally distributed returns, which may not always reflect real-world conditions and can sometimes overlook extreme events or tail risks. Alternatives like the Sortino ratio, which focuses on downside risk, value at risk (VaR), which estimates potential loss, and maximum drawdown, which measures the most significant peak-to-trough decline, offer different perspectives but do not integrate return and risk as comprehensively as the Sharpe ratio.

Model

Model Features	Daily closing prices.
Predicted Label	Daily closing prices over the next 3 months (3 * 21 days).
Model	Amazon Chronos.

Amazon Chronos is a state-of-the-art machine-learning model specialized for financial market predictions, offering high accuracy, scalability, and ease of use.

This example implements two trading strategies, one using the base and one with a fine-tuned Amazon Chronos model.

The critical alternative forecasting models are ARIMA, Prophet, LSTM, support vector machines, and XGBoost:

- Autoregressive integrated moving average (ARIMA) is a widely used time-series forecasting model that is particularly effective for stationary data with linear patterns.
- Prophet (by Facebook) is a model designed to handle seasonality and trends.
- Long short-term memory (LSTM) is a neural network model that captures long-term dependencies in sequential data. LSTM is a type of recurrent neural network.
- Support vector machines (SVM) is a machine-learning model effective for forecasting time series by handling high-dimensional data and capturing non-linear relationships through kernel functions.

- XGBoost is a gradient-boosting algorithm that excels at handling tabular data and can be customized for time-series forecasting.

Choosing a suitable forecasting model depends on the specific use case, and exploring alternative models is always recommended.

Trading Universe

At the beginning of each month, the algorithm selects the universe of the top five most liquid assets from SPY, an ETF tracking the S&P 500 index.

Portfolio Construction

Model Training Time	The first trading strategy uses the base Amazon Chronos model with no training.
	The second trading strategy fine-tunes the Amazon Chronos model at midnight on the first trading day of each month.
Portfolio Rebalancing Time	Midnight on the first trading day of every third month (quarterly).
Portfolio Weights	The weights are determined by maximizing the forward Sharpe ratio.

Trading Logic

The first trading strategy downloads the history of closing prices of the assets in the universe for the last year, calculates the median predicted price for each day in the next 3 months, and sets the portfolio weights from the portfolio optimization results by maximizing the Sharpe ratio.

The second trading strategy enhances the first trading strategy by retraining the Amazon Chronos model before predicting the closing daily prices for the next 3 months.

The portfolio optimization we are solving aims at finding the best combination of assets to maximize returns for a given level of risk.

Formally, the objective function is

$$\max \left(\frac{R_p - R_f}{\sigma_p} \right).$$

Subject to these constraints:

- The sum of portfolio weights equals 1: $\Sigma w_i = 1$.
- No short selling: $0 \leq w_i \leq 1$.

Where:

- R_p is the return of the portfolio.
- R_f is the risk-free rate, which is the primary credit rate from the Federal Open Market Committee.

- σ_p is the standard deviation of the portfolio's returns.
- w_i are the portfolio weights.

In Python, we solve using SciPy's `minimize` function: we convert the maximization problem into a minimization problem by multiplying the objective function by −1. Sequential least squares programming is a popular algorithm for this task, effectively handling the constraints and finding the optimal weights.

Tearsheet

The pretrained HuggingFace models may contain lookahead bias if they were originally trained on data after January 1, 2019.

Trading Strategy 1 (Base Model):

- See Figures 6.56 and 6.57.

Trading Strategy 2 (Fine-Tuned Model):

- The `context_length` argument defines the length of the context window, which determines how many past tokens are used to predict the subsequent tokens. The default is 512, but we reduced it to 126 (6 months) since we only provided the model with 252 data points (1 year) for each asset.
- The `max_steps` argument defines the maximum number of training steps to perform. Training stops after this number of steps. The default is 200,000, but we reduced it to 3 to ensure the algorithm finishes training within the 10-minute quota.
- See Figures 6.58 and 6.59.

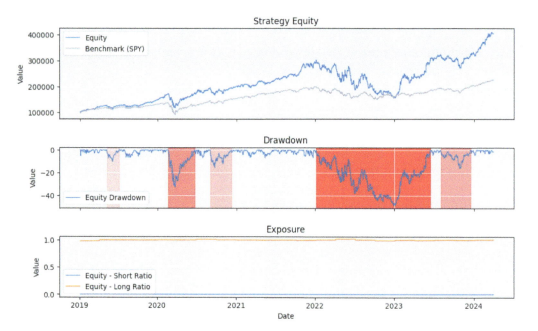

Figure 6.56 Equity curve and performance plots for Example 18.1.

Chapter 6. Applied Machine Learning 269

Figure 6.57 Monthly returns and crisis event for Example 18.1.

Figure 6.58 Equity curve and performance plots for Example 18.2.

Figure 6.59 Monthly returns and crisis event for Example 18.2.

Implementation Insights

The Amazon Chronos model produces a range of forecasted values for each future close price, with each value assigned its probability. For simplicity, we take the median forecast.

```
# Get historical equity curves.
history = self.history(symbols, self._lookback_period)['close'].unstack(0)

# Forecast the future equity curves.
all_forecasts = self._pipeline.predict(
    [
        torch.tensor(history[symbol].dropna())
        for symbol in symbols
    ],
    self._prediction_length
)

# Take the median forecast for each asset.
forecasts_df = pd.DataFrame(
    {
        symbol: np.quantile(
            all_forecasts[i].numpy(), 0.5, axis=0   # 0.5 = median
        )
        for i, symbol in enumerate(symbols)
    }
)
```

Chapter 6. Applied Machine Learning

Where the model is either a pretrained default model (the base model).

```python
# Load the pre-trained model.
self._pipeline = ChronosPipeline.from_pretrained(
    "amazon/chronos-t5-tiny",
    device_map="cuda" if torch.cuda.is_available() else "cpu",
    torch_dtype=torch.bfloat16,
)
```

Or is the output of the fine-tuned model trained on the actual data considered in this example.

```python
# Gather the training data.
training_data_by_symbol = {}
for symbol in symbols:
    df = history[[symbol]].dropna()
    if df.shape[0] < 10: # Skip this asset if there is very little data
        continue
    adjusted_df = df.reset_index()[['time', symbol]]
    adjusted_df = adjusted_df.rename(columns={str(symbol.id): 'target'})
    adjusted_df['time'] = pd.to_datetime(adjusted_df['time'])
    adjusted_df.set_index('time', inplace=True)
    adjusted_df = adjusted_df.resample('D').asfreq()
    training_data_by_symbol[symbol] = adjusted_df
tradable_symbols = list(training_data_by_symbol.keys())

# Fine-tune the model.
output_dir_path = self._train_chronos(
    list(training_data_by_symbol.values()),
    context_length=int(252/2), # 6 months
    prediction_length=self._prediction_length,
    optim=self._optimizer,
    model_id=self._model_name,
    output_dir=self._model_path,
    learning_rate=1e-5,
    # Requires Ampere GPUs (e.g., A100)
    tf32=False,
    max_steps=3
)

# Load the fine-tuned model.
pipeline = ChronosPipeline.from_pretrained(
    output_dir_path,
    device_map=self._device_map,
    torch_dtype=torch.bfloat16,
)
```

Where the method _train_chronos executes the training.

The portfolio optimization is implemented by maximizing the forecasted Sharpe ratio of the portfolio:

```python
optimal_weights = self._optimize_portfolio(forecasts_df)
```

Where the method `_optimize_portfolio` runs the SciPy's minimize function:

```python
def _sharpe_ratio(
        self, weights, returns, risk_free_rate, trading_days_per_year=252):
    # Define how to calculate the Sharpe ratio so we can use
    # it to optimize the portfolio weights.

    # Calculate the annualized returns and covariance matrix.
    mean_returns = returns.mean() * trading_days_per_year
    cov_matrix = returns.cov() * trading_days_per_year

    # Calculate the Sharpe ratio.
    portfolio_return = np.sum(mean_returns * weights)
    portfolio_std = np.sqrt(np.dot(weights.T, np.dot(cov_matrix, weights)))
    sharpe_ratio = (portfolio_return - risk_free_rate) / portfolio_std

    # Return negative Sharpe ratio because we minimize this
    # function in optimization.
    return -sharpe_ratio

def _optimize_portfolio(self, equity_curves):
    returns = equity_curves.pct_change().dropna()
    num_assets = returns.shape[1]
    initial_guess = num_assets * [1. / num_assets,]
    # Find portfolio weights that maximize the forward Sharpe
    # ratio.
    result = minimize(
        self._sharpe_ratio,
        initial_guess,
        args=(
            returns,
            self.risk_free_interest_rate_model.get_interest_rate(self.time)
        ),
        method='SLSQP',
        bounds=tuple((0, 1) for _ in range(num_assets)),
        constraints=(
            {'type': 'eq', 'fun': lambda weights: np.sum(weights) - 1}
        )
    )
    return result.x
```

Example 19—FinBERT Model

Predicting	News sentiment
Technology	LLM
Asset Class	US equities
Difficulty	Hard
Type	Full strategy
Source Code	qnt.co/book-example19

Summary

This algorithm demonstrates applying a pretrained "ProsusAI/finbert" HuggingFace model to assess the sentiment of the latest news releases related to an asset. At the beginning of each month, the algorithm selects the most volatile asset from the top 10 most liquid assets and computes an aggregated sentiment score based on news releases from the past 10 days. If the sentiment is more positive than negative, the algorithm initiates a long position; otherwise, it enters a short position. Similar to Example 18, we demonstrate the base model and then fine-tuned the model.

Motivation

Leveraging advanced natural language processing (NLP) models to analyze market sentiment can provide a significant edge, especially in uncovering upcoming trends. Positive sentiment typically leads to price increases, while negative sentiment can signal potential declines.

This algorithm utilizes the pre trained "ProsusAI/finbert" model from HuggingFace to assess the sentiment of the latest news releases related to the most volatile asset of the top 10 most liquid assets in the S&P 500 index. Volatility serves as an indicator of potential significant price movements. The algorithm ensures it can capitalize on the highest potential for substantial returns by targeting the most volatile assets. Additionally, selecting from the most liquid assets ensures ease of entry and exit from positions, minimizing slippage and transaction costs.

Model

Model Features	News article.
Predicted Label	Confidence probabilities for each sentiment category: positive, neutral, negative.
	The positive sentiment indicates a favorable outlook for the asset in the text. The negative sentiment indicates an unfavorable outlook, while the neutral sentiment indicates an indifferent outlook.
Model	FinBERT.

In Example 16, we have covered sentiment analysis with OpenAI's GPT-4 model. When comparing FinBERT or Bidirectional Encoder Representations from Transformers (BERT) models with OpenAI's GPT-4 models, several distinctions emerge in terms of performance and cost:

- Performance—FinBERT, a variant of BERT fine-tuned specifically for financial sentiment analysis, excels in understanding the context and nuances of financial news. FinBERT and BERT models typically provide faster inference speeds because they are smaller than larger models like GPT-4.

  On the other hand, GPT-4, as a general-purpose model, enables deeper contextual understanding and generates more nuanced interpretations of news articles. However, this comes at the cost of increased computational resources and processing time.
- Costs—FinBERT and BERT models are more cost-effective, requiring less computational power for training and inference, which translates to lower operational costs.

Their implementation is also more straightforward, reducing development time and associated costs.

Conversely, the larger size and complexity of GPT-4 demands more computational resources, leading to higher operational costs. While GPT-4's versatility is advantageous, integrating it for financial sentiment analysis might require additional fine-tuning, further increasing development costs.

We implement the trading strategy in both the base FinBERT model (using the pre trained model) and a fine-tuned FinBERT model. (We retrain the model using the actual articles and judging the sentiment by the following stock return.)

Trading Universe

On the first trading day of each month, we select the most volatile stock from the top 10 most liquid S&P Index components.

Portfolio Construction

Model Training Time	For the base model, no further training is performed.
	For the fine-tuned model, we retrain the model at midnight on the first trading day of each month.
Portfolio Rebalancing Time	At midnight on the first trading day of each month.
Portfolio Weights	If the aggregate sentiment is more likely positive than negative, we hold 100% of our portfolio in the asset. Otherwise, we short ¼ of our portfolio in the asset.

Trading Logic

In the base FinBERT model, we get the last 10 days of news articles related to the asset in the universe from TiingoNews, tokenize the articles, and apply the pre trained model.

```
# Get the target security.
security = self.securities[list(self._universe.selected)[0]]

# Get the latest news articles.
articles = self.history[TiingoNews](security.dataset_symbol, 10, Resolution.DAILY)
article_text = [article.description for article in articles]
if not article_text:
    return

# Prepare the input sentences.
inputs = self._tokenizer(article_text, padding=True, truncation=True,
return_tensors='tf')

# Get the model outputs.
outputs = self._model(**inputs)
```

```
# Apply softmax to the outputs to get probabilities.
scores = tf.nn.softmax(outputs.logits, axis=-1).numpy()
self.log(f"{str(scores)}")
scores = self._aggregate_sentiment_scores(scores)

# Rebalance the portfolio.
weight = 1 if scores[2] > scores[0] else -0.25
self.set_holdings(security.symbol, weight, True)
self._last_rebalance_time = self.time
```

Where `_aggregate_sentiment_scores` calculates an exponentially weighted score for the articles, giving more importance to the recent sentiment scores (latest news is more valuable), and then aggregates it into a single score.

In the fine-tuned FinBERT model, we get the last 30 days of close prices and the 30 days of articles.

In the training dataset we generate, we label each day's sentiment using this logic:

1. We calculate the daily return of the close prices.
2. We sort the positive daily returns in descending order and select the first 75% as having the positive label.
3. Similarly, we sort the negative daily returns in ascending order and select the first 75% as having the negative label.
4. The non-assigned values are labeled with the neutral label.

We retrain the model using this training dataset and proceed like in the Base Model.

Tearsheet

The pretrained HuggingFace models may contain lookahead bias if they were originally trained on data after January 1, 2019.

Trading Strategy 1 (Base Model):

- See Figures 6.60 and 6.61.

Trading Strategy 2 (Fine-Tuned Model):

- See Figures 6.62 and 6.63.

Implementation Insights

FinBERT uses a random numbers generator for data splits, weight initialization, and training. For reproducibility, we recommend setting the initial random seed, for example, like this:

```
set_seed(1, True)
```

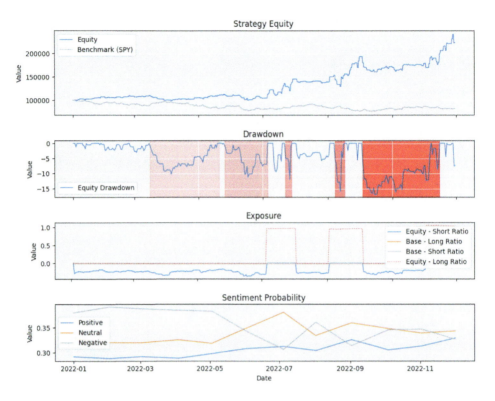

Figure 6.60 Equity curve, performance plots, and custom plots for Example 19.1.

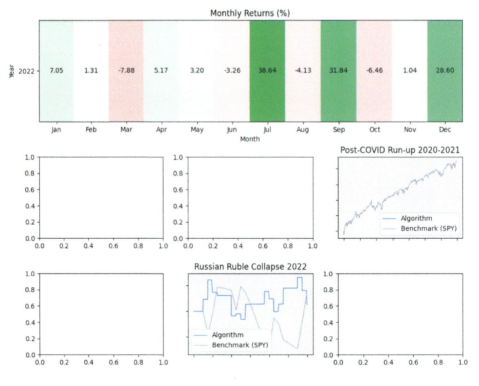

Figure 6.61 Monthly returns and crisis events for Example 19.1.

Chapter 6. Applied Machine Learning 277

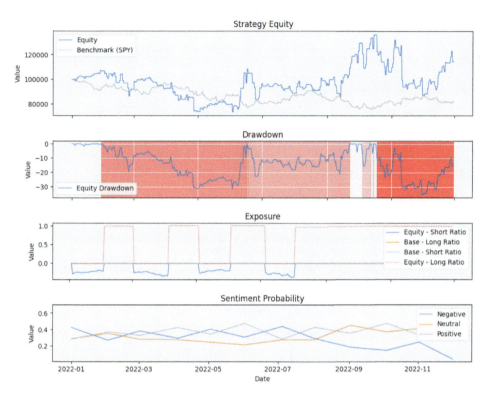

Figure 6.62 Equity curve, performance plots, and custom plots for Example 19.2.

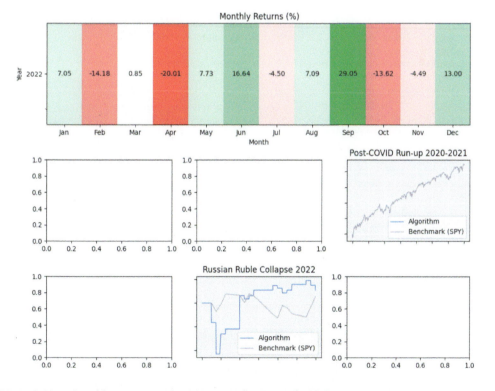

Figure 6.63 Monthly returns and crisis events for Example 19.2.

We aggregate the sentiment scores using exponential weighting to ensure the latest news sentiment has the most significant weight in the aggregated score.

```python
def _aggregate_sentiment_scores(self, sentiment_scores):
    n = sentiment_scores.shape[0]

    # Generate exponentially increasing weights.
    weights = np.exp(np.linspace(0, 1, n))

    # Normalize weights to sum to 1.
    weights /= weights.sum()

    # Apply weights to sentiment scores.
    weighted_scores = sentiment_scores * weights[:, np.newaxis]

    # Aggregate weighted scores by summing them.
    aggregated_scores = weighted_scores.sum(axis=0)

    return aggregated_scores
```

In Trading Strategy 2 (Fine-Tuned Model), we create the training dataset, train the model, and proceed as in Trading Strategy 1 (Base Model).

```python
security = self.securities[list(self._universe.selected)[0]]

# Get samples to fine-tune the model
samples = pd.DataFrame(columns=['text', 'label'])
news_history = self.history(security.dataset_symbol, 30, Resolution.DAILY)
if news_history.empty:
    return
news_history = news_history.loc[security.dataset_symbol]['description']
asset_history = self.history(
    security.symbol, timedelta(30), Resolution.SECOND
).loc[security.symbol]['close']
for i in range(len(news_history.index)-1):
    # Get factor (article description).
    factor = news_history.iloc[i]
    if not factor:
        continue

    # Get the label (the market reaction to the news).
    release_time = self._convert_to_eastern(news_history.index[i])
    next_release_time = self._convert_to_eastern(news_history.index[i+1])
    reaction_period = asset_history[
        (asset_history.index > release_time) &
        (asset_history.index < next_release_time + timedelta(seconds=1))
    ]
    if reaction_period.empty:
        continue
    label = (
        (reaction_period.iloc[-1] - reaction_period.iloc[0])
        / reaction_period.iloc[0]
    )
```

```python
        # Save the training sample.
        samples.loc[len(samples), :] = [factor, label]

samples = samples.iloc[-100:]

if samples.shape[0] < 10:
    self.liquidate()
    return

# Classify the market reaction into positive/negative/neutral.
# 75% of the most negative labels => class 0 (negative)
# 75% of the most positive labels => class 2 (positive)
# Remaining labels                 => class 1 (neutral)
sorted_samples = samples.sort_values(
    by='label', ascending=False
).reset_index(drop=True)
percent_signed = 0.75
positive_cutoff = (
    int(percent_signed
    * len(sorted_samples[sorted_samples.label > 0]))
)
negative_cutoff = (
    len(sorted_samples)
    - int(percent_signed * len(sorted_samples[sorted_samples.label < 0]))
)
sorted_samples.loc[
    list(range(negative_cutoff, len(sorted_samples))), 'label'
] = 0
sorted_samples.loc[
    list(range(positive_cutoff, negative_cutoff)), 'label'
] = 1
sorted_samples.loc[list(range(0, positive_cutoff)), 'label'] = 2

# Load the pre-trained model.
model = TFBertForSequenceClassification.from_pretrained(
    self._model_name, num_labels=3, from_pt=True
)
# Compile the model.
model.compile(
    optimizer=tf.keras.optimizers.Adam(learning_rate=3e-5),
    loss=tf.keras.losses.SparseCategoricalCrossentropy(from_logits=True)
)
# Create the training dataset.
dataset = Dataset.from_pandas(sorted_samples)
dataset = dataset.map(
    lambda sample: self._tokenizer(
        sample['text'], padding='max_length', truncation=True
    )
)
dataset = model.prepare_tf_dataset(
    dataset, shuffle=True, tokenizer=self._tokenizer
)
# Train the model.
model.fit(dataset, epochs=2)
```

Chapter 7

Better Hedging with Reinforcement Learning

Introduction

A New AI Trading Assistant

When we began writing this book in 2023, it marked the 50th anniversary of the publication of the seminal work by Black and Scholes (1973) and Merton (1973) on the pricing of options. The Black-Scholes Merton (BSM) pricing model ushered in a new era in quantitative finance and capital markets. The impact of their treatise was immediately felt both in academic research and on the market prices of options. It was indeed in the 1970s and 1980s that traders in the options pit acquired a new weapon—the Black-Scholes (*abbr.* BS, which will prove to be a versatile abbreviation) option pricing model, later programmed into a desktop computer, or the Rolodex of personal computing devices, the HP financial calculators. The earliest documented Black-Scholes program for HP calculator was written by Peter Carr, then a doctoral student at UCLA on HP-12C, published in 1988 (Carr, 1988). Type in a few inputs—stock price, expiration date, rate on treasury bills, and a guesstimate volatility—the trusty HP would spit out a price instantaneously. A new "AI" trading assistant had just arrived! To the traders' surprise, or to some much delight, the prices of options they were trading with each other were...

wrong!?

The fact that the market prices were much different from BS prices was an opportunity for windfall profits, but only if the traders knew how to hedge their positions and wait for prices to converge to the "arbitrage-free" BS prices. This was a problem because the BSM model assumes continuous hedging in a frictionless (i.e., zero transaction cost) market with fractional shares. This market did not exist at the time, has not come to being since, and we can state with a high degree of certainty, will not exist in the near future—even with zero-commission, miniscule bid-ask spread, fractional shares, and high-frequency trading technologies, we are still qualitatively away from the ideal. But no matter, the pit traders who normally would look down on, or rather as one former pit trader would quip, "look up and thumb their noses at" the academics and dismiss their fantastical models became infatuated with the BS (as we said earlier, this abbreviation is versatile). As a result, the BS price became a self-fulfilling prophesy. The rest is history. BSM now permeates unexpected corners of financial economics, accounting, and corporate finance, from pricing employee stock options, evaluating merger and acquisition deals, to justifying the stratospheric valuations of unicorn startup ventures.

Continuous Hedging Is Not Required

To be fair, BSM does not necessarily require that one carries out continuous and frictionless hedging. In fact, you do not need to hedge at all. If a market is reasonably efficient, everyone agrees on the probability of distribution of outcomes at expiration of the option contracts, and the "implied" volatility during the contract's lifetime is constant, then market prices should converge to BS prices. Note, this convergence has a random distribution and is not arbitrage-free. That is because, in finance, we discount future cash flows based on uncertainty and risk of such expected cash flows. BSM is consistent with the discount cash flow analysis. And the one-price theory predicts that in a perfectly competitive market, traders will converge on the same set of "equilibrium" expectations about prices, volatilities, and risk premia. Still there are many assumptions here that are fundamentally the same as those of BSM.

Already, practitioners noticed inconsistencies in the assumptions of BSM. For example, when using BSM to calculate the "implied volatility (vol)" of a particular stock from the market price of options, one notices that implied vol are different at different strike prices. Indeed, there appears a "volatility smile" where implied vol seems to increase further in (or out) of the money (Figure 7.1). The volatility smile is inconsistent with the "constant volatility" assumption. There is also a volatility skew, normally negative, that is, the implied vol for an out-of-money put is higher than implied vol of an out-of-money calls with the same "money-ness" (i.e., the difference between strike and underlying prices), and equivalently, the implied vol of an out-of-money call is higher than the implied volatility of in-the-money call with the same absolute moneyness (Figure 7.1). This skew is not explained by the skew in the return distribution of the underlying prices, and hints at risk premium skew or more fashionably, a behavioral bias, which can only persist if they cannot be arbitraged away.

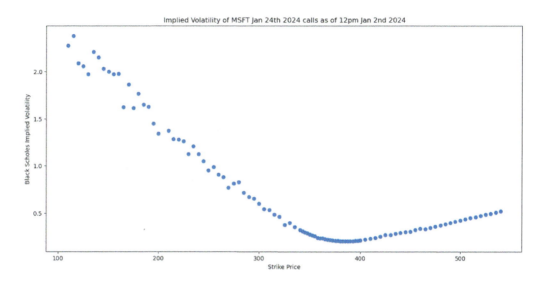

Figure 7.1 The volatility "smile" and "skew": implied volatility of MSFT call options expiring on January 24, 2024, as of 12:00 pm on January 2, 2024. MSFT stock price was about $375/share. Implied volatility calculated using BSM from the mid-prices of call options.

Continuous hedging makes the assumptions of asset return distribution unnecessary in theory. (You still must deal with the distribution of asset price paths, which relies on a similar set of assumptions.) Advocates of Black-Scholes and Merton's approach, therefore, would tweak the underlying assumptions; for example, Heston (1993) proposed a stochastic process for the volatility of the underlying asset and a numerical algorithm to calibrate model parameters to observed market prices of options. Empirically, the Heston model fits observed market data quite well. But the improvement comes at the cost of increased model complexity, which is harder and more costly to work with, as numerical calibration tends to consume a lot of computational resources. And there is a big problem with these calibrated models: they tend to be more complex and have more parameters. For Heston, the parameter values for different stocks turned out to be different, hence the risk of overfitting!

Then, there are costs associated with hedging trades, including commissions, exchange fees, bid-ask spreads, impact of trades on market prices, and over- and under-hedging due to share count rounding. To properly account for these costs, one needs to simulate potential trading costs realistically. Since different traders face different trading costs, a robust estimation of the distribution of trading costs is also needed.

Deeper and deeper into the rabbit hole goes Alice!

Machine Learning Comes to the Rescue

With the onset of machine learning (ML), particularly with reinforcement learning (RL), it is now feasible to predict option prices without the structural models like BSM or Heston. We can now incorporate fundamental and empirical features previously ignored in these models, such as transaction costs, liquidity, market sentiment, and so on, into a deep neural network (DNN). We let the DNN learn from market data, and then price arbitrary options through interpolation and extrapolation.

Not only can an artificial intelligence (AI) "agent" learn a realistic pricing model (although we may not know exactly how it does so), we can also use reinforcement learning to train the AI agent to construct an optimal hedging policy *ex ante*, incorporating aforementioned practical considerations of transaction costs and market friction. The result is a much more robust hedging policy that market makers and options dealers can deploy programmatically to hedge the risk of taking on inventory, thereby increasing the overall liquidity and efficiency of the options market.

Furthermore, the method we describe here can be generalized to combinations of options (i.e., combos) or structured notes. Structured notes are complex securities, usually mature in 3–5 years, and make coupon and principal payments that are indexed to individual stock prices or market indices, and such coupon and principal payments are usually contingent upon the future prices of reference stocks or indices reaching certain threshold. The contingent payment structure are embedded options. For example, a structured note issued by Barclays referenced to the S&P 500 Index has the following conditional principal value matrix:

$$V = \begin{cases} V_0 + (x - V_0) * 1.105 & \text{if } x > V_0 \\ \min(0, x - 0.8 \times V_0) & \text{if } x \leq V_0 \end{cases},$$

where V_0 and x are the initial and final value of the reference indices, respectively. This note provides leverage (1.105) of the reference index return and a protective buffer of 20%, which is effectively a long and short pair of put options: a long an at-the-money put, and a short an out-of-money put, with a strike price at 80% of initial value of the reference index, V_0. Like options market makers, issuers of such notes have a need to hedge.

In this chapter, we will describe a "simplified" reinforcement learning algorithm, implemented and made available on QuantConnect.com for practitioners of options trading. We will discuss the underlying algorithmic framework, present example codes, and investigate the performance of the reinforcement learning hedging algorithm, compared to more traditional hedging based on matching delta, or, delta hedging. Before proceeding with the rest of the chapter, we encourage the readers to familiarize themselves with the basic option pricing theory like the BSM and machine-learning concepts of neural network (NN) and reinforcement learning (RL).

A Simplified but Effective Reinforcement Learning Approach

First things first, due to the complexity and cost of large RL models required to train an industrial-strength AI hedging algorithm, a comprehensive treatment of state-of-the-art AI hedging is beyond the scope of this book, and beyond the capability and resources of lone-wolf quant traders. Instead, the author and his research team have developed an approach that simplifies RL, with a reduced NN architecture, and reliant on a much smaller dataset, that can be implemented effectively by the reader.

The models and algorithms presented here have been incorporated into the online algorithmic trading library of the QuantConnect.com platform, which seamlessly integrates with the platform's extensive market data for options and equities. In what follows, we shall use the source code implemented on QuantConnect.com as examples. However, if readers so choose, they can implement the code in a Python environment on a local computer with a GPU and a minimum of 16 GB of RAM. Readers will also need access to daily options and equities data for individual tickers of their choice. The entire Python files associated with this example are available in the book's GitHub repository at qnt.co/book-repo. For instructions on how to clone the repository, please refer to "Part III Part Overview."

Overview of the Reinforcement Learning

In general, a typical RL AI hedging program contains these steps:

1. Identification
2. Training with simulated data
3. Training or refinement with "real" market data
4. Testing and implementation

We will describe these steps conceptually in this section and illustrate them with code examples in the following section.

Identification

This step identifies and specifies the price processes of underlying stocks. For brevity and readability, we shall use the term "stock" to describe all reference assets or indices of options. The underlying stocks are risky assets, and their price processes are stochastic in nature. Since we shall admit potentially different asset classes as the underlying, price dynamics can differ significantly. Therefore, it is important in this step to identify the specific process(es) and estimate or calibrate parameters that are sufficiently accurate in describing the process and distribution of outcomes.

Without loss of generality, in the following example, we adopt the Geometric Brownian Motion (GBM) as the underlying process for stocks:

$$dS_t = \mu S_t dt + \sigma S_t dW_t$$

where S_t is the stock price at time t, μ is the mean drift of the stock return, σ is the volatility of the stock return, and W_t is a Wiener process (Brownian motion). The return of the stock is distributed with a mean of μ and standard deviation of σ.

Other stochastic processes of underlying stocks can be adopted as well. For example, the Heston model (Heston, 1993) posits:

$$dS_t = \mu S_t dt + \sqrt{v_t} S_t dW_t^S.$$

The Heston model relaxes the assumption that the volatility of stock return is invariant. Instead, the model added an additional time-dependent stochastic process for volatility, $\sigma_t = \sqrt{v_t}$.

$$d\sqrt{v_t} = -\theta\sqrt{v_t}\,dt + \delta dW_t^v$$

The volatility is modeled as an Ornstein-Uhlenbeck process, with parameters θ and δ, the variance of the Wiener process for volatility. The negative sign in front of θ suggests that this is an auto regressive process. Indeed, Ornstein-Uhlenbeck is the continuous-time version of discrete autoregressive process of order 1, AR(1). The two Wiener processes for stock, W_t^S and volatility W_t^v are independent. This double-stochastic process provides a more market consistent way to model stock prices but at a (much) higher cost of computation, for calibration of parameters from market data, and for numerical estimation of options prices and other analytics (Greeks). Therefore, in this simplified model, we have chosen the more analytically appealing GBM, which requires only traditional statistics to estimate parameters and has closed-form solutions for option prices and Greeks, that is, the Black-Scholes Merton model.

Simulation

It is a good idea to simulate training data, when the hedged instrument (in this example, a call option) is a derivative of an underlying security (in this example, a stock) where a theoretical no arbitrage relationship can be specified. Despite the appearance of large data, historical financial market data is actually quite inadequate for reinforcement learning. This is because financial markets are competitive. Any "innovation," i.e., deviations from fundamental price relationships, that may reasonably persist (e.g., in a time frame that an algorithm can react to and trade on) are usually very hard to detect. Or put it another way, the signal-to-noise ratio of such a tradeable innovation is very low. Therefore, most financial datasets contain only low information content for models to reliably learn persistent innovation that are not already known to structural models. If our goal is to train a hedging policy to respond to some known, persistent non-structural behavior, then we can simulate these "known unknowns," as long as we correctly identify them.

In the example here, the persistent and fundamental behavior we want the model to learn is dominated by the no-arbitrage relationship between the prices of options and underlying stocks: no arbitrage relationship can be approximated using different models (we discussed BSM and Heston in the last section). We identified one, BSM with GBM, as the core relationship between options and stock prices. Hence, we will simulate copious amounts of data using BSM with GMB, and first train the model to find the best hedging strategy under these assumptions. We had earlier discussed the shortcomings of theoretical models and clarified the motivation of using RL to learn more realistic aspects of hedging. So, what do we gain from training a model on simulated data?

The answer is nuanced. The first part of the answer is that one aspect of "realism" is discrete hedging, as opposed to continuous hedging that underlies BSM. With simulated data, we simulate discrete steps in asset prices (daily in this example) and discrete hedging (daily also in this example). It is possible to determine analytically the "optimal" discrete hedging strategy. But the computation is quite complex, requiring solving stochastic partial differential equations that, in most cases, can only be performed numerically. This makes it impractical to implement, as the latency between an update to input states and the decision of appropriate hedge action is unacceptably long if the trading frequency is minutes or seconds. An ML policy network, on the other hand, once learned, can respond to current market conditions (states) and derive "actions" with very low latency.

The other answer is, because we are simulating data, any known variation or innovation to the fundamental pricing model, such as liquidity, market trend or other predictive models, transaction cost model, and so on, can be built into the simulator. The caveat is they must be "known unknowns." RL models will not be able to learn from simulated data, those processes that have not been seen. This brings us to the next topic: refinement training on actual market data.

Refinement Training on Actual Market Data

In situations where we believe large datasets of historical market prices contain persistent innovation or processes unknown to us, we can train the model on "real" market data. As we discussed previously, the competitive nature of the financial markets makes it unlikely for any known or unknown unknowns to persist and to be noticeable in data. In certain situations, where there are a lot of data and the market is not perfectly competitive, for example, in high-frequency (HF) trading, where the investments in high-end computing and information technology hardware required make the HF market place less competitive, ML/RL models trained on real data, tick-by-tick or high-frequency time-bar data, can yield significant advantages over competitors' rule-based algorithms. But even in this case, simulation can play an important role in priming the model with a theoretical and fundamental prior. Then, the model can be refined on precious real market data to incorporate real-world challenges and additional "unknown unknowns."

In this example, we incorporate market data in the second "refinement" stage of training a hedging policy network. In this refinement stage, a short window of historical market data is used to fine-tune the policy network to recent information. We chose a short and recent historical window because option markets have been evolving rapidly, and the features, such as liquidity, transaction costs, and market trends, which we want the RL agent to learn do not stay stationary. We will discuss details of the implementation in the next section.

Testing and Implementation

As with all machine-learning efforts, it is best practice to split sample data into training, validation, and out-of-sample testing. In the case of financial market applications, since the market is continuously generating new data, we have the opportunity to conduct out-sample tests using new market data. This is the age-old tradition of running a "paper" portfolio to continuously monitor the out-sample performance of algorithmic trading models (or fundamental investment processes) and use results of the out-sample to (in)validate, refine, and enhance the model.

Even upon implementation of a trading algorithm with real money, we should continue to systematically analyze performance results. It is important to understand the variance between what is expected of a model performance conditioned on the current market state (*ex ante*), and what we experience in real money trading (*ex post*), to help identify blind spots, inaccuracies, or even errors in our models. We will not cover this part of the AI hedging process, as the details depend on application. We would like to emphasize that no AI hedging should be implemented without a well-thought-out plan for continuous testing, attribution, and model refinement in place.

Now we proceed to illustrate AI hedging with the code example implemented on QuantConnect.com.

Implementation on QuantConnect

This example is implemented on QuantConnect.com and uses PyTorch's NN interface for RL. We will not cover the basics of PyTorch in this book. The readers are directed to the excellent online documentation and tutorial at pytorch.org.

The objective of this project is to obtain an optimal hedging policy that minimizes the variance of the profit and loss (PnL) of a hedged portfolio containing the asset to be hedged, in this case a call option, and the hedging instrument, in this case, the underlying stock. The example demonstrates the process of training an agent, or hedging policy network with AAPL (Apple, Inc.) call options and stock. In the following text, we use the terms "agent" and "policy network" interchangeably. But there is a slight distinction: the policy network refers to the NN whose parameters are tuned through RL, where the input is the current market state, and the output is the hedging decision for the next period. The "agent" refers to the trading algorithm armed with the policy network to make real-time decisions and trades on those decisions. In other words, the "agent" is the AI.

The reader will find the entire project on QuantConnect.com's code library under "aihedging." The organization of the files is as follows:

AI Delta Hedging. This is the main project:

- **research.ipynb:** the main model to run the two-stage training, test the model, and generate the results.
- **main.py:** defines the class, `AIDeltaHedgingAlgorithm`, which contains the initialization of training and sets up general parameters. The class can be called in the backtest environment on QuantConnect.com.

- **aihedging:** a separate project containing the class and function definitions of components of the main research notebook.
  - **model.py:** defines the classes and functions called by the main research notebook.
  - **policy.py:** the "policy" class that defines the architecture of the policy neural network.

We will describe each component next.

Primary Research Notebook

In the research notebook, research.ipynb, we will illustrate the process of the two-stage training, and some simple tests of the model performance. The first cell in the research notebook creates the model, fixes the random seed to ensure reproducibility, and chooses the processor, e.g., CPU or GPU. We will look at the details of the `AIDeltaHedgeModel` class later.

[research.ipynb/Cell 1]

```python
from aihedging.model import AIDeltaHedgeModel

qb = QuantBook()

model = AIDeltaHedgeModel(
    qb, timedelta(qb.get_parameter('min_contract_duration', 30)),
    timedelta(qb.get_parameter('max_contract_duration', 120)),
    timedelta(qb.get_parameter('min_holding_period', 14)))
```

The second cell trains the base model, or the first stage of training the policy network to mimic delta hedging. We will look at the details of the `model.train_base_model` function later.

[research.ipynb/Cell 2]

```python
model.train_base_model(plot=True, epochs=1000)
```

The third cell runs the refinement stage, where we apply a penalty function based on PnL of the hedged portfolio, and refine the policy network with daily closing prices of AAPL (Apple Inc.) from December 19, 2023, to February, 17, 2024. We will look at the details of the `model.train_asset_model()` function later.

[research.ipynb/Cell 3]

```python
start_date = datetime(2023, 12, 19)
end_date = datetime(2024, 2, 17)
model.train_asset_model("AAPL", start_date, end_date,
    epochs=40, save=False, in_research_env=True)
```

The last cell runs tests of the performance of the model. We will look at the details of the `model.research_test()` function later.

[research.ipynb/Cell 4]

```
model.research_test(strike_level=-1, start=start_date, end=end_date)
```

The Policy Network

In the policy network, policy.py, we define a hedging "policy" class on a NN directly, `Policy(nn.Module)`. It takes a three-dimensional state as input, which includes (1) moneyness, defined next, (2) time-to-maturity, and (3) previous hedging position in the underlying stock (e.g. AAPL). And it outputs two parameters, the hedging position for the next step, and the respective uncertainty denoted as **mu** and **sigma** of a normal probability distribution. Note, for code readability, we shall avoid using Greek letters in the text, except for detailed mathematical equations. Readers should not confuse **mu** and **sigma** of hedging positions with the mean and volatility of asset returns.

Moneyness is defined as the maximum between zero and the difference between the strike price and underlying stock price. For a call option, the option is in the money, that is, moneyness is positive, if the stock price is above the strike price. For a put option, the option is in the money, or moneyness is positive, if the strike price is above the stock price.

A careful reader might have noticed that option price itself is not a feature in the state vector. In the first stage of training, we will simulate option price as a no-arbitrage price based on BSM with GBM of the underlying stocks as discussed previously. Therefore, the option price is totally dependent on the other state variables.

We also did not include other possible features, such as market structure, (e.g., overall trading volume, bid-ask spread, macro-economic backdrops). Readers are encouraged to enrich the state vector with additional features. However, for simulation, you will need to identify and model the data generation process that simulates these additional features.

Let's take a look at the code:

[policy.py]

```python
from torch import nn
from torch import optim
from torch import distribution

class Policy(nn.Module):
    def __init__(self, device):
        super(Policy, self).__init__()

        # Define the network layers.
        self._fcin = nn.Linear(3, 256)
        self._fc1 = nn.Linear(256, 256)
        self._fcout = nn.Linear(256, 1*2)

        # Define the optimizer.
        self.optimizer = optim.Adam(self.parameters(), lr=3e-4)
```

```python
    # Move the network's parameters and buffers to the correct
    # device (CPU or GPU).
    self.to(T.device(device))

def forward(self, state):
    x = F.relu(self._fcin(state))
    x = F.relu(self._fc1(x))
    x = self._fcout(x)
    lmu, lsig = x.split(1,dim=-1)
    return F.sigmoid(lmu), F.sigmoid(lsig)+1e-12

def sample(self, state):
    mu, sig = self.forward(state)
    d = D.normal.Normal(mu, sig)
    sample = d.rsample()
    return sample, d.log_prob(sample).sum(axis=-1)
```

Here, the policy NN is constructed with three layers. We define the input layer self.fcin = nn.Linear(3, 256) to have three input features corresponding to the three state dimensions discussed previously with 256 nodes in this hidden layer. Therefore, there are 256 interim output features from the input layer that will be fed into the nodes of the second hidden layer [Code: self.fc1 = nn.Linear(256, 256)]. The second hidden layer then has 256 interim outputs that will be passed to the output layer [Code: self.fcout = nn.Linear(256, 1*2)]. And the final output layer consists of the hedging position, **mu** and the uncertainty of the decision **sigma** of the next period as discussed earlier.

The hedging position, **mu**, along with an update to the moneyness and time-to-maturity for the next time period, will be passed **forward** to the next time period to determine the hedging policy **mu**, and **sigma** for the period after next. The ReLU function is used for activation between layers.

Readers are at the liberty of designing their own NN architecture and choosing the appropriate activation function. The author here makes no claim that a three-layer NN is adequate for the complex function of hedging. It is however quite an efficient NN for training a model on simulated data as described next.

Out of the three state dimensions, time-to-maturity is not a random variable, as it will simply be decremented by the length between periods, in this case 1 day, each time we step forward. However, moneyness is a stochastic variable that needs to be calculated based on the dynamics of underlying stock. To capture the dynamics of the underlying stock, we can (a) simulate stock price processes, and (b) use historical stock prices. Option (a) offers the advantage of potentially generating an unlimited amount of data for training purposes. In the follow section, we set up a data generation process using BSM, which assumes stocks follow GBM with fixed drifts, (i.e., average returns), and fixed volatilities of returns. There are more sophisticated models such as Heston (1993) described earlier, where the stationarity of stock return distribution is relaxed by introducing a stochastic process for the volatility itself. For reasons already stated, we shall stick with GBM and hence, BSM, in this example.

Model Functions

The entire model is encapsulated in the model.py class, `AIDeltaHedgeModel`. We will not print and describe every definition contained in the entire class, nor is it necessary. We will review the following definitions:

- `_init_()`: class initialization.
- `train_base_model()`: the delta-mimicking training stage with simulated data and a loss function defined as mse between delta and the policy action.
- `train_asset_model()`: the refinement training stage with historical market data and a penalty function based on pnl of the hedged portfolio.
- `research_test()`: a simple test of hedging performance for an option on a single stock for illustration.

[model.py/AIDeltaHedgeModel/_init_()]

```
def __init__(
        self, algorithm, min_contract_duration=timedelta(30),
        max_contract_duration=timedelta(120),
        min_holding_period=timedelta(14), size=(10_000, 1),
        commission=0.01):
    self._algorithm = algorithm
    self._min_contract_duration = min_contract_duration
    self._max_contract_duration = max_contract_duration
    self._min_holding_period = min_holding_period
    self._size = size
    self._commission = commission
    self._pos = 0
    self._policy = None
    self.enable_automatic_indicator_warm_up = True
    # Set the random seeds to enable reproducibility.
    seed_value = 1
    os.environ['PYTHONHASHSEED'] = str(seed_value)
    random.seed(seed_value)
    np.random.seed(seed_value)
    T.manual_seed(seed_value)
    # Set the default tensor type.
    T.set_default_dtype(T.float32)
    # Set the device type (CPU/GPU).
    self._device = 'cuda:0' if T.cuda.is_available() else 'cpu'
```

This initializes the `AIDeltaHedgeModel` object and specifies the maximum/minimum contract duration (120/30 days), minimum holding period (14 days), commission (0.01) used to simulate data, and filter historical data. And it fixes the random seed for reproducibility.

We would like to train our model on a GPU available on QuantConnect.com for premium accounts. The last line of code checks to see if a GPU, torch.cuda is available. If so, we set the device to 'cuda:0.' Otherwise, we default to "cpu."

[model.py/AIDeltaHedgeModel/train_base_model()]

```python
def train_base_model(self, plot=True, epochs=1000):
    # Create the policy.
    self._policy = Policy(self._device)
    # Define the loss function.
    mse = nn.MSELoss()

    # Set the volatility and risk-free interest rate arguments.
    # The base model is trained with generated data, which doesn't
    # have a start and end date, so let's just use 2013-2018.
    vol, rf = self._get_vol_and_rf(
        Symbol.create("SPY", SecurityType.EQUITY, Market.USA),
        self._earliest_options_date, datetime(2018, 1, 1)
    )

    # Train the model to replicate the underhedged Black-Scholes'
    # delta.
    in_sample_loss_values = []
    oos_loss_values = []
    for E in range(epochs):
        # Get the data we need to run the network.
        ttm, moneyness, delta, position = self._generate_data(vol, rf)
        states, y, test_states, test_y = self._forge_batch(
            moneyness, ttm, delta, position
        )
        # Get the in-sample action and loss.
        action, _ = self._policy.sample(states)
        loss = mse(action, y)
        inloss = loss.item()
        # Update the network parameters.
        self._policy.optimizer.zero_grad()
        loss.backward()
        self._policy.optimizer.step()
        # Get the out-of-sample action and loss.
        action, _ = self._policy.sample(test_states)
        outloss = mse(action, test_y).item()
        # Record the loss value of this epoch.
        in_sample_loss_values.append(inloss)
        oos_loss_values.append(outloss)

    # Plot the training loss values of each epoch.
    if plot:
        x = list(range(1, epochs+1))
        go.Figure(
            [
                go.Scatter(x=x, y=in_sample_loss_values, name='In-sample'),
                go.Scatter(x=x, y=oos_loss_values, name='Out-of-sample')
            ],
            dict(
                title='Training Loss of the Base Model',
                xaxis_title='Epoch', yaxis_title='Loss', showlegend=True
            )
        ).show()

    # Save the base model to the Object Store.
    joblib.dump(
        self._policy,
        self._algorithm.object_store.get_file_path(self._base_model_key)
    )
```

As we discussed, the loss function at this stage is the mean square error (MSE) between BS delta, y, and the policy "action," as in this line:

```
loss = mse(action, y)
```

where `mse` is assigned `nn.MSELoss()`, which is a method in PyTorch. In each training epoch, we have the following four stages: (1) simulating data for training, (2) splitting data into training and testing sets, (3) training model with the train dataset and validating with test dataset, and (4) calculating respective loss function value. In the `generate_data()` function, we obtain the three state variables (time-to-maturity, moneyness, and delta), which is then passed into the `forge_batch()` function to split the simulated data into train/test datasets.

The plotting function outputs the convergence graph of the loss function at this stage, which we will discuss in the "Results" section.

Generating Training Data Using Black-Scholes

We define the BS function here. These are standard BSM equations with GBM. The `norm.cdf()` function takes the risk-neutral equivalent of moneyness d1 and out-of-moneyness d2 to compute the net risk-neutral expected value of the call option discounted to the present with risk-free rate. The readers are encouraged to look up the derivation of BS formula and BSM model available in numerous textbooks and resources, including an excellent entry on Wikipedia.org.

[model.py/AIDeltaHedgeModel/]

```
def black_scholes_call(S,K,sig,r,t):
    d1 = np.log(S/K) + (r+sig**2/2)*t
    d2 = d1 - sig * np.sqrt(t)
    return S * norm.cdf(d1) - K * np.exp(-r * t) * norm.cdf(d2)

def black_scholes_delta(m,sig,r,t):
    d1 = np.log(m+1.) + (r+sig**2/2)*t
    return norm.cdf(d1)
```

Note, the parameters for the underlying stock distribution and risk-free rate are estimated using historical prices of actual stocks, that is, AAPL, and the primary credit rate from the Federal Open Market Committee as the risk-free rate. We will omit the description of the code that estimates the parameters here as they are straightforward. The code is contained within "model.py." Price history of the stocks and risk-free rate are retrieved from market data on QuantConnect.com, using predefined data query functions available on the platform. Without loss of generality, we will train the policy network by considering a fixed volatility level of the individual stock (i.e., AAPL in our example). It is entirely likely that the parameters of the best hedging policy may depend on the stock's volatility. Readers are encouraged to train their models on multiple stock volatility assumptions.

The functions for generating training data and splitting data into train and test subsets are defined next. Note the features that define the state vector is forged into a tensor using PyTorch's method `tensor()`.

[model.py/AIDeltaHedgeModel/]

```
def generate_data(size):
    ttm = np.random.uniform(size=size) * 31 / 252
    moneyness = np.random.uniform(size=size) * 2 - 1
    delta = black_scholes_delta(moneyness,vol,rf,ttm)
    position = np.random.uniform(size=size)
    return ttm, moneyness, delta, position


def forge_batch(moneyness, ttm, delta, position, ratio=0.75):
    cut = int(moneyness.size * ratio)
    tmp = delta * 0.9 + position * 0.1
    states = T.tensor(np.concatenate((moneyness.flatten()[:cut,np.newaxis],
np.sqrt(ttm.flatten())[:cut,np.newaxis],
position.flatten()[:cut,np.newaxis]), axis=1)).float().to(DEVICE)
    y = T.tensor(tmp.flatten()[:cut,np.newaxis]).float().to(DEVICE)

    test_states =
T.tensor(np.concatenate((moneyness.flatten()[cut:,np.newaxis],
np.sqrt(ttm.flatten())[cut:,np.newaxis],
position.flatten()[cut:,np.newaxis]), axis=1)).float().to(DEVICE)
    test_y = T.tensor(tmp.flatten()[cut:,np.newaxis]).float().to(DEVICE)

    return states, y, test_states, test_y
```

Target and Loss Function with Simulated Data

To recap, in this stage of the learning algorithm, we allow the policy network to learn or "mimic" the behavior of "under-hedged" Black-Scholes delta. The term "under-hedged" refers to the fact that the simulated and real hedging strategies are discrete and not continuous. Since delta changes continuously as the underlying stock's volatility and price change, any discrete delta-hedge is insufficient to match the PnL of the option position.

Here, the simulation assumes a BSM process, and therefore, the BS delta is used as a target for learning. In other words, in this step, the policy network will learn to estimate delta, without knowing the underlying mathematics. One can also train the policy network by targeting the PnL of the option position, in which case the policy network will learn the BS prices. In practice, delta is a first derivative of stock price, and it is bounded between 0 and 1 for a call or put option. The policy network will converge more quickly and more robustly with a bounded target like delta.

To generalize the method here with other (derivatives, underlying) pair dynamics that do not have a closed form delta, one can compute delta numerically using the finite-difference method from simulated prices. It is important to note that the policy learned will not be identical to deltas at present nor next period, as the policy hedge ratio for the next period is determined based on the current state (see earlier discussion). Given the stochastic nature of underlying stock, one can only assess the probability distribution of the next period delta, and therefore, there will be finite loss between policy hedge ratio and the BS delta. The example code minimizes MSE, between the policy "action" and target delta, "y."

To avoid confusion, it may be helpful to point out that the purpose of this stage of training is not simply to learn delta from simulated data. It is to "prime" the policy network by mimicking the behavior of delta hedging. Subsequent to learning "delta," the policy network will then learn from historical market data. At this second stage of the training, we will specify a "penalty" function that is based on the variance of the PnL of the hedged portfolio to fine tune, or "reinforce" the policy network.

Fine-tuning with Market Data

In this section, we will fine-tune or reinforce the policy network, with recent historical market data. The purpose of this training stage is to inject a source of "realism." As the previous stage trains the policy network to mimic the behavior of delta hedging, the policy network has only learned the "textbook" rules of hedging. In this stage, we train the policy network on actual market prices, which are presumed to incorporate recent market conditions, such as transaction costs, liquidity, and market trends. In order to fully incorporate information latent in market prices, we define a penalty function on the change of the PnL of the hedged portfolio. The objective of the refinement learning is to minimize the changes in PnL, defined as follows:

$$\Delta_{t+1} = a_{t+1}(S_{t+1} - S_t) - c * (a_{t+1} - a_t) - (C_{t+1} - C_t)$$

where Δ_{t+1} is the "change" in the total value of the hedged portfolio between time t and $t + 1$; a_{t+1}, which is the hedging action, or quantity of the underlying stocks to hold, determined at time t and held until $t + 1$; S_t, which is the price of underlying stock at time t; c is the commission rate of trading the underlying stock, and C_t is the "invoice" price of the call option. Note, the call's invoice price is adjusted from the quoted price by multiplying the quoted price by 100, as per convention of listed options. The loss function is computed by applying a ReLU function to the negative of the "change" in PnL, that is, Δ_{t+1} as a percentage of "wealth," that is, total value of the hedged portfolio, written in code:

```
penalty =  T.relu( - change / wealth)
wealth += change.item()
```

The use of ReLU functional form for the penalty function is an efficient method as ReLU is used as an activation function in the refinement stage. This makes the activation more direct and loss function more likely to converge, as there is no need to compute a separate gradient of descent on the loss function. In addition, the ReLU function penalizes negative changes in wealth but not positive changes. This has the benefit of encouraging learning of potential "alpha" opportunities. Although the objective of hedging is not to generate alpha, it never hurts to pick up the dollar bill lying on the sidewalk when we see one.

Pick Your Poison: Price or Delta?

More seriously, we will pause here to discuss an important design decision in reinforcement learning for hedging options. The central challenge of any training program is an unstable and unbounded target or loss function that does not converge. Option and stock prices are unbounded, and the option price is a non-linear function of the underlying stock price. Even if the underlying stock returns are GBM, which implies that the return is normally distributed, the option prices and returns are not normally distributed, and has extreme skew and kurtosis. Therefore, a PnL-based loss function will likely require large amounts of high-quality data, a (very) large policy network, and many epochs of training to converge, if at all. In order to reduce the variance of loss functions, several choices are available.

First, regularization, a method of "clipping" the loss function in the context of Q-learning, has been tested in academic research. It has been shown to stabilize loss functions during training and speed up convergence (e.g., Du et al., 2020). This is the chosen method on the research platform at the author's firm, Adaptive Investment Solutions, LLC. This is only feasible if the researcher has access to a large amount of high-quality historical market data, and high-end machine-learning processors and GPUs.

The second choice is what we are presenting in this book. Here as we have demonstrated, we start with a policy network primed with "delta hedging" using simulated data. That is, the policy network has already gone to "school" to learn the delta from BSM. We then fine-tune the policy network with recent market data. Effectively, this is a two-step regularization procedure: the policy network is primed with a prior that mimics delta hedging in the first step and will then learn to adjust its actions based on recent market data in the second step. One consequence of this design is that the policy network will be more dynamic but also potentially make more mistakes, that is, taking recent history as an indication of the future. However, the dynamic change in policy is small compared with the core policy behavior of discrete delta hedging. We can make the policy network more stable by simulating more data in the first training stage, if we desire. Figure 7.2 illustrates the two stages of consecutive training and the process of updating the policy forward in time.

Lastly, it is possible to combine the two loss functions into one and train the model on a large amount of historical market data. That is, construct a loss function with a term to minimize the variance between the policy and delta hedging and another term minimizing the variance of the PnL of the hedged portfolio, with a regularization factor to reduce the influence of the PnL term. This method will require hyperparameter tuning. If applied to only historical data, the parameter tuning could result in in-sample overfitting. We did not adopt this method.

Refinement with Real Data

The second stage of training is the refinement of policy network with real market data. The code example for the second stage, `train_asset_model()` is shown here.

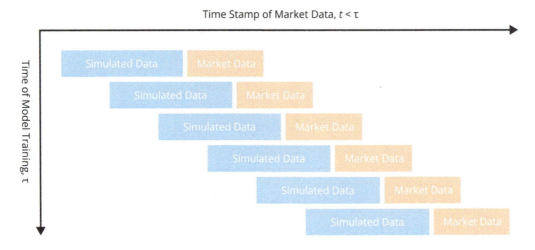

Figure 7.2 Illustrative diagram of the continuous two-stage RL. The RL model can be updated and retrained continuously. At each model update/retraining at time, τ, we will use a short window of market option prices date at $\tau - \Delta t < t < \tau$ for the refinement stage. The simulated dataset can also be updated using a longer historical window of stock prices prior to $\tau - \Delta$ to determining the distribution of stock returns.

[model.py/AIDeltaHedgeModel/]

```python
def train_asset_model(
        self, ticker, start_date, end_date, epochs=20,
        save=False, in_research_env=False):
    # If there is no base model in the Object Store yet, add one.
    if not self._algorithm.object_store.contains_key(self._base_model_key):
        print("No base model in the Object Store. Let's create one first.")
        self.train_base_model()

    # Adjust the QuantBook date to avoid look-ahead bias.
    if in_research_env:
        self._algorithm.set_start_date(end_date)
    # Add a security initializer so that `self._equity.price`
    # isn't zero in research and so we can trade Option contracts
    # right after we subscribe to them while trading.
    self._algorithm.set_security_initializer(
        BrokerageModelSecurityInitializer(
            self._algorithm.brokerage_model,
            FuncSecuritySeeder(self._algorithm.get_last_known_prices)
        )
    )
    # Subscribe to the underlying Equity.
    self._equity = self._algorithm.add_equity(
        ticker, data_normalization_mode=DataNormalizationMode.RAW
    )
    # Create a member on the Equity object to track the current
    # Option contract.
    self._equity.option_contract = None

    self._asset_model_key = "ai-hedging-" + ticker
    epoch_penalties = self.refit(save, epochs)
    # Plot the training penalties.
    if in_research_env:
```

Chapter 7. Better Hedging with Reinforcement Learning

```
            go.Figure(
                go.Scatter(
                    x=list(range(1, epochs+1)), y=epoch_penalties,
                    name='Total Penalty'
                ),
                dict(
                    title='Training Penalties of the Refined Model<br><sub>'
                        + f'Refined the base model for {ticker}</sub>',
                    xaxis_title='Epoch', yaxis_title='Total Pentality',
                    showlegend=True
                )
            ).show()

    if not in_research_env:
        return self._equity.symbol
```

The code is self-explanatory. The function `refit()` is used to compute the penalty function at each epoch as described earlier:

[model.py/AIDeltaHedgeModel/]

```
def refit(self, save=False, epochs=20, lookback=timedelta(2*365)):
    # Load the base model from the Object Store.
    self._policy = joblib.load(
        self._algorithm.object_store.get_file_path(self._base_model_key)
    )
    contract_list_date = self._algorithm.time - lookback
    # Train the base model to be specific to this asset.
    contract_symbols, selected_strikes, data = self._get_data(
        None, contract_list_date, self._algorithm.time
    )
    # Reset the optimizer and run the epochs.
    self._policy.optimizer = optim.AdamW(self._policy.parameters(), lr=1e-5)
    epoch_penalties = []
    for E in range(epochs):
        total_pen = 0
        for k in selected_strikes:
            # Get the closest expiry.
            next_expiry = min(
                [
                    symbol.id.date for symbol in contract_symbols
                    if symbol.id.strike_price == k
                ]
            )
            # Get the Option sequence data.
            path = self._get_option_seq(
                data, k, next_expiry, contract_list_date,
                self._algorithm.time
            )
            s = path['close_underlying']
            c = path['close_option']
            if c.empty:
                continue
            moneyness = s / k - 1
            ttm = np.array(
                [path.shape[0] - i for i in range(path.shape[0])]
            ) / 252
            position = T.zeros([1], device=self._device, dtype=T.float32)
            wealth = c.iloc[0]
```

```python
            self._policy.optimizer.zero_grad()

            for t in range(path.shape[0]-1):
                state = T.cat(
                    (
                        T.tensor(
                            [moneyness.iloc[t], ttm[t]],
                            device=self._device, dtype=T.float32
                        ),
                        position
                    )
                ).unsqueeze(0)
                new_position, _ = self._policy.sample(state)
                change = (
                    new_position * (s.iloc[t+1] - s.iloc[t])
                    - self._commission * (new_position - position)
                    - (c.iloc[t+1] - c.iloc[t])
                )
                penalty =  T.relu( - change / wealth)
                wealth += change.item()
                (penalty).backward()
                total_pen += penalty.item()

            self._policy.optimizer.step()
        epoch_penalties.append(total_pen)

# Save the model to the Object store.
if save or self._algorithm.live_mode:
    joblib.dump(
        self._policy,
        self._algorithm.object_store.get_file_path(self._asset_model_key)
    )
return epoch_penalties
```

Results

The code for forward testing is straightforward and is contained within model.py, which is published in the book's GitHub repository along with other project files used in this example. Here we shall summarize some results, illustrated by the graphs plotted in the training and testing phases.

This demonstration code uses AAPL stock and AAPL call option prices to train the policy network. Figure 7.3 shows the daily closing price of AAPL and AAPL call options from December 2023 and February 2024, the period used for the refinement part of the training. The training is based on the front call options (live options with the closest expiry). As front call options expire, the price series switches to the contract with the next closest expiry. As the graph demonstrates, there is a price discontinuity at each roll. This is not a problem for the RL, as the state variables are updated with the next contract's expiration. Implicitly, calendar roll is in the training data, and the RL may incorporate price dynamics specific to calendar rolls when tuning the policy network.

The convergence of the loss function in the first stage of delta-mimicking training on simulated data is rapid, as shown in Figure 7.4.

Chapter 7. Better Hedging with Reinforcement Learning   301

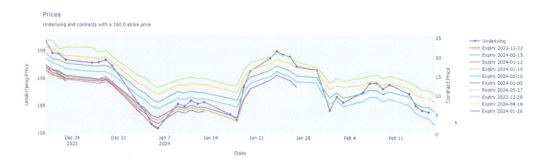

Figure 7.3 Daily closing price of AAPL (Apple, Inc.) shares and APPL Call options with 180 Strike from December 2023 to February 2024.

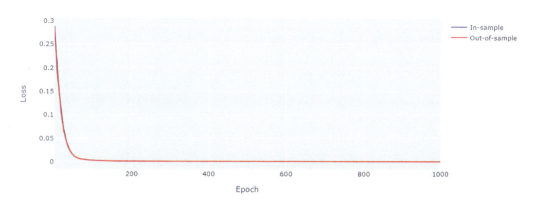

Figure 7.4 Convergence of loss function of the base model, that is, delta-mimicking stage of training. Recall the loss function is the MSE between policy action and delta of the options computed with simulated data. The graph shows rapid convergence both in-sample and out-of-sample. Note, it is not surprising that the convergence of the in-sample and out-of-sample loss functions appear identical. This is because, at this stage, the model is trained on simulated data that are identically distributed between in-sample and out-of-sample.

In the second refinement stage of training with historical market data, the penalty function also converges in a robust manner as Figure 7.5 shows.

Figure 7.6 compares the hedging decision (or action) from the trained policy network to BS delta. The plot shows that the hedging decisions in this case are correlated with BS delta, but the AI policy deployed a lower hedge ratio than the theoretical delta. This makes sense, as in discrete hedging, there is a large variance of potential outcome in the future prices of stocks and call options, as well as delta values. The uncertainty pushes the policy network to take a smaller position in the underlying, since it is less costly to catch up than overshoot the ideal delta, when trading is costly. Also, AAPL price has been in decline earlier in this period. Since delta of a call option declines when underlying stock price decline, the effective forward delta will have been lower than theoretical spot delta.

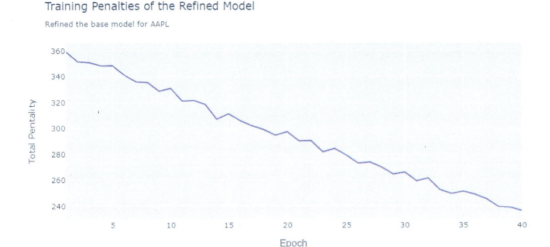

Figure 7.5 Convergence of the PnL-based penalty function (loss function) during the refinement stage. This shows a rapid convergence of penalty function.

Figure 7.6 Comparison of the decision evolution of the full model compared to the evolution of delta of an AAPL call with a 180 strike and a 2024-05-17 expiry. In this case, AI hedging policy appears to under-hedge compared delta. This is likely as AAPL prices have been in decline earlier in this period. Therefore, the effective forward delta would have been lower than theoretical spot delta.

The following two charts, Figures 7.7 and 7.8, show comparisons of the wealth of the hedging portfolio (i.e., the stock portfolio) and the wealth of the hedged portfolio (i.e., call option + stock). These illustrate that the AI hedging policy outperforms all alternative hedging policies. It also has lower variance than numerical hedging, and similar variance to Delta hedging strategies (Hold and Discrete Delta hedging).

Chapter 7. Better Hedging with Reinforcement Learning

Figure 7.7 Cumulative changes of the total wealth of the hedging portfolios of static hedging, that is, "Hold" the original hedging position, the AI hedging portfolio, the delta hedging portfolio, and a numerical hedging portfolio (i.e., hedged with delta calculated using finite difference method with market data).

Figure 7.8 Cumulative changes of the net wealth of the hedged portfolio (i.e., the option + hedging position) of static hedging ("Hold"), the AI hedging portfolio, the delta hedging portfolio, and a numerical hedging portfolio (i.e., hedged with delta calculated using finite difference method with market data).

Conclusion

AI hedging is still in its infancy but has already demonstrated huge potential. This chapter demonstrates that with some care, simple reinforcement learning models can be implemented for practical use. The two-stage process of first priming the policy network with a textbook delta hedging policy on simulated data, followed by refining the policy with a PnL-based penalty function using actual market data, works quite well for small-scale learning models. The methodology is agnostic to the assumptions of the underlying stochastic dynamics of the hedged and hedging assets. Therefore, readers can test various stochastic models for the underlying assets.

A bonus of a robust hedging policy is that, through finding the best optimal hedging policy, one may shed some light on the true underlying security price processes as well, and in turn help with refining the pricing model for the hedged and hedging assets. Indeed, in some advanced RL models of AI hedging, a "pricing" kernel is a natural output of the hedging policy and can be used to predict market prices of options.

Another encouraging result is, through machine learning, we are able to incorporate realistic market conditions, by simply "refining" the learning process on market data. The policy network adjusts to market conditions consistent with the sample data. This is because the hedging policy is agnostic to any structural model of option prices. Therefore, any known or unknown non-fundamental processes or innovations in option prices are admissible, and potentially "learnable." Of course, market conditions evolve over time. It is important to update the model forward. This rolling forward strategy is an age-old learning and fine-tuning strategy of quant finance. We simply updated it for this new generation of AI agents.

Chapter 8

AI for Risk Management and Optimization

The most successful application of artificial intelligence (AI) to asset management may not be the most obvious one. Sometimes, AI should be used to correct human decisions, instead of making them autonomously à la *The Terminator*. AI can also be used for optimizing resource allocation that adapts to the changing environment. We call the former technique Corrective AI, and the latter Conditional Parameter Optimization (CPO). At Predictnow.ai and QTS Capital Management, we have put both techniques into production with significant commercial success.

What Is Corrective AI and Conditional Parameter Optimization?

The holy grail of machine learning (ML) is Artificial General Intelligence: essentially cloning a silicon version of a human being that can make all autonomous decisions. Unfortunately (or fortunately depending on your point of view), that day is still far off. For example, despite the billions of R&D dollars spent on building fully autonomous vehicles, we don't yet find too many of them driving around our neighborhoods. (For a sobering assessment of Tesla Fully Self-driving capability, check out qnt.co/book-tesla-autopilot.) On the other hand, we can hardly buy a new car these days without a fully loaded set of assisted driving technologies.

The same is true in asset management. I have spent decades, starting at IBM's Watson Lab, later at various financial institutions such as Morgan Stanley's AI group, and finally at QTS Capital Management, researching machine learning and then applying it to fully autonomous trading systems. If it were a resounding success, I would have been too busy sipping champagne on my super yacht to write about this. The reality is that few funds have found success in this endeavor (López de Prado, 2017). But a few years ago, we learned that there was a much more pragmatic way to deploy machine learning to commercial problems that does not involve waiting for decades. It is already here.

We believe that AI is much more effective in correcting erroneous decisions made by humans or other simple algorithms than in making them from scratch. That's what we call "Corrective AI."

When we learned of this concept from the financial machine-learning expert Dr. Marcos Lopez de Prado who described it as "meta-labeling" (López de Prado, 2018), we immediately tested it on our fund's crisis alpha strategy in late 2019. To our amazement, it made three consequential, and correct, predictions on that strategy. From November 2019 to January 2020, Corrective AI told us that we shouldn't expect any crisis in the market, and therefore shouldn't run our crisis alpha strategy. Investors thought we were asleep in those 3 months and grew concerned. Starting in early February 2020, it suddenly flashed red and told us to expect a crisis and recommended trading at full leverage. The subsequent COVID-induced financial crisis led to about 80% gross return in the next few months. But Corrective AI wasn't done yet. In early November 2020, it once again told us that we shouldn't expect any more crises. A few days later, on November 9, Pfizer and BioNTech announced their vaccine.

Because of the shocking effectiveness and the general applicability of this approach, we launched Predictnow.ai to commercialize this technique beyond finance. After all, asset management is the most challenging use case for AI (López de Prado, 2017). If Corrective AI worked for us in asset management with its ultra-low signal-to-noise and ultra-competitive arbitrage environment, surely it would work charmingly in other enterprise applications.

Beyond correcting decisions, we also found that AI can provide a way to optimize any business process, especially in resource allocation, more effectively than traditional optimization methods. Traditional optimization methods involve finding the parameters that generate the best results based on past data for a given business process, such as a trading strategy or stocking a retail shelf. However, when the objective function is dependent on external time-varying and stochastic conditions, traditional optimization methods may not produce optimal results. For example, in the case of a trading strategy, an optimal stop loss may depend on the market regime, which may not be clearly defined. In the case of retail shelf space optimization, the optimal selection may depend on whether it is a back-to-school season or a holiday season. Furthermore, even if the exact set of conditions is specified, the outcome may not be deterministic. Machine learning is a better alternative to solving this problem. Using machine learning, we can approximate this objective function by training its many nodes using historical data. We call this novel optimization method Conditional Parameter Optimization, or more specifically Conditional Portfolio Optimization (CPO either way), when the objective is to optimize capital allocation of a portfolio.

Encouragingly, these ideas were well-received across multiple industries. We spoke to the principals of an oil exploration firm. They used a simple formula with just a small handful of variables to predict the productivity of an oil well. We showed them how machine learning can exploit a much larger set of variables, discover their non-linear dependencies, and correct the predictions of their simple formula. Note that we are not asking them to replace their existing formula, which is well-known and well-trusted in the oil industry—we are only correcting it.

Similarly, semiconductor manufacturers often use an expert system, handcrafted with many rules created by process engineers, to predict the outcome of a manufacturing process. We spoke to the head of production control and the head of AI of a major semiconductor manufacturer and discussed how Corrective AI can learn from a much larger set of predictors and make real-time adjustments to their manufacturing process.

In practically every enterprise, there will be an opportunity for Corrective AI and CPO to improve their process. We deliver this service to all verticals via a common Software-as-a-Service (SaaS) platform but with bespoke input features specific to each vertical.

Naturally, because of our domain expertise in finance, we have created our earliest product and found the earliest success in the asset management industry. We launched our SaaS platform for asset managers to correct their investment decisions and optimize their capital allocations, and to date our many clients range from professional traders to institutional fund managers, spanning both traditional and crypto asset classes.

New users to our platform are often surprised to find that we don't always need to use deep learning techniques. Researchers have found that deep learning, while enormously successful in image and speech recognition and other natural language processing tasks, is not well-suited to most commercial datasets (including most financial data sets). Such data are often "heterogeneous" (Shwartz-Ziv and Armon, 2021). Furthermore, deep learning tends to require a much larger dataset than is available in commercial use cases, and it often requires a much longer time to train than the technique we use. Another advantage of our technique is "explainability": we have published multiple papers on how we can offer better intuition to the human operators of what input features are really important to the predictions (Man and Chan, 2021a, 2021b). We have ultimately gone beyond merely "correcting decisions" to "improving decisions," that is, optimizing the parameters of a commercial process via CPO.

In the process of serving asset managers, we learned another key success factor in commercializing AI. No matter how good your algorithm is, it is useless to the customer unless we also provide pre-engineered input features, customized to each application domain. For asset managers, we created more than 600 such features in traditional markets (Nautiyal and Chan, 2021) and more than 800 such features in crypto markets (Viville, Sawal, and Chan, 2022). It requires our deep domain expertise to create these features, but many of our customers find them to be our most compelling value proposition. The same is true for our proof-of-concept with our oil exploration partner. They thought they had just a handful of input features to predict oil well productivity. One of our data scientists with geological engineering expertise showed them how we can create tens of thousands of them. In the next section, we will summarize some of the features used in asset management.

Feature Engineering

Features are inputs to supervised machine-learning models (Figure 8.1). In traditional finance, they are typically called "factors," and they are used in linear regression models to either explain or predict returns. In the former usage, the factors are contemporaneous with the target returns, while in the latter the factors must be from a prior period.

Figure 8.1 All these names are synonymous.

There are generally two types of factors: cross-sectional vs. time-series (Ruppert and Matteson, 2015). If you are modeling stock returns, cross-sectional factors are variables that are specific to an individual stock, such as its earnings yield, dividend yield, and so on. For example, Predictnow.ai has created 40 stocks' fundamental features, free to all QuantConnect subscribers. These cross-sectional features are sourced from the Sharadar stock fundamental dataset. This dataset contains more than 6,000 US listed companies and nearly 10,000 delisted companies. We have carefully vetted this list to ensure it is survivorship-bias-free and that all the data is captured point-in-time, without restatements. (You might be surprised to find that some much more expensive commercial datasets from well-known vendors are *not* point-in-time, and thus cannot be used for machine learning or backtesting.) This data is available quarterly, yearly, and for trailing 12 months (these are called the three "dimensions" in Sharadar's terminology). The original Sharadar dataset has around 140 raw data fields. We have arrowed and filtered this down to 40 essential features for users, as many of the features in the original set were redundant or highly correlated.

To use this data for machine learning, the time series data has been made stationary. For indicators that are denominated in dollars, such as total assets or capex (capital expenditure), we compute the percentage change between a given filing and the next. For indicators that are already in percentages like gross margin or net margin, we simply take the difference between the values for successive filings. These conversions are done for each of the three dimensions: quarterly, yearly and trailing 12 months.

We have also normalized this data cross-sectionally to facilitate easy comparisons across different stocks. This allows users to merge data from different stocks into a single training data set for easy input into our application program interface (API). We multiply ratios like "earnings-per-share" or "debt-per-share" with the total number of common shares outstanding, divide by the enterprise value, then finally take the difference between consecutive filings. To reiterate, this normalization is done for each of the three dimensions.

Predictnow.ai has also ensured that a reused ticker symbol is assigned to the last company that uses that ticker, not to a delisted company that previously had that ticker. This is to avoid any kind of survivorship biases. All reused ticker symbols are available with a numeric counter as a postfix at the end. For example, Australia Acquisition corporation and Ares Acquisition corporation both have the ticker symbol AAC. Australia Acquisition corporation was delisted in 2012, so it is available as AAC1 in our database. In contrast, Ares Acquisition corporation is still actively listed as AAC. Conversely, in the case where the ticker symbol for a company has changed over time, all its data is tied to its last valid ticker.

As Securities and Exchange Commission (SEC) filings generally happen at arbitrary times on any given day, to avoid look-ahead biases during backtests, the date of the associated data has been shifted to the next trading day to guarantee its availability long before the market opens.

Predictnow.ai enables automatic merging of this fundamental data with your own technical or higher frequency data as one single input dataset for machine learning. When merging the Sharada fundamental features with higher frequency data, the fundamental features are forward filled until the next valid filing date. For example, gross margin for quarterly filings will be forward filled for all dates until the gross margin for the next quarter is available on the date of its filing.

But as we advocate using ML for risk management and capital allocation purposes (i.e., Corrective AI and CPO), not for returns predictions, you may wonder how these factors can help predict the returns of your trading strategy or portfolio. For example, if you have a long-short portfolio of tech stocks, such as AAPL, GOOG, AMZN, and so on, and want to predict whether the portfolio as a whole will be profitable in a certain market regime, does it really make sense to have the earnings yields of AAPL, GOOG, and AMZN as individual features? We will discuss how they can be used soon.

Meanwhile, time-series factors are typically market-wide or macroeconomic variables such as the familiar Fama-French (1995) three factors: market (simply, the market index return), SMB (the relative return of small cap vs. large cap stocks), and HML (the relative return of value vs. growth stocks). These time-series factors are eminently suitable for Corrective AI and CPO because they can be used to predict your portfolio or strategy's returns.

Cross-sectional Factors	Time-series Factors
Stock-specific	Market-wide
e.g., P/E, B/M, DivYld, ...	e.g., HML, SMB, WML, ...
Use that to explain/predict stocks' returns	Use that to explain/predict portfolio's/strategy's returns
Regression models	Classification models

Figure 8.2 Cross-section vs. time-series features.

Given that many more obvious cross-sectional factors than time-series factors are available (Figure 8.2), it seems a pity that we cannot use cross-sectional factors as features for Corrective AI and CPO. Actually, we can; Eugene Fama and Ken French themselves showed us how. If we have a cross-sectional factor on a stock, all we need to do is to use it to rank the stocks, form a long-short portfolio using the rankings, and use the returns of this portfolio as a time-series factor. The long-short portfolio is called a hedge portfolio.

We show the process of creation of a hedge portfolio with the help of an example, starting with Sharadar's fundamental cross-sectional factors (which we generated as shown in Nautiyal and Chan, 2021). There are 40 cross-sectional factors updated at three different frequencies: quarterly, yearly, and 12 month trailing. In this example, however, we use only the quarterly cross-sectional factors. Given a factor like capex (capital expenditure), we consider the normalized (the normalization procedure was discussed earlier) capex of approximately 8,500 stocks on particular dates from January 1, 2010, until the current date. Four particular dates are of interest every year: January 15, April 15, July 15, and October 15. We call these the ranking dates. On each of these dates we find the percentile rank of the stock based on normalized capex. The dates are carefully chosen to capture changes in the cross-sectional factors of the maximum number of stocks post the quarterly filings.

Once the capex across stocks is ranked at each ranking date (four dates) each year, we obtain the stocks present in the upper quartile (i.e., ranked above 75 percentile) and the stocks present in the lower quartile (i.e., ranked below 25 percentile). We take a long position on the ones that showed highest normalized capex and take a short position on the ones with the lowest. Both these sets together make our long-short hedge portfolio.

Once we have the portfolio on a given ranking date, we generate the daily returns of the portfolio using risk parity allocation (i.e., allocate proportional to inverse volatility). The daily returns of each chosen stock are calculated for each day till the next ranking date. The portfolio weights on each day are the normalized inverse of the rolling standard deviation of returns for a 2-month window. These weights change on a daily basis and are multiplied to the daily returns of individual stocks to get the daily portfolio returns. If a portfolio stock is delisted in between ranking dates, we simply drop the stock and do not use it to calculate the portfolio returns. The daily returns generated in this process are the capex time series factors. This process is repeated for all other Sharadar cross-sectional factors.

So, voila! Forty cross-sectional factors become forty time-series factors, and they can be used as input to Corrective AI or CPO applications for any portfolio or trading strategy, whether it trades stocks, futures, FX, or anything at all.

Following are a number of other notable features we created:

NOPE (net options pricing effect; Francus 2020) is a normalized measure of the net delta imbalance between the put and call options of a traded instrument across its entire option chain, calculated at the market close for contracts of all maturities. This indicator was invented by Lily Francus and is normalized with the total traded volume of the underlying instrument. The imbalance estimates the amount of delta hedging by market markers needed to keep their positions delta-neutral. This hedging causes price movement in the underlying, which NOPE should ideally capture. The data for this has been sourced from deltaneutral.com, and the instrument we applied it to was SPY ETF options. The SPX index options weren't used because the daily traded volume of the underlying SPX index "stock" was ill-defined. It was calculated as the traded volume of the constituents of the index.

Canary is an indicator that acts similar to a canary in a coal mine and will raise an alarm when there's an impending danger. This indicator comes from the dual momentum strategies of Keller and Keuning (2017). The canary value can be either 0, 1, or 2. This is a daily measure of which of the two bond or stock ETFs has a negative absolute momentum: (1) BND, Vanguard Total Bond Market ETF; (2) VMO, Vanguard Emerging Markets Stock Index Fund ETF. The momentum is calculated using the 13612W method where we take a proportionally weighted average of percentage change in the bond/stock ETF returns in the last 1 month, 3 months, 6 months, and 1 year. In the paper, the values of "0,""1," or "2" of the canary portfolio represent what percentage of the canary is bullish. This indicates what proportion of the asset portfolio was allocated to global risky assets (equity, bond, and commodity ETFs) and what proportion was allocated to cash. For example, a "2" would imply 100% cash or cash equivalents, while a "0" would imply 100% allocation to the global risky assets. Alternatively, a value of "1" would imply 50% allocation to global risky assets and 50% to cash.

Carry (Koijen et al. 2016) defined a carry feature as "the return on a futures position when the price stays constant over the holding period." (It is also called "roll yield" or "convenience yield.") We calculate carry for (1) global equities, calculated as a ratio of expected dividend and daily close prices; (2) SPX futures, calculated from price of front month SPX futures contract and spot price of the index; and (3) currency, calculated from the two nearest months' futures data.

Order flow. The underlying reason for the price movement for an asset is the imbalance of buyers and sellers. An onslaught of market sell orders portends a decrease in price and vice versa. Order flow is the signed transaction volume aggregated over a period and over many transactions in that period to create a more robust measure. It's also positively correlated with the price movement. This feature is calculated using tick data from Algoseek with aggressor tags (which flag the trade as a buy or sell market order). The data is time-stamped at milliseconds. We aggregate the tick-based order flow to form order flow per minute.

Consider the following example.

Order flow feature with time stamp 10:01 am ET will consider trades from 10:00:00 am ET to 10:00:59 am ET, as shown in Table 8.1.

Table 8.1 Example trade ticks

Time	Trade Size	Aggressor Tag
10:00:01 am	1	B
10:00:03 am	4	S
10:00:09 am	2	B
10:00:19 am	1	S
10:00:37 am	5	S
10:00:59 am	2	S

The order flow would be $1 - 4 + 2 - 1 - 5 - 5 = -9$. This would be reflect in our feature as Time:10:01, Order flow: −9

Applying Corrective AI to Daily Seasonal Forex Trading

Let us now illustrate how Corrective AI can improve the Sharpe ratio of a daily seasonal Forex trading strategy. This trading strategy takes advantage of the intraday seasonality of forex returns. Breedon and Ranaldo (2012) observed that foreign currencies depreciate versus the US dollar during their local working hours and appreciate during the local working hours of the US dollar. We first backtested the results of Breedon and Ranaldo on recent EUR/USD data from September 2021 to January 2023, and then applied Corrective AI to this trading strategy to achieve a significant increase in performance. (Portions of this section were published in Belov, Chan, Jetha, and Nautiyal, 2023).

Breedon and Ranaldo (2012) described a trading strategy that shorted EUR/USD during European working hours (3 am ET to 9 am ET, where ET denotes the local time in New York, accounting for daylight savings) and bought EUR/USD during US working hours (11 am ET to 3 pm ET). The rationale is that large-scale institutional buying of the US dollar takes place during European working hours to pay global invoices and the reverse happens during US working hours. Hence, this effect is also called the "invoice effect."

There is some supportive evidence for the time-of-the-day patterns in various measures of the forex market like volatility (Andersen and Bollerslev, 1998), turnover (Hartmann, 1999), and return (Cornett, Schwarz, and Szakmary, 1995). Essentially, local currencies depreciate during their local working hours for each of these measures and appreciate during the working hours of the United States.

Figure 8.3 describes the average hourly return of each hour in the day over a period starting from 2019-10-01 17:00 ET to 2021-09-01 16:00 ET. It reveals the pattern of returns in EUR/USD. The return pattern in the previously described "working hours" reconciles with the hypothesis of a prevalent "invoice effect" broadly. Returns go down during European working and up during US working hours.

As this strategy was published in 2012, it offers ample time for true out-of-sample testing. We collected 1-minute bar data of EUR/USD from Electronic Broking Services (EBS) and performed a backtest over the out-of-sample period October 2021–January 2023. The Sharpe ratio of the strategy in this period is 0.88, with average annual returns

Chapter 8. AI for Risk Management and Optimization   313

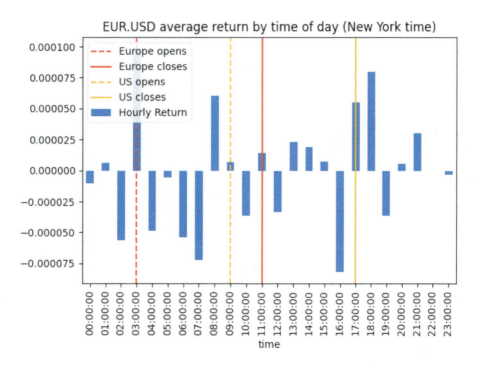

Figure 8.3 Average EURSUD return by time of day (New York time).

of 3.5%, and a maximum drawdown of −3.5%. The alpha of the strategy apparently endured. (For the purpose of this article, no transaction costs are included in the backtest because our only objective is to compare the performances with and without Corrective AI, not to determine if this trading strategy is viable in live production.)

Figure 8.4 shows the equity curve ("growth of $1") of the strategy during the out-of-sample period. The cumulative returns during this period are just below 8%. We call this the "Primary" trading strategy, i.e., the strategy before any Corrective AI was applied.

Figure 8.4 Equity curve of Primary trading strategy in out-of-sample period.

The sample backtest code for this Primary trading strategy is shown in qnt.co/bookcai-backtesting. (The code cannot actually be executed without input data, and license agreement would not allow us to share the input data.)

Code for Primary Trading Strategy

```
FOREX Strategy using Corrective Artificial Intelligence (CAI)

# This notebook connects to PredictNow, trains a model, and generates
# predictions. The model hypothesis is that USD will rise against
# the EUR during EUR business hours and # all during the USD business
# hours. This is called the time of the day effect and seen due to
# HF OF and returns.

# Connect to PredictNow
from AlgorithmImports import *
from QuantConnect.PredictNowNET import PredictNowClient
from QuantConnect.PredictNowNET.Models import *
from datetime import datetime, time
from io import StringIO
import pandas as pd

qb = QuantBook()
client = PredictNowClient("account@email.com", "your_username")
client.connected

#Prepare the Data
# In this notebook, we will create a strategy that short EURUSD when
# Europe is open and long when Europe is closed and US is open. We
# will aggregate the daily return of this static strategy that is
# activate everyday, and use CAI to predict if the strategy is
# profitable for a given date. We will follow this On and Off signal
# to create a dynamic strategy and benchmark its performance.

# load minute bar data of EURUSD
symbol = qb.add_forex("EURUSD").symbol
df_price = qb.History(symbol, datetime(2020,1,1),
datetime(2021,1,1)).loc[symbol]

# resample to hourly returns
minute_returns = df_price["close"].pct_change()
hourly_returns = (minute_returns + 1).resample('H').prod() - 1
df_hourly_returns = hourly_returns.to_frame()
df_hourly_returns['time'] = df_hourly_returns.index.time

# generate buy and sell signals and get strategy returns
# Sell EUR.USD when Europe is open
sell_eur = ((df_hourly_returns['time'] > time(3)) &
(df_hourly_returns['time'] < time(9)))

# Buy EUR.USD when Europe is closed and US is open
buy_eur = ((df_hourly_returns['time'] > time(11)) &
(df_hourly_returns['time'] < time(15)))
```

```
# signals as 1 and -1
ones = pd.DataFrame(1, index=df_hourly_returns.index, columns=['signals'])
minus_ones = pd.DataFrame(-1, index=df_hourly_returns.index,
columns=['signals'])
signals = minus_ones.where(sell_eur, ones.where(buy_eur, 0))

# strategy returns
strategy_returns = df_hourly_returns['close'] * signals['signals']
strategy_returns = (strategy_returns + 1).resample('D').prod() - 1
df_strategy_returns = strategy_returns.to_frame().ffill()

#Save the Data
# We will label the data and save it to disk (ObjectStore) with the
# model name. This file will be uploaded to PredictNow.
# Define the model name and data label
model_name = "fx-time-of-day"
label = "strategy_ret"

# Label the data and save it to the object store
df_strategy_returns = df_strategy_returns.rename(columns={df_strategy_returns.
columns.to_list()[0]: label})
parquet_path = qb.object_store.get_file_path(f'{model_name}.parquet')
df_strategy_returns.to_parquet(parquet_path)
```

Suppose we have a trading model (like the Primary trading strategy just described) for setting the side of the bet (long or short). We just need to learn the size of that bet, which includes the possibility of no bet at all (zero sizes). This is a situation that practitioners face regularly. A machine-learning algorithm can be trained to determine that. To emphasize, we do not want the machine-learning algorithm to learn or predict the side, just to tell us what the appropriate size is. This is an application of Corrective AI because we want to build a secondary machine-learning model that learns how to use a primary trading model.

We train an machine-learning algorithm to compute the "Probability of Profit" (PoP) for the next minute-bar. If the PoP is greater than 0.5, we will set the bet size to 1; otherwise, we will set it to 0. In other words, we adopt the step function as the bet sizing function that takes PoP as an input and gives the bet size as an output, with the threshold set at 0.5. This bet sizing function decides whether to take the bet or pass, a purely binary prediction.

The training period was from 2019-01-01 to 2021-09-30 while the out-of-sample test period was from 2021-10-01 to 2023-01-15, consistent with the out-of-sample period we reported for the Primary trading strategy. The model used to train ML algorithm was done using the predictnow.ai Corrective AI API, with more than a hundred pre-engineered input features (predictors). The underlying learning algorithm is a gradient-boosted decision tree.

After applying Corrective AI, the Sharpe ratio of the strategy in this period is 1.29 (an increase of 0.41), with average annual returns of 4.1% (an increase of 0.6%) and a maximum drawdown of −1.9% (a decrease of 1.6%). The alpha of the strategy is significantly improved.

The equity curve of the Corrective AI filtered secondary model signal can be seen in Figure 8.5.

The sample training, testing, and backtest codes for this Corrective AI-enhanced trading strategy are shown in qnt.co/book-cai-research. (The code cannot actually be executed without a Premium Subscription to Predictnow.ai's API.)

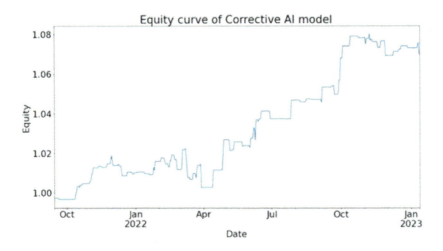

Figure 8.5 Equity curve of Corrective AI model in out-of-sample period.

Features used to train the Corrective AI model include technical indicators generated from indices, equities, futures, and options markets. Many of these features were

Corrective AI Code
```
# Create the Model
# Create the model by sending the parameters to PredictNow
model_parameters = ModelParameters(
    mode=Mode.TRAIN,
    type=ModelType.CLASSIFICATION,
    feature_selection=FeatureSelection.SHAP,
    analysis=Analysis.SMALL,
    boost=Boost.GBDT,
    testsize=42.0,
    timeseries=False,
    probability_calibration=False,      # True  to refine your probability
    exploratory_data_analysis=False,    # True to use exploratory analysis
    weights="no")                       # yes, no, custom

create_model_result = client.create_model(model_name, model_parameters)
str(create_model_result)
# Train the Model
# Provide the path to the data, and its label. This task may take
# several minutes.
train_request_result = client.train(model_name, parquet_path, label)
```

```python
str(train_request_result)
# Get the training result
# The training results include dataframes with performance metrics
# and predicted probability and labels.
training_result = client.get_training_result(model_name)
str(training_result)

# Predicted probability (float between 0 and 1) for
# validation/training data set the last column notes the probability
# that it's a "1", i.e. positive return
predicted_prob_cv = pd.read_json(StringIO(training_result.predicted_prob_cv))
print("predicted_prob_cv")
print(predicted_prob_cv)

# Predicted probability (float between 0 and 1) for
# the testing data set
predicted_prob_test = pd.read_json(StringIO(training_result.
predicted_prob_test))
print("predicted_prob_test")
print(predicted_prob_test)

# Predicted label, 0 or 1, for validation/training data set.
# Classified as class 1 if probability > 0.5
predicted_targets_cv = pd.read_json(StringIO(training_result.
predicted_targets_cv))
print("predicted_targets_cv")
print(predicted_targets_cv)

# Predicted label, 0 or 1, for testing data set.
# Classified as class 1 if probability > 0.5
predicted_targets_test = pd.read_json(StringIO(training_result.
predicted_targets_test))
print("predicted_targets_test")
print(predicted_targets_test)

# Feature importance score, shows what features are being
# used in the prediction. More helpful when you include your features
# and only works when you set feature_selection to
# FeatureSelection.SHAP or FeatureSelection.CMDA
if training_result.feature_importance:
    feature_importance = pd.read_json(StringIO(training_result.
feature_importance))
    print("feature_importance")
    print(feature_importance)

# Performance metrics in terms of accuracies
performance_metrics = pd.read_json(StringIO(training_result.
performance_metrics))
print("performance_metrics")
print(performance_metrics)
# Start Predicting with the Trained Model
predict_result = client.predict(model_name, parquet_path,
exploratory_data_analysis=False, probability_calibration=False)
str(predict_result)
```

created using Algoseek's high-frequency futures and equities data. More discussions of these features can be found in Nautiyal and Chan (2021).

By applying Corrective AI to the time-of-the-day Primary strategy, we were able to improve the Sharpe ratio and reduce drawdown during the out-of-sample backtest period. This aligns with observations made in the literature on meta-labeling.

What Is Conditional Parameter Optimization?

Every trader knows that there are market regimes that are favorable to their strategies and others that are not. Some regimes are obvious, like bull vs. bear markets, calm vs. choppy markets, and so forth. These regimes affect many strategies and portfolios (unless they are market-neutral or volatility-neutral portfolios) and are readily observable and identifiable (but perhaps not predictable). Other regimes are more subtle and may only affect a specific strategy. Regimes may change every day, and they may not be observable. It is often not as simple as saying the market has two regimes, and we are currently in regime 2 instead of 1. For example, with respect to the profitability of your specific strategy, the market may have an infinite number of regimes ranging from very favorable to very unfavorable. For example, a momentum trading strategy's returns could be positively correlated with market volatility, which is obviously a continuous, not a discrete, variable.

Regime changes sometimes necessitate a complete change of trading strategy (e.g., trading a mean-reverting instead of momentum strategy). Other times, traders just need to change the parameters of their existing trading strategy to adapt to a different regime. As we mentioned earlier, PredictNow.ai has come up with a novel way of adapting the parameters of a trading strategy called CPO. This invention allows traders to adapt their trading parameters as frequently as they like—perhaps for every trading day or even every single trade. (This section is substantially the same as that in Chapter 7 of Chan 2021 and is reprinted here for completeness and ease of reference.) CPO uses machine learning to place orders optimally based on changing market conditions (regimes) in any market. Traders in these markets typically already possess a basic trading strategy that decides the timing, pricing, type, and/or size of such orders. This trading strategy will usually have a small number of adjustable trading parameters. Conventionally, they are often optimized based on a fixed historical data set ("train set"). Alternatively, they may be periodically reoptimized using an expanding or rolling train set. (The latter is often called "Walk Forward Optimization.") With a fixed train set, the trading parameters clearly cannot adapt to changing regimes. With an expanding train set, the trading parameters still cannot respond to rapidly changing market conditions because the additional data is but a small fraction of the existing train set. Even with a rolling train set, there is no evidence that the parameters optimized in the most recent historical period generate better out-of-sample performance. A too-small rolling train set will also give unstable and unreliable predictive results, given the lack of statistical significance. All these conventional optimization procedures can be called unconditional parameter optimization, as the trading parameters do not intelligently respond to rapidly changing market conditions. Ideally, we would like trading parameters that are much more sensitive to the market conditions and yet are trained on a large enough amount of data.

To address this adaptability problem, we apply a supervised machine-learning algorithm (we have used random forest with boosting, but the CPO methodology is indifferent to the specific learning algorithm) to learn from a large feature set that captures various aspects of the prevailing market conditions, together with specific values of the trading parameters, to predict the outcome of the trading strategy. (An example outcome is the strategy's future one-day return.) Once such machine-learning model is trained to predict the outcome, we can apply it to live trading by feeding in the same features that represent the latest market conditions as well as various combinations of the trading parameters. The set of parameters that results in the optimal predicted outcome (e.g., the highest future one-day return) will be selected as optimal and will be adopted for the trading strategy for the next period. The trader can make such predictions and adjust the trading strategy as frequently as needed to respond to rapidly changing market conditions.

In the example in the next section, we apply CPO using PredictNow.ai's financial machine-learning API to adapt the parameters of a Bollinger Band-based mean reversion strategy on GLD (the gold ETF) and obtain superior results.

The CPO technique is useful in industry verticals other than finance as well; after all, optimization under time-varying and stochastic condition is a very general problem. For example, wait times in a hospital emergency room may be minimized by optimizing various parameters, such as staffing level, equipment and supplies readiness, discharge rate, and so on. Current state-of-the-art methods generally find the optimal parameters by looking at what worked best on average in the past. There is also no mathematical function that exactly determines wait time based on these parameters. The CPO technique can employ other variables, such as time of day, day of week, season, weather, whether there are recent mass events, and so on, to predict the wait time under various parameter combinations, and thereby find the optimal combination under the current conditions to achieve the shortest wait time.

Applying Conditional Parameter Optimization to an ETF Strategy

To illustrate the CPO technique, we next describe an example trading strategy on an ETF.

This strategy uses the lead-lag relationship between the GLD and GDX ETFs using 1-minute bars from January 1, 2006, until December 31, 2020, splitting it 80%/20% between train/test periods. The trading strategy has three trading parameters: the hedge ratio (GDX_weight), entry threshold (entry_threshold), and a moving lookback window (lookback). The spread is defined as follows:

$$Spread(t) = GLD\_close(t) - GDX\_close(t) * GDX\_weight. \qquad (1)$$

We may enter a trade for GLD at time t, and exit it at time $t + 1$ minute, hopefully realizing a profit. We want to optimize the three trading parameters on a $5 \times 10 \times 8$ grid. The grid is defined as follows:

$$GDX\_weight = \{2, 2.5, 3, 3.5, 4\}$$
$$entry\_threshold = \{0.2, 0.3, 0.4, 0.5, 0.7, 1, 1.25, 1.5, 2, 2, 5\}$$
$$lookback = \{30, 60, 90, 120, 180, 240, 360, 720\}$$

To be clear, even though we are using GLD and GDX prices and functions of these prices to make trading decisions, for simplicity of illustration we only trade GLD, unlike the typical long-short pair trading setup.

Every minute we compute Spread(t) in equation (1), and compute its "Bollinger Bands," conventionally defined as follows:

$$Z\_score(t) = \frac{Spread(t) - Spread\_EMA(t)}{\sqrt{Spread\_VAR(t)}} \qquad (2)$$

where Spread_EMA is the exponential moving average of the Spread, and Spread_VAR is its exponential moving variance (see Definitions of Spread_EMA & Spread_VAR at the end of this chapter for their conventional definitions).

Similar to a typical mean-reverting strategy using Bollinger Bands, we trade into a new GLD position based on these rules:

a. Buy GLD, if Z_score < -entry_threshold (resulting in long position).
b. Short GLD, if Z_score > entry_threshold (resulting in short position).
c. Liquidate long position, if Z_score > exit_threshold.
d. Liquidate short position, if Z_score < -exit_threshold.

The exit_threshold can be anywhere between entry_threshold and −entry_threshold. After optimization in the train set, we set exit_threshold = −0.6*entry_threshold and keep that relationship fixed when we vary entry_threshold in our future (unconditional or conditional) parameter optimizations. We trade the strategy on 1-minute bars between 9:30 and 15:59 ET, and liquidate any position at 16:00. For each combination of our three trading parameters, we record the daily return of the resulting intraday strategy and form a time series of daily strategy returns, to be used as labels for our machine-learning step in CPOs. Note that since the trading strategy may execute multiple round trips per day before forced liquidation at the market close, this daily strategy return is the sum of such round-trip returns.

Unconditional vs. Conditional Parameter Optimizations

In conventional, unconditional, parameter optimization, we select the three trading parameters (GDX_weight, entry threshold, and lookback) that maximize cumulative in-sample return over the three-dimensional parameter grid using exhaustive search. (Gradient-based optimization did not work due to multiple local maxima). We use that fixed set of three optimal trading parameters and use them to specify the strategy out-of-sample on the test set.

With conditional, parameter optimization, the set of trading parameters used each day depends on a predictive machine-learning model trained on the train set. This model will predict the future one-day return of our trading strategy, given the trading parameters and other market conditions. Since the trading parameters can be varied at will (i.e., they are control variables), we can predict a different future return for many sets of trading parameters each day, and select the optimal set that predicts the highest future return. That optimal parameter set will be used for the trading strategy for the next day. This step is taken after the current day's market close and before the market open of the next day.

In addition to the three trading parameters, the predictors (or "features") for input to our machine-learning model are eight technical indicators obtained from the Technical Analysis Python library: Bollinger Bands Z-score, Money Flow, Force Index, Donchian Channel, Average True Range, Awesome Oscillator, and Average Directional Index. We choose these indicators to represent the market conditions. Each indicator actually produces 2 × 7 features, since we apply them to each of the ETFs GLD and GDX price series, and each was computed using seven different lookback windows: 50, 100, 200, 400, 800, 1600, and 3200 minutes. (Note: This is not the same as the trading parameter "lookback" described earlier.) Hence, there are a total of 3 + 8 × 2 × 7 = 115 features used in predicting the future 1-day return of the strategy. But because there are 5 × 10 × 8 = 400 combinations of the three trading parameters, each trading day comes with 400 rows of training data that looks something like Table 8.2 (labels—future returns—are not displayed):

After the machine-learning model is trained, we can use it for live predictions and trading. Each trading day after the market closes, we prepare an input vector, which is structured like one row of Table 8.2, populated with one particular set of the trading parameters and the current values of the technical indicators, and use the machine-learning model to predict the trading strategy's return on the next day. We do that 400 times, varying the trading parameters, but obviously not the technical indicators' values,

Table 8.2 A 1-day slice of features table as input to the machine-learning model.

GDX_weight	entry_threshold	lookback	Z-score-GLD(50)	Z-score-GDX(50)	Money-Flow-GLD(50)	Money-Flow-GDX(50)	...
2	0.2	30	0.123	0.456	1.23	4.56	...
2	0.2	60	0.123	0.456	1.23	4.56	...
2	0.2	90	0.123	0.456	1.23	4.56	...
...							
4	5	240	0.123	0.456	1.23	4.56	...
4	5	360	0.123	0.456	1.23	4.56	...
4	5	720	0.123	0.456	1.23	4.56	

and find out which trading parameter set predicts the highest return. We adopt that optimal set for the trading strategy next day. In mathematical terms,

$$\begin{aligned}(GDX\_weight\_optimal, &entry\_threshold\_optimal, lookback\_optimal) \\ = argmax(GDX\_weight, &entry\_threshold, lookback)\{\ldots \\ predict(GDX\_weight, &entry\_threshold, lookback, technicalindicators)\}\end{aligned} \quad (3)$$

where predict is the predictive function available from predictnow.ai's API, which uses random forest with boosting as the machine-learning model.

It is important to understand that unlike a naïve application of machine learning to predict GLD's one-day return using technical indicators, we are using machine learning to predict the return of a trading strategy applied to GLD given a set of trading parameters and using those predictions to optimize these parameters on a daily basis. The naïve approach is less likely to succeed because everybody is trying to predict GLD's (i.e., gold's) returns and inviting arbitrage activities, but nobody is predicting the returns of this particular GLD trading strategy (unless they take this toy example too seriously!). Furthermore, many traders do not like using machine learning as a black box to predict returns. In CPO, the trader's own strategy is making the actual predictions. Machine learning is merely used to optimize the parameters of this trading strategy. This provides for much greater degree of transparency and interpretability.

Performance Comparisons

We compare out-of-sample test set performance of unconditional vs. conditional parameter optimization on the last three years of data ending on December 31, 2020, and find the cumulative three-year return to be 73% and 83%, respectively. All other metrics are improved using conditional parameter optimization. See Table 8.3 and Figure 8.6.

Table 8.3 Out-of-sample performances of unconditional vs. conditional parameter optimization

	Unconditional Optimization	Conditional Optimization
Annual Return	17.29%	19.77%
Sharpe Ratio	1.947	2.325
Calmar Ratio	0.984	1.454

Conditional Portfolio Optimization

Regime Changes Obliterate Traditional Portfolio Optimization Methods

While CPO showed promise in optimizing the operating parameters of trading strategies, its greatest potential lies in its potential to optimize *portfolio allocations*. We

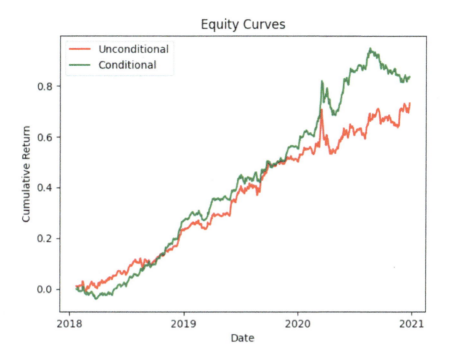

Figure 8.6 Cumulative returns of strategies based on conditional vs. unconditional parameter optimization.

refer to this approach as Conditional **Portfolio** Optimization (which, fortuitously, shares the same acronym).

To recap, traditional optimization methods involve finding the parameters that generate the best results based on past data for a given business process, such as a trading strategy. For instance, a stop loss of 1% may have yielded the best Sharpe ratio for a trading strategy tested over the last 10 years, or stocking a retail shelf with sweets generate the best profit over the last 5 years. Although the numerical optimization process can be complex due to various factors, such as the number of parameters, the non-linearity of objective functions, or the number of constraints on the parameters, standard methods are available to handle such difficulties. However, when the objective function is dependent on external time-varying and stochastic conditions, traditional optimization methods may not produce optimal results. Machine learning is a better alternative to solve this problem.

In the context of financial portfolio optimization, where the parameters to optimize are the capital allocations to various components of a portfolio to achieve the best financial performance objective, there are several competing machine learning approaches. As far as we know, all of them (e.g., Tomasz and Katarzyna, 2021; or Cong et al., 2021) involve using cross-sectional features to predict the returns of individual components of a portfolio. This is a highly challenging task with uncertain success. More problematically, such cross-sectional features are also often unavailable for portfolios with components whose identities are undisclosed in commercial applications, rendering such cross-sectional returns predictions even more difficult. We will elaborate on this advantage of CPO in the following section. (Portions of this section were published in Chan, Fan, Sawal, and Ville, 2023.)

Learning to Optimize

Machine learning (especially neural networks, see Hornik, Stinchcombe, and White, 1989) can be used to approximate any function, including the objective function for our portfolio optimization, by training on historical data. (We will henceforth refer to this machine-learning model as the ML model. We primarily use gradient-boosted trees, but neural networks or other algorithms can be equally effective.) The inputs to this ML model will not only include the parameters that we originally set out to optimize, but also the vast set of features that measure the external conditions. For example, to represent a "market regime" suitable for portfolio optimizations, we may include market volatility, behaviors of different market sectors, macroeconomic conditions, and many other input features. The output of this ML model would be the outcome you want to optimize. For example, maximizing the future 1-month Sharpe ratio of a portfolio is a typical outcome. In this case, you would feed historical training samples to the ML model that include the capital allocations of the various components of the portfolio, the market features, plus the resulting forward 1-month Sharpe ratio of the portfolio as "labels" (i.e., target variables). Once trained, this ML model can then predict the future 1-month Sharpe ratio based on any hypothetical set of capital allocations and the current market features. The components of the portfolio could be stocks in a mutual fund or trading strategies in a hedge fund. For example, in Table 8.4, we display the input features for one day of a portfolio optimization problem:

Table 8.4 A 1-day slice of features table as input to the neutral network

GOOG	MSF	AAPL	VIX	Oil 30d Return	GDP Growth	VIX	...
20%	60%	20%	15.3	0.456%	1.23%	4.56%	...
25%	60%	15%	15.3	0.456%	1.23%	4.56%	...
30%	60%	10%	15.3	0.456%	1.23%	4.56%	...
...							
40%	50%	10%	15.3	0.456%	1.23%	4.56%	...
45%	50%	5%	15.3	0.456%	1.23%	4.56%	...
50%	50%	0%	15.3	0.456%	1.23%	4.56%	

Control Features | Market Features

Assuming that the features that measure market regimes (denoted "Market features" in Table 8.4) have a daily frequency, a 1-day slice of the features table nevertheless contains many rows (samples). Each row represents a unique capital allocation—we call them "control features." For a portfolio that holds S&P 500 stocks, for instance, there will be up to 500 parameters (if cash is included). In this case, we are supposed to feed into the neural network *all possible combinations* of these 500 parameters, plus the market features, and find out what the resulting forward 1-month Sharpe ratio (or whatever performance metric we want to maximize) is. *All possible combinations?* If we represent the capital weight allocated to each stock as $w_s \in [0, 1]$, assuming we are not allowing short positions, the search space has $[0, 1]^{500}$ combinations. Even discretizing to a grid search, our computer will need to run till the end of time to finish. And that is just for one day; training the neural net will require many days of such samples that include the features and the resulting labels (forward 1-month Sharpe ratio). Overcoming this curse of dimensionality by intelligently sampling the grid is one of the major breakthroughs Predictnow.ai has accomplished. Intelligent sampling involves, for example, not sampling those parts of the 500-dimensional grid that are unlikely to generate optimal portfolios, or not sampling those parts of the grid that result in portfolios that are too similar to an existing sample.

Perhaps the following workflow diagrams (Figures 8.7, 8.8, and 8.9) can illuminate the process:

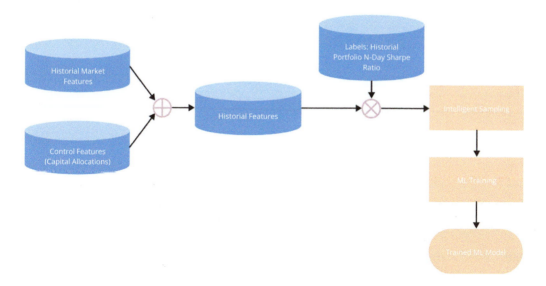

Figure 8.7 Training a portfolio performance prediction machine.

Ranking Is Easier Than Predicting

Some readers may argue that if a ML model can predict the Sharpe ratio of a portfolio based on its parameters and market features, why not use the model to directly predict the underlying assets' returns and replace the original portfolio altogether? However, with our CPO method, you don't need to predict the portfolio's Sharpe ratio accurately; you just need to predict which set of parameters give the *best* Sharpe

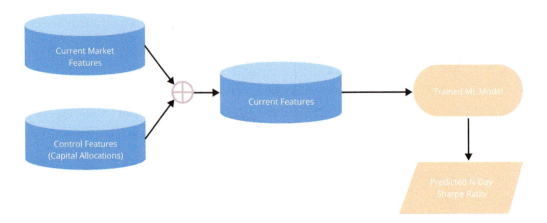

Figure 8.8 Live prediction of portfolio performance (inferences).

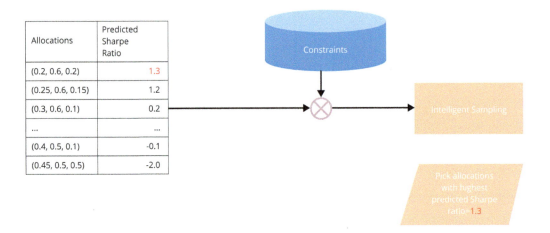

Figure 8.9 Optimization step.

ratio. Even if the Sharpe ratio predictions come with huge error bars, it is the *ranking* of predicted Sharpe ratio that matters. The situation is analogous to many alpha models for stock selection: to form a profitable long-short portfolio of stocks, an alpha model doesn't need to predict the cross-sectional returns accurately, but only needs to rank them correctly. We don't have an alpha model to predict or even rank such cross-sectional returns. (If we did, we wouldn't be offering that to clients as a technology product; we would offer it as a performance-fee-based managed account service.) Our client has used its own alpha model to select the portfolio components for us already. All we need to do is to rank the various capital allocations applied to a client's portfolio based on their predicted Sharpe ratios. It is a much less demanding predictive model if we only care that it gets the ranking of the labels correctly (Poh et al., 2020).

The Fama-French Lineage

With CPO, not only is it unnecessary to predict cross-sectional returns, but we also don't need to use any cross-sectional features as input to our optimizer. Instead, we only use market features that are sometimes called "time series factors" (Ruppert and Matteson, 2015). Can a ML model really predict portfolio returns without any cross-sectional features? Let's draw an analogy with the Fama-French three-factor model (Fama and French, 1995). Recall that Fama and French proposed that we can explain (not predict) a portfolio's returns using just three factors: the market index return, SMB which measures the outperformance of small cap stocks over large cap stocks, and HML, which measures the outperformance of value stocks over growth stocks. (Note that these factors can be negative, where "outperformance" becomes "underperformance.") The explanatory model is just a linear regression fit using these three factors as independent variables against the current-period portfolio return, hopefully with a decent R^2. But if we use these as predictive factors (or features) to forecast the next-period portfolio return, the R^2 of such a regression fit will be poor. This may be because we have too few factors. We can try to improve it by adding hundreds of factors (e.g., using our "factor zoo"; Nautiyal and Chan, 2021), capturing all manners of market regimes and risks. But many of these factors will be collinear or insignificant and will continue to cause high bias and variance (Murphy, 2012). So finally, we are led to the application of non-linear machine-learning model that can deal with such multicollinearity and insignificance, via standard techniques such as features selection (Man and Chan, 2021a, 2021b) and regularization. If we also add to the input "control features" that *condition* the prediction on the capital allocation in the portfolio, we have come full circle and arrive at Conditional Portfolio Optimization.

Comparison with Conventional Optimization Methods

To assess the value of Conditional Portfolio Optimization, we need to compare it with alternative portfolio optimization methods. The default method is Equal Weights, which involves allocating equal capital to all portfolio components. Another simple method is Risk Parity, where the capital allocation to each component is inversely proportional to its return volatility. It is called Risk Parity because each component is supposed to contribute an equal amount of risk, as measured by volatility, to the overall portfolio's risk. This method assumes zero correlations among the components' returns, which is of course unrealistic. Then there is the Markowitz method, also known as Mean-Variance optimization. This well-known method, which earned Harry Markowitz a Nobel prize, maximizes the Sharpe ratio of the portfolio based on the historical means and covariances of the component returns through a quadratic optimizer. The optimal portfolio that has the maximum historical Sharpe ratio is also called the *tangency portfolio*. One of us wrote about this method in a previous blog post (Chan, 2014) and its equivalence to the Kelly formula. It certainly doesn't take into account market regimes or any market features. It is also a vagrant violation of the familiar refrain, "Past performance is not indicative of future results," and is known to be highly sensitive to slight variations of input and to produce all manners of unfortunate instabilities (see Ang, 2014; López de Prado, 2020). Nevertheless, it is the standard portfolio optimization method that many asset managers use. Finally, there is the Minimum Variance portfolio, which uses Markowitz's method not to maximize the Sharpe ratio, but to minimize the variance (and hence volatility) of the portfolio's returns. Even though this approach does not maximize a portfolio's past Sharpe ratio, it often achieves better forward Sharpe ratios than the tangency portfolio! Another case of "past performance is not indicative of future results."

Some researchers compute expected cross-sectional returns using an alpha model, and then use Markowitz's optimization by inputting these returns (Tomasz and Katarzyna, 2021). However, in practice most alpha models do not produce expected cross-sectional returns accurately enough as input for a quadratic optimizer. As we explained before, the beauty of our method is that we don't need cross-sectional returns nor cross-sectional features of any kind as input to the ML model. Only "time series" market features are used.

Let's see how our Conditional Portfolio Optimization method stacks up against these conventional methods.

Based on a client's request, we tested how our CPO performed for an ETF (TSX: MESH) given the constraints that we cannot short any stock, and the weight w_s of each stock s obeys $w_s \in [0.5\%, 10\%]$, but we can allocate a maximum of $w_c=10\%$ of the portfolio to cash, with $\sum_s w_s + w_c = 1$. See Table 8.5.

Table 8.5 MESH ETF

Period	Method	Sharpe Ratio	CAGR
2021-08–2022-07	Equal Weights	−0.76	−30.6%
(Out-of-sample)	Risk Parity	−0.64	−22.2%
	Markowitz	−0.94	−30.8%
	Minimum Variance	−0.47	−14.5%
	CPO	−0.33	−13.7%

In the bull market, CPO performed similarly to the Markowitz method. However, it was remarkable that CPO was able to switch to defensive positions and outperformed the Markowitz method in the bear market of 2022. Overall, it improved the Sharpe ratio of the Markowitz portfolio by more than 60%. That is the whole rationale of *Conditional Portfolio Optimization*: it adapts to the expected future external conditions (market regimes) instead of blindly optimizing on what happened in the past. Because of the long-only constraint and the tight constraint on cash allocation, the CPO portfolio still suffered negative returns. But if we had allowed the optimizer to allocate a maximum of 50% of the portfolio NAV to cash, it would have delivered positive returns. The dramatic effect of cash allocation will be evident in the next example.

In the next example, we tested the CPO methodology on a private investor's tech portfolio, consisting of seven US and two Canadian stocks, mostly in the tech sector.

We call this the Tech Portfolio. The constraints are that we cannot short any stock, and the weight w_s of each stock s obeys $w_s \in [0\%, 25\%]$, and we can allocate a maximum of $w_c = 50\%$ of the portfolio to cash, with $\sum_s w_s + w_c = 1$. See Table 8.6.

Table 8.6 Tech Portfolio

Period	Method	Sharpe Ratio	CAGR
2021-08–2022-07	Equal Weights	0.39	6.36%
(Out-of-sample)	Risk Parity	0.49	7.51%
	Markowitz	0.40	6.37%
	Minimum Variance	0.23	2.38%
	CPO	0.70	11.0%

CPO performed better than both alternative methods under all market conditions. It improves the Sharpe ratio over the Markowitz portfolio by 75% as the market experienced a regime shift around January 2022. Figure 8.10 shows the comparative equity curves.

Figure 8.10 Comparative performances of various portfolio optimization methods on Tech Portfolio. (Out-of-sample period starts August 2021.)

Even though this portfolio is tech-heavy, it was able to generate a positive return during this trying out-of-sample period of 2021-08–2022-07. The reason is that it can allocate 50% of the NAV to cash, as one can see by looking at the time evolution of the cash component in Figure 8.11.

In Figure 8.11, the highlighted time periods indicate when CPO allocated maximally to cash. The overlay of the S&P 500 Index reveals that these periods are highly correlated with the drawdown periods of the market index, even during out-of-sample

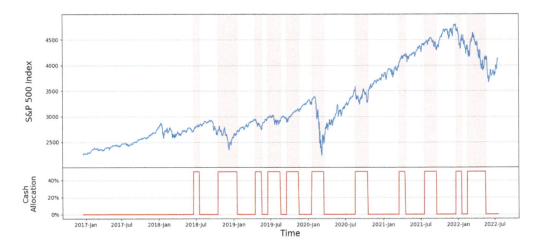

Figure 8.11 Cash allocation vs. market regime of tech portfolio.

period. This supports our hypothesis that CPO can rapidly adapt to market regime changes.

We also tested how CPO performs for some non-traditional assets: a portfolio of eight crypto currencies, again allowing for short positions and aiming to maximize its 7-day forward Sharpe ratio. See Table 8.7.

Table 8.7 Crypto portfolio

Method	Sharpe Ratio
Markowitz	0.26
CPO	1.00

(These results are over an out-of-sample period from January 2020 to June 2021, and the universe of cryptocurrencies for the portfolio are BTCUSDT, ETHUSDT, XRPUSDT, ADAUSDT, EOSUSDT, LTCUSDT, ETCUSDT, XLMUSDT). CPO improves the Sharpe ratio over the Markowitz method by a factor of 3.8.

Finally, to illustrate that CPO doesn't just work on portfolios of assets, we apply it to a portfolio of FX trading strategies managed by a FX hedge fund WSG; see Table 8.8. (WSG is our client, and we published these results with their permission.) It is a portfolio of seven trading strategies s, and the allocation constraints are $w_s \in [0\%, 40\%]$, $w_c \in [0\%, 100\%]$, with $\sum_s w_s + w_c = 1$. See Table 8.8.

Table 8.8 WSG's FX strategies portfolio

Method	Sharpe Ratio
Equal Weights	1.44
Markowitz	2.22
CPO	2.65

(These results are over an out-of-sample period from January 2020 to July 2022.) CPO improves the Sharpe ratio over the Markowitz method by 19%. WSG has decided to deploy CPO in production starting July 2022. Since then, CPO has added about 60bps per month to the portfolio over their previous proprietary allocation method.

In all four cases, CPO outperformed both the naive Equal Weights portfolio and the Markowitz portfolio during a market downturn, while generating similar performance during the bull market. It is important to note that we do not claim CPO can outperform *all* other allocation methods for *all* portfolios in *all* periods. Some portfolios may be constructed to be so factor-neutral that CPO can't improve on any conventional allocation method. For other portfolios, CPO may underperform a conventional allocation method for a certain period with the benefit of hindsight (*ex post*), but nevertheless outperform the best conventional allocation method selected at the beginning of the period (*ex ante*). We provide an illustration of this effect through the following model portfolio.

Model Tactical Asset Allocation Portfolio

The purpose of studying a model tactical asset allocation (TAA) portfolio is not only to investigate whether CPO can outperform conventional allocation methods, but also to observe how CPO allocates across different asset classes over evolving market regimes. The model portfolio we selected comprises five ETFs representing various asset classes: GLD (gold), IJS (small cap stocks), SPY (large cap stocks), SHY (1–3 year Treasury bonds), and TLT (20+ year Treasury bonds). This portfolio is inspired by the Golden Butterfly portfolio created by (Tyler, 2016). To train our ML model, we use the period January 2015 to December 2018, while the out-of-sample test period covers January 2019 to December 2022. The portfolio rebalances every 2 weeks, and CPO aims to maximize the Sharpe Ratio over the forward 2-week period. The constraint is $w_s \in [0\%, 100\%]$, $\sum_s w_s = 1$, with no cash allocation allowed (since SHY is practically cash).

Table 8.9 In- and Out-of-sample performance of TAA portfolio

Period	Method	Sharpe Ratio	CAGR
2015-01–2018-12 (In-sample)	Equal Weights	0.51	3.60%
	Risk Parity	0.62	1.87%
	Markowitz	0.59	5.26%
	Minimum Variance	0.47	1.13%
	CPO	0.63	3.93%

Period	Method	Sharpe Ratio	CAGR
2019-01–2022-12 (Out-of-sample)	Equal Weights	0.62	6.61%
	Risk Parity	0.22	1.16%
	Markowitz	-0.13	-2.09%
	Minimum Variance	-0.05	0.39%
	CPO	0.42	3.83%

Table 8.9 shows during the out-of-sample period, CPO generates the second-highest Sharpe ratio, trailing only the Equal Weights method. However, selecting Equal Weights ex ante would not have been an obvious choice, since it generated the second-lowest Sharpe ratio during the in-sample period. If we were to choose a conventional allocation method ex ante, Risk Parity would have been our choice, but it underperformed CPO out-of-sample as measured by both the Sharpe ratio and CAGR, the latter by more than threefold.

To gain more transparency into the CPO method, we can examine its allocations at various times in Figure 8.12.

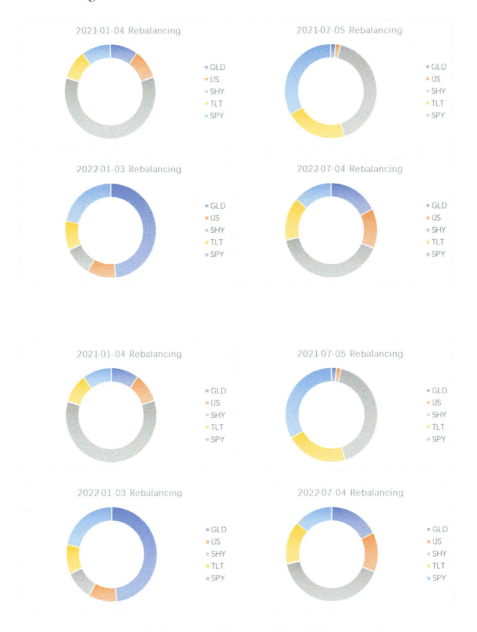

Figure 8.12 Time evolution of allocations of TAA portfolio. (GLD is deep blue.)

It is noteworthy that the portfolio had a high allocation to large-cap stocks beginning in July 2019, just before the market experienced a period of calm appreciation over the next 6 months. The high allocation to short-term treasuries in January 2020 proved to be prescient in light of the COVID-induced financial crisis that followed. The portfolio also had a high allocation to gold at the beginning of 2022, which fortuitously anticipated the surge in commodity prices due to the war in Ukraine. Finally, the allocation to small-cap stocks increased in mid-2022, which performed better than large-cap stocks during that year.

CPO Software-as-a-Service

For clients of Predictnow.ai's CPO Software-as-a-Service (SaaS) platform, we can optimize any objective function, not just Sharpe ratio. For example, we have been asked to minimize Expected Shortfall and UPI. We can also add specific constraints to the desired optimal portfolio, such as average ESG rating, maximum exposure to various sectors, or maximum turnover during portfolio rebalancing. The only other input we require is the historical returns of the portfolio components (unless these components are publicly traded assets, in which case clients only need to tell us their tickers). If these components changed over time, we will also need the historical components.

We will provide pre-engineered market features (Nautiyal and Chan, 2021) that capture market regime information. If the client has proprietary market features that may help predict the returns of their portfolio, they can merge those with ours as well. Clients' features can remain anonymized. We will be providing an API for clients who wish to experiment with various constraints and hyperparameters (such as the frequency of portfolio rebalancing) and their effects on the optimal portfolio.

In the two code examples below, we show a sample client-side Jupyter Notebook and calls on our CPO API. (The code cannot actually be executed without input data, and license agreement would not allow us to share the input data.) (qnt.co/book-cpo-research) (qnt.co/book-cpobacktesting)

CPO Code

```
# Generate Portfolio Weights to Run a LEAN Backtest
# This notebook connects to PredictNow, optimizes the portfolio
# weights for each rebalance, and then saves the rebalancing weights
# for each month into the Object Store. After you run the cells in
# this notebook, you can run the algorithm in main.py, which uses
# the portfolio weights from PredictNow in a LEAN backtest.

# Connect to PredictNow

from QuantConnect.PredictNowNET import PredictNowClient
from QuantConnect.PredictNowNET.Models import *
from time import sleep
from datetime import datetime
algorithm_start_date = datetime(2020, 2, 1)
algorithm_end_date = datetime(2024, 4, 1)
```

```python
qb = QuantBook()
client = PredictNowClient("test@quantconnect.com")
client.connected

# Upload Asset Returns
# The returns file needs to have sufficient data to cover
# the backtest period of the algorithm in main.py and the in-sample
# backtest, which occurs before algorithm_start_date.
# Calculate the daily returns of the universe constituents.
tickers = [
    "TIP", "BWX", "EEM", "VGK", "IEF", "QQQ", "EWJ", "GLD",
    "VTI", "VNQ", "TLT", "RWX", "SPY", "DBC", "REM", "SCZ"
]
symbols = [qb.add_equity(ticker).symbol for ticker in tickers]
df = qb.history(
    symbols, datetime(2019, 1, 1), algorithm_end_date, Resolution.Daily
).close.unstack(0)

# Save the returns data into the Object Store.
df.rename(lambda x: x.split(' ')[0], axis='columns', inplace=True)
returns_file_name = "ETF_return_Test.csv"
returns_file_path = qb.object_store.get_file_path(returns_file_name)
df.pct_change().dropna().to_csv(returns_file_path)

# Upload the returns file to PredictNow.
message = client.upload_returns_file(returns_file_path)
print(message)

# List the return files you've uploaded.
return_files = client.list_returns_files()
','.join(return_files)

# Upload Constraints
# The constraints must contain a subset of the assets in the returns file. The CPO system only
# provides portfolio weights for assets that have constraints.
# Define the constraints.
constraints_by_symbol = {
    Symbol.create(ticker, SecurityType.EQUITY, Market.USA).ID: contraint
    for ticker, contraint in {
        "SPY": (0, 0.5),
        "QQQ": (0, 0.5),
        "VNQ": (0, 0.5)
    }.items()
}

# Create the constraints file.
content = "component,LB,UB"
for symbol, boundaries in constraints.items():
    content += f'\n{symbol},{boundaries[0]},{boundaries[1]}'

# Save the constraints file in the Object Store.
constraints_file_name = "ETF_constrain_Test.csv"
qb.object_store.save(constraints_file_name, content)

# Upload the constraints file to PredictNow.
constraint_file_path = qb.object_store.get_file_path(constraints_file_name)
message = client.upload_constraint_file(constraint_file_path)
print(message)
```

```python
# List the constraint files you've uploaded.
constraint_files = client.list_constraint_files()
','.join(constraint_files)

# Define the Portfolio Parameters
portfolio_parameters = PortfolioParameters(
    name=f"Demo_Project_{datetime.now().strftime('%Y%m%d')}",
    returns_file=returns_file_name,
    constraint_file=constraints_file_name,
    #feature_file=feature_file_name,
    max_cash=1.0,
    rebalancing_period_unit="month",
    rebalancing_period=1,
    rebalance_on="first",
    training_data_size=3,
    evaluation_metric="sharpe"
)

# Run the In-Sample Backtest
# The in-sample period must end before the set_start_date in main.py.
# Since our algorithm does monthly rebalancing at the beginning
# of each month, the training_start_date argument should align with
# the start of the month and the training_end_date should be one day
# before the start date in main.py.
in_sample_result = client.run_in_sample_backtest(
    portfolio_parameters,
    training_start_date=datetime(2019, 1, 1),
    training_end_date=algorithm_start_date-timedelta(1),
    sampling_proportion=0.3,
    debug="debug"
)
print(in_sample_result)

def wait_for_backtest_to_finish(id_, sleep_seconds=60):
    job = client.get_job_for_id(id_)
    while job.status != "SUCCESS":
        job = client.get_job_for_id(id_)
        print(job.status)
        sleep(sleep_seconds)
    return job

job = wait_for_backtest_to_finish(in_sample_result.id)
print(job)
# Run the Out-Of-Sample Backtest
# The out-of-sample period should match the start and end dates
# of the algorithm main.py. It is important to keep the
# training_start_date parameters have the same format
# for in-sample and out-of-sample tests. For this example, we are
# working on a portfolio that takes monthly rebalance on the first
# market day of the month, so we will keep training_start_date
# to the 1st of the month in the out-of-sample test.

out_of_sample_result = client.run_out_of_sample_backtest(
    portfolio_parameters,
    training_start_date=algorithm_start_date,
    training_end_date=algorithm_end_date,
    debug="debug"
)
print(out_of_sample_result)
```

```python
job = wait_for_backtest_to_finish(out_of_sample_result.id)
print(job)

# Get the Backtest Weights

# Let's get the portfolio weights from the preceding out-of-sample
# backtest. These are the weights you will use to run the LEAN
# algorithm in main.py. Save the portfolio weights into the Object
# Store so that you can load them in the algorithm.
weights_by_date = client.get_backtest_weights(
    portfolio_parameters,
    training_start_date=algorithm_start_date,
    training_end_date=algorithm_end_date,
    debug= "debug"
)
print(weights_by_date)

# Save the weights into the Object Store.
qb.ObjectStore.Save("ETF_Weights_Test1.csv", json.dumps(weights_by_date))
```

CPO Code

```python
# region imports
from AlgorithmImports import *

from QuantConnect.PredictNowNET import PredictNowClient
from QuantConnect.PredictNowNET.Models import *
from time import sleep
from datetime import datetime
# endregion


class PredictNowCPOAlgorithm(QCAlgorithm):
    """
    This algorithm demonstrates how to use PredictNow.ai to perform
    Conditional Portfolio Optimization (CPO). CPO utilizes the trailing
    asset returns and hundreds of other market features from PredictNow
    to determine weights that will maximize the future 1-month Sharpe
    ratio of the portfolio. The algorithm rebalances at the beginning
    of each month. To backtest this algorithm, first run the cells in
    the `research.ipynb` notebook.
    """

    def initialize(self):
        self.set_start_date(2020, 2, 1)
        self.set_end_date(2024, 4, 1)
        self.set_cash(100000)

        # Define the universe.
        tickers = [
            "TIP", "BWX", "EEM", "VGK", "IEF", "QQQ", "EWJ", "GLD",
            "VTI", "VNQ", "TLT", "RWX", "SPY", "DBC", "REM", "SCZ"
        ]
        self._symbols = [self.add_equity(ticker).symbol for ticker in tickers]

        if self.live_mode:
            # Connect to PredictNow.
            self._client = PredictNowClient("jared@quantconnect.com")
            if not self._client.connected:
                self.quit(f'Could not connect to PredictNow')
```

```python
        # Define some parameters.
        self._in_sample_backtest_duration = timedelta(
            self.get_parameter("in_sample_days", 365)
        )
        self._out_of_sample_backtest_duration = timedelta(
            self.get_parameter("out_of_sample_days", 365)
        )
    else:
        # Read the weights file from Object Store.
        self._weights_by_date = pd.read_json(
            self.object_store.Read("ETF_Weights_Test1.csv")
        )
    # Schedule training and trading sessions.
    self.train(
        self.date_rules.month_start(self._symbols[0].symbol),
        self.time_rules.after_market_open(self._symbols[0].symbol, -10),
        self._rebalance
    )
    # Add a warm-up period to avoid errors on the first rebalance.
    self.set_warm_up(timedelta(7))

def _rebalance(self):
    # Don't trade during warm-up.
    if self.is_warming_up:
        return
    # In live mode, get the weights from PredictNow.
    date = self.time.date()
    if self.live_mode:
        self._get_live_weights(date)

    # Create portfolio targets.
    targets = []
    for symbol, weight in self._weights_by_date[str(date)].items():
        self.log(f"Setting weight for {symbol.value} to {weight}")
        targets.append(PortfolioTarget(symbol, weight))

    # Rebalance the portfolio.
    self.set_holdings(targets, True)

def _get_live_weights(self, date):
    self.log(f"Loading live weights for {date}")

    # Upload the returns file to PredictNow.
    # Note: the history request includes an extra 2 months of data
    # so that we can move the start and end dates of the in-sample
    # and out-of-sample backtests so that they align with the start
    # and end of each month.
    self.debug(f"Uploading Returns file")
    returns_file_name = f"ETF_return_{str(date)}.csv"
    file_path = self.object_store.get_file_path(returns_file_name)
    returns = self.history(
        self._symbols,
        (self._in_sample_backtest_duration
        + self._out_of_sample_backtest_duration
        + timedelta(60)),
        Resolution.DAILY
    ).close.unstack(0).pct_change().dropna()
    returns.to_csv(file_path)
```

```python
        self._client.upload_returns_file(file_path)
        self.debug(f"Uploaded file: {file_path}")

        # Create the asset weight constraints.
        content = "component,LB,UB"
        constraints_by_symbol = {
            Symbol.create(ticker, SecurityType.EQUITY, Market.USA).id: contraint
            for ticker, contraint in {
                "SPY": (0, 0.5),
                "QQQ": (0, 0.5),
                "VNQ": (0, 0.5),
                "REM": (0, 0.33),
                "IEF": (0, 0.5),
                "TLT": (0, 0.5)
            }.items()
        }

        # Upload the contraints file to PredictNow.
        self.debug(f"Uploading Contraints file")
        for symbol, boundaries in constraints_by_symbol.items():
            content += f'\n{symbol},{boundaries[0]},{boundaries[1]}'
        constraints_file_name = f"ETF_constraint_{str(date)}.csv"
        self.object_store.save(constraints_file_name, content)
        file_path = self.object_store.get_file_path(constraints_file_name)
        self.debug(f"Uploaded file: {file_path}")
        self._client.upload_constraint_file(file_path)

        # Define the portfolio parameters.
        portfolio_parameters = PortfolioParameters(
            name=f"Demo_Project_{str(date)}",
            returns_file=returns_file_name,
            constraint_file=constraints_file_name,
            max_cash=1.0,
            rebalancing_period_unit="month",
            rebalancing_period=1,
            rebalance_on="first",
            training_data_size=3,
            evaluation_metric="sharpe"
        )

        # Calculate the dates of the in- and out-of-sample backtests.
        oos_start_date, oos_end_date = self._get_start_and_end_dates(
            date, self._out_of_sample_backtest_duration
        )
        is_start_date, is_end_date = self._get_start_and_end_dates(
            oos_start_date-timedelta(1), self._in_sample_backtest_duration
        )

        # Run the in-sample backtest.
        self.debug("Running in-sample backtest")
        in_sample_result = self._client.run_in_sample_backtest(
            portfolio_parameters,
            training_start_date=is_start_date,
            training_end_date=is_end_date,
            sampling_proportion=0.3,
            debug="debug"
        )
        in_sample_job = self._client.get_job_for_id(in_sample_result.id)
```

```python
        # Run the out-of-sample backtest.
        self.debug("Running out-of-sample backtest")
        out_of_sample_result = self._client.run_out_of_sample_backtest(
            portfolio_parameters,
            training_start_date=oos_start_date,
            training_end_date=oos_end_date,
            debug="debug"
        )
        out_of_sample_job = self._client.get_job_for_id(out_of_sample_result.id)

        # Wait until the backtests finish running.
        self.debug("Checking if the backtests are done")
        while (in_sample_job.status != "SUCCESS" or
               out_of_sample_job.status != "SUCCESS"):
            in_sample_job = self._client.get_job_for_id(in_sample_result.id)
            out_of_sample_job = self._client.get_job_for_id(
                out_of_sample_result.id
            )
            self.debug(f"In Sample Job: {in_sample_job.status}")
            self.debug(f"Out of Sample Job: {out_of_sample_job.status}")
            sleep(60)

        # Run the live prediction.
        self.debug("Running Live Prediction")
        exchange_hours = self.securities[self._symbols[0]].exchange.hours
        live_prediction_result = self._client.run_live_prediction(
            portfolio_parameters,
            rebalance_date=date,
            next_rebalance_date=exchange_hours.get_next_market_open(
                Expiry.end_of_month(self.time), extended_market_hours=False
            ).date(),
            debug="debug"
        )
        live_job = self._client.get_job_for_id(live_prediction_result.id)

        # Wait until the live prediction job is done.
        self.debug("Checking Live prediction job status")
        while live_job.status != "SUCCESS":
            live_job = self._client.get_job_for_id(live_prediction_result.id)
            self.debug(f"Live Prediction status: {live_job.status}")
            sleep(60)

        # Get the prediction weights.
        self._weights_by_date = self._client.get_live_prediction_weights(
            portfolio_parameters,
            rebalance_date=date,
            debug="debug"
        )

    def _get_start_and_end_dates(self, date, duration):
        start_date = end_date - duration
        start_date = datetime(start_date.year, start_date.month, 1)
        return start_date, end_date
```

Conclusion

In this chapter, we first demonstrated the power of machine learning to correct decisions made by an expert system, in this case an algorithmic Forex trading strategy, via our Corrective AI implementation. The key ingredients for success in Corrective AI are not so much the underlying machine-learning algorithm, but the proprietary input features one must engineer for a specific business process. Secondly, we demonstrated the success of Conditional Parameter Optimization (CPO) in optimizing the parameters of a business process, in this case an algorithmic ETF trading strategy. Thirdly, we demonstrated the superiority of Conditional Portfolio Optimization (also abbreviated as CPO) in optimizing resource allocation over conventional methods, in this case the capital allocation to portfolios of financial instruments.

It is intuitively obvious that the optimal solution to a problem depends on the environment in which it occurs, whether the problem is the optimal way to stock a retail shelf (back-to-school or holiday sales) or optimal asset allocation (risk-on or risk-off). Unfortunately, most conventional optimization methods cannot consider the environmental context, as it is often ill-defined and may involve hundreds of variables. However, machine-learning algorithms excel in dealing with big data inputs that may contain redundant and insignificant variables. Our CPO method leverages machine learning and Big Data to provide an optimal solution to many commercial problems such as portfolio optimization that adapts to the environment. We have demonstrated in multiple use cases that it can outperform conventional portfolio optimization methods and have shown an example in tactical asset allocation where historical allocations were timely.

Definitions of Spread_EMA & Spread_VAR

$Spread\_EMA(0) = Spread(0)$

$SpreadEMA(t + 1) = 2lookback\_periodSpreadt + 1$
$\qquad\qquad\qquad + (1 - 2lookback\_period)Spread\_EMA(t),$

$Spread\_VAR(1) == (Spread(1) - Spread(0))2,$

$Spread\_VAR(t + 1) = 2lookback\_period(Spread(t + 1) - Spread\_EMA(t + 1))\,2$
$\qquad\qquad\qquad + (1 - 2lookback\_period) * Spread\_VAR(t)$

Chapter 9

Application of Large Language Models and Generative AI in Trading

Role of Generative AI in Creating Alpha

The most valuable resource in conducting equity research is time. Equity analysts must pick actionable investment insights from vast amounts of data from many sources: equity research reports, investor presentations, earnings reports, industry research, industry research, reports from industry competitors, and more. Thus, there is a need to be more efficient with time to be able cover more information and uncover greater insights efficiently. Generative artificial intelligence (AI) applications, powered by large language models (LLMs), have introduced a new paradigm in increasing human efficiency by lowering the effort required to accomplish many text-based generative tasks: summarization, question answering, classification, text generation, and many more. In this chapter, we will go over the concepts and a few real-world applications of generative AI in the field of investment analysis to help create an edge for the readers. With these applications, you can save weeks of investment research effort annually and expand the scope and depth of your coverage by across industries and companies, gleaning deeper insights from text information and spending more time analyzing information rather than finding the right information.

Selecting an LLM for Building a Generative AI Application

There is no one size fits all kind of model that is ideally suited across all tasks, use cases, and data types. This is because the training data is not common across all models, which makes a model more or less performant than the others on a given domain or topic. Further, the internal weights or parameters for different models are designed differently impacting the way these models interpret data to uncover relationships to make predictions.

Generally, within a model family (e.g., GPT [ChatGPT], Gemini, Claude, Llama, and Mistral), a larger size model will be more performant, and hence also costlier to use than a smaller model. Similarly, a newer version of model family, say Llama 3 vs. Llama 2, will be more performant for the same size. Notably, these rules apply only to the base versions, with no fine-tuning, of the models under comparison. That is to say a pretrained or base version of Llama3 70B will generally perform better than a pretrained Llama3 8B, simply because the higher parameter size allows a larger model to understand more complex relationships and concepts within the data, and to make more nuanced predictions and generalizations using new, unseen data. However, with fine-tuning using proprietary data, a smaller model can also perform at par or even better a larger pretrained or base version of the model that has not been fine-tuned with the proprietary data. But this does not mean that using a smaller fine-tuned model is more cost effective than using a larger base version of a model. This is because model fine-tuning is typically extremely expensive. Instead, users should start with applying effective prompt engineering techniques (discussed later in this chapter) to improve model performance, followed by using retrieval-augmented generation techniques (for QnA and customer chatbot use cases) and only use model fine-tuning in exceptional cases when the data belongs to unique domains requiring expert knowledge of the concepts and terminology, such as biology, medicine, and legal domains.

Further, for question-answering and chat applications (the most common use of generative AI applications today), most LLM providers, such as Anthropic, Meta, and Mistral, also release "Instruct" versions of their pretrained or base models. These "Instruct" versions are trained by model providers to improve their instruction following abilities, improving their performance for multi-turn conversations by allowing them to retain prior context and follow the instructions through the conversation. So, for chat or questions answering use cases, these "Instruct" models are a good choice.

With lots of comparable models, choosing a model can become a subjective exercise, so let us try to give it some shape to aid model selection.

Step 1: Use popular LLM leaderboards to pick a few of the top performing models as a starting point. Leaderboards have their different niches where they evaluate and rank models on different criteria, and hence their applicability to different use cases. Table 9.1 provides a few of the more popular leaderboards today with their respective niches.

Table 9.1 Popular LLM by use case.

Popular LLM Leaderboards

Use Case	Leaderboard
Chatbot/QnA/Multi-turn conversations	Chatbot Arena (qnt.co/book-chat-lmsys)
	HELM Instruct (qnt.co/book-helm-instruct)
Generic/Multipurpose	MMLU (qnt.co/book-mmlu)
	HELM Lite (qnt.co/book-helm-lite)
	HuggingFace Open LLM (qnt.co/book-open-llm)
	AlpacaEval (qnt.co/book-alpaca-eval)
Embeddings	Massive Text Embedding Benchmark (qnt.co/book-mteb)
Emotional Intelligence	EQ Bench (qnt.co/book-eqbench)

Step 2: Short-list the top model options by testing those using different prompt engineering techniques and your proprietary dataset to evaluate which models perform better for your use case.

Step 3: Evaluate performance vs. cost trade-off for selected models, to select the final model for building your application. For reference, the pricing information for some of the more popular models in Amazon Bedrock is given in Table 9.2.

Table 9.2 On-demand pricing on Amazon Web Services (AWS) for popular models.

On-Demand Pricing on AWS Bedrock (as of June 2024)

Model	Price per 1,000 input tokens	Price per 1,000 output tokens
Anthropic models		
Claude 3.5 Sonnet	$0.0030	$0.0150
Claude 3 Opus	$0.0150	$0.0750
Claude 3 Haiku	$0.0003	$0.0013
Claude 3 Sonnet	$0.0030	$0.0150
Claude 2.1	$0.0080	$0.0240
Claude 2.0	$0.0080	$0.0240
Claude Instant	$0.0008	$0.0024
Meta models		
Llama 3 Instruct (8B)	$0.0003	$0.0006
Llama 3 Instruct (70B)	$0.0027	$0.0035
Llama 2 Chat (13B)	$0.0008	$0.0010
Llama 2 Chat (70B)	$0.0020	$0.0026

(Continued)

Table 9.2 (*Continued*)

On-Demand Pricing on AWS Bedrock (as of June 2024)

Model	Price per 1,000 input tokens	Price per 1,000 output tokens
Mistral models		
Mistral 7B	$0.0002	$0.0002
Mixtral 8*7B	$0.0005	$0.0007
Mistral Small	$0.0010	$0.0030
Mistral Large	$0.0040	$0.0120
Cohere models		
Command	$0.0015	$0.0020
Command-Light	$0.0003	$0.0006
Command R+	$0.0030	$0.0150
Command R	$0.0005	$0.0015
Embed - English	$0.0001	N/A
Embed - Multilingual	$0.0001	N/A

*Token sizes differ by models, but for rough conversions 1 token = 0.75-word size, and one page text is about 1,000 tokens.

Prompt Engineering

Prompts, in reference to generative AI applications or LLMs, refer to specific inputs provided to a model with the intention to generate a desired response or output. These could be questions, instructions, guidance, or even hints or examples to help the model understand the task, format, and the intent of the input. There are prompting techniques, with various levels of complexity, that can be used to guide the model to produce a desired output. This is done by designing, adjusting, and iterating on the text prompts, from simple questions to elaborate scenarios including examples, format, and structure, to teach the model on how to think about and execute the task at hand.

Prompts play a crucial role in leveraging the full potential of a large language model (LLM). When sending inputs, users should think of LLMs as young children, who, even when they know the answer, must be guided with instructions or examples to answer the question correctly. Without these detailed instructions, the answers, just as from young children, could be too short, or too long and winding, irrelevant, and often include some element of fantasy or wild imagination not grounded in facts. This element of adding nonfactual information is referred to as "hallucination" and is a frequent problem with LLMs (more on this momentarily). As such, thinking of LLMs as young children, when trying to elicit a response, helps in getting the best out of them.

Just as with young children, two key prompting tenets to follow are providing clear and detailed instructions and being patient by allowing or even encouraging the model to take time to think and process the information and task at hand. Let's discuss a few of the popular prompting techniques considering the earlier statement. The most common approach is *N*-shot prompting (zero-shot prompting and few-shot prompting). Here, N refers to the number of examples given to the model to help understand the task and format of the output. For example, zero-shot prompting refers to a scenario where the model generates outputs without any explicit examples provided in the prompt, whereas few-shot prompting typically uses a set of two to eight examples to guide the model on the task. Zero-shot prompting is suitable for relatively simpler tasks such as classification (e.g., sentiment analysis), while few shot promptings should be employed for more complex tasks, where the output needs to adhere to a context or desired format. Advance levels of prompting techniques involve coaching the model to pause and take time to think and process the instructions to generate a better response. Three important techniques here are system prompting (highly suitable for Llama family models), chain-of-thought (CoT) prompting, and tree of thought prompting (Figure 9.1). System prompting acts as a framework, guiding the model's responses by setting the context, style, or tone and steering its thought process by trying to maintain a certain persona (e.g., teacher, judge, financial analyst, sports enthusiast, or assistant) while performing the task. CoT prompting asks the model to break down the task into intermediate steps, and then tackle then sequentially as a multistep process before arriving at the final output. For example, given a task to summarize an earnings report, the model would break it down into five sequential steps of summarizing the top line (revenue), expenses (gross, operational, one-time), bottom line (profit margins, cash flow, CapEx, working cap), and the balance sheet, before stitching these summaries together cohesively to generate the final summary. Tree of thought prompting guides the LLM to explore different ideas and reevaluate when needed to provide the optimal solution.

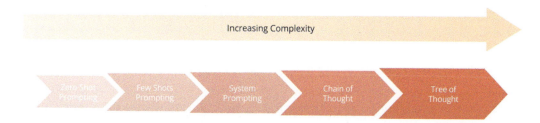

Figure 9.1 Prompt engineering complexity.

Prompt Engineering in Practice

The three key components of a prompt framework are instruction, context, and desired output format:

1. Instruction refers to the task to be performed such as summarization or question and answering (QnA) and also any specific character profile (system prompting) to be assumed to perform the task. Instructions should be followed with context where your model is provided with the information needed to perform the task (e.g., the passage to be summarized or the text to find the answer to the question posed).
2. Context includes style, tone, and specifics of the information needed and breaking down a complex task into smaller steps with stepwise guidance to be followed.

Here, the model can also be encouraged to come up with its own steps using CoT technique. These steps also allow the model to take time to think and follow a logical line of reasoning to generate a better response.
3. Output format should indicate the format of response—list, sentence, or any other structure—as well examples of good outputs if available (*N*-shot prompting).

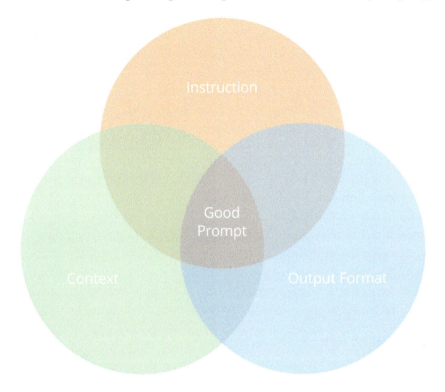

Figure 9.2 Intersection of the prompt components.

Prompt engineering is an iterative process to keep improving the model output (Figure 9.2). The model's response to the initial prompt should be evaluated to gauge the prompt's effectiveness and its capacity to understand and follow instructions. Users should iterate and refine the prompt using instructions and output examples to keep improving the output quality to acceptable levels.

Addressing Model "Hallucination"

LLM hallucination refers to model responses that are either factually incorrect, incoherent, or disconnected from the input context. While fictional creativity could be useful for certain tasks—writing poems or stories—it could have severe consequences in financial analysis and decision-making if the model response are not based on accurate and factual information.

There are two sets of methods that users can employ to reduce model hallucination. The first is using LLM settings to restrict randomness or creativity in responses.

This can be done by lowering "temperature" and "Top005Fp" parameter values or model deployment configurations in SageMaker or Bedrock API or SDK. Lower values for these parameters make the responses more deterministic and fact-based. The second set of methods include providing the ground truth (i.e., reliable), and factual information to use for the task, adding clear instructions to stick to the context provided in input, and providing examples for both what can and cannot be inferred from the text provided in the context. The information can also be provided by pointing the model to the S3 location of the documents as in the case of RAG applications. Instructing the model to admit lack of sufficient information to generate response can also help reduce hallucination. Finally, continuous response monitoring and evaluation as a standard practice is key to ensuring factual accuracy.

We will now go through a few real-world applications of Generative AI, such as querying a proprietary database for specific information using a Retrieval Augmented Generation (RAG) application and summarizing a text passage to highlight the key takeaways. These applications can help reduce the time spent in finding the right information and gleaning the right insights, allowing analysts to spend more time in analyzing the data, thereby saving weeks of effort annually.

Question Answering Using a Retrieval Augmented Application in SageMaker Canvas

A very important and certainly the most popular use of Generative AI is to search for the correct information from within a large database (e.g., question answering applications or customer service chatbots use cases). These applications can quickly sift through vast amounts of data and find the correct information. Imagine the power of finding any information, from within a large proprietary database, at your fingertips. Analysts can quickly search for information from old earning call transcripts, analyst reports, and industry research papers and glean insights, saving them hours if not days of effort each time.

When presented with a query and an accompanying piece of text that has the answer within it, an LLM can search for the right information from within the text and give it back to the user. The challenge with this context-based approach is that LLMs typically come with a limited context size (i.e., there is a cap on the amount of information [words] you can provide as an input at a time). This limits our ability to include all relevant documents as context, as it might exceed the allowed context size for that model. Further, models that allow for larger context windows typically also cost more.

To overcome this challenge, we can use a RAG solution with LLMs. A RAG solution retrieves the relevant context from within the entire database and sends only the relevant part, along with the original prompt query to the LLM. This enables the solution to fit the prompt and the context within the allowed context window for the model, which can then easily reference the context to generate the answer. For example, given an earnings call transcript, if you ask the LLM to find the organic revenue growth rate and the impact of currency fluctuations on the earnings, the

RAG solution will find only the relevant paragraphs referencing this information and send it to the LLM to generate the answer. Thus, by dynamically retrieving relevant information from your database, RAG solutions enable AI models to produce more accurate results.

Since having a functioning knowledge of underlying fundamentals is a key tenet of equity research, let us try and unpack, in brief, the components and architecture of a RAG solution. A RAG solution consists of a document database, an embedding model, a vector database, and an LLM. The embeddings model converts the document text into vector embeddings, which are numerical representations of the text. These vectors are then stored and maintained in a vector store in a manner where similar vectors are stored in proximity, meaning words with similar meanings are stored near each other, making it easier to search for words with similar meaning. When a user poses a question prompt to a RAG solution, the prompt is converted into embeddings and quickly matched with document embeddings stored in the vector store to find the most pertinent information to answer the question. The matched information is then retrieved from the vector store and sent to the LLM, along with the original prompt, to generate an answer using the prompt and the retrieved relevant context from the documents in the database.

Let's try to put this into practice by building our RAG solution in AWS (Figure 9.3). We will use AWS services for the different components of a RAG application and an LLM in SageMaker Canvas to generate to answer a query based on the information present in our database.

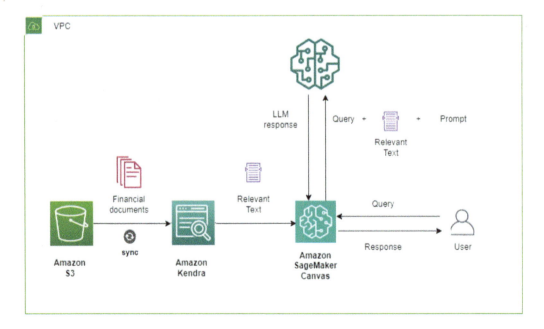

Figure 9.3 Amazon AWS architecture for LLM.

For these examples, I have uploaded a few analyst reports on Marriott (ticker: MAR) and Hyatt (ticker: H) from March 2024. The reports have the usual sections on a summary, investment thesis, recent developments, earnings and growth analysis, financial strengths, and risks. The reports also carry infographics and tables apart from the passages in text form. We will now walk through the steps to set up a RAG application and ask the application specific questions based on the information in the report and evaluate the accuracy of the results.

Step 1: The first step is to store the data that we want to query. We will use Amazon S3 for storage (Figure 9.4), where we upload the analyst reports in pdf format into a S3 bucket.

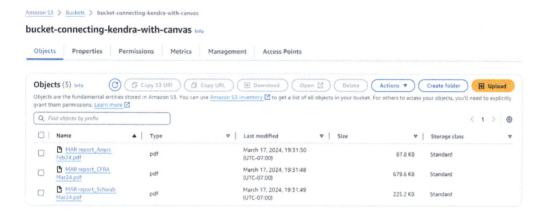

Figure 9.4 Amazon S3 dashboard.

Step 2: To create and store embeddings we will use Amazon Kendra, which is a machine-learning (ML)–powered enterprise search service from AWS. Kendra creates embeddings for the text in documents stores that in a vector index, which I named "rag-index" (Figure 9.5).

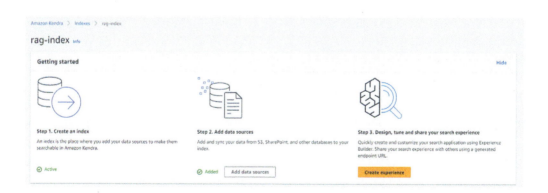

Figure 9.5 Amazon Kendra wizard.

Step 3: Connect SageMaker Canvas with Kendra by "enabling document query using Amazon Kendra" for your domain in Canvas settings in SageMaker console (Figure 9.6).

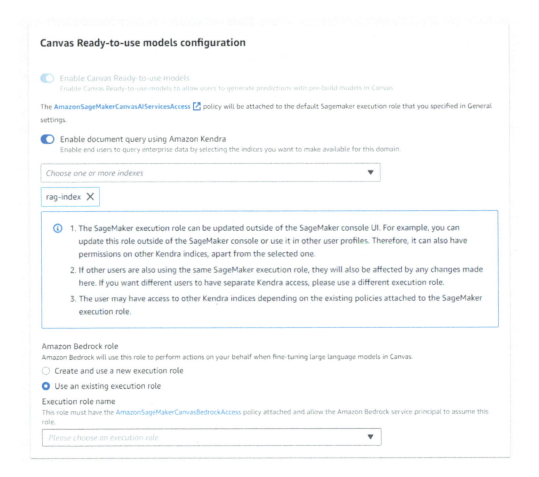

Figure 9.6 Amazon SageMaker wizard.

RAG Application Costs and Optimization Techniques

This solution incurs the expenses shown in Table 9.3 for using the previously described services. Note that these expenses will only apply if the application is kept running for an entire month. As a best practice, you should turn off any resources that you are not using actively to save costs from running idle resources.

Table 9.3   RAG application monthly cost.

Service	Service Tier	Resource	Price per month
S3	Standard	Storage per GB	$0.02
Kendra	Developer Edition	Index	$810
SageMaker Canvas	Standard	Workplace instance	$1,368
SageMaker Inference	Standard	ml.G5.12xl	$5,105

As a general best practice to save costs, it is important to delete any resources deployed as part of developing the application when not in use.

1. Canvas: Log out of the Amazon SageMaker Canvas application to stop the consumption of SageMaker Canvas workspace instance hours. This will release all resources used by the workspace instance.
2. Kendra: Delete the index if not needed further. If you intend to use the index in the future, make sure to turn off auto sync to crawl and index any new documents by itself. You can always run a manual sync to add any documents to the index.
3. SageMaker instances: Turn off any running instances hosting the model that was deployed through Canvas. This will prevent any usage charges from running any idle instances.

Testing Our Infrastructure

Now, let us put the prompt engineering lessons from the previous section to effectively query our documents and see how the output varies, as we iterate on the prompts to guide the model to generate a desirable result. For model selection, I followed the same process described earlier in this chapter. Since this book describes examples using AWS services and platforms, I narrowed down the most popular LLMs in AWS to the Claude, Mistral, and Llama model families. But given that my workload is not too complex and the high cost of Claude models, I shortlisted Llama 2 and Mistral 7B models for further evaluation. The performance was comparable between Llama 2 and Mistral, but I finally selected Llama-2-7b-instruct model because of its large context window (allows larger input-output text length) and its "instruct" capability that makes it better at following instructions (good for multi-turn conversations).

Example 1: Analysis on Marriot International Stock

We will ask the application to perform stock analysis on Marriott International stock (ticker: MAR) using the equity research reports that we have uploaded to our document repository in S3. We will iteratively increase prompt complexity (using prompt engineering concepts explained earlier) going from a simple question-answering prompt to asking the model to come up with its own steps to evaluate investment factors and provide an investment advice on the stock.

Prompt 1: What is the financial outlook for Marriott International in 2024?

Model Response (Figure 9.7):
Based on the provided documents, the financial outlook for Marriott International in 2024 is positive. The company expects to achieve RevPAR growth of 3%–5% and adjusted EPS of $9.15–$9.52 in 2024, which is higher than the previous guidance provided in February 2024. Additionally, the company has raised its 2024 EPS estimate to $9.72 from $9.61 and set a 2025 estimate of $10.90, both above consensus.

The documents also mention that Marriott's global operating model, which allows it to expand room capacity anywhere in the world, is a positive factor for earnings growth in 2024. Furthermore, the company's emphasis on corporate travel and profitable fee-based business is expected to continue driving growth.

However, it is important to note that there are some concerns around the outlook for travel in 2H 2023, which may impact Marriott's financial performance in the second half of the year. Additionally, the documents mention that the company's net new rooms growth guidance (ex-MGM & City Express deals) was trimmed, which may also affect the company's growth prospects.

Overall, while the financial outlook for Marriott International in 2024 is positive, there are some factors that may impact the company's performance in the second half of the year.

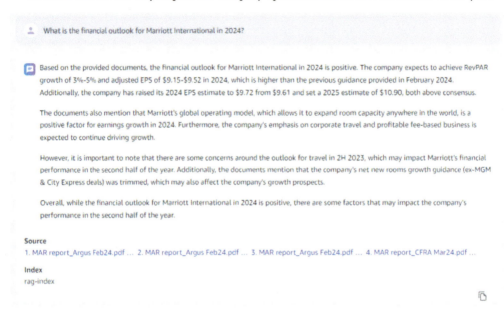

Figure 9.7 Snapshot from SageMaker Canvas.

Here, we see that with a simple one-line prompt, the model provides us with only factual information from the documents, which is not very useful for us in evaluating the investment potential in the stock.

Let's now increase the prompt complexity to increase model response usefulness for us. We will do this by asking the model to assume the character profile of a financial analyst and asking for its investment advice on the stock by providing it with specific instructions on which factors to consider in forming its opinion.

Prompt 2: You are a financial analyst analyzing equity research reports on Marriott International, which is a lodging company. Based on the documents, outline the financial outlook for the company in 2024, highlighting the EBITDA and RevPAR growth. Also provide your expert investment advice on the stock considering the recent development, growth prospects, and risks.

Model Response:
Based on the equity research reports provided, here is the financial outlook for Marriott International in 2024:

EBITDA Growth: Marriott International expects RevPAR growth of 4%–5% in 2024, which translates to an EBITDA growth of 8%–10%.

Chapter 9. Application of Large Language Models and Generative AI in Trading 353

RevPAR Growth: The company expects RevPAR growth of 4%–5% in 2024, driven by the expansion of room capacity, growth in the company's loyalty program, and the recovery of the lodging industry.

Stock Advice: After considering the recent developments, growth prospects, and risks, I would advise investors to BUY Marriott International stock with a target price of $270. Here are the reasons behind this recommendation:

1. Strong growth prospects: Marriott International has a proven track record of delivering strong earnings growth, and the company's focus on expanding its fee-based business, growing its loyalty program, and increasing its room capacity should continue to drive growth in 2024.
2. Cautious guidance: While Marriott International's guidance for 2024 may appear cautious, the company's expectations for RevPAR growth of 4%–5% are still above the peer average, indicating that the company has a positive outlook for the lodging industry.
3. Valuation: Marriott International's shares are trading at 24.0-times our revised EPS estimate for 2024, which is below the peer average of 31.

In the previous example, we see that by asking the model to think like a financial analyst (system prompting), we provided it with a framework to steer its thought process. This helped the model to identify the relevant pieces of information from the documents to create an investment thesis on the stock and provide us with an investment recommendation along with the rationale for the recommendation including growth factors, risks, and the valuation. But the model still doesn't cover a few quantitative and qualitative factors—balance sheet, competitive positioning, industry trends, market sentiments—and the response seems synthetic in presentation.

We will now try to improve the model response quality by encouraging the model to use its own reasoning to decide investment factors by first asking it to come up with the steps or factors to form an investment opinion. We will then ask the model to use the steps and the information in the documents to provide us with its investment advice along with the rationale or reasoning behind it.

Prompt 3, Part 1: You are a financial analyst analyzing equity research reports on Marriott. Outline the steps to form an investment opinion on the stock.

Model Response:
To form an investment opinion on Marriott International, Inc. (MAR), I would follow these steps:

1. Analyze the company's financial statements to evaluate its financial health, including revenue growth, profitability, and cash flow.
2. Review the company's valuation multiples, such as price-to-earnings ratio (P/E) and price-to-book ratio (P/B), to determine if the stock is overvalued or undervalued.
3. Assess the company's growth prospects by analyzing its historical growth rates, industry trends, and competitive position.
4. Evaluate the company's risk profile by analyzing factors such as its exposure to economic cycles, regulatory risks, and geopolitical risks.
5. Consider the overall market sentiment and investor expectations towards the company and its industry.

Prompt 3, Part 2: You are a financial analyst analyzing equity research reports on Marriott. Using the following steps and the information in the documents, provide your expert investment advice on the stock highlighting the financial and growth metrics used to form the advice.

1. Analyze the company's financial statements to evaluate its financial health, including revenue growth, profitability, and cash flow.
2. Review the company's valuation multiples, such as price-to-earnings ratio (P/E) and price-to-book ratio (P/B), to determine if the stock is overvalued or undervalued.
3. Assess the company's growth prospects by analyzing its historical growth rates, industry trends, and competitive position.
4. Evaluate the company's risk profile by analyzing factors such as its exposure to economic cycles, regulatory risks, and geopolitical risks.
5. Consider the overall market sentiment and investor expectations toward the company and its industry.

Model Response:
Based on the information provided in the equity research reports, I have analyzed Marriott International's (MAR) financial and growth metrics to provide an expert investment advice.

Financial Health: Marriott's financial statements indicate a strong financial position, with steady revenue growth, high profitability, and adequate cash flow. In 2024, the company expects RevPAR growth of 4%–5% and adjusted EPS of $9.15–$9.52, which is cautiously optimistic given the current economic uncertainty. Marriott's adjusted EBITDA margin rose to 19.6% in 4Q23 from 18.4% in 4Q22, indicating improved profitability. The company's total debt was $11.9 billion, and cash and cash equivalents totaled $300 million, which provides a reasonable balance between debt and cash.

Valuation Multiples: Marriott's valuation multiples, such as its price-to-earnings ratio (P/E) and price-to-book ratio (P/B), are reasonable compared to its peers and the broader market. As of March 16, 2024, Marriott's P/E ratio was 24.6x, which is slightly lower than the industry average of 26.1x. Its P/B ratio was 4.3x, which is in line with the industry average of 4.2x. These valuation multiples suggest that Marriott's stock is slightly undervalued compared to its peers and the broader market.

Here we see how CoT prompting helps improve the response quality by allowing the model to think first about the sequential order of tasks or factors to consider while forming an investment thesis on a stock, and then use those steps to guide its decision-making. This results in a more cohesive and organic response with stronger rationale for the recommendation covering both qualitative and quantitative aspects for stock analysis including comparison with peers and balance sheet metrics.

Example 2: Expanded Competitive Analysis Between Companies

We will ask the model to do competitive analysis on Marriott (MAR) vs. Hyatt (H) and help make an investment choice between the two stocks. For this we will ask the application to form separate investment thesis on Hyatt and Marriott, using equity research reports uploaded in S3, and then use the theses and any other relevant factors to compare the two stocks and suggest the better investment along with the rationale for it.

Chapter 9. Application of Large Language Models and Generative AI in Trading

Prompt 1: You are an experienced hedge fund manager. What is your investment thesis on Hyatt stock? Provide the rationale behind your opinion.

Model Response:
Based on the information available in the provided documents, Hyatt appears to be a company with a solid balance sheet, a strong brand portfolio, and a clear strategy to transition to an asset-light business model. This transition should help the company to reduce its debt levels and improve its profitability, as it will no longer be burdened by the heavy debt load associated with its asset-heavy exposure.

Furthermore, Hyatt's investment efforts, such as committing more of its own capital, culling unprofitable properties, investing in its digital platform, launching new brands, and maintaining recent cost savings extracted during the pandemic, are expected to support continued economic profits. The company's shareholder distribution is also considered appropriate, and its dividend as a percentage of net income is expected to expand from historical levels as it continues to shift to an asset-light business model.

Prompt 2: You are an experienced hedge fund manager. What is your investment thesis on Marriott stock? Provide the rationale behind your opinion.

Model Response:
Based on the provided documents, my analysis, and interpretation of the information, my investment thesis on Marriott stock is as follows:

1. Profitable Fee-Based Business: Marriott's fee-based business model is a significant positive factor, as it generates steady income and provides a hedge against economic downturns. The company's loyalty program and strong brand presence also contribute to its competitive advantage in the industry.
2. Strong Liquidity: Marriott has a solid balance sheet with low debt levels, which provides the company with the flexibility to invest in its business, pursue strategic opportunities, and return capital to shareholders through dividends and share repurchases.
3. Emphasis on Corporate Travel: Marriott's focus on corporate travel, which accounts for a significant portion of its revenue, positions the company well for earnings growth in 2024 and beyond. The company's global operating model allows it to expand room capacity anywhere in the world, further enhancing its competitive advantage.
4. Rising Expenses and Borrowing Costs: While Marriott's expenses and borrowing costs are expected to rise, the company's strong cash flow generation and liquidity position should help it navigate these increases. Management has guided for adjusted EPS growth of 3%–5% in 2024, which is cautious and may be surpassed.
5. Shareholder Distribution: Marriott has a history of supporting its solid balance sheet by keeping debt at conservative levels and distributing capital to shareholders through dividends and share repurchases. The company's shareholder distribution strategy is appropriate and aligned with its long-term growth strategy.

In the two examples just provided, we use system prompting, by asking the model to assume the role of a hedge fund, to help define a framework for its thinking. This allows the model to generate a response that is not merely a factual regurgitation of information in the documents but a well-reasoned answer that relies on the information to form its own opinion.

Now, let's leverage chain of though prompting to ask the model to retain context from its previous answers and combine with new information to provide an investment recommendation between the two stocks.

Prompt 3: How does Hyatt room growth compare to that of Marriott for the next decade?

Model Response:
According to the provided documents, Hyatt is expected to have a higher room growth rate than Marriott for the next decade.

The document titled "H report_MS May24.pdf" states that Hyatt's room growth is expected to average 4%–5% annually over the next decade, which is above the 1%–2% supply increase estimated for the US industry during the same period.

In contrast, the document titled "MAR report_MS May24.pdf" notes that Marriott's annual room growth is expected to be 4%, which is comfortably above the US industry forecast of 1%–2% growth.

Prompt 4: In light of the room growth estimates and based on your investment thesis for Hyatt and Marriott provided above, which one is a better stock?

Model Response:
Based on the information provided in the documents, both Hyatt and Marriott have strong growth potential, but Marriott appears to have a slight edge in terms of room growth estimates. Marriott expects to achieve revenue per available room (revPAR) growth at the high end of its 12% to 14% range for 2023, with an average lift of 3% to 6% in 2024–2025. This suggests that Marriott is expected to experience higher growth in the near term compared to Hyatt.

Additionally, Marriott's global operating model, which allows it to expand room capacity anywhere in the world, is a significant positive factor for the company's growth prospects. This, combined with its industry-leading 7% global room share and leadership in luxury hotels, positions Marriott well for earnings growth in 2024.

However, it's important to note that Hyatt also has a strong loyalty program and is well-positioned to post industry-leading room growth for the next decade, according to the documents. Hyatt's room pipeline represents 38% of its existing base, and its portfolio averages just 4 rooms per US market, which is lower than Marriott's 14 rooms per market. This suggests that Hyatt has a significant opportunity for growth, particularly in the US market.

So, we see here how the model used the retained context and incorporated additional factors to provide us with definitive answer on its pick between the two stocks and the rationale behind it. Importantly, the model evaluated both industry trends (macro) and company specific (micro) factors to formulate its opinion and provided us with metrics-based rationale for it. This kind of analysis would be really helpful in screening phases for an investment analyst with a fundamental approach to stock analysis.

Summarization

Equity analysts today have access to vast amounts of information and data, and the challenge becomes how to cover everything with the limited time available, to make the best use of time, and find the right insights to create alpha.

Another important Generative AI use case is document summarization to help readers focus on key points of a document and transforming unstructured text into standardized formats to highlight important attributes.

Now let's try to put this into practice to see how we can use generative AI to summarize passages to help increase our efficiency by covering more information in a lesser amount of time. For the following examples, I've used text from one of the analyst reports we used in the earlier Question Answering example and leverage LLMs (Llama2-7b-chat) in SageMaker Canvas to summarize the reports. We will also see how prompt engineering plays a crucial role in guiding the model to generate the desired response.

Example: Summarize Analyst Report for Insights

In this example, we will summarize an analyst report, gleaning insights that are more relevant and important for investment analysis.

> **Prompt 1:** Summarize the following report on Marriott stock, highlighting the growth analysis and risks:
>
> "INVESTMENT THESIS We are maintaining our BUY rating on Marriott International Inc. (NYSE: MAR) and raising our target price to $270 from $261. We believe that Marriott's profitable fee-based business, strong liquidity, and emphasis on corporate travel position it well for earnings growth in 2024. The company's global operating model, --Marriott's adjusted EBITDA margin rose to 19.6% in 4Q23 from 18.4% in 4Q22. The company pays a quarterly cash dividend. In May 2023, Marriott raised its quarterly dividend to $0.52 per share from $0.40. Our dividend estimates are $2.50 for 2024 and $2.64 for 2025. RISKS The company is at risk from weak economic conditions, rising operating expenses, and the threat of terrorism, which could hurt both business and leisure travel."
>
> **Model Response:**
> Thank you for sharing the report on Marriott International Inc. (NYSE: MAR). Based on the information provided, here are some key points and potential risks to consider:
> Key Points:
>
> 1. Strong financial performance: Marriott International reported adjusted EPS of $3.57 in 4Q23, up from $1.96 in 4Q22, driven by strong growth in incentive management fees and higher franchise fees. Revenue rose 3% to $6.1 billion, driven by low-teens growth in base management fees and 7% higher franchise fees.
> 2. Robust growth prospects: The company issued first-quarter guidance for RevPAR growth of 4%–5%, indicating a continued recovery in the hospitality industry. Marriott expects adjusted EBITDA of $1.12–$1.15 billion in 1Q24, driven by increased credit card fees and higher base management and incentive management fees.
> 3. Shareholder-friendly policies: Marriott returned $4.5 billion to shareholders in 2023 through share buybacks and dividend payments, and the company has a history of paying a quarterly cash dividend.
> 4. International growth potential: The company's global operating model allows it to expand room capacity anywhere in the world, which could lead to growth opportunities in international markets.
>
> Potential Risks:
>
> 1. Economic uncertainty: The company is at risk from weak economic conditions, which could impact both business and leisure travel. A decline in demand could lead to lower occupancy rates and revenue growth.

2. Rising operating expenses: Marriott's operating expenses have been increasing, which could neg (answer truncated since context length reached)

Let's now add a character profile, context scenario, and specific instructions on the task.

Prompt 2: You are an experienced hedge fund manager. Use the following analyst report to explain the investment thesis on Marriott stock to your clients. Make sure to highlights the superior financial performance of the company, it's market strength and growth prospects:

"INVESTMENT THESIS We are maintaining our BUY rating on Marriott International Inc. (NYSE: MAR) and raising our target price to $270 from $261. We believe that Marriott's profitable fee-based business, strong liquidity, and emphasis on corporate travel position it well for earnings growth in 2024. The company's global operating model, ---Marriott's adjusted EBITDA margin rose to 19.6% in 4Q23 from 18.4% in 4Q22. The company pays a quarterly cash dividend. In May 2023, Marriott raised its quarterly dividend to $0.52 per share from $0.40. Our dividend estimates are $2.50 for 2024 and $2.64 for 2025. RISKS The company is at risk from weak economic conditions, rising operating expenses, and the threat of terrorism, which could hurt both business and leisure travel."

Model Response:
Thank you for providing the analyst report on Marriott International Inc. (MAR). Based on the information provided, here are some key points that I can highlight as an experienced hedge fund manager:

1. Strong Financial Performance: Marriott International has demonstrated strong financial performance in recent years, with adjusted EPS of $9.99 in 2023, representing a 36% increase from the previous year. The company's adjusted EBITDA margin also improved to 19.6% in 4Q23 from 18.4% in 4Q22.
2. Market Strength: Marriott's global operating model and strong loyalty program have positioned the company well for earnings growth in 2024. The company's international RevPAR rose 17% year-over-year, driven by recovery in all regions, including the Middle East/Africa and European markets.
3. Growth Prospects: Marriott expects RevPAR growth of 4%–5% in 1Q24, driven by increased credit card fees and higher base management and incentive management fees. The company's long-term earnings growth rate forecast is 12%, which is above the consensus estimate.
4. Financial Strength: Marriott's financial strength rating is Medium, with Standard & Poor's rating the company's debt as investment grade with a rating of BBB. The company's total debt was $11.9 billion at the end of 4Q23, and cash and cash equivalents totaled $300 million.

In these examples, we see how system prompting can also help with efficient text summarization by providing the model with a framework for guiding its actions. By assuming the role of a hedge fund manager and following the additional context provided in the prompt, the model generated a response going beyond just stating facts to using those facts to formulate a more contextual summary keeping in mind the relevant information to be highlighted for the intended audience.

Useful AI Platforms and Services

Finally, let's go over a few GenAI services and platforms that can help you provide the right products to help get started and build scalable Generative AI applications.

ChatGPT

ChatGPT gives developers innovative text capabilities with an easy-to-use UI (chatbot) as well as an API option GPT-3.5 Turbo API for developers to integrate the AI tool into their own applications, products, or services. It was developed by OpenAI, an AI research company, and released in November 2022. The LLMs powering ChatGPT, GPT 3.5, and GPT4 are some of the most performing models available today.

Gemini

Google Gemini is a family of AI models developed by Google DeepMind, powering many of Google's products, including Gmail, Docs, Sheets, and its search engine. Also available through an API, Gemini models come in three sizes: ultra, pro, and nano. Gemini is multimodal, meaning it can understand and generate text, images, audio, videos, and code. Gemini as an AI tool can help with writing, planning, and learning.

Bedrock

Amazon Bedrock is a fully managed service that offers a choice of high-performing foundation models from leading AI companies like AI21 Labs, Anthropic, Cohere, Meta, Mistral AI, Stability AI, and Amazon through a single API, along with a broad set of capabilities to build generative AI applications with security, privacy, and responsible AI. Since Amazon Bedrock is serverless, users don't have to manage any infrastructure and can securely integrate and deploy generative AI capabilities into applications using other AWS services.

SageMaker

Amazon SageMaker allows users to build, train, and deploy machine-learning models for any use case with fully managed infrastructure, tools, and workflows. SageMaker JumpStart is the machine-learning (ML) hub, on SageMaker, offering state-of-the-art foundation models for generative AI use cases, where users can discover, explore, experiment, fine-tune, and deploy the models using the GUI Amazon SageMaker Studio or using the SageMaker Python SDK for JumpStart APIs. SageMaker Canvas offers users a no-code interface to create highly accurate machine-learning models without any machine-learning experience or writing a single line of code. Canvas also provides access to ready-to-use models, including foundation models from Amazon Bedrock or Amazon SageMaker JumpStart.

Q Business

Amazon Q Business is a fully managed, generative-AI powered assistant that users can configure to answer questions, provide summaries, generate content, and complete tasks based on their enterprise data. It allows end users to receive immediate, permissions-aware responses from enterprise data sources with citations. Amazon Q generates code, tests, debugs, and has multistep planning and reasoning capabilities that can transform and implement new code generated from developer requests.

References

Andersen, T.G. and Bollerslev, T. (1998). Answering the skeptics: Yes, standard volatility models do provide accurate forecasts. *International Economic Review* 39(4): 885–905. Doi: http://dx.doi.org/10.2307/2527343

Ang, A. (2014). *Asset Management: A Systematic Approach to Factor Investing*. Oxford: Oxford University Press.

Belov, S., Chan, E., Jetha, N., and Nautiyal, A. (2023). *Applying Corrective AI to Daily Seasonal Forex Trading*. Retrieved from https://predictnow.ai/applying-corrective-ai-to-daily-seasonal-forex-trading-paper/

Black, F. and Scholes, M. (May–Jun, 1973). The pricing of options and corporate liabilities. *The Journal of Political Economy* 81(3): 637–654.

Breedon, F. and Ranaldo, A. (April 3, 2012). *Intraday Patterns in FX Returns and Order Flow*. Retrieved from https://ssrn.com/abstract=2099321

Carr, P. (1988). HP 12 CPGM. *hp12cpgm.pdf*. Retrieved from http://www.math.nyu.edu/research/carrp/papers/pdf/hp12cpgm.pdf

Chan, E. (August 18, 2014). Quantitative trading. Retrieved from http://epchan.blogspot.com/2014/08/kelly-vs-markowitz-portfolio.html

Chan, E., Fan, H., Sawal, S., and Viville, Q. (2023). Conditional Portfolio Optimization: Using Machine Learning to Adapt Capital Allocations to Market Regimes. Available at https://ssrn.com/abstract=4383184

Cong, L. W., Tang, K., Wang, J., & Zhang, Y. (2021). AlphaPortfolio: Direct construction through deep reinforcement learning and interpretable AI. Available at https://ssrn.com/abstract=3554486

Cornett, M.M., Schwarz, T.V., and Szakmary, A.C. (1995). Seasonalities and intraday return patterns in the foreign currency futures market. *Journal of Banking & Finance* 19(5): 843–869.

Du, J., Jin, M., Kolm, P. et al. (2020). Deep reinforcement learning for option replication and hedging. *The Journal of Financial Data Science* 2(4): 44–57.

Fama, E.F. and French, K.R. (1995). Size and book-to-market factors in earnigns and returns. *Journal of Finance* 50(1): 131–155.

Francus, L. (December, 2020). *Investigating Delta-Gamma Hedging Impact On SPY Returns 2007–2020*. Retrieved from https://www.scribd.com/document/487296659/Investigating-Delta-Gamma-Hedging-Impact-on-SPY-Returns-2007-2020#

Hartmann, P. (1999). Trading volumes and transaction costs in the foreign exchange market: Evidence from daily dollar–yen spot data. *Journal of Banking and Finance* 23(5): 801–824.

Heston, S.L. (1993). A closed-form solution for options with stochastic volatility with applications to bond and currency options. *Review of Financial Studies* 6(2): 327–343.

Hornik, K., Stinchcombe, M. and White, H. (1989). Multilayer feedforward networks are universal approximators. *Neural Networks* 2(5): 359–366.

Keller, W.J. and Keuning, J.W. (2017). *Breadth Momentum and Vigilant Asset Allocation (VAA): Winning More by Losing Less*. Retrieved from https://ssrn.com/abstract=3002624

Koijen, R.S.J., Moskowitz, T.J., Pedersen, L.H. et al. (2016). *Carry: Fama-Miller Working Paper*. Retrieved from https://ssrn.com/abstract=2298565

López de Prado, M. (2017). *The 7 Reasons Most Machine Learning Funds Fail*. Retrieved from https://ssrn.com/abstract=3031282

López de Prado, M. (2018). *Advances in Financial Machine Learning*. Hoboken: John Wiley & Sons.

López de Prado, M. (2020). *Machine Learning for Asset Managers*. Cambridge: Cambridge University Press.

Kaczmarek, T. and Perez, K. (2021). Building portfolios based on machine learning predictions. *Economic Research-Ekonomska Istraživa*nja 35(1): 19–37.

Man, X. and Chan, E. (2021). The best way to select features? Comparing MDA, LIME, and SHAP. *The Journal of Financial Data Science* 3(1): 127–139.

Man, X. and Chan, E.P. (2021). Cluster-based feature selection. *Market Technician* 90: 11–22.

Merton, R.C. (September, 1973). An intertemporal capital asset pricing model. *Econometrica* 41(5): 867–887.

Mordo Intelligence. (2021). *Global AI in Oil and Gas Market - Growth, Trends, COVID-19 Impact, and Forecasts (2023–2028)*. Retrieved from https://www.mordorintelligence.com/industry-reports/ai-market-in-oil-and-gas

Murphy, K.P. (2012). *Machine Learning: A Probabilistic Perspective*. Cambridge: The MIT Press.

Nautiyal, A. and Chan, E. (2021). New additions to the PredictNow.ai factor zoo. Retrieved from https://predictnow.ai/new-additions-to-the-predictnow-ai-factor-zoo/

Poh, D., Lim, B., Zohren, S. et al. (2020). *Building Cross-Sectional Systematic Strategies By Learning to Rank*. Retrieved from https://arxiv.org/abs/2012.07149

Ruppert, D. and Matteson, D.S. (2015). *Statistics and Data Analysis for Financial Engineering with R Examples*, 2e. Ithaca: Springer.

Shwartz-Ziv, R. and Armon, A. (2021). *Tabular Data: Deep Learning is Not All You Need*. Retrieved from https://arxiv.org/abs/2106.03253

Tomasz, K., and Katarzyna, P. (2021). Building portfolios based on machine learning predictions. *Economic Research-Ekonomska Istraživanja* 35(1): 19–37.

Tyler. (2016). *Portfoliocharts*. Retrieved from https://portfoliocharts.com/portfolio/golden-butterfly/

Viville, Q., Sawal, S. and Chan, E. (2022). *800+ New Crypto Features*. Retrieved from Predictnow.ai: https://predictnow.ai/800-new-crypto-features/

Subject Index

Page numbers followed by f and t refer to figures and tables, respectively.

A

AAPL (Apple) stock, 193, 288–290, 294, 300–302, 301f, 302f, 309. *See also* Apple, Inc.
Absolute order quantity, 221–222
Adam (adaptive moment estimation) optimization algorithm, 123, 156
Adaptive Investment Solutions, LLC, 297
Adaptive portfolio rebalancing, 50–51
ADF (Augmented Dickey-Fuller) test, 64–65
AI, *see* Artificial intelligence (AI)
AI21 Labs, 361
aihedging, 288–289
Algorithmic trading strategies:
   AI and ML in, 47–48
   AI-based, 48
   building robust, 26
   and limit order books, 4
   market declines from, 8
   out-of-sample performance of, 288
   and risk management, 141
   trend prediction using, 143
Algoseek, 14, 15, 311, 318
Alpha:
   in capital allocation, 31–32
   cross-sectional return prediction by, 326, 328
   in daily seasonal forex trading, 313
   generative AI creation of, 343
   by hidden Markov models, 158–170
   in lasso regression, 93
   and meta-labeling, 306
   in portfolio management, 32
   in ReLU functions, 296
   removing, 44
   in ridge regression, 96
Amazon:
   Amazon AWS, 345t, 346t, 350–351, 350f, 353, 361
   Amazon Bedrock, 345, 345t, 346f, 349, 361–362
   Amazon Chronos model, 88, 135–137, 137f, 265–272
   Amazon Kendra, 351–353, 351f
   Amazon Q Business, 362
   Amazon S3, 349, 351, 351t, 353, 356
   Amazon SageMaker, 349–351, 352f, 353, 354f, 359, 361–362
AMZN (Amazon) stock, 309
Anthropic, 344, 361

364　SUBJECT INDEX

Apple, Inc., 9, 38, 42, 288–290, 294. *See also* AAPL (Apple) stock
Area under the curve (AUC) value, 117
Ares Acquisition corporation, 309
ARIMA (autoregressive integrated moving average), 266
Artificial General Intelligence, 305
Artificial intelligence (AI):
　algorithmic trading strategies of, 47–48
　corrective, *see* Corrective AI
　delta hedging, 288–289. *See also* Delta hedging
　generative, *see* Generative AI
　generative AI alpha creation, 343
　hedging, 284–285, 288, 302, 303–304, 303f
　relation to machine learning (ML), 47
Assets, 15–23, 37–40
　constituents, 39
　cryptocurrency, 23
　dollar-volume, 40
　equities, 15–19
　equity options, 19–21
　fundamental, 38–39
　futures, 21–23
　index options, 21
　mapped, 22
AUC (area under the curve) value, 117
Augmented Dickey-Fuller (ADF) test, 64–65, 67–69, 72
Australia Acquisition corporation, 309
Auto-identification of features, 48, 76, 78
Automatic indicators, 41
Autoregressive integrated moving average (ARIMA), 266
Average daily volume, 221–222
Average Directional Index, 321
Average true range (ATR), 154, 155, 157, 215, 219, 222, 321
Awesome Oscillator, 321

B

Backtesting:
　in AI delta hedging, 288
　for asset identification, 13
　in coding process, 28–29
　for corrective AI, 312–314, 316, 318
　in data clustering, 211
　and debugging, 27, 27f
　in dividend harvesting, 180
　in feature engineering, 308
　in Gaussian Naive Bayes (GNB) classifiers, 245, 253, 254
　in hidden Markov models, 162–164
　in H&S trading, 261, 265
　in inverse volatility ranking, 217
　logging during, 27
　and look-ahead bias, 29–30
　in Object Store, 28
　point-in-time, xixf
　in positive-negative splits, 182
　in QuantConnect, xviii
　in research process, 25
　in statistical arbitrage mean reversion, 232, 238, 239
　in stop loss options, 187–188, 190
　and survivorship bias, 38–39
　in trading costs optimization, 224
　uses for, 26
　in wavelet forecasting, 174
　while adjusting parameters, 34
Bagging, 110–111
Barclays, 284
Belov, Sergei, 312
Berkshire Hathaway, 16
BERT (bidirectional encoder representations from transformers) model, 137, 273
Bid-ask spread, 8, 282, 283, 290
Binary flags, 31
Binary signals, 31
BioNTech, 306
Bitcoin (BTCUSD), 146, 222–223
Black-Scholes Merton (BSM) pricing model, 281–284, 286, 290–291, 294–295, 297
Bloomberg, 13
Bollinger Bands, 50, 319–321
Bootstrap aggregating, *see* Bagging
Box plots, 58, 58f
Breedon, F., 312
Brokerages, 3, 10–12, 17, 21, 23, 35–37
BSM, *see* Black-Scholes Merton (BSM) pricing model
BTCUSD (Bitcoin), 146
Build tests, 26, 28

C

CAGR, 332
Calendar roll, 300
Call option payoff, 161
Canary, 311
Candidate algorithm, 223
Canonical contracts, 22
Capital allocation, 31–32, 35, 37, 307, 309, 323–327, 340
Capital expenditure (capex), 308, 310, 347
Capital markets:
   assets and derivatives in, 15–23
   brokerages in, 10–13
   data feeds in, 7–10
   foundations of, 3–23
   mechanics of, 3–4
   participants in, 4–7
   security identifiers for, 13–15
   transaction costs in, 10–13
Carr, Peter, 281
Carry features, 311, 351
Cash accounts, 23, 35–36
CBOE (Chicago Board of Option Exchange), 6, 21
Chain-of-thought (CoT) prompting, 347–348, 356
Chan, Ernest, 312, 318
Charting programs, 27–28
ChatGPT, 253–254, 344, 361
Chicago Board of Option Exchange (CBOE), 6, 21
Chicago Mercantile Exchange (CME) Group, 6, 21
Chohere, 361
City Express, 354
Claude, 344, 353
Clustering, 130–132
   OPTICS, 88, 130–132, 132*f*, 197–199
   stock selection through, 207–214
CME (Chicago Mercantile Exchange) Group, 6, 21
CNN, *see* Convolutional neural networks (CNN)
Coding process, 28–29
Coinbase, 15
Cointegrated time series, 48, 70–75
Cointegration, 70, 73, 197–198, 202
Conditional parameter optimization (CPO). *See also* Conditional portfolio optimization (CPO); Unconditional parameter optimization
   applying, 319–320
   and corrective AI, 305–308
   definition of, 318–319
   performance comparisons of, 322–323
   unconditional vs., 321–322
Conditional portfolio optimization (CPO), 307, 323–340. *See also* Conditional parameter optimization (CPO); Portfolio allocations
   conventional optimization methods vs., 327–331
   CPO software-as-a service in, 333–340
   Fama-French three-factor model in, 327
   machine learning in, 324–325
   model tactical asset allocation in, 331–333
   ranking vs. predicting in, 325–326
   regime changes vs., 323–324
Confusion matrix, 113*f*, 116–117
Consolidated data, 9
Constituents asset selection, 39
Continuous front contracts, 22
Continuous hedging, 282–283
Continuous signals, 31
Contract multipliers, 15, 20, 21, 37, 216
Contrarian strategies, 144
Control features, 325, 327
Convenience yield, 311
Convolutional layers, 123, 234–235, 257
Convolutional neural networks (CNN), 88, 122, 233–234, 242, 256–265. *See also* Temporal CNN model
Corrective AI, 305–310, 312–318, 340
Correlation analysis, 48, 76
CoT (chain-of-thought) prompting, 347–348
COVID-19 pandemic, 6, 27, 35, 306, 333
CPO, *see* Conditional parameter optimization (CPO); Conditional portfolio optimization (CPO)
CPO Software-As-A-Service, 333
Cross-sectional factors, 308–310, 309*f*, 324
Cross-sectional returns, 324, 326, 327–328
Cross-validation, 48, 85–86
Cryptocurrency, xv, 23, 30, 307, 330, 330*t*
CUSIP, xvii, 13. *See also* Securities Information Processor (SIP)

D

Daily seasonal forex trading, 312–318
Data collection, 53
Data-driven investing, 44
Data feeds, 7–10
  consolidated, 9
  custom, 9–10
  in extended market hours, 40
  indicator warm up for, 42
  manual indicators for, 41
  quote ticks, 8
  trade ticks, 8
Data normalization mode, 18, 41, 232
Data preprocessing, 54–75
Data resolution, 41
Data splitting, 83–86
Dataset preparation, 53–86
  data collection in, 53
  exploratory data analysis (EDA) in, 53–54
  feature selection in, 76–83
  preprocessing, 54–75
  splitting, 83–86
Davies-Bouldin index, 132
Debt-per-share ratios, 309
Debugging, 26–29
Decentralized exchanges (DEX), 23
Decision tree regression, 88, 103–105, 104f, 105f, 176. *See also* Regression
Decision trees, 87, 110, 234, 315
Deep neural networks (DNNs), 284
Delistings, 13, 16, 18–19, 22
Delta hedging, 288–289, 296–297, 302, 303f, 311. *See also* Hedging
Delta-mimicking training, 292, 300, 301f
Derivatives, 14, 15, 19, 23, 215, 286, 295
DEX (decentralized exchanges), 23
Dimensionality reduction, 80
Direct market access (DMA), 3–4
Diversification, 31, 37–38, 50, 215
Dividend harvesting, 176–180
Dividend payout ratio, 16, 176
Dividends:
  backtesting of, 26
  in company life cycles, 16
  in data normalization, 18
  definition of, 17–18
  harvesting of, 176–180
DMA (direct market access), 3–4

DNNs (deep neural networks), 284
Dollar-volume asset selection, 40
DOW 30 E-Mini, 216
Drawdowns, 32, 37, 185, 266, 313, 316, 318, 329
Dropout, 122
Dropout layers, 123
Dynamic stop-loss distance, 186

E

Earnings-per-share ratios, 308–309
EBS (Electronic Broking Services), 312
EDA (exploratory data analysis), 53–54
Eigenvectors, 81
Electronic Broking Services (EBS), 312
Engle-Granger Test, 48, 55, 70–75, 202
Ensemble learning, 110
Equal weights method, 327, 331–332
Equities. *See also* Equity options
  asset allocation of, 32
  backtests in, 13
  carry calculations for, 311
  and corrective AI, 318
  delisting of, 19
  forms of, 35–37
  in low-volatility regimes, 159
  options data on, 20
  problems with, 49
  RL approach to, 285
  selection of, 208
  short-biased, 32
Equity corporate events, 13, 16–17, 26
Equity options, 15–21, 36, 166, 168. *See also* Equities
Exchange traded funds (ETFs), 38, 39, 51
Expiration date, 19–21, 161, 186, 281
Explained variance ratio, 81
Exploratory data analysis (EDA), 53–54

F

Facebook, 266
False Negative (FN), 116
False Positive (FP), 116
Fama, Eugene, 310
Fama-French three-factor model, 309, 327
Feature engineering, 61–62, 103, 242, 308–312

Feature extraction, 234
Feature importance analysis, 77–80, 79f, 114f
Feature selection, 76–83, 93
  correlation analysis, 76
  dimensionality reduction, 80
  feature importance analysis, 77–80
  principal component analysis, 80–83
Federal Open Market Committee, 267, 294
FIGI, xvii, 13
FinBERT model, 88, 137–139, 272–279
FINRA, 10, 35
Fixed percentage-based stop-loss order, 186
Flash Crash (2010), 8
FN (False Negative), 116
Force Index, 321
Forex (FX) markets, 170, 256, 312
FP (False Positive), 116
Fractional differentiation technique, 67, 69f, 70f
Francus, Lily, 311
Free-cash flow, 176
Free cash flow percent, 16, 176
French, Kenneth R., 155, 310
Frictionless markets, 282
Front-month contracts, 22, 216
Fundamental asset selection, 38–39
Fundamental traders, *see* Liquidity traders
Futures contracts, 22, 37, 214–221
Futures markets, 21–23, 30–31
FX markets, *see* Forex (FX) markets
FX SVM wavelet forecasting, *see* Wavelet forecasting

G

Gaussian Naive Bayes (GNB) classifiers, 119–121, 121f, 242, 261
GBM, *see* Geometric Brownian Motion (GBM)
GDX EFT, 319–322
Generative AI, 343–362
  in alpha creation, 343
  and prompt engineering, 346–349
  question answering applications for, 349–358
  selecting LLM for, 344–346

Geometric Brownian Motion (GBM), 285–286, 290–291, 294, 297
GLD (gold) ETF, 319–322, 331
GNB classifiers, *see* Gaussian Naive Bayes (GNB) classifiers
Golden butterfly portfolio, 331
GOOG (Google stock), 309
Google, 14
  Google DeepMind, 361
  Google Gemini, 344, 361
GPT-4 model, *see* OpenAI GPT-4 model
Gradient-based optimization, 321
Grid search, 34, 108, 175, 325

H

Half-lives, 197–198, 203
Head-and-shoulder (H&S) trading pattern, 256–265
Hedge portfolios, 310
Hedging, 282–285, 288, 302, 303–304, 303f. *See also* Delta hedging
Heston, S. L., 283, 291
Heston model, 283, 285–286
Hidden Markov models (HMM), 88, 117–119, 119f, 158–170
High-frequency (HF) trading, 287
High-volatility regimes, 159
Historical price data, 49–50, 53, 230, 232
HML, 309, 327
HMM, *see* Hidden Markov models (HMM)
HuggingFace, 265–266, 268, 272–273, 275, 345
Hurst coefficient, 73
Hurst exponent, 75, 197–198, 202–203
Hyatt (H), 350, 356–358
Hyperparameters, 83, 108, 110–111, 122, 175, 208, 297, 333
Hypothesis-driven testing, 43–44

I

IBM's Watson Lab, 306
ICE (Intercontinental Exchange) Group, 21
Idea sourcing, 42–44

IJS ETF, 331
Imputation, 57
In-sample accuracy, 297, 301f, 321–322. *See also* Out-of-sample (OOS) accuracy
In the money (ITM) options, 20, 195
Indicator events, 42
Indicator warm up, 42
Informed traders, 6–7, 13
Initial public offerings (IPOs), 14, 16, 18
Intercontinental Exchange (ICE) Group, 21
Internal Revenue Service, 21
Interquartile range (IQR), 58–59
Inverse volatility, 214–221, 310
Investor's Business Daily, 7
IPOs, *see* Initial public offerings (IPOs)
ISIN, xvii, 13
ITM (in the money) options, 20

J
Jetha, E., 312
JumpStart, 361–362
Jupyter notebooks, xviii, 25–26, 221, 223–224, 333

K
K eigenvectors, 81
k-fold cross-validation, 85
k-means, 87, 130
K-nearest neighbors (KNN) imputation, 57
Keller, W. J., 311
Kelly formula, 32, 327
Keras deep learning library, 155, 235
Keras prediction model, 241–242, 257
Keras/TensorFlow framework, 123
Keuning, J. W., 311
KO stock, 187–188, 190–193, 195
Kraken, 15

L
LambdaRank, 127–128, 214
Large language models (LLMs), 87, 132–139
　Amazon Chronos model, 88, 135–137, 265–272
　AWS for, 350f, 353
　For building generative AI applications, 344–346
　in ChatGPT, 361
　FinBERT model, 88, 137–139, 272–279
　hallucination, 348–349
　in look-ahead bias, 29
　OpenAI language model, 88, 132–134
　and prompts, 346–347
　retrieval augmented generation using, 349–350
　summarization example of, 250–256
Lasso regression, 88, 91, 93–95, 95f, 185–187, 192, 229. *See also* Regression
LEAN, 195
LEAN architecture, xxif
LEAN CLI, xvii, xx
Learning-to-rank algorithm, 127, 208, 214
LGBMRanker, 128, 208, 214
LGBRanker, 88, 127–130, 213
LightGBM library, 127
LightGBM model, 111
Limit order books, 4–5
Linear regression. *See also* Regression
　in clustering, 208
　description of, 89–90
　example of, 90f, 145f
　in Fama-French model, 327
　in feature engineering, 308
　in lasso regression, 93
　in MLFinlab, 144–145
　in polynomial regression, 91
　in positive-negative splits, 181, 185
　in ridge regression, 96
　in statistical arbitrage mean reversion, 228–234
Liquidity traders, 5–7
Live trading, xviii–xix, xxf. *See also* Paper trading
　backtesting in, 26
　in bid-ask spread, 12
　debugging during, 27
　indicators for, 42
　ML models for, 319
　in Object Store, 28
　and paper trading, 26

in research process, 25
during rolling, 22
Llama, 344, 347, 353
LLM hallucination, 348–349
LLMs, *see* Large language models (LLMs)
Logging, 27
Logistic regression, 114–117. *See also* Regression
Long short-term memory (LSTM) layers, 123, 266
Look-ahead bias, 26, 29–30
Lookback window periods, 34, 144, 162, 321
López de Prado, Marcos, 67, 144, 152, 306
Loss function:
and adam optimizer, 156
clipping of, 297
in delta hedging, 294
in delta-mimicking training, 300, 301*f*
in Lasso regression, 93
in polynomial regression, 91
in recurrent neural networks, 122
in ridge regression, 96
with simulated data, 295–297
Low-volatility regimes, 159
LSTM (long short-term memory) layers, 123, 266

M

MA, *see* Moving averages (MA)
Machine learning (ML):
algorithmic trading strategies of, 47–48
and Amazon Kendra, 351
and Amazon SageMaker, 361
and artificial general intelligence, 305
and automatic merging, 309
best practice for, 287
CPO use of, 318, 319–320
and data splitting, 83
deployment of, 306–307
and ensemble learning, 110
in feature engineering, 61
and feature standardization, 55, 62–63
hyperparameter settings of, 83
and imputation, 57
learning-to-rank technique in, 208
live trading models, 319

non-linear, 327
option price prediction with, 283–284
for parameter removal, 34
primary trading model in, 315
promises of, 7
and random forest regression, 322
relation to AI, 47
supervised, 87, 308, 319
SVM model of, 266
trading cost reduction via, 221
tree-based, 77
unsupervised, 87
using cross-sectional features, 323–324
main.py, 288
Manual indicators, 41–42
Many alpha approach, 32, 326
Mapped assets, 22
Margin accounts, 36
Margin modeling, 35–37
Market hours, 15, 30, 40
Market makers, 3, 5–7, 10, 13, 23, 284
Market-neutral portfolios, 32, 73
Market participants, 4–7
AI actors, 7
informed traders, 6–7
liquidity traders, 5
market makers, 5–6
Market regimes. *See also* Regimes
cash allocation vs., 330*f*
in feature engineering, 309
and hidden Markov models, 117–118
and Markov regression, 160
and MLFinab, 144
and OPTICS clustering, 130–131
optimizing for, 324–325, 327–328
and portfolio strategy, 32–33
and stop loss, 306
in TAA portfolios, 331, 333
Market volatility regimes, 158
Markov regression model, 158–159
Markov switching dynamic regression (MSDR), 88, 99–102, 102*f*, 160. *See also* Regression
Markowitz, Harry, 37, 327–328
Markowitz portfolios, 328–329, 331
Marriott (MAR), 350, 353–360
Mean/median/mode imputation, 57
Mean reversion strategies, 32, 198, 203, 228–229
Mean-variance optimization, 327

Mergers, 13, 14, 16, 19, 138, 282
Merton model, 282, 283. *See also* Black-Scholes Merton (BSM) pricing model
MESH ETF, 328*t*
Meta, 344, 361
Meta-labeling, 306, 318
MGM, 354
MICE (multivariate imputation by chained equations), 57
Minimum Variance portfolios, 328
Mistral, 344, 353, 361
ML, *see* Machine learning (ML)
MLFinlab, 143–144, 198
Model retraining, 30, 164, 185, 267, 274–275, 298*f*
Model training, 48, 220–221
model.py, 289, 292
Modern portfolio theory, 31, 266
Momentum strategies, 30, 154, 311, 318
Money Flow, 321
Moneyness, 282, 290–291, 294
Morgan Stanley, 306
Morningstar, 181, 243
Moving averages (MA), 50, 62, 215, 320
MSDR, *see* Markov switching dynamic regression (MSDR)
Multiclass random forest model, 110–117, 148–149, 187. *See also* Random forest model
Multicollinearity, 96, 187, 215, 327
Multivariate imputation by chained equations (MICE), 57

N

N-shot prompting, 346–348
Nasdaq 100 E-Mini, 216
National Association of Securities Dealers Automated Quotations System (NASDAQ), 3, 8, 21, 50
National best bid or offer (NBBO), 3, 8, 12
Natural language processing (NLP), 122, 137, 273, 307
Nautiyal, Akshay, 312, 318
NDCG (normalized discounted cumulative gain), 129–130
NDX index, 21

Net options pricing effect (NOPE), 310–311
Netting, 5, 10
Neural network model, 122, 156, 264, 266, 284
New York Stock Exchange (NYSE), 3, 5, 6, 8
NLP, *see* Natural language processing (NLP)
Non-linear machine learning, 327. *See also* Machine learning (ML)
Non-linear relationships, 103, 171, 234, 266
NOPE (net options pricing effect), 310–311
Normalization. *See also* Standardization
  in AI-based algorithmic trading, 48
  in Amazon Chronos model, 135
  in convolutional neural networks, 122
  in decision tree regression, 103
  definition of, 62
  in feature engineering, 309–310
  in FinBERT model, 137–138
  in Gaussian naive Bayes, 119–120
  in hidden Markov models, 114, 117–118
  in lasso regression, 93
  and LGBRanker, 128
  in linear regression, 89
  in logistic regression, 114
  in Markov regression, 99
  in multiclass random forest regression, 110
  in OpenAI language model, 133
  in OPTICS clustering, 130–131
  in polynomial regression, 91
  possible combinations of, 22
  in preprocessing phase, 54–55
  in ridge regression, 96
  in SVM regression, 105–106
  z-score, 63
Normalized discounted cumulative gain (NDCG), 129–130
NVIDIA, 38
NYSE, *see* New York Stock Exchange (NYSE)

O

OLS (ordinary least squares) model, 230
OOS, *see* Out-of-sample (OOS) accuracy
Open-high- low-close (OHLC) bar, 9, 233–235, 238
Open/high/low/close/volume (OHLCV) stock data, 233–234, 238
OpenAI GPT-4 model, 133, 250, 273–274, 361, 364
Operating cash flow, 16, 176
Operational constraints, 49–51
OPTICS clustering, 88, 130–132, 132*f*, 197–199
OPTICS (ordering points to identify the clustering structure), 130
Optimal trade entry/exit, 144
Optimization, *see* Conditional parameter optimization (CPO); Conditional portfolio optimization (CPO)
Optimizers, xix, 122, 327–328
Option rights, 19
Options Price Reporting Authority (OPRA), 20
Order flow, 10, 311–312
Order tickets, 11
Ordering points to identify the clustering structure (OPTICS), 130
Ordinary least squares (OLS) model, 230
Ornstein-Uhlenbeck process, 286
OTM (out-of-the-money) options, 20
Out-of-sample (OOS) accuracy. *See also* In-sample accuracy
  and conditional parameter optimization, 319
  in convergence of loss function, 301*f*
  and corrective AI, 312, 315, 316*f*, 318
  definition of, 16
  in equity curve of primary trading strategy, 313*f*
  and look-ahead bias, 29
  and overfitting, 86
  in parameter sensitivity testing, 34
  performance comparisons of, 322, 322*t*, 329–331
  positive-negative, 180–185
  in regime testing, 149–153, 156
  and reinforcement learning, 285
  reverse, 17
  in TAA portfolios, 331–332, 331*f*

Out-of-the-money (OTM) options, 20, 195
Overfitting. *See also* Underfitting
  in backtesting, 28
  in decision tree regression, 103
  dropout layers for, 123
  in feature selection, 76
  Heston's view of, 283
  and in-sample accuracy, 297
  in lasso regression, 88, 93
  in multiclass random forest model, 110
  in neural networks, 122
  in parameter optimization, 26
  in polynomial regression, 91
  in portfolio strategies, 32
  problems with, 33*f*
  reasons for, 33
  reducing chances of, 33–34, 44
  in ridge regression, 96, 215
  and splits, 86
  in SVM regression, 106
  testing for, 83
  through regularization, 187, 215
  and validation loss, 127

P

P-value, 72–73
Pandas code, 26, 54, 211
Paper trading, 25, 26. *See also* Live trading
Parameter sensitivity testing, xviii, 33–35
Parameters. *See also* Conditional parameter optimization (CPO)
  in AI delta hedging, 288, 294
  in corrective AI, 306
  of data splits, 84–85, 182
  definition of, 33
  Heston's approach to, 283
  hyper-, *see* Hyperparameters
  in LLMs, 344
  of Markov switching dynamic regression, 99
  in ML model, 324–325
  in model hallucination, 348
  model training of, 48
  in neural networks, 122
  optimization of, xviii, 26
  and overfitting, 33–35

of policy networks, 290
in portfolio allocation, 323
of put options, 186
in RL, 285
and Sharpe ratio prediction, 325–326
of SVM regression, 106, 108
in Wiener process, 286
PC, see Principal components (PC)
PCA, see Principal component analysis (PCA)
PE Ratio, 16, 176
Pfizer, 306
PnL, see Profit and loss (PnL)
Policy networks, 287–301
policy.py, 289
Polynomial regression, 91–92, 92f, 106. See also Regression
PoP (Probability of Profit), 315
Portfolio allocations, 31–32, 158, 160, 323. See also Conditional portfolio optimization (CPO)
Portfolio margin, 36
Portfolio rebalancing, see Adaptive portfolio rebalancing
Portfolios:
　conditional, see Conditional portfolio optimization (CPO)
　golden butterfly, 331
　hedge, 310
　market-neutral, 32, 73, 318
　tactical asset allocation (TAA), 32
　tangency, 327–328
　tech, 328–329, 329f, 330f
　volatility-neutral, 318
Positive-negative splits, 180–185
Predicted ranking, 130f, 214. See also Ranking
Predictnow.ai, 305–306, 308–309, 315–316, 318–319, 322, 325, 333
Preprocessing, see Data preprocessing
Principal component analysis (PCA):
　in clustering, 87, 199, 208, 211, 213
　description of, 81–82
　example of, 82f
　in factor standardization, 152–154
　in regime detection, 148–149
　statistical arbitrage mean reversion, 228–229, 232
　in trading pairs selection, 197

Principal components (PC), 81–83, 153f, 197–198, 213, 230
Probabilistic Sharpe Ratio (PSR), 35. See also Sharpe ratio
Probability of Profit (PoP), 315
Profit and loss (PnL), 288–289, 292, 295–297, 302f, 304
Prompt engineering, 346–349
Prophet, 266
ProsusAI/FinBERT model, 272–273
PSR (Probabilistic Sharpe Ratio), 35. See also Sharpe ratio
Put option payoff, 161
Put options, 186–187, 190, 194–195, 197, 284, 290
Python:
　ADF testing with, 65, 67
　EDA in, 54
　local usage of, 285
　OPTICS in, 131
　pandas in, 56
　PCA implementation in, 81
　PyWavelets library in, 106
　SciPy in, 268
　Technical Analysis library of, 321
Python's duck typing, 42
PyTorch, 288, 294–295

Q

QQQ ETF, 177–178, 237
QTS Capital Management, 305–306
QuantConnect:
　AI hedging implementation on, 288–300
　assets and derivatives treatment by, 15–23
　backtesting by, 224, 254
　cloud platform of, xvi–xx
　data consolidation by, 8
　data sets of, 9–10
　data transformations by, 41–45
　debugging mode of, 27–28, 27f
　diversification and asset selection by, 37–41
　fee models of, 11–12
　frameworks of, xv–xvi
　implementation on, 157
　liquid asset treatment by, 13
　margin modeling by, 35–37

model deployment on, 142
open-source core of, xx
order types of, 11
parameter sensitivity testing by, 34–35
scheduling by, 30
security identifiers of, 14
use of Algoseek, 15
QuantConnect Explorer, 45
QuantConnect Object Store, 28, 223, 253–254
QuantConnect Research, 45
Quantitative trading:
  diversification in, 37–41
  foundations of, 25–45
  idea generation in, 42–45
  indicators for, 41–42
  and look-ahead bias, 29–30
  margin modeling for, 35–37
  parameters for, 33–35
  platforms for, xvi–xvii
  research process for, 25–26
  strategies for, 30–33
  testing, 26–29
Quantpedia, 44
Question and answering (QnA), 344, 347, 349–362
Quote ticks, 8

R

RAG, *see* Retrieval augmented generation (RAG) application
Ranaldo, A., 312
Random forest model, 77, 88, 103, 208, 234, 319, 322. *See also* Multiclass random forest model
Random forest regression, 229. *See also* Regression
Ranking, 127–130
  in capital allocation, 31
  Fama-French use of, 310
  inverse volatility method of, 215
  in LGBR algorithm, 213
  predicted, 130f, 214
  predicting vs., 325–326
  supervised, 87
Ranking dates, 310
Raw mode, 18
Receiver operating characteristic (ROC) curve, 117

Rectified linear units (ReLU), 296
Recurrent neural networks (RNNs), 122, 266
Recursive feature elimination (RFE), 78
Refinement training, 287
Regime change:
  in conditional parameter optimization, 318
  in conditional portfolio optimization, 330
  in model retraining, 164
  and MSDR models, 99
  in portfolio allocation optimization, 323–325
  portfolio bias during, 33
  trading algorithm for, 166
Regime detection, 148–154
Regimes. *See also* Market regimes
  in hidden Markov models, 118
  high-volatility, 159–160, 165–166
  low-volatility, 159–160, 166
  market volatility, 155, 158–159
  in Markov regression, 99, 102f
  and portfolio strategy, 148–154
  trading logic for, 161
Regression, 88–109
  decision tree, 103–105
  lasso, 93–95
  linear, 89–90
  logistic, 114–117
  Markov switching dynamic, 99–102
  polynomial, 91–92
  random forest, 229
  ridge, 96–99
  support vector machines, 105–109
Regularization, 91, 93, 96, 106, 122–123, 187, 297, 327
Regularization terms, 215
Regulatory constraints, 50–51
Reinforcement learning (RL), 281–304
  definition of, 88
  for identification, 285–286
  implementation of, 287–288
  overview of, 285–288
  for refinement training, 287
  simplified approach to, 284–285
  for simulation, 286–287
  trade execution with, 51

Relative strength index (RSI), 50, 154–155, 157
ReLU (rectified linear units), 296
Renaissance Technologies, 32
Renames, 13–14, 19
research.ipynb, 288
Retrieval augmented generation (RAG) application, 349–353, 352t
Revenue growth, 16, 176, 349, 355, 356, 359
Reverse splits, 16–17
Reversion risk strategies, 154
RevPAR growth, 354–356, 358–360
RFE (recursive feature elimination), 78
Ridge regression, 88, 96–99, 98f, 214–215, 229. See also Regression
Risk management:
 in Amazon Chronos model, 135
 and conditional parameter optimization, 305–308, 318–319
 conditional parameter optimization for, 305–308, 321–322
 conditional portfolio optimization for, 323–340
 corrective AI for, 305–308
 in daily seasonal forex trading, 312–318
 ETF strategies for, 319–320
 feature engineering for, 308–312
 in FinBERT model, 137
 in linear regression, 89
 LLMs for, 133
 in Markov switching dynamic regression, 99
 PCA use for, 81
 performance comparisons of, 322–323
 and stop loss orders, 185–186
 unconditional parameter optimization for, 321–322
Risk parity, 310, 327, 332
RL, see Reinforcement learning (RL)
RNNs (recurrent neural networks), 122, 266
Robustness to noise, 234
ROC (receiver operating characteristic) curve, 117
Roll yield, 311

Rolling, 22–23, 34, 239
Rolling train set, 318–319
RSI, see Relative strength index (RSI)

S

Scheduling, 30, 40
SciPy package, 265, 268, 272
SDK, 349, 361
Securities and Exchange Commission (SEC), 3, 10, 16, 25, 309
Securities Information Processor (SIP), 3, 23. See also CUSIP
Security identifiers, 13–15
Selection bias, 38
Semi-supervised learning, 87. See also Supervised learning; Unsupervised learning
Sentiment analysis:
 in convolutional neural networks, 122
 in data collection, 53
 in FinBERT model, 88, 137–138, 273–274
 forecasting with, 50–51
 in LLM summarization, 250
 LLM use for, 133
 parameter replacement with, 34
 in zero shot prompting, 347
Sequential neural networks, 155, 264
Sharadar dataset, 308–310
Sharpe ratio:
 in adaptive portfolio rebalancing, 50
 in Amazon Chronos model, 265–267, 271
 in capital allocation, 31–32
 in clustering, 209
 in conditional portfolio optimization, 323–325, 328–331
 in corrective AI, 312–313, 316, 318
 and CPO software-as-a-service, 333
 in dividend harvesting, 177
 in H&S trading, 260
 in inverse volatility, 215
 in Markov regression, 160
 in mean-variance optimization, 327–328
 in positive-negative splits, 182
 ranking using, 325–326
 in ridge regression, 216
 in statistical arbitrage mean reversion, 230
 in stop loss, 187–188

in TAA portfolios, 331–332
in temporal CNN, 243
in wavelet forecasting, 172–173
SHY ETF, 331
Silhouette score, 132
SIP (Securities Information Processor), 3, 23. *See also* CUSIP
Sklearn library, 81, 83–84
Slippage, 12–13, 13f, 26, 51, 222–223, 273
SMB, 309, 327
Sortino ratio, 266
S&P 500:
   company rankings in, 31
   control features in, 325
   CPO correlation with, 329
   in deep neural networks, 284
   ETFs in, 39
   in FinBERT model, 274
   options in, 21
   ProsusAI/FinBERT model in, 273
   SPX tracking in, 161, 168, 267
   SPY tracking in, 154, 160
S&P 500 E-Mini, 216
Spin-offs, 19
Splits:
   backtesting of, 26
   in data normalization, 18, 41, 232
   description of, 16–17
   effect on share price, 17f
   and overfitting, 86
   positive-negative, 180–185
   reverse, 16–17
   stock, 181–185, 193
Spread-crosses, 198
Spread percentage, 221–222
SPX index, 21, 161, 168, 311
SPY market index, 148–149, 154–161, 164, 166, 168
Stability AI, 361
Standardization. *See also* Normalization
   in convolutional neural networks, 122
   in data preprocessing, 55
   in decision tree regression, 103
   definition of, 63
   in FinBERT model, 137–138
   in Gaussian naive Bayes, 119–120
   in hidden Markov models, 117–118
   importance in PCA, 81, 93
   in lasso regression, 93

   and LGBRanker, 128
   in linear regression, 89
   in logistic regression, 114
   in Markov regression, 99
   in multiclass random forest regression, 110
   in OpenAI language model, 133
   in OPTICS clustering, 130–131
   in polynomial regression, 91
   in regime detection, 149
   in ridge regression, 96
   in SVM regression, 105–106
   testing, 152
Stationary factors, 149, 152, 152f, 154
Statistical arbitrage mean reversion, 32, 73, 154, 197–198, 203, 228–233, 319
Statistical arbitrage strategy, 228–233
Stock splits, 181–185, 193
Stop loss, 185–197
   dynamic distance of, 186
   fixed percentage-based, 186, 187–188, 190–191
   ML placed, 188–194
Straddle options strategy, 158, 160f, 161, 166
Strategy selection, 143, 154–158
Strike price, 19–20, 161, 186, 195, 282, 284, 290
Supervised learning, 87–88, 105, 152, 308, 319. *See also* Semi-supervised learning; Unsupervised learning
Supervised machine learning, 87, 308, 319. *See also* Machine learning (ML)
Supervised ranking, 87. *See also* Ranking
Support vector machines (SVM) regression, 63, 87, 88, 105–109, 108f, 229. *See also* Regression
Support vector machines (SVMs), 170–175, 234, 266
Survivorship bias, 38, 308–309
Sweetviz, 54–55, 54f, 55f

T

Tactical asset allocation (TAA) portfolios, 32, 331, 331f, 332t
Tangency portfolios, 327–328

Target variables, 49–51, 76–77, 85, 93, 324
Tech portfolios, 328–329, 329f, 330f
Technical Analysis Python library, 321
Temporal CNN model, 233–242, 236f. See also Convolutional neural networks (CNN)
Temporal patterns, 234
The Terminator (film), 305
Tesla, 305
Testing sets, 83, 294. See also Training sets; Validation sets
TiingoNews, 9–10, 253, 274
Time-of-the-day primary strategy, 312, 318
Time series factors:
    in Amazon Chronos model, 135, 266
    cointegrated, 48, 70–74
    in conditional parameter optimization, 319
    cross-sectional vs., 308–310, 309f, 328
    differenced, 69
    in Fama-French model, 327
    in forecasting models, 266–267
    in hidden Markov models, 117–118
    in Hurst exponent, 198, 203
    in Markov switching dynamic regression, 99
    in MLFinlab, 143, 145
    and model predictions, 151f–153f
    in neural networks, 122
    non-stationary, 66f, 69f, 202
    in polynomial regression, 91
    in regression models, 88
    short-term reversal factor, 155
    stationary, 70f
    stationary transition of, 55, 64
    in temporal CNN, 234, 239
    in wavelet forecasting, 105–106, 170–171
TLT (Treasury) bonds, 154, 157, 158, 160–161, 164
TN (True Negative), 116
Top-of-book size, 222
TP (True Positive), 116
Trade reporting facility (TRF), 3

Trade routing, 22, 32
Trade ticks, 8, 29, 312t
Trading costs optimization, 221–228
Trading fees, 11
Trading pairs selection, 197–207
Trading Signals, 31
Trading volumes, 49–50, 53, 222, 290
Training sets, 83, 106, 256, 261, 264, 294. See also Testing sets; Validation sets
Transaction costs, 10–13
    bid-ask spread, 12
    in frictionless markets, 282
    and machine learning, 283–284
    and market data, 296
    minimizing, 51, 131, 273
    operational constraints as, 50
    simulations for, 287
    slippage, 12–13
    trading fees, 11
Treasury (TLT) bonds, see TLT (Treasury) bonds
Tree-based machine learning models, 77
Trend following, 144
Trend scanning, 143–147
True Negative (TN), 116
True Positive (TP), 116
TSLA stock, 251–253

U

UCI Machine Learning Repository, 85
Unconditional parameter optimization, 319–323, 323f. See also Conditional parameter optimization (CPO)
Under-hedged strategy, 295
Underfitting, 83, 96. See also Overfitting
    problems with, 33f
Underlying assets, 15, 19–20, 161, 168, 186, 283, 304, 325
United States Treasury bonds, 154, 331
Universe selection, 38–41, 208
Universe settings, 40–41
Unsupervised learning, 87–88. See also Semi-supervised learning; Supervised learning

V

Validation sets, 83. *See also* Testing sets; Training sets
Value at risk (VaR), 51, 266
Vanguard Total Bond Market ETF, 311
VanguardEmerging Markets Stock Index Fund ETF, 311
VIX index, 154–155, 186, 191, 193, 262
Volatility, 159
Volatility model features, 218
Volatility-neutral portfolios, 318
Volume-weighted average price (VWAP), 60–51

W

Walk forward optimization, 318
Walk-the-book process, 4, 12
Wall Street Journal, 7
Wang, Xindi, 127
Warm up, *see* Indicator warm up
Wavelet decomposition, 106, 170
Wavelet forecasting, 88, 105–108, 170–175
Wiener process for volatility, 285–286
World Quant, 32
WSG hedge fund, 330–331

X

XGBoost, 266–267
XLK benchmark, 181–182

Z

Z-score, 58–59, 63, 229, 321
Zero shot prompting, 347

Code Index

A
add_data method, 10
add_future method, 22
AIDeltaHedgeModel class, 289, 292
AIDeltaHedgingAlgorithm, 288
alpha_exponent, 188, 190
arrays parameter, 84
atr, std_of_close_returns, 219
atr_months parameter, 217

B
bagging_fraction hyperparameter, 111
bagging_freq hyperparameter, 111
benchmark_order_fills, 224
binary_crossentropy loss function, 156
boosting_type hyperparameter, 111

C
CategoricalCrossentropy parameter, 237
close_roc, 220
components parameter, 209, 211
confidence_threshold parameter, 260
context_length argument, 269
contract.ask_price, 195
correct_predictions, 147
_create_model() method, 239

D
days_per_sample parameter, 244
DecisionTreeRegressor model, 180, 221, 223
deduplicated_articles_by_date, 254

E
epsilon parameter, 106
expected_volatility_by_security, 221

F
factors_to_use list, 211
feature_fraction hyperparameter, 111
features_by_day data structure, 247
ffill, 221
final_universe_size parameter, 210–211
.flatten(), 213

G
gamma parameter, 106
GridSearchCV, 111

H
hold_duration parameter, 183
holding_period parameter, 260

I

indicator_history, 219–220
indicator_lookback_months parameter, 188–189
init(): class initialization, 292
initialize() method, 212, 245
InteractiveBrokersFeeModel, 195

K

kernal type parameter, 106

L

label_history variable, 219
labels_by_day data structure, 247
learning_rate hyperparameter, 111
lightgbm multiclass classifier model, 150
liquid_universe_size parameter, 211
live_mode, 245
lookback_days parameter, 230, 232
lookback_period parameter, 211
lookback_years parameter, 179

M

make_classification method, 111
max_open_trades parameter, 182
max_steps argument, 268
minimum_order_margin_portfolio_percentage setting, 216
model.train_asset_model() function, 289
MyFactorDataset class, 10

N

NaN (dropna), 220
nn.MSELoss(), 294
num_components parameter, 230–231
num_leaves hyperparameter, 111

O

on_end_of_algorithm method, 180, 245
open_roc, 220
open_roc.update(), 220
_optimize_portfolio method, 272
_order_fills data frame, 223
oss_accuracy method, 150

P

Policy(nn.Module), 290
predicted_low_price + contract.ask_price, 195
prediction method, 241
previous_opens data structure, 247

R

random_state parameter, 85
refit(), 299
regularization parameter, 106
research_test(), 292
roc_window data structure, 247

S

_samples data frame, 192
security.features_by_day, 246
security.labels_by_day, 246
self._stop_loss_buffer, 194
shuffle parameter, 85
sklearn.datasets.make_blobs method, 131
SpreadSlippageModel, 223
std_months parameter, 188
std_of_open_returns, 220
stop_loss_buffer parameter, 188–189
stop_loss_percent parameter, 188
stratify parameter, 85
_svm_forecast method, 175
SymbolData class pattern, 40

T

tensor() method, 295
test_size parameter, 84
torch.cuda, 292
tradable_symbols list, 211
_trades_by_symbol, 182–183
_train method, 185
train_asset_model(), 292, 297
train_base_model(), 292
_train_chronos method, 271
training_lookback_years parameter, 183
training_samples parameter, 238
train_size parameter, 84

U

universe_size parameter, 178, 232, 238, 244
Universe.UNCHANGED, 22
update() method, 220
utils.to_categorical function, 237

V

.values, 213

W

weight_threshold, 173–174

Y

y_train.rank(axis=1, method='first'), 213
y_wavelet, 107

Z

z_score_threshold parameter, 232